D1743125

Legal Issues of Services of General Interest

Series Editors

Johan Willem van de Gronden
Markus Krajewski
Ulla Neergaard
Erika Szyszczak

For further volumes:
http://www.springer.com/series/8900

Erika Szyszczak · Johan Willem van de Gronden
Editors

Financing Services of General Economic Interest

Reform and Modernization

Editors
Erika Szyszczak
School of Law
University of Leicester
Leicester
UK

Johan Willem van de Gronden
Faculty of Law
Radboud University
Nijmegen
The Netherlands

ISBN 978-90-6704-905-4   ISBN 978-90-6704-906-1   (eBook)
DOI 10.1007/978-90-6704-906-1

Library of Congress Control Number: 2012951138

Published by T.M.C. ASSER PRESS, The Hague, The Netherlands www.asserpress.nl
Produced and distributed for T.M.C. ASSER PRESS by Springer-Verlag Berlin Heidelberg

Printed on acid-free paper

Springer is part of Springer Science+Business Media (www.springer.com)

Series Information

The aim of the series *Legal Issues of Services of General Interest* is to sketch the framework for services of general interest in the EU and to explore the issues raised by developments related to these services. The Series encompasses, inter alia, analyses of EU internal market, competition law, legislation (such as the Services Directive), international economic law and national (economic) law from a comparative perspective. Sector-specific approaches will also be covered (health, social services). In essence, the present Series addresses the emergence of a European Social Model and will therefore raise issues of fundamental and theoretical interest in Europe and the global economy.

Series Editors

Johan Willem van de Gronden
Faculty of Law
Radboud University
Comeniuslaan 4
6525 HP Nijmegen
The Netherlands
e-mail: J.vandeGronden@jur.ru.nl

Markus Krajewski
Fachbereich Rechtswissenschaft
Universität Erlangen-Nürnberg
Schillerstraße 1
91054 Erlangen
Germany
e-mail: markus.krajewski@jura.
uni-erlangen.de

Ulla Neergaard
Faculty of Law
University of Copenhagen
Studiestræde 6
1455 Copenhagen K
Denmark
e-mail: ulla.neergaard@jur.ku.dk

Erika Szyszczak
School of Law
University of Leicester
University Road, Leicester
LE1 7RH
UK
e-mail: ems11@leicester.ac.uk

Editors' Note

We have used the modern referencing introduced by the Treaty of Lisbon 2009, referring to the European Court of Justice as 'CJEU' and the General Court as 'GC' and using the Treaty Articles from the TFEU and TEU throughout, with only occasional references to old numbering of the Treaties. We have used the term European Union (EU) to denote the political entity—with only occasional references to 'Community' or 'European Economic Community' or 'European Community'. We feel this makes the text easier to read for a modern audience.

We are aware that the four criteria/conditions of the *Altmark* are repeated in every chapter of the book. We have not edited this duplication because the chapters may be read as 'stand alone' chapters by some readers.

On a final reading of the chapters it became clear that the detailed analysis of the Almunia Package required an in-depth explanation of its content in the **Introduction** and this explains why the **Introduction** is much longer than is normally the case in the books in this series.

We have also used a 'light touch' in editing individual chapters, changing linguistic phrases and language only where we felt it was necessary to ease the reading and understanding of the text.

Tristan Naber complied the Table of European Court cases and Commission Decisions. We also thank him, along with Dr Anne Witt, for help in translating some of the German language titles.

Contents

Contributors

José Luís Buendía Sierra obtained his degree in Law and subsequently his Ph.D at the University of Zaragoza, Spain. He also holds a Master's in European Legal Studies from the College of Europe (Bruges, Belgium). José Luís is currently Partner at GARRIGUES and leads the Brussels office of this law firm, where he regularly works in antitrust and State aid cases. He previously worked at the European Commission (Legal Service, DG Competition, Internal Market and Cabinet of Commissioner Oreja) intensively advising and litigating for the Institution before the Court of Justice of the European Union. He is currently visiting professor at King's College London and he has also been visiting lecturer at Vrije Universiteit Brussels. José Luís Buendía is a widely respected practitioner on antitrust and State aid issues and has taken part in a number of conferences in Brussels, London, Paris and Madrid. He regularly publishes on State aid and other competition law issues. Among his publications special mention must be made to his book, '*Exclusive Rights and State Monopolies under EC Law*', published by Oxford University Press.

Ian Clarke is a Ph.D candidate in Procurement Law at the University of Leicester. Since October 2011, he has been working on a research project entitled: *Procurement Directives*: *Rising to the Challenges of a New Commercial Environment*. He obtained his first Master's degree at the University of Leicester in 2006 and followed this with an LLM degree in European Commercial Law in 2010. He is a procurement practitioner specialising in EU public procurement rules and the Managing Director of Excalibur Procurement Services Limited in the UK.

Albert Sanchez Graells LL.B, BA (Business), DEA (Law), Ph.D (Eur) (Law) is a Lecturer in Law at the University of Hull, UK, specialising in EU Economic Law and, more specifically, in EU Competition Law and EU Public Procurement Law. Prior to this appointment, Albert was Lecturer in European and Commercial Law at the Law Faculty of the Comillas Pontifical University (Madrid, Spain), as well as Director of its Master in International and European Business Law. Albert has spent significant research time at the Library of Congress (Washington, USA), the

Centre for Competition Law and Policy of the University of Oxford (UK) and the Law Department of the Copenhagen Business School (DK). His research interests are in law and economics, especially regarding competition and public procurement law, on which he completed his Ph.D (Eur) and has recently published *Public Procurement and the EU Competition Rules* (Oxford, Hart Publishing, 2011). His working papers and some of his most recent publications are available at http://ssrn.com/author=542893.

Johan W. van de Gronden is Professor of European law at the Radboud University of Nijmegen, the Netherlands, since September 2007. He teaches European and competition law. His research focuses on EU free movement, internal market and competition law. His publications concern *inter alia* the relationship between internal market and competition law and issues of general interest, the impact of EU law on healthcare, and the Services Directive. He has published in many leading European law journals, *inter alia, the ECLRev, European Constitutional Law Review* and *LIEI*. He is one of the editors of the TMC Asser Press Series, *Legal Issues of Services of General Interest*. Until September 2007 he worked at the Europa Institute of Utrecht University (from 2003 to 2007 as senior lecturer). The subject of his Ph.D thesis was the implementation of EC Environmental law by decentralised authorities. He is also a deputy judge at the district court of Rotterdam (competition law). Furthermore, he is a member of the Committee for Consumer Affairs of the Social and Economic Council of the Netherlands (Sociaal-Economische Raad) and of the Committee International Affairs of this council. He is one of the founding members of the ToMas research project.

Leigh Hancher LL.B, MA, Ph.D is a professor of European law at the University of Tilburg and was a member of the Scientific Council for Government Policy (WRR). Prior to 1997, she was a professor of European law at the Erasmus University Rotterdam and a visiting professor of Natural Resources Law at the University of Calgary, Canada. Leigh has written extensively on EU law and healthcare issues. Leigh was admitted as advocate, in the Netherlands in 1996 and is Of Counsel at Allen & Overy in Amsterdam. She has regularly acted as adviser to the European Commission and the European Parliament on energy law issues.

Marijn Holwerda LL.M, MA, is a Ph.D researcher at the Groningen Centre of Energy of the University of Groningen, the Netherlands. His research focuses on legal issues associated with the cross-border application of carbon capture and storage (CCS) technology in the EU. Prior to working as a Ph.D researcher at the University of Groningen, he worked for the Dutch government as an advisor on EU climate and energy policy for nearly three years.

James Kavanagh BA, MSc is a Managing Consultant at Oxera, an economics consultancy based in Oxford, UK. He has worked on economic and finance issues in competition, State aid and damages cases before authorities and courts in the UK and Europe. James has published in several competition journals on abuse of dominance and other competition topics. He runs Oxera's training course, Using

Economics in Competition Law, and contributes to the post-graduate Diploma in Economics for Competition Law at King's College London. He is a co-author of Economics for Competition Lawyers (Oxford, OUP, 2011).

Max Klasse Ph.D is a member of the antitrust and competition practice group of Freshfields Bruckhaus Deringer, Berlin office. He advises clients on European and German antitrust law, merger control and State aid law. Recent experience includes: acting for several clients in the energy sector in merger control proceedings before the European Commission; advising clients in State aid proceedings; and acting for several clients in the pharmaceutical sector. Max was educated at Humboldt University of Berlin and holds a Doctor of Laws from the University of Cologne. He has worked in the European Commission's DG Competition in Brussels (2005). Max is co-author of the book "Kartellrecht im Pharma- und Gesundheitssektor" (Competition Law in the Pharmaceutical and Healthcare Sector, first published in 2007, together with Thomas Lübbig).

José Manuel Panero Rivas holds an LL.M in European Law at the College of Europe, Bruges, a PGD in Economics for Competition Law at King's College, London as well as an LL.M in Business Law at Centro de Estudios Garrigues, Madrid. He obtained his degree in Law at the University of Las Palmas de Gran Canaria, Spain, having studied part of it at the University of Bologna, Italy. José Manuel currently provides his services as associate working with Garrigues Brussels' office, where he deals with EU Law and Competition Law cases. Jose Manuel has broad interests in EU Law and Competition Law and Economics, being a regular contributor in specialised journals devoted to EU Law and, particularly, EU State aid law.

Stéphane Rodrigues Ph.D is an Avocat, member of the Paris Bar, established to the Brussels' Bar, Partner, Lallemand, Legros & Associés (since 2003). Stéphane is also Senior Lecturer in Public and Community Law (University Paris I, Panthéon-Sorbonne). Stéphane has a Ph.D in Public Community Law, University Paris I (1999, « Public service utilities and EC Law »). Stéphane has published, and among others : « La nouvelle régulation des services publics en Europe : énergie, postes, télécommunications et transports », éditions Lavoisier-Tec&Doc, Paris, 2000 - « Les services d'intérêt économique général et l'Union européenne », co-editor with Jean-Victor Louis, Bruylant, Brussels, 2006. He is a member of the Editorial Committee of « Cahiers de droit européen », Bruylant, Brussels, and former Member of the TEPSA Executive Board (Trans-European Policy Studies Association, Brussels, 1999–2005).

Tim Maxian Rusche LL.M, MPA, maître en droit, is a Member of the Legal Service of the European Commission. He joined the European Commission in 2004. Prior to joining the Commission's Legal Service in 2010, he worked in the Commission's DG for Energy and Transport, first in the unit in charge of competition and internal market and then as coordinator for the relations with the European Parliament and the Council. Tim holds a joint law degree from the

University Paris 1 (Panthéon-Sorbonne) and the University of Cologne, and a Master in Public Administration from Harvard University. He has published a number of articles and book chapters on EU law, with a focus on State aid, regulation of energy and transport and environmental law. In the leading German commentary of EU law (Grabitz/Hilf/Nettesheim, *Das Recht der Europäischen Union*), he is co-author of the section on Articles 90 to 100 TFEU (transport).

Catalin Stefan Rusu LL.B, MA, LL.M, Ph.D is assistant professor of European law at Radboud University, Nijmegen. He obtained his Ph.D from the Faculty of Law, Economics and Governance from Molengraaff Institute, Utrecht University. Catalin was also educated at the International Faculty of Comparative Law, Strasbourg and the Universitatea Babeş-Bolyai in Cluj-Napoca, Romania. His research interests are in the field of EU competition law.

Silvia Schmidt LL.B, MA, graduated in Law and French from Trinity College Dublin with First Class honours in 2009. During her undergraduate degree she was awarded an Entrance Exhibition, received a Law School Prize, was elected Scholar of the university and was awarded membership and a scholarship by the German National Academic Foundation. She holds a Master's degree from University College London where she concentrated on legal theory, with particular emphasis on the development and application of a Foucauldian framework of governmentality on the European Union. She presented part of this research at the Institute for Cultural Diplomacy in Berlin. Following her studies she worked as a trainee at the European Commission's Legal Service in the department of State aid. Silvia is currently a trainee soliciter at Clifford Chance, London.

Wolf Sauter Ph.D has a research interest in economic law, competition law and sector specific regulation, with a specialisation in telecommunications law. His doctoral thesis 'The Relationship between Industrial and Competition Policy under the Economic Constitution of the European Union, with a Case Study of Telecommunications' was defended at the EUI, Fiesole, in 1996. From 1998 to 2002 he was Professor of economic law, University of Groningen and is now a professor and member of TILEC, University of Tilburg and a competition expert at the Dutch Healthcare Authority (NZa). The current focus of his research is on national and European healthcare regulation. Further published research can be found at his author page: http://ssrn.com/author=857260

Erika Szyszczak LL.B, LL.M, Ph.D is Jean Monnet Professor of European Law ad personam at the University of Leicester, where she is the Director of the Centre for European Law and Internationalisation. She is a practising barrister at Littleton Chambers, Temple, London and an ADR accredited mediator. She sits on the Editorial Boards of the Modern Law Review, European Law Review, European Journal of Social Law and The International Journal of Discrimination and the Law. She is one of the founding members of the ToMas research project and is interested in the relationship between free movement rules, competition and liberalisation in the EU. She is currently writing a second edition of her book *The Regulation of the State in Competitive* Markets in the EU (Hart Pub). She recently edited: *Research Handbook on European State Aid Law*, published by Edward Elgar in 2011.

Hans Vedder is an Honorary Judge at the Leeuwarden Appeals Court and member of the advisory committee on administrative appeals to the Netherlands Competition authority and conducts research and gives courses for a number of parties such as law firms, the Netherlands centre for the training of the judiciary. He was involved in contract research for various public bodies and private parties.

Abbreviations

AG	Advocate General
CFEU	Charter on the Fundamental Rights of the European Union
CJEU	Court of Justice of the European Union
ERP	Equity risk premium
GC	General Court
NACM	Net avoided cost methodology
MEAT	Most economically advantageous tender
OJ	Official Journal of the European Union
PSC	Public service compensation
PSO	Public service obligation
SGEI	Service of general economic interest
SGI	Service of general interest
SME	Small & medium sized companies
SSGI	Social service of general interest
TEU	Treaty on European Union
TFEU	Treaty on the Functioning of the European Union
USO	Universal service obligation
WACC	Weighted average cost of capital

Chapter 1
Introduction

Erika Szyszczak

Abstract This chapter provides an introduction to the background to recent reforms for financing SGEI, known as the 'Almunia package'. It traces the reaction to the *Altmark* ruling from the European Commission and the European Courts and sets the legal and political debate on how to finance SGEI in its modern economic and constitutional context. The chapter introduces and summarises the arguments made in the subsequent chapters of the book.

Contents

E. Szyszczak (✉)
School of Law, University of Leicester, Leicester, LE1 7RH, United Kingdom
e-mail: ems11@le.ac.uk

E. Szyszczak and J.W. van de Gronden (eds.), *Financing Services of General Economic Interest*, Legal Issues of Services of General Interest, DOI: 10.1007/978-90-6704-906-1_1, © T.M.C. Asser press, The Hague, The Netherlands, and the authors 2013

1.1 Introduction

On 20 December 2011, the Commission adopted a package of measures to regulate the relationship between the State aid rules and the financing of services of general economic interest (SGEI) in the EU. The measures comprise two Communications[1] and a Decision.[2] There was also the promise of a Regulation on *de minimis* aid,[3] after further consultation. Such a Regulation was adopted on 25 April 2012.[4] Accompanying the measures was an Impact Assessment[5] and a Quality Framework.[6] The Package of measures was also explained in a Press Release and a

---

[1] *Communication from the Commission on the application of the European Union State aid rules to compensation granted for the provision of services of general economic interest, OJ 2012 C 8/ 4; Communication from the Commission, European Union framework for State aid in the form of public service compensation, OJ 2012 C 8/15.*

[2] Commission Decision of 20 December on the application of Article 106(2) of the Treaty on the Functioning of the European Union to State aid in the form of public service compensation granted to certain undertakings entrusted with the operation of services of general economic interest, *OJ* 2012 L 7/3.

[3] Draft Commission Regulation on the application of Articles 107 and 108 of the Treaty on the Functioning of the European Union to *de minimis* aid granted to undertakings providing services of general economic interest, *OJ* 2012 C 8/23.

[4] Commission Regulation on the application of Articles 107 and 108 of the Treaty on the Functioning of the European Union to *de minimis* aid granted to undertakings providing services of general economic interest, *OJ* 2012 L 114/8.

[5] Available at: http://ec.europa.eu/governance/impact/ia_carried_out/cia_2011_en.htm#comp.

[6] The idea of a quality framework, avoiding binding legislation, was mooted by the Commission as part of the initial ideas for modernising the single/internal market: European Commission, *services of general interest, including social services of general interest: a new European commitment* COM (2007) 725 final. See the chapter by Maxian Rusche.

powerpoint presentation, an analysis tree and a table comparing the new and old rules, but oddly there was no document of 'Frequently Asked Questions (FAQs).[7]

This has become known as the 'Almunia Package'.[8] According to the Press Release of the Commission:

> The new package clarifies key state aid principles and introduces a diversified and proportionate approach with simpler rules for SGEIs that are small, local in scope or pursue a social objective, while taking account of competition considerations for large cases.[9]

The measures were implemented in a changing economic and constitutional climate as well as a modernisation process and a 'more economic' approach towards regulating the financing and operation of SGEI in Europe. The measures also reflect the changing policy towards the regulation of state aid by the European Commission, and, indeed, were described by the Vice President of the Commission Almunia as part of the Commission's learning process.[10] The measures are also part of a process, beginning with the landmark ruling of *Altmark*,[11] and followed up in the Monti Report 2010,[12] of initiatives to reboost the single market and the subsequent modernisation of state aid and procurement programmes, by integrating SGEI into the broader framework of EU law and policy.

This book analyses the 'Almunia Package' from different perspectives, legal, political and economic, analysing how new regulatory frameworks for the modernisation of SGEI in the European Union (EU) are emerging. The book is divided into three Parts. The **Introduction** sets the context for the original *Altmark* ruling and the reactions to the ruling by the Commission and the European Courts, outlining the Almunia Package. **Part I** examines the legacy of the *Altmark* ruling. **Part II** examines, from various critical perspectives, the new Almunia reforms of the initial measures taken by the Commission in what is

---

[7] Available at: http://ec.europa.eu/competition/state_aid/legislation/sgei.html. Articles were also published in the Competition Policy Newsletter 2012:1: http://ec.europa.eu/competition/publications/cpn/cpn_2012_1_en.html.

[8] For commentary see: Sinnaeve 2012, Buendía Sierra 2012. This Introduction is based (in part) upon Szyszczak 2012a.

[9] *State aid: Commission adopts new rules on services of general economic interest (SGEI)* IP/11/1571, 20/12/2011. For an early application of the new package see: State aid SA.33054 (2012/N)— United Kingdom Post Office Limited (POL): Compensation for net costs incurred to keep a non-commercially viable network for the period 2012–2015 and the continuation of a working capital facility, C(2012) 1905 fin. 28 March 2012.

[10] Joaquín Almunia Vice President of the European Commission responsible for Competition Policy, 'The State Aid Modernisation Initiative', speech at The State Aid Modernisation Initiative EStALI— European State Aid Law Institute 10th Experts' Forum on New Developments in European State Aid Law Brussels, 7 June 2012. Available at: http://europa.eu/rapid/pressReleasesAction.do?reference=SPEECH/12/424&format=HTML&aged=0&language=EN&guiLanguage=en (last accessed on 1 August 2012).

[11] CJEU, Case 280/00 *Altmark Trans GmbH and Regierungspräsidium Magdeburg v. Nahverkehrsgesellschaft Altmark GmbH, and Oberbundesanwalt beim Bundesverwaltungsgericht* [2003]*ECR* I-7747.

[12] Mario Monti, *A New Strategy for the Single Market, At the Service of Europe's Economy and Society, Report to the President of the European Commission Jose Manuel Barroso*, May 9 2010.

known as the '*Altmark*-Monti-Kroes' Package. **Part III** addresses areas where special exemptions, or special treatment, is accorded to SGEI. *Van de Gronden* offers a **Conclusion,** addressing problems and issues that remain to be resolved within, and after, the Almunia reforms.

1.2 The Background

1.2.1 The Awkwardness of Public Services

Bauby notes that, with the exception of what is now Article 93 TFEU, the original EEC Treaty declined to acknowledge the role of traditional public services in the European integration project.[13] Instead the EEC Treaty reinvented the concept of public services as SGEI, in what is now Article 106(2) TFEU, as a *derogation* from the fundamental economic policy provisions of the EEC.

Article 106(1) and Article 37 TFEU allowed for challenges to state monopolies in general and the focus of (sporadic) litigation was upon the anti-competitive effects of the operation of commercial state monopolies, with some discussion of the impact upon free movement of goods and services.[14] The late 1980s saw the emergence of liberalisation programmes of commercial public monopolies at the national level, followed by EU-level responses.[15] This period also saw the recognition that core public services in commercial sectors could be provided by non-state bodies and concepts of universal service obligations (uso) were used in the liberalisation processes to protect such services and enhance the rights of consumers.[16]

From the 1990s, a new phase of litigation emerged where the *funding* of public services became the focus of challenge to Member State policies as public markets were opened up to competition. The legal issues of the role of public services turned to the financing mechanisms of these services and their compatibility with the EU state aid measures. This turn of events created the legal problems for the policy makers of today in relation to the correct legal base to regulate public services in the EU. Originally, Article 106(3) TFEU was considered a possible legal base. The Treaty of Lisbon 2009 created a new legal base for measures in Article 14 TFEU and this gave rise to a debate discussed by *Maxian Rusche* as to the correct use of such regulatory measures. A cautious approach has been taken by the Commission, with greater resort to the flexibility of soft law. The Almunia Package used the legal base of Article 106(3) TFEU, focusing upon the state aid

---

[13] Bauby 2011. On special measures for transport see the chapter by *Maxian Rusche and Schmidt*.

[14] For a deeper discussion of the earlier phases of litigation see Buendia Sierra 1999 and Szyszczak 2007.

[15] See Szyszczak 2007, Chap. 1.

[16] Davies and Szyszczak 2011.

jurisdiction of the EU. Indeed, shortly before the Treaty of Lisbon 2009 was ratified the Commission announced that it would not use the new legal base of Article 14 TFEU for measures to modernise SGEI and instead adopted a more expansive soft law and soft governance process.[17] The legal constraints upon the Commission in the Almunia modernisation process are discussed by *Maxian Rusche*. Arguably, the measures introduced by the Commission affect the quality of public services, and the manner in which they are delivered, extending the role of state aid regulation in the EU.

As *Kavanagh* points out, from an economist's perspective, the continued provision of a protected public service may not be commercially attractive (or viable) where the cost of the provision of a public service exceeds the revenues, or, where the public service cannot be provided at a socially acceptable (for e.g., uniform) price. Thus even with a liberalisation agenda, there was the need for continued state involvement in subsidising some, or all, of the costs of public services. However, state financial provision for public services was not necessarily efficient. Lack of transparency in the award of public service contracts (favouring local suppliers or repaying national favours) the provision of a uso by a liberalised state incumbent, excessive gold plating of public services, are but examples of the lack of attention, and commitment, towards the modernisation of the funding and operation of public services.

EU state aid law provided the legal means whereby challenges could be brought to the continued state involvement in the provision of goods and services. Difficulties emerged as a state aid approach looked to the distortive effects of a subsidy where an undertaking obtains an advantage from the funding ostensibly granted for the provision of a public service. The Commission was not consistent in its handling of such subsidies and in the early years of litigation the European Courts joined the Commission in oscillating between taking a 'state aid' approach and a 'compensation' approach in scrutinising the compatibility of public services and EU law.[18]

In a 'state aid' approach subsidies are seen as state aids, unless they fall within one of the exemptions set out in Articles 107(2) and (3) TFEU, secondary legislation and soft law communications. In contrast, a 'compensation' approach sees the subsidy as covering the extra costs of providing a public service. While the Commission and the General Court preferred to see the payment for public services as a state aid issue, EU state aid rules contained few escape clauses to capture the range and level of state funding for public services. In contrast, Article 106(2) TFEU contains a 'Community' (now EU) concept of 'services of general economic interest' and is seen as an exception, a justification, derogation, escape clause or a switch rule[19] to the free market and competition rules of the EU.[20]

---

[17] Szyszczak 2012b.

[18] Szyszczak 2004.

[19] Baquero Cruz 2002.

[20] The availability of Article 106(2) TFEU as a derogation or justification from the free movement rules is contentious, see Bekkedal 2011. See the strict interpretation of when Article 106(2) TFEU can apply in relation to a free movement of capital (golden shares) infringement: CJEU, Case C-543/08 *Commission v. Portugal* [2010] *ECR* I-0000.

This can be used to allow the funding of public services by reading across the exemption into the state aid rules.

The Commission allowed the Member States to control the definition of an SGEI (by only allowing for review in cases of manifest error) and the European Courts developed concepts of 'economic' and 'non-economic' activity to capture the wider range of public services being delivered in competitive markets but to avoid 'social' SGEI from being brought into EU competence. Despite the growing influence of EU law over SGEI there was no consensus for binding EU *regulation* of public services.[21]

In the absence of EU regulation,[22] the increasing threats posed by ad hoc litigation were mitigated by the Commission using soft law communications to create a policy framework, and a framework for discussion of how public services fitted with EU law. In hindsight this was an astute political move, placing the Commission at the centre of policy making in a sensitive, and controversial area not fully within the legislative competence of the EU, nor fully immune from challenge by EU law. Thus, state aid policy became a central tool for the assessment of *how* public services should be provided in the EU, but with a limited capacity to accommodate the range of public services, especially where the activity was of a social nature.

Viewing public subsidies to pay for public services as a state aid issue was a tough stance to take. This harsh approach was eventually mitigated by the CJEU in the ruling of 23 July 2003 in *Altmark*.[23] The reference was from the German Bundesverwaltungsgericht (the highest German administrative law court) and concerned an issue of a small amount of subsidy granted in East Germany for regional transport services. A competitor sought annulment of licences granted to Altmark Trans GmbH to provide regional transport services. Altmark Trans had shown that the routes realised a loss of 0.58 DM per km and received compensation for this loss. As *Maxian Rusche and Schmidt* show the transport sector had been excluded from earlier de minimis rules and this explains why, given the small amount of local aid, the case could be challenged as contrary to the EU state aid rules.

The CJEU set out four prescriptive criteria[24] whereby a Member State could finance an SGEI *without* incurring the application of the state aid rules of the EU.[25] The four criteria comprise:

---

[21] European Commission, *Green Paper on Services of General Interest*, COM (2003) 270 final (21 May 2003); European Commission, *White Paper on Services of General Interest*, COM (2004) 374 final (12 May 2004).

[22] European Commission, *Green Paper on Services of General Interest*, COM (2003) 270 final (21 May 2003); European Commission, *White Paper on Services of General Interest*, COM (2004) 374 final (12 May 2004).

[23] CJEU, Case C-280/00 *Altmark* [2003] *ECR* I-7747.

[24] Also termed 'conditions' by some commentators.

[25] CJEU, Case C-280/00 *Altmark* [2003] *ECR* I-7747, adopting a compensation approach following the earlier ruling in CJEU, Case C-53/00 *Ferring v ACOSS* [2001] *ECR* I-9067. For background on the vacillation between a state aid and compensation approach in the earlier case law and Commission policy see Szyszczak 2004.

(1) the recipient undertaking has clearly defined public service obligations (pso) to perform;
(2) the parameters on which public service compensation (psc) is calculated are established in advance in a transparent and objective manner;
(3) the compensation does not exceed the cost of performing the obligations, taking into account relevant receipts and a reasonable profit;
(4) the recipient undertaking was chosen to perform the SGEI in a public procurement procedure allowing performance of the services at the lowest cost or, if not, the level of compensation needed is based upon the costs of a typical, well-run undertaking with adequate funding.

The criteria were not entirely new. The first three conditions were already contained in the European Courts' case law. The fourth criterion created a standard to calculate the psc without further clarification but also added a rider that the Member State should control public expenditure 'at least cost to the community'.[26] As most chapters in this book show, this has proved to be the most problematic of the criteria. The conditions/criteria applied cumulatively and as *Klasse* points out, were interpreted strictly by the Commission in its subsequent decision-making practice.

The *Altmark* ruling was an important turning point for the modernisation of state aid, addressing the financing of SGEI (particularly avoiding overcompensation of what were often viewed as inefficient 'gold-plated' public services that had not been subject to market testing) but also addressing the quality and delivery of public services in a competitive environment. It can be argued that *Altmark* created a pathway for the modernisation of the funding of public services, as well a debate on *how* such services should operate in a competitive market.

1.2.2 The Significance of Altmark

The *Altmark* criteria provided a set of conditions to be applied *ex ante* diminishing the necessity to rely upon Article 106(2) TFEU which can provide a derogation for anti-competitive measures which allow for SGEI to operate.[27] *Altmark* also diminished the necessity for the Member State to notify financing for SGEI to the Commission under Article 108(3) TFEU: *Altmark* opened the possibility for self-assessment of financing schemes. A parallel aspect of *Altmark* was a response to a need to increase efficiency because of international competitiveness. As *Vedder*

---

[26] An application of this condition is seen Commission Decision Energy Supply Slovenia, *OJ* 2007 L 219/9, paras 111ff where the Commission was satisfied that Slovenia had chosen an option that did not strictly fulfil the fourth criterion but was the option which incurred the least cost for the State.

[27] See, for example, GC, Case T-289/03 *BUPA v Commission* [2008] *ECR* II-81. Cf Klasse 2009, who argues that Article 106(2) TFEU is restricted to assessing a possible over-compensation where psc is evaluated, whereas the *Altmark* criteria apply a stricter regime, requiring also a judgment of efficiency.

and Holwerda argue, *Altmark* can also be seen as a drive to develop new mechanisms that will increase efficiency and competitiveness of public services whilst protecting the interests underlying the SGEI, in an ever more fine-tuned balancing act between these interests.

The ruling in *Altmark* can be placed within an historical context of removing the qualitative conditions for the provision of public services away from the competence of the Member States and modernising the conceptual framework within which public services are funded. Hancher and Larouche see this as a significant shift from the formalist paradigm inherent within Article 106(2) TFEU towards, what they describe as 'a more integrative paradigm', which can accommodate the funding of public services without a harsh and formal rule/exception relationship.[28]

Altmark is of significant importance in the implicit recognition that state monopolies are no longer privileged undertakings operating in a *sui generis* 'market'. Public services can be (and often are) economic activities that are delivered in competitive markets and the EU competition rules can be used to foster competition, efficiency and consumer satisfaction. It is prescriptive approach in guiding the Member States towards the *ex ante* regulation of public services, rather than the old model of abolition, or adaptation, of existing State monopolies when challenged and measured against EU law in litigation. Thus, *Altmark* sits between the regulatory approach of the EU in creating universal service obligations and the state aid rules which favour efficiency and transparency in competitive markets.

As the chapters in this book show, the response to the *Altmark* ruling from has had a wide impact, and allowed for the modernisation of public services and a debate on *how* public services should function in the EU.

1.3 The Reaction of the Commission

While the *Altmark* ruling attracted much critical attention, the significance of *Altmark* lies more in the Commission's handling of Decisions following the case and its management of the subsequent reform process.[29] At a practical level, overnight the *Altmark* ruling questioned the funding, and thereby the operation of, SGEI across the EU, opening them to potential litigation. The European Court had endorsed the Commission's approach to the funding of SGEI but it had also opened the door for the Member States to self-assess their own funding operations and avoid scrutiny by the Commission of the proportionality of national measures.

The Commission reacted to the ruling in a pragmatic manner. It seized back the scrutiny of potential state aid by encouraging notification of proposed funding for SGEI for analysis against the *Altmark* criteria and continuing to offer the opportunity of using Article 106(2) TFEU (and the principle of proportionality) to

---

[28] Hancher and Larouche 2011.

[29] Szyszczak 2011.

review funding for SGEI enabling a balance between competing public service interests against economic (competition) interests. The Commission seized back the control over monitoring the financing of SGEI by adopting the 2005 Package comprising a Decision[30] and a Framework.[31] While the Commission cannot alter the four criteria set out by the Court, a restrictive interpretation of these measures has ensured that the Commission retained control over the financing of pso and *how* the Commission's decision-making practice did this is analysed by *Klasse.*

The Framework and Decision were accompanied by a revision of the Transparency Directive[32] imposing an obligation to keep separate accounts for undertakings benefiting from psc that also engage in activities outside of the SGEI, irrespective of whether they were receiving state aid, and a Commission Press Release of FAQ.[33] This collection of measures, known as the 'Monti-Kroes package', or the '*Altmark*-Monti-Kroes Package' added to a prescriptive ex ante approach towards financing of public services with safe havens for certain kinds of social and transport services.[34]

Klasse argues that the Commission, by interpreting its own measures restrictively, was, at times, at odds with the policy of the European Courts towards SGEI. This is seen, for example, in the Commission expanding its review of the definition of an SGEI beyond 'manifest error' on the part of a Member State towards, what *Klasse* describes as, 'second guessing' the Member State definitions, a practice at odds with the General Court approach in cases such as *BUPA*.[35] The Commission has consolidated this approach in its new package of measures where it attaches a number of conditions to the definition of an SGEI, for example, the notion that it would not be appropriate to attach specific pso to activities provided by undertakings operating under normal market conditions.

Klasse shows that the criteria set out in *Altmark* for psc to be free of state aid elements have been met only on rare occasions in the Commission Decisions as a consequence of the Commission taking a very strict reading of the *Altmark* criteria. Additionally, the 2005 SGEI Package, adopted by the Commission is limited.

---

[30] Commission, *Commission Decision of 28 November 2005*, C(2005) 2673 *on the Application of Article 86(2) of the EC Treaty to State Aid in the Form of* **Public Service Compensation** *Granted to Certain Undertakings Entrusted With the Operation of Services of General Economic Interest, OJ* 2005 L 312/67.

[31] Community Framework for State Aid in the Form of Public Service Compensation, *OJ* 2005 C 297/4.

[32] Commission Directive 2006/111/EC of 16 November 2006 on the transparency of financial relations between Member States and public undertakings as well as on financial transparency within certain undertakings *OJ* 2006 L 318/17.

[33] State aid: Commission provides greater legal certainty for financing services of general economic interest, Press Release IP/05/937, Reference: MEMO/05/258 Date: 15/07/2005. Available at: http://europa.eu/rapid/pressReleasesAction.do?reference=IP/05/937&format= HTML&aged=0%3Cuage=EN&guiLanguage=en. Of particular significance are the reasons set out as to why social services are excluded from the State aid rules.

[34] See Szyszczak 2012b.

[35] GC, T-289/03 *BUPA* v. *Commission* [2008] *ECR* II-81.

His chapter charts the Commission's practice in relation to each of the four *Altmark* criteria. While the first three criteria are generally considered to be relatively straightforward to apply, his analysis shows that the Commission's case law has confined the Member States' room for manoeuvre in relation to each criterion. Even where the Commission acknowledges a margin of discretion on the part of the Member States which is subject only to review for manifest error (for e.g. in relation to the definition of a public service mission) the Commission has interpreted its powers widely. *Klasse* notes that the main challenging factor, remains the assessment of the fourth *Altmark* criterion, namely, in the absence of a competitive tender, a benchmarking analysis is required. Save for in exceptional circumstances, the benchmarking exercise has never been successful. He argues that it is difficult to reconcile the Commission's decision-making approach with the jurisprudence of the European Courts.

1.4 The Reaction of the European Courts

Few cases on funding SGEI have reached the European Courts in the post-*Altmark* era and the ad hoc nature of the case law has led to an uneven application of the *Altmark* criteria.

This case law is analysed in the chapter by *Vedder and Holwerda*. Their analysis is from the perspective of the constitutional and judicial protection implications of *Altmark* in order to determine the purpose of *Altmark*. They argue that while the judgment in *Altmark* was groundbreaking, it can be seen as part of an evolutionary trend emerging from the earlier judgment in *Ferring*.[36] Significantly, the era of post-*Altmark* litigation is marked by the fact that that most cases were brought by competitors of the undertakings entrusted with the SGEI, taking the opportunity to use EU law to challenge national preferences for the organisation of SGEI. The response of the European Courts is mixed. *Vedder and Holwerda* state that some 20 European Court judgments have been handed down since the ruling in *Altmark* and that the majority of these judgments contain a simple and straightforward application of *Altmark* ruling.[37] There are also a number of judgments that point at the difficulties of applying *Altmark* in practice. A significant case is the judgment of the General Court in *BUPA*[38] which has been interpreted as a modification of,[39] and withdrawal from, the strict efficiency

---

[36] CJEU, Case C-53/00 [2001] *ECR* I-9067.

[37] Cf. Szyszczak 2011.

[38] GC, T-289/03 [2008] *ECR* II-81.

[39] Hancher and Larouche 2011, p. 765.

approach taken in *Altmark*.[40] It has also been argued that *BUPA* must be seen as evidence of the flexibility offered by the *Altmark* exception to SGEI.[41] This idea of flexibility in the application of *Altmark* is also found in the judgment in *Chronopost*.[42] *Vedder and Holwerda* conclude that European Court judgments can be viewed as deference being afforded to the historical and cultural specificity of certain kinds of national SGEI. However, the Almunia Package may have made significant inroads into the deference afforded to Member State competence in the area of public services.

1.5 The Review of the *Altmark*-Monti-Kroes Package

The Commission Decision of 2005 provided for an impact assessment of the *Altmark* package by December 2009 (Article 9). But, by 2009, the appraisal of SGEI had entered a different economic and political phase and a different constitutional context. **Part II** of the book provides different perspectives of the process of review of the Monti-Kroes Package and the content of the Almunia Package. First, for the purposes of this **Introduction** the process of reform is set in context.

1.5.1 The Changing Constitutional Context Towards SGEI

The Treaty of Lisbon 2009 created a new concept of a 'highly competitive social market economy' as an objective of the Union (Article 3(3) TEU). Competition policy was moved from the main body of the Treaties to Protocol No. 27 where competition is absorbed into a principle of the internal market.[43] The Commission acknowledged the concerns of the Member States that a better balance should be achieved between social and economic objectives of European integration and that *social* services of general interest (SSGI) may be better provided at the local level and not fully exposed to market principles.[44]

In 2007, the Commission had started a review of the internal market balancing the aim of removing barriers to trade towards a greater recognition of the needs of

---

[40] Hancher and Larouche 2011, p. 764. See also Sauter and van de Gronden 2011, p. 618. Who state that the GC substantially amended the *Altmark* criteria and that it, by moderating the fourth criterion, called into question the strict efficiency approach that the Commission adopted in four healthcare decisions.

[41] Ross 2009, p. 138.

[42] CJEU, Joined Cases C-341/06 P and C-342/06 P *Chronopost II* [2008] *ECR* I-4777.

[43] For more detailed discussion of the constitutional significance of these changes to the basic Union Treaties and their use in soft law see Szyszczak 2012c.

[44] The Treaty of Lisbon 2009 recognised for the first time the role of subnational governments in the Union, see: Article 4(2) TEU; Protocol No. 2, Articles 2, 5; Article 5(3) TEU.

consumers, with a new language of citizenship and new values of solidarity, inclusion and sustainability. In the communication *Towards A Single Market Act*, the Commission emphasised that public services were a key aspect of the economic recovery of Europe and should be accessible, easy to operate, adhere to clear financing rules and be of the highest quality.[45] Thus SGEI were brought in from the cold, where they had been seen as a 'persistent irritant' and acknowledged as a tool of the new single market programme.[46]

The Treaty also delivered a revised Article 16 EC in the form of Article 14 TFEU, stressing that SGEI were the shared responsibility of the Member States and the Union. The new Article 14 TFEU provided a legal base for EU legislation on SGEI. Surprisingly after years of discussion as to whether the EU should take competence for legislation in the field of SGEI the Commission declined to use the new legal base and instead has focussed upon delivering tougher soft law communications in the area.

Additionally, SGI were addressed in Protocol No. 26 to the TEU and TFEU 2009. This makes explicit recognition of the competence of the Member States to regulate *non-economic* services of general interest. The Protocol also recognises the need for diversified and local services as well as 'a high level of quality, safety and affordability, equal treatment and the promotion of universal access and of user rights.'

Mention should also be made of the Charter of Fundamental Rights of the Union which contains a number of provisions of relevance to SGEI. For example: Article 29 (right of access to placement services); Article 34 (social security and social assistance); Article 35 (health care); Article 37 (environmental protection); Article 38 (consumer protection). Of special significance is Article 36 of the Charter which states:

> The Union recognises and respects *access* to SGEIs as provided for in national laws and practices, in accordance with the Treaties in order to promote the social and territorial cohesion of the Union [my emphasis].

The Charter is not incorporated into any of the EU Treaties or the Protocols but Article 6(1) TEU states that the Charter 'shall have the same legal value as the treaties'.

1.5.2 The Review Process

This was the new constitutional and economic setting for the review of the 'Monti-Kroes' package. *Rodrigues'* chapter explores the complementary link between EU competition rules and SGEI which is clearly confirmed by the Treaty of Lisbon 2009 in the new Article 14 TFEU, Protocol No. 26 on SGI and Article 36 CFREU. *Rodrigues* argues that among the competition rules, state aids rules play a very

---

[45] COM (2007) 724 final; COM (2007) 725 final, COM (2007) 726 final.

[46] Mario Monti, *A New Strategy for the Single Market. At the Service of Europe's Economy and Society. Report to the President of the European Commission Jose Manuel Barroso*, 9 May 2010, 73. (The Monti Report).

important role in order to ensure a sustainable financing of SG(E)I by the Member States. According to *Rodrigues* such a balanced approach is the key milestone of the European Commission's strategy to reform the rules applicable to psc, by giving them greater clarification and more adaptability, in order to promote higher quality of service. His chapter concludes with a remaining question after the reforms: whether such a strategy is sufficient to ensure an effective implementation of these rules by the public authorities, notably local entities.

The post-*Altmark* era may be regarded as a transitional and experimental period where the Member States and the EU (particularly through Commission practice) have brokered a new relationship towards the regulation of public services using the state aid rules. This has resulted in many elements of uncertainty in both Commission practice and Court jurisprudence. There is both a Member State and EU benefit in the fluidity of application of the legal rules. Where there is no sector-specific legislation there is greater flexibility to negotiate the evolution and recalibration of the provision of public services. The Commission reviewed the new relationship through a stakeholder consultation, eliciting feedback on three broad issues related to stakeholders' interests:

1. From public bodies: is the package sufficiently user friendly and does it allow provision of SGEI to citizens?
2. From SGEI users: does the package allow for provision of good-quality and cost-effective services?
3. From providers: does the package ensure a level playing field with competitors without creating unnecessary obstacles?[47]

The Member States were asked to report on the implementation of the Monti-Kroes package during 2009. This element of review reveals the weaknesses of self-reporting. Many reports are not very detailed; the Member States must be reluctant to expose their internal organisation of SGEI to too much scrutiny. Some Member States express concerns over issues of legal certainty connected to the *Altmark* ruling and the Monti-Kroes Package, especially around the notions of economic activity, effect on trade, the relationship between state aid/public procurement and how to control of overcompensation.[48]

The lack of legal certainty raised concerns, both for the Member States, and the Commission, as to whether rules were always applied correctly. Additionally, many Member States would have liked to see the *de minimis* threshold raised and the creation of more safe harbours, especially for SSGI.

As *Maxian Rusche* explains there was no legal obligation for the Commission to enter the consultation exercise. The extensive consultation would seem to be part of the Commission's strategy to position itself in the centre of an area of

---

[47] *The Application of EU State Aid rules on Services of General Economic Interest since 2005 and the Outcome of the Public Consultation*, SEC (2011) 397.
[48] *The Application of EU State Aid rules on Services of General Economic Interest since 2005 and the Outcome of the Public Consultation*, SEC (2011) 397.

policy where EU competence is shaky and to create a constellation of stakeholders in its policy-making strategy.[49] This was not an easy task. The Commission was also faced with a growing interest in the regulation of SGEI and different views on how to regulate SGEI at the EU level. *Maxian Rusche* explains that the political debate on SGEI has different facets in the EU. First, there is a clear divide between the political right and the left in the European Parliament. Second, only a few Member States, composed of the six founding members of the EEC, dominate the debate. Third, local and regional actors are of particular importance, as they fund the bulk of the services. Notably absent from the general policy debate are the potential beneficiaries of stricter state aid control.

The Commission adopted a Communication in which it set out the broad themes it envisaged for the reform of the *Altmark* Package.[50] The Commission launched a second round of consultations by inviting the other EU Institutions, the Member States and stakeholders to react to the broad themes set out in its Communication. The European Parliament,[51] Committee of the Regions[52] and Economic and Social Committee[53] responded with reports that were supportive of the policy proposed by the Commission, but requested more generous notification exemptions.

The contentious point for all of the Institutions was whether the Commission should use the new legal base of Article 14 TFEU. The Committee of the Regions and the Economic and Social Committee supported this idea, and invited the Commission to use the legal base, rather than a Communication (from the Commission), to clarify the concept of state aid and the precise meaning of the *Altmark* ruling.[54]

In September 2011, the Commission published the draft texts for the four instruments, and again invited comments from the other EU Institutions, Member States and stakeholders. The response was similar as the one that was given to the earlier Communication but the only institution to formally adopt an opinion was the Committee of the Regions.[55]

In another process, the Commission engaged in a dialogue with the legal community at the European State Aid Law Institute[56] and Vice President Almunia presented the draft texts at an academic conference at the College of Europe in Bruges.[57]

---

[49] See Szyszczak 2012b.

[50] *Reform of the EU State Aid Rules on Services of General Economic Interest*, COM (2011) 146 final.

[51] Resolution A7 0371/2011 of 24 October 2011.

[52] Opinion COR/2011/150, *OJ* 2011 C 259/40.

[53] Opinion EESC/2011/1008, *OJ* 2011 C 248/149.

[54] Recital 4.11 of Opinion EESC/2011/1008; Recitals 12 to 14 of Opinion COR/2011/150.

[55] Opinion COR/2011/27, *OJ* C 9 of 11 January 2012, p. 45. See Lambertz and Hornung 2012.

[56] See Regner 2011; Jääskinen 2011.

[57] The conference proceedings edited by Messola 2011. They were available on the College of Europe web pages at the time of writing (1 August 2012):
    http://www.coleurope.eu/content/gclc/documents/GCLC%20-%20SGEI%20Conference%20 Booklet.pdf

The results of the extensive consultations are reflected in the impact assessment accompanying the Almunia Package.[58]

Maxian Rusche notes that there were only two main legal constraints for the Commission in the review of the 2005 Package: the interpretation of Article 107 (1) TFEU given by the Court in *Altmark*, and the legal base provided in the TFEU. The first constraint was unchanged since the Monti-Kroes Package, whereas the second constraint may have been affected by the Treaty of Lisbon 2009. There has been a debate amongst academic commentators on the legal base for regulation of SGEI and this debate is explored by *Maxian Rusche*. He concludes that the entry into force of the Treaty of Lisbon 2009 has not changed the exclusive competence of the Commission for authorising state aid for SGEI compensation: Article 14 TFEU does not provide a legal basis for legislating on the concept, the compatibility or the notification exemption for state aid in the form of SGEI compensation.

1.6 The Almunia Package: A New Hierarchy

The Commission adopted the Almunia Package without a statement of how the measures work with each other. There are differences in language and the use of different methodology in the calculation of psc among the various measures. There is now a hierarchy of measures, with the hard law de minimis Regulation No. 360/2012 as a starting point for any inquiry of whether there is state aid that is compatible/ incompatible with the Single Market.

If the measure is protected by the de minimis Regulation then the measure is not caught by the state aid rules. If the measure does not fall within the Regulation then the application of the *Altmark* criteria (as explained by the new Communication) applies. Again if all four criteria are met the measure is not caught by the state aid rules. If the criteria are not met in full then the new Commission Decision applies to determine if there is compatible state aid. There is, albeit a remote, possibility that even if a measure fails to pass through the various parts of the Package the underlying application of Article 106(2) TFEU may be possible.

1.7 The *De Minimis* Regulation

Regulation No. 360/2012[59] is a residual measure that applies to SGEI that are not already covered by specific sectoral rules, as outlined in Article 1. The Regulation will remain in force until 31 December 2018.

---

[58] SEC (2011) 1581.

[59] Commission Regulation on the application of Articles 107 and 108 of the Treaty on the Functioning of the European Union to *de minimis* aid granted to undertakings providing services of general economic interest, *OJ* 2012 L/8.

Questions were raised as to *why* a specific SGEI *de minimis* measure was necessary. The Commission's justification of the new measure is that the threshold is higher than the general de minimis thresholds in the field of state aid (EUR 200,000 over 3 years) because it can be assumed that the support measures are at least in part compensating for the extra costs incurred for the provision of a public service.[60]

Original ideas of defining 'local' *de minimis* criteria according to the size of the local authority, size of the provider or the amount of compensation were dropped in favour of a simple threshold of EUR 50,000 over three fiscal years. *De minimis* aid under the Regulation cannot be cumulated with state aid for the same eligible costs if the cumulating would result in an aid intensity exceeding that stipulated in the specific circumstances of each case by a Block Exemption, Regulation of Decision adopted by the Commission. However, *de minimis* may be cumulated with other *de minimis* aid under other *de minimis* regulations up to the EUR 500,000 threshold. It may not be cumulated with any compensation in respect of the same SGEI, regardless of whether or not it is state aid.

Article 2 sets out the detail of the financial accounting periods. The fiscal year will be determined according to the criteria used by the undertaking in the Member State concerned. The threshold is measured as a cash grant, using gross figures, but where the State aid is in a form other than a grant the gross equivalent of the aid shall be used and where aid is paid in instalments the discount rate applicable at the time of the grant shall apply. The *de minimis* Regulation only applies where it is possible to calculate precisely the gross equivalent of ex ante aid without the necessity to undertake a risk assessment. Specific forms of this transparent aid are identified:

(a) aid comprised in loans shall be considered as transparent *de minimis* aid when the gross grant equivalent has been calculated on the basis of the reference rate applicable at the time of the grant;

(b) aid comprised in capital injections shall not be considered as transparent *de minimis* aid, unless the total amount of the public injection does not exceed the *de minimis* ceiling;

(c) aid comprised in risk capital measures shall not be considered as transparent *de minimis* aid, unless the risk capital scheme concerned provides capital only up to the *de minimis* ceiling to each target undertaking;

(d) individual aid provided under a guarantee scheme to undertakings which are not undertakings in difficulty shall be treated as transparent *de minimis* aid when the guaranteed part of the underlying loan provided under such scheme does not exceed EUR 37,50,000 per undertaking. If the guaranteed part of the underlying loan only accounts for a given proportion of this ceiling, the gross grant equivalent of that guarantee shall be deemed to correspond to the same proportion of the ceiling laid down in paragraph 2. The guarantee shall not exceed 80 % of the underlying loan. Guarantee schemes shall also be considered as transparent if:

(i) before the implementation of the scheme, the methodology to calculate the gross grant equivalent of the guarantees has been accepted following notification of this methodology to the Commission under a regulation adopted by the Commission in the State aid area, and

---

[60] European Commission Press Release IP/12/402, State aid: Commission adopts *de minimis* Regulation for SGEI, 25 April 2012.

      (ii) the approved methodology explicitly addresses the type of guarantees and the type of underlying transactions at stake in the context of the application of this Regulation.

Article 3 imposes a set of monitoring conditions.

1.8 The Interpretative Communication

The aim of the Communication[61] is to clarify the European Courts' case law and Commission practice. The use of the Communication follows a new trend of the Commission adopting weightier forms of soft law to act as a guide, or handbook, for practitioners, the judiciary and other actors, particularly central and local government officials engaged in state aid decisions.[62] As a piece of soft law, it is nevertheless included under the heading 'Legislation in Force' on the European Commission Competition web pages.[63] The Communication is an interpretative document for the new Regulation, Decision and Framework as well as the application of the *Altmark* criteria.

1.8.1 Definition of Basic Terms

After the introduction explaining the purpose and scope of the Communication Part 2 outlines the General Principles. This part of the Communication explains the case law relating to the definition of economic activity, an undertaking, the exercise of public power, the indicators for a solidarity-based social security scheme. The Communication has some inconsistent statements. For example, the Communication states that national decisions could influence whether a particular activity is 'economic'[64] but in other parts is very direct in stating that national classifications/provision of certain activities cannot influence the EU classification of an activity.[65]

---

[61] *Communication from the Commission on the application of the European Union State aid rules to compensation granted for the provision of services of general economic interest, OJ* 2012 C 8/4.

[62] See the earlier: European Commission, *Guide to the application of the European Union rules on state aid, public procurement and the internal market to services of general economic interest, and in particular to social services of general interest*, SEC (2010) 1545, Brussels, 7 December 2010 (a document of 84 pages).

[63] http://ec.europa.eu/competition/state_aid/legislation/sgei.html

[64] See paras 12 and 14.

[65] See, for eg, paras 13 (on in-house provision of services) and 37 (exclusive rights and hybrid markets). On stating that in-house provision has no particular relevance for the economic nature of an activity the Commission bases its interpretation *not* on CJEU case law but on its Decision 2011/501/EU *Verkersverbund Rhein Ruhr, OJ* 2011 L210/1.

Special consideration is provided for the newer and more problematic 'social' SGEI issues that are emerging in the fields of health and education. The Communication then moves on to explain the law on 'State resources' and 'effect on trade' as understood in the state aid rules and policy. This part is not new law but drawn from Commission practice and the European Courts' case law.

1.8.2 De Minimis and Effect on Trade

In relation to the effect on trade criteria the Commission acknowledges that the Court has stated that there is no general *de minimis* rule to be applied in the field of state aid.[66] Balanced against this position the Commission then illustrates four examples from its *own practice* where activities that have a purely local character were found not to affect trade in the EU: swimming pools to be used predominantly by the local population; local hospitals aimed exclusively at the local population; local museums unlikely to attract cross-border visitors; local cultural events whose potential audience is restricted locally. The Commission also notes that there is a general *de minimis* Regulation[67] and that specific *de minimis* rules apply in the transport, fisheries and agricultural sectors.

1.8.3 The Conditions Under Which PSC Does Not Constitute State Aid

The Communication explains the *Altmark* criteria, providing further interpretation. First, the definition of an SGEI is discussed. It is recognised that SGEI are not static concepts and are evolving in specific contexts, depending upon, *inter alia*, the needs of citizens, technological and market developments and the social and political preferences in each Member State. The Commission is of the opinion that for a service to be classified as an SGEI it must be addressed to citizens or be in the interest of society as a whole (para 50). The Court has established that SGEI have special characteristics as compared with other economic activities.[68] In the absence of specific sectoral rules, the Commission acknowledges that the Member States have a wide margin of discretion in defining a service as an SGEI and the Commission's power is limited to checking whether the Member State has made a manifest error in definition and assessing that any psc is not a State Aid.

---

[66] See CJEU, Case C-280/00 *Altmark* [2003] *ECR* I-7747.

[67] Regulation (EC) No 1998/2006, *OJ* 1998 L 379/5.

[68] See for example, CJEU, Case C-179/90 *Merci convenzionali porto di Genova* [1991] *ECR* I-5889, para 27.

The question of whether a service can be provided by the market may only be assessed by the Commission by investigating if there has been a manifest error. The Commission gives the example of the types of activity that may be an SGEI in the broadband sector, drawn from its own 2009 Guidelines.[69] It illustrates that where private investors have already invested in the broadband network infrastructure and providing competitive broadband services setting up a parallel broadband structure would *not* be an SGEI. However, where investors are not in a position to provide adequate broadband coverage SGEI compensation could be granted under certain conditions.

Thus, in paras 48–50, the Commission adds two *new* criteria to limit the Member States' discretion. First, the Commission considers that it would be inappropriate to attach pso to an activity which is already provided (or can be satisfactorily provided and under conditions such as price, objective quality characteristics, continuity and access to the service) consistent with the public interest, as defined by the State, by undertakings operating under normal market conditions. Second, an SGEI must be addressed to citizens or be in the interests of society as a whole.

1.8.4 Entrustment

Hancher and Larouche[70] observe that the evolution of public services at the national level may result in a 'pot pourri' of historical entrustments without clearly defined regulation, and often without market testing. The Communication points out that for Article 106(2) TFEU to apply the Court has held that the undertaking must have been entrusted with a special task by the State. *Altmark* confirmed that the undertaking must have a pso to discharge. The Communication then enumerates five *minimum* criteria to be satisfied in the act of entrustment:

(a) The content and duration of the pso;
(b) The undertaking and, where applicable, the territory concerned;
(c) The nature of any exclusive or special rights assigned to the undertaking by the authority in question;
(d) The parameters for calculating, controlling and reviewing the psc; *and*
(e) The arrangements for avoiding and recovering any overcompensation.

These criteria narrow down the wide discretion of the Member States and create a set of *ex ante* prescriptive provisions for scrutiny when payment for pso services is challenged. The Commission acknowledges that it is not unusual for the pso provider to be involved in the act of entrustment (and the legal form is irrelevant) but a national authority must approve the provider's proposal for a pso before psc is granted.[71]

---

[69] *Communication from the Commission Community Guidelines for the application of State Aid rules in relation to rapid deployment of broadband networks, OJ* 2009 23/7.

[70] Hancher and Larouche 2011, p. 24.

[71] See GC, Case T-17/02 *Fred Olsen* [2005] *ECR* II- 2031, para 188.

The Commission adds other conditions (para 57). First, where the undertaking is offered a reasonable profit as part of its compensation, the entrustment act must also establish the criteria for calculating that profit (para 57). Second, where a review of the amount of compensation during the entrustment period is provided for, the entrustment act must also specify the arrangements for the review and any impact it may have on the total amount of compensation (para 58).

Following the second *Altmark* criterion the parameters of psc must be established in advance in an objective and transparent manner in order to ensure that they do not confer an economic advantage that could favour the recipient undertaking over competing undertakings. However, the Commission points out that the need to establish the compensation parameters in advance does not mean that the compensation has to be calculated on the basis of a specific formula (for example, a certain price per day, per meal, per passenger or per number of users). It should be clear from the outset *how* the compensation is to be determined. The Commission then clarifies that where the authority decides to compensate all cost items of the provider, it must determine at the *outset* how those costs will be determined and calculated. Only the costs directly associated with the provision of the SGEI can be taken into account in that context. All the revenue accruing to the undertaking from the provision of the SGEI must be deducted. If the SGEI is assigned under a tendering procedure, the method for calculating the compensation must be included in the information provided to all the undertakings wishing to take part in the procedure.

1.8.5 Avoiding Overcompensation

The third *Altmark* criterion is explained at para 61, broken down into a number of components. *Reasonable profit* should be taken to mean the rate of return on capital that would be required by a typical company considering whether or not to provide the SGEI for the whole duration of the period of entrustment, taking into account the level of risk.

The *level of risk* will depend on the sector concerned, the type of service and the characteristics of the compensation mechanism. The rate should be determined (where possible) by reference to the rate of return on capital that is achieved on similar types of public service contracts under competitive conditions (for example, contracts awarded under a tender).

In the difficult scenario of sectors where there is no undertaking comparable to the undertaking entrusted with the SGEI, reference can be made to comparable undertakings situated in other Member States, or, if necessary, in other sectors, provided that the particular characteristics of each sector are taken into account.

In determining what constitutes a reasonable profit, the Member States may introduce *incentive criteria* relating, in particular, to the quality of service provided and gains in productive efficiency. However, efficiency gains cannot be achieved at the expense of the quality of the service provided.

Any mechanism concerning the selection of the pso provider must be taken in such a way that the level of compensation is determined on the basis of these elements.

1.8.6 Selection of the pso Provider

The Commission argues that the simplest way for national authorities to meet the fourth *Altmark* criterion is to conduct an open, transparent and non-discriminatory public procurement procedure in line with Directive 2004/17/EC[72] and Directive 2004/18/EC.[73] *Altmark* did not include this as a mandatory process but merely provided *incentives* for the Member States to adopt procurement procedures. The Commission points out that the use of such a public procurement procedure is often a mandatory requirement under existing EU rules. In cases where it is not a legal requirement, an open, transparent and non-discriminatory public procurement procedure is an appropriate method to compare different potential offers and set the compensation so as to exclude the presence of aid. Relying on the dicta in *Altmark* the Commission notes that a public procurement procedure only excludes the existence of state aid where it allows for the selection of the tenderer capable of providing the service at 'the least cost to the community'.

Both an open procedure in line with the requirement of the public procurement rules and also a restricted procedure can satisfy the fourth *Altmark* criterion, unless interested operators are prevented to tender without valid reasons. In contrast, a competitive dialogue or a negotiated procedure with prior publication confer a wide discretion upon the adjudicating authority and may restrict the participation of interested operators. Therefore, the Commission argues, they can only be deemed sufficient to satisfy the fourth *Altmark* criterion in *exceptional* cases. The negotiated procedure without publication of a contract notice cannot ensure that the procedure leads to the selection of the tenderer capable of providing those services at the least cost to the community.

In relation to the award criteria, the 'lowest price' criterion obviously satisfies the fourth *Altmark* criterion, but also the 'most economically advantageous tender' is deemed sufficient, provided that the award criteria, including environmental or social criteria, are closely related to the subject-matter of the service provided and allow for the most economically advantageous offer to match the value of the market. This is an important development clarifying when considerations other than price may be used as award criteria. Where such circumstances occur, a claw-back mechanism may be appropriate to minimise the risk of overcompensation *ex ante*. The awarding authority is not prevented from setting qualitative standards to be met by all economic operators, or from taking qualitative aspects related to the different

---

[72] *OJ* 2004 L 134/114.

[73] *OJ* 2004 L 134/1.

proposals into account in its award decision. There can be circumstances where a procurement procedure cannot allow for 'the least cost to the community' as it does not give rise to a sufficient open and genuine competition. Examples are given such as the particularities of the service in question, existing intellectual property rights or necessary infrastructure owned by a particular service provider. Similarly, in the case of procedures where only one bid is submitted, the tender cannot be deemed sufficient to ensure that the procedure leads to the least cost for the community.

Thus, on the one hand, the Commission appears to be toughening up the fourth *Altmark* criterion, and on the other, allowing a softening of the award criteria to accommodate factors other than lowest price.

1.8.7 Where a Tendering Procedure is Not Used

The final part of the Communication addresses the difficult situation of assessing the remuneration given for a pso where procurement procedures are not used. Here, the Commission draws upon its own practice and economic advice to establish clearer criteria to be applied.

The Commission starts with an (obvious) point that where a generally accepted market remuneration exists for a given service, that market remuneration provides the best benchmark for the compensation in the absence of a tender. Where no such market remuneration exists, then the *Altmark* criterion insists that the amount of compensation must be determined on the basis of an analysis of the costs that a typical undertaking, well run and adequately provided with material means so as to be able to meet the necessary public service requirements, would have incurred in discharging those obligations, taking into account the relevant receipts and a reasonable profit for discharging those obligations. The aim is to ensure that the high costs of an inefficient undertaking are not taken as the benchmark. The concept of 'well run undertaking' is given further precision. In the absence of any official definition, the Member States should apply objective criteria that are economically recognised as being representative of satisfactory management.

The Commission considers that simply generating a profit is not a sufficient criterion for deeming an undertaking to be 'well run'. Account should also be taken of the fact that the financial results of undertakings, particularly in the sectors most often serviced by SGEI, may be strongly influenced by their market power or by sectoral rules. The Commission takes the view that the concept of 'well run undertaking' entails compliance with the national, Union or international accounting standards in force. The Member States may base their analysis, *inter alia*, on analytical ratios representative of productivity (such as turnover to capital employed, total cost to turnover, turnover per employee, value added per employee or staff costs to value added).

The Member States may also use analytical ratios relating to the quality of supply as compared with user expectations. An undertaking entrusted with the operation of an SGEI that does not meet the qualitative criteria laid down by the

Member State concerned does not constitute 'a well run undertaking' even if its costs are low. Undertakings with such analytical ratios representative of efficient management may be regarded as representative typical undertakings. But, the analysis and comparison of the cost structures must take into account the size of the undertaking in question and the fact that in certain sectors undertakings with very different cost structures may exist side by side.

The reference to the costs of a 'typical undertaking' in the sector under consideration implies that there are a sufficient number of undertakings whose costs may be taken into account (the undertakings may be located in the same Member State or in other Member States). However, the Commission takes the view that reference cannot be made to the costs of an undertaking that enjoys a monopoly position or receives psc granted on conditions that do not comply with Union law, as in both cases the cost level may be higher than normal. The costs to be taken into consideration are all the costs relating to the SGEI: the direct costs necessary to discharge the SGEI and an appropriate contribution to the indirect costs common to both the SGEI and other activities. If the Member State can show that the cost structure of the undertaking entrusted with the operation of the SGEI corresponds to the *average* cost structure of efficient and comparable undertakings in the sector under consideration, the amount of compensation that will allow the undertaking to cover its costs, including a reasonable profit, this will comply with the fourth *Altmark* criterion. The expression 'undertaking adequately provided with material means' should be taken to mean an undertaking which has the resources necessary for it to discharge immediately the public service obligations incumbent on the undertaking to be entrusted with the operation of the SGEI.

'Reasonable profit' should be taken to mean the rate of return on capital that would be required by a typical company considering whether or not to provide the service of general economic interest for the whole duration of the period of entrustment, taking into account the level of risk.

1.9 Commission Decision 2012/21/EU

The revised Decision[74] replaces Decision 2005/842/EC[75] and continues to set out the conditions under which state aid in the form of psc is not subject to prior notification to the Commission under Article 108(3) TFEU. The objective of

---

[74] Commission Decision of 20 December on the application of Article 106(2) of the Treaty on the Functioning of the European Union to State aid in the form of public service compensation granted to certain undertakings entrusted with the operation of services of general economic interest, *OJ* 2012 L 7/3.

[75] Commission, *Commission Decision of 28 November 2005*, C(2005) 2673 *on the Application of Article 86(2) of the EC Treaty to State Aid in the Form of Public Service Compensation Granted to Certain Undertakings Entrusted With the Operation of Services of General Economic Interest*, *OJ* 2005 L 312/67.

creating a diversified and proportionate approach is achieved by a simplification of the rules for social services: there are no thresholds for the exemption of the majority of social services, thus extending the exemption for social housing and hospitals found in the 2005 Decision. Specific mention is made of Article 14 TFEU in the preliminary explanations, as is special mention of social SGI at para 11.

A proportionate approach to psc is achieved by a reduction of the compensation ceiling to EUR 15 million per annum (down from EUR 30 million) for SGEI (other than in transport and transport infrastructure). Simplification is introduced by abolishing the turnover threshold of EUR 100 million over the previous 2 years. Thus, the emphasis is upon the amount of the psc, not the size of the undertaking. Where the amount of psc varies over time the annual amount is to be calculated as the average per annum over the period of the entrustment. Article 7 provides that for the purposes of transparency any psc above EUR 15 million granted to an undertaking which also has activities outside the scope of the SGEI the Member State shall publish on the Internet (or by other appropriate means) the entrustment act (or a summary provided that it includes the elements of entrustment set out in Article 4 and the amounts of aid granted to the undertaking on a yearly basis. The period of entrustment of the pso must be limited to 10 years, unless significant investment is required.

Article 2(1)(b) and (c) creates the safe haven (and a broad exemption) for social SGI discussed by *van de Gronden and Rusu*. The explanation for this broad exemption is found in para 11 of the preliminary explanations:

(11) Hospitals and undertakings in charge of social services, which are entrusted with tasks of general economic interest, have specific characteristics that need to be taken into consideration. In particular, account should be taken of the fact that, in the present economic conditions and at the current stage of development of the internal market, social services may require an amount of aid beyond the threshold in this Decision to compensate for the public service costs. A larger amount of compensation for social services does thus not necessarily produce a greater risk of distortions of competition. Accordingly, undertakings in charge of social services, including the provision of social housing for disadvantaged citizens or socially less advantaged groups, who due to solvency constraints are unable to obtain housing at market conditions, should also benefit from the exemption from notification provided for in this Decision, even if the amount of compensation they receive exceeds the general compensation threshold laid down in this Decision. The same should apply to hospitals providing medical care, including, where applicable, emergency services and ancillary services directly related to their main activities, in particular in the field of research. In order to benefit from the exemption from notification, social services should be clearly identified services, meeting social needs as regards health and long-term care, childcare, access to and reintegration into the labour market, social housing and the care and social inclusion of vulnerable groups.

Article 2 (d) and (e) creates special rules for certain transport SGEI (discussed by *Maxian Rusche and Schmidt*):

(d) compensation for the provision of services of general economic interest as regards air or maritime links to islands on which the average annual traffic during the 2 financial years preceding that in which the service of general economic interest was assigned does not exceed 300,000 passengers;

(e) compensation for the provision of services of general economic interest as regards airports and ports for which the average annual traffic during the 2 financial years preceding that in which the service of general economic interest was assigned does not exceed 200,000 passengers, in the case of airports, and 300,000 passengers, in the case of ports.

Article 4 of the Decision sets out the requirements of the entrustment of the pso, as previously explained in the Communication.

Articles 5 and 6 set out the parameters for calculating compensation and overcompensation, as set out in the Communication.

One difference between the *Altmark* criterion and the Decision (and also the Framework) is that under the latter all costs actually incurred by the undertaking may be compensated. The Decision introduces a new methodology: Net Avoided Cost Methodology (NACM) which takes a comparison between the net cost for the undertaking of operating with a pso and the net cost (or profit) of the undertaking operating without a pso. Other methodology may also be used. This is discussed by *Kavanagh.*

The simplification of the procedure is seen in the extension of regular checks of overcompensation to at least every 3 years, but this is balanced by provision for the recovery of overcompensation and an update of the parameters for the psc (with the possibility of a 10 % carry forward). Safe harbours are created for the calculation of a reasonable profit, defined as: the return on capital equals the swap rate + 100 basis points (and for risk-free cases this is also the maximum). Flexibility is introduced by allowing the use of other profit indicators for determining the reasonable profit if return on capital is not feasible (for e.g: return on equity, return on assets, return on sales).

1.10 The Framework

The revised Framework, adopted as a Communication,[76] sets out the circumstances in which psc that constitutes State aid not covered by Decision 2012/21/EU can be found compatible with the internal market under Article 106(2) of the Treaty. Such aid should be notified to the Commission under Article 108(3) TFEU. The Commission appears to have introduced another new criterion by stating that Member States should show that they have given proper consideration to the public service needs through a public consultation (or other appropriate instruments) to take the interests of users into account.

The Commission will look for competition and efficiency criteria to decide whether the use of psc is proportionate, as well as ensuring that there is no discrimination between the treatment of several pso providers. The Commission outlines where additional conditions or commitments can be necessary to reduce the risk of serious distortions of trade and competition, for example, education of

---

[76] *Communication from the Commission, European Union framework for State aid in the form of public service compensation, OJ* 2012 C 8/15.

duration/scope/territory of the entrustment of a pso; reduction of the compensation, taking account of excessive profit on activities not in the SGEI using the same network; limitation of special or exclusive rights; an obligation to grant access to third parties to infrastructure or network financed by the compensation at appropriate conditions.

A direct—and controversial—link with the procurement rules is made in para 19 when the Commission states that when entrusting an SGEI the Member State should comply with the EU procurement rules. This requirement is discussed by *Clarke* and by *Sanchez Graells* in greater detail. This would seem to alter the fourth *Altmark* criterion in making competitive tendering *compulsory* if psc for an SGEI is to be approved under the Framework. The transparency requirement element is emphasised in that the Member States must publish basic information on SGEI on the internet or other appropriate means.

The Framework adopts similar methodology to that contained in the Decision on the calculation of compensation. NACM is the preferred methodology but cost allocation methodology may be used where NACM cannot. The Framework (unlike the Decision) addresses the criteria to be used for defining the contribution to the common cost: 'to determine the appropriate contribution to the common costs, market prices for the use of the resources, where available, can be taken as a benchmark'.

Overcompensation will be monitored at the end of the period of entrustment and at intervals of a maximum of every 3 years (or 2 years for concession and in-house contracts where a procurement procedure is not used).

The Framework is tougher than the Decision in that the Commission may make a closer examination of psc and ask for 'commitments' where there is:

(i) a longer duration than is objectively necessary;
(ii) a series of tasks which are bundled together;
(iii) where similar services to those of the SGEI are provided or can be expected to be provided in the near future in the absence of the SGEI;
(iv) where there are special or exclusive rights that seriously restrict competition within the internal market;
(v) where the aid allows the undertaking to finance the creation of an essential facility; or
(vi) if distortions of competition are a consequence of the entrustment hindering effective implementation or enforcement of Union legislation aimed at safeguarding the proper functioning of the internal market.

1.11 The Aim of the Almunia Package

Maxian Rusche states that in relation to the *content* of the Almunia Package, the Commission has opted for clarification of the rules on financing SGEI through a restatement of the case law and the Commission's decision-making practice; simplification of the rules through a total notification exemption of social services and the use of the principle of proportionality by creating stricter rules for certain sectors and larger scale compensation for SGEI above EUR 15 million.

Maxian Rusche argues that whereas under the Monti-Kroes package, all SGEI where essentially treated the same way, with verification for absence of over-compensation, the Almunia package tightens the rules for large SGEI. For example, it excludes undertakings in difficulty from the benefit of SGEI compensation if they do not, at the same time, undergo in-depth restructuring (including usually compensatory measures in the form of disposals of assets and market share); it requires award of the SGEI by tender (except for *in-house* situations) and efficiency incentives in the compensation mechanism (so as to become *Altmark* compliant over time); and it reserves the right for the Commission to ask for additional commitments in situations where there is particular risk of trade being affected to an extent contrary to the interest of the Union.

Buendía Sierra and Panero Rivas draw upon the historical context of the Almunia reform package to analyse the thought processes of the Commission and what it hopes to achieve in the new measures. Their analysis argues that the Commission has made an attempt to introduce flexibility into the rules for small-scale SGEI and created a practical framework for assessing larger scale SGEI. They argue that, combined with the application of the EU competition and procurement rules the new package would appear to have substantially limited the Member States' discretion to organise larger SGEI. The new rules are complex, with some overlap. Thus *Buendía Sierra and Panero Rivas* conclude that the Commission must exercise its discretion in applying the rules in a consistent and predictable manner if the objectives of clarification and simplification are to be achieved.

1.12 A 'More Economic Approach' Towards State Aid Control in the EU

The Almunia Package of measures establishes a more prescriptive methodology for determining the compensation to an undertaking entrusted with offering an SGEI, alongside enhanced efficiency incentives. *Kavanagh* surveys the revised financial and economic tests for determining appropriate SGEI compensation, analysing the theoretical basis and practical implementation of these tests. The Commission's revised Framework employs a strengthened set of economic tests with the purpose of ensuring that SGEI providers earn only a reasonable profit and have strong incentives to deliver efficiency and innovation.

In line with the general move in EU competition law to allow the Commission to prioritise enforcement of the more significant effects of anti-competitive conduct the Almunia reform brings a greater degree of European Commission control over SGEI compensation, and with it, an increased obligation on Member States to justify the financial terms of large SGEI contracts. This will require adjustment by competent national authorities making major entrustments of an SGEI. *Kavanagh* argues that, to a certain extent, the Commission is encouraging a form of economic regulation in relation to SGEI provision with an ensuing more sophisticated model for SGEI compensation. Potentially, the compliance obligation will encourage Member States to use competitive tenders for SGEI contracts, with the result that those contracts may be deemed to fall under the *Altmark* criteria (no State aid) rather than the SGEI Framework (compatible State aid).

1.13 The Broader Modernisation Agenda

Taking the uncertainties left by the fourth *Altmark* condition as the point of departure, the chapter by *Sanchez Graells* describes and critically appraises the position of the European Commission regarding the use of procurement procedures as a device to exclude the existence of State aid, or, where State aid exists, to contribute to its compatibility with the internal market and, at any rate, as a mechanism of control of contracting entities' 'market' behaviour.

His chapter stresses that there may be a disconnection between the two aspects of the modernisation agenda, in that the reform of public procurement rules currently underway[77] may diminish the effectiveness of the recent SGEI 'Almunia' reform or, in some instances, even lead to a clash with some of its basic assumptions—which may call for a major revision of a system of oversight of public expenditure that is currently in crisis in most of the EU.

1.14 Exclusions from, and Special Treatment in, the Package

Part III of this book addresses the exclusions from the package for certain kinds of SGEI.

1.14.1 Transport

The chapter by *Maxian Rusche and Schmidt* explores the complexities of the transport sector and the way it has been influenced by recent legislative developments on SGEI. Starting on the different legislative bases, the authors examine Article 93 TFEU which applies to land transport and Article 106 TFEU which applies to air and maritime transport. It is argued that Article 93 TFEU takes a more permissible view on State aid. There is a lack of harmonisation in the transport sector in the EU and thus the remainder of the chapter is divided between

---

[77] For discussion of the modernisation programme see Ølykke et al. 2012.

an initial discussion on the applicable rules and case law in land transport and, then, air and maritime transport.

In relation to land transport, *Maxian Rusche and Schmidt* argue that while the Commission is restricted by Articles 93, 91 and 109 TFEU, there are indications that the Commission has started taking a more assertive role. This part of the chapter focuses on the applicable secondary legislation, including the new *de minimis* Regulation which exempts small local transport undertakings from notification under certain circumstances. The last part of the chapter examines air and maritime transport with particular focus on the new SGEI Decision which has lowered the notification thresholds and this is felt particularly with regards to airports. The new SGEI Framework applies, other than the 2005 framework, to air and maritime transport. The possible effects of the new rules are assessed on the basis of available figures from the transport sector as well as Commission Decisions and case law.

1.14.2 Social Services of General [Economic] Interest

The approach of *Altmark*, set in the context of public services delivered in a commercial environment, became the benchmark for addressing the funding requirements of *all* SGEI in the EU where sector-specific rules are absent. In areas where *social* public services are provided, and hence greater political sensitivity is required, the *Altmark* framework required adaptation. These issues are discussed in detail in the chapters by *van de Gronden and Rusu* and *Hancher and Sauter.*

In recent years, *Social* Services of General Interest (SSGI) have emerged as an important issue on the political agenda.[78] The 2011 Almunia package exempts only particular social services from the State aid notification requirement embedded in Article 108 (3) TFEU. Thus Member States must bring the financing of other social services into line with the conditions set out in the 2011 Commission Decision[79] by adapting key features of the national measures regulating and governing social services. This creates inroads into the autonomy of the Member States to organise national SSGI and may become a sensitive matter, given the role of social services in the context of specific historical and cultural contexts at the national level.

Van de Gronden and Rusu explore the intricacies of the developments brought about by the 2011 Almunia Package by analysing, *inter alia* the relevant case law of the European Courts and decisional practice of the Commission, the applicable soft law documents and the relationship between SSGI and competition and free movement rules. In their contribution, the 2011 Commission Decision is explored in detail, the focus being directed at the Decision's main provisions on matters relating to definitions, act of entrustment, compensation and overcompensation, transparency and information, as well as the role of Article 106 (2) TFEU in the

---

[78] See Neergaard et al. 2012.

[79] Supra n 2.

context of social services. They argue that hard law with a bearing on social services is scarce in EU law. Therefore, the 2011 Commission Decision is of great interest for social services and, as a result, for the national social welfare states, especially since, it may be argued that the Decision provides for some aspects of a comprehensive model for the social services delivery. Thus, they conclude that the adoption of the Almunia Package constitutes a significant step towards an EU approach to social services. They also argue that a new pathway has been created for binding EU measures designed to build an EU model for social services based on a balance between State involvement and social needs, on the one hand and considerations of efficiency and competition, on the other hand.

Healthcare issues have caught the attention of EU competition and free movement law[80] and in the 2005 Monti-Kroes Package hospital care was given a special exemption. The safe haven for hospital services has been broadened in the 2011 Almunia package to cover not only hospital care but all (curative) healthcare, as well as long-term care, irrespective of the amount of aid or turnover. Using the IRIS-H decision (concerning the financing of public hospitals in the Brussels capital region of Belgium, adopted by the Commission prior to the 2011 Almunia Package) *Sauter and Hancher* argue that it proves a useful illustration of the way the Commission applies the rules on State aid and SGEI compensation in practice. Both the Almunia Package and State aid practice show that the Commission is content to abandon a stringent application of the State aid rules based on economic analysis in the hospital sector, and indeed, in healthcare and long-term care at large: net costs are assumed as given, and only the scope for reasonable profits is restrained. *Sauter and Hancher* argue that the Commission could, presumably, reverse this trend by bringing its own practice into line with a more ambitious interpretation of its recent legislation, and insisting that Member States do the same.

1.15 Conclusion

The idea of a review of the original *Altmark*-Monti-Kroes Package envisaged for 2009 could not have anticipated the demanding and changed economic context in the EU: of the need to reign in inefficient public expenditure and create a climate for efficiency and effectiveness in the delivery of public services in global competitive markets. In 2012, the EU struggles to balance a new constitutional dimension of a 'highly competitive social market economy' with a modernisation of the Single Market programme (which pays closer attention to the State aid and procurement dimension) aiming to integrate SGEI into the mainstream of EU law and policy.

---

[80] On the application of competition law to healthcare see Hancher and Sauter 2012. In relation to SGEI see van de Gronden et al. 2011.

The rest of the chapters of this book use this changing political and economic context to explore in greater, and critical, detail the different components of the Almunia Package, offering a review of the measures and highlighting where the future direction of the regulation of public services may lead.

References

Bauby P (2011) From Rome to Lisbon: SGIs in primary law. In: Szyszczak E et al (eds) Developments in services of general economic interest. TMC Asser Press, The Hague

Bacquero Cruz J (2002) Between competition and free movement. Oxford University Press, Oxford

Bekkedal T (2011) Article 106 TFEU is dead. Long live Article 106 TFEU! In: Szyszczak E et al (eds) Developments in services of general economic interest. TMC Asser Press, The Hague

Buendía Sierra JL (1999) Exclusive rights and state monopolies under EC Law. Oxford University Press, Oxford

Buendía Sierra JL (2012) A turn of the screw, comment on the Almunia package on the blog 'chilling competition', http://chillingcompetition.com/2012/03/14/a-turn-of-the-screw-jl-buendia-on-sgeis/

Davies J, Szyszczak E (2011)' Universal service obligations: fulfilling new generations of services of general economic interest'. In: Szyszczak E et al. (eds.) Developments in services of general economic interest, TMC Asser Press, The Hague

Van de Gronden JW, Szyszczak E, Neergaard U, Krajewski M (eds) (2011) Health care and EU law. TMC Asser Press, The Hague

Hancher L, Larouche (2011) Community, state and market. In: Craig P, De Búrca G (eds) The evolution of EU law, 2nd edn. Oxford University Press, Oxford

Hancher L, Sauter W (2012) EU competition and internal market law in health care. Oxford University Press, Oxford

Jääskinen N (2011) The new rules on SGEI, EStAL, 599

Lambertz K-H, Hornung M (2012) State aid rules on services of general economic interest: for the committee of the regions the glass is half-full ESTAL 329

Klasse M (2009) Services of general economic interest Ch 7. In: Heidenhain M (ed) European State aid law Verlag Ch Beck/Hart. Munich & Oxford, Munich

Messola M (ed) (2011) The reform of State aid rules on services of general economic interest: from the 2005 Monti-Kroes package to the 2011 Almunia Package. College of Europe, Bruges

Neergaard U, Szyszczak E, van de Gronden J, Krajewski M (eds) (2012) Social services of general interest in the EU. TMC Asser Press, The Hague

Ølykke G, Risvig C, Tvarnø C (eds) (2012) EU public procurement-modernisation, growth and innovation. DJØF, Copenhagen

Regner E (2011) Reform of the legal framework for services of general interest: where do we stand? What should a reform look like? ESTAL 597

Ross M (2009) Article 16 E.C. and services of general economic interest: from derogation to obligation? ELRev 25 22

Sauter W, Van de Gronden J (2011) State aid, services of general economic interest and universal service in healthcare. ECLRev 32(12):615

Sinnaeve A (2012) What's new in SGEI in 2012?—An overview of the commission's SGEI package ESTAL 347

Szyszczak E (2004) Financing of services of general economic interest. MLR 67:982

Szyszczak E (2007) The regulation of the state in competitive markets in the European Union. Hart, Oxford

Szyszczak E (2011) Altmark assessed. In: Szyszczak E (ed) Research handbook on European State aid law. Edward Elgar, Cheltenham

Szyszczak E (2012a) Modernising State aid and the financing of SGEI. JCL&P 3:332

Szyszczak E (2012b) Soft law and safe havens. In: Neergaard U, Szyszczak E, Van de Gronden J, Krajewski M (eds) Social services of general interest in the EU. TMC Asser Press, The Hague

Szyszczak E (2012c) Building a socioeconomic constitution: a fantastic object? Fordham INT'L L.J. 35:1364

Chapter 2
The Impact of *Altmark*: The European Commission Case Law Responses

Max Klasse

Abstract This chapter analyses the case law of the European Commission in relation to State aid granted to companies entrusted with public service missions following the landmark ruling in *Altmark*. *Klasse* shows that the criteria laid down by the CJEU for public service compensation to be free of State aid elements have been met only on rare occasions in the case law. The author notes that this is a consequence of the difficulties the Commission has faced when applying the *Altmark* test which resulted in a very strict reading by the Commission of the *Altmark* criteria. According to his interpretation, the 2005 SGEI Package, adopted by the Commission to provide stakeholders with legal certainty on the application of the State aid rules, clarified that the room for financing public service missions without the necessity for Member States to notify the financing to the Commission is rather limited. His chapter charts the Commission's practice in relation to each of the four *Altmark* criteria. While the first three criteria are generally considered to be relatively straightforward to apply, his analysis shows that the Commission's case law has confined the Member States' room for manoeuvre in relation to each criterion. Even where the Commission acknowledges a margin of discretion on the part of the Member States, which is subject only to review for manifest errors, such as in relation to the definition of a public service mission, it has interpreted its powers widely. *Klasse* notes that the main challenging factor remains the assessment of the fourth *Altmark* criterion, according to which, in the absence of a competitive tender, a benchmarking analysis is required. Save for in exceptional circumstances, the benchmarking exercise has never been successful. He argues that it is difficult to reconcile the Commission's approach emanating from its case law with the jurisprudence of the European Courts.

M. Klasse (✉)
Freshfields Bruckhaus Deringer LLP, Potsdamer Platz 1, 10785 Berlin, Germany
e-mail: max.klasse@freshfields.com

E. Szyszczak and J.W. van de Gronden (eds.), *Financing Services of General Economic Interest*, Legal Issues of Services of General Interest, DOI: 10.1007/978-90-6704-906-1_2, © T.M.C. ASSER PRESS, The Hague, The Netherlands, and the authors 2013

Contents

2.1 Introduction

This chapter analyses the case law of the European Commission law in relation to State aid in the form of compensation granted to companies entrusted with public service obligations (pso). It covers the period starting with the *Altmark* ruling in 2003,[1] which laid down specific criteria in order for public service compensation to be free of State aid elements, and thus be exempt from the notification requirement under Article 108(3) TFEU, and ends with recent Commission decisions on the subject.

Written shortly after the entry into force of the new EU rules on services of general economic interest (SGEI) that will be dealt with in subsequent chapters of this book, the aim of this chapter is twofold: (i) it sums up the Commission's experience with the application of the *Altmark* criteria across different sectors after 2003 and in particular since the Commission adopted its first SGEI Package in 2005; and (ii) it analyses critically the Commission's case law. It is hoped that the experiences which have emerged will help readers to better understand the concerns of Member States and general stakeholders in the reform process that has led to the adoption of the new SGEI Package.

As will be detailed in the following sections, the Commission has applied the *Altmark* criteria very strictly. As a result, scarcely any public service compensation (psc) granted by Member States have been regarded as aid-free by the Commission. There are only very few Commission decisions in which the Commission came to the conclusion that the *Altmark* test was satisfied.[2] Most of the cases under

---

[1] CJEU, Case C-280/00 *Altmark Trans* [2003] *ECR* I-7747.

[2] The notable exceptions include Commission, 16 December 2003, State aid N 475/2003 *Security of Supply Ireland (CADA)*; Commission, 16 November 2004, State aid N 381/2004 *Broadband Infrastructure Project Pyrénées-Atlantiques*; Commission, 3 May 2005, State aid N 382/2004 *Broadband infrastructure project Limousin (Dorsal)*; Commission, 30 September 2009, State aid N 331/2008 *Broadband Hauts de Seine*; Commission, 24 May 2007 *Energy supply Slovenia* OJ 2007 L 219/9; Commission, 15 September 2009, State aid N 206/2009 *Financing of the public transport services in district of Anhalt-Bitterfeld*; Commission, 15 September 2009, State aid N 207/2009, *Financing of the transport services in district of Wittenberg.*

scrutiny, lacked one or more of the criteria of the *Altmark* ruling as interpreted by the Commission.

This chapter is organised as follows: after recalling the main elements of the *Altmark* judgment and the Commission's 2005 SGEI Package (Sect. 2.2), this chapter critically analyses the Commission decision-making practice in relation to each of the four *Altmark* criteria (Sect. 2.3). Section 2.4 draws some conclusions as to the overall approach taken by the Commission in its case law.

2.2 The *Altmark* Ruling and the 2005 SGEI Package

In its well-known ruling in the *Altmark* case, the CJEU held that the discharge of pso is *not* caught by Article 107(1) TFEU where it merely compensates the provider of a public service mission for the costs that arise due to the performance of the pso.[3] For that to be the case, four cumulative criteria have to be met:

1. the recipient undertaking must actually have pso to discharge, and the obligations must be clearly defined;
2. the parameters on the basis of which the compensation is calculated must be established in advance in an objective and transparent manner;
3. the compensation cannot exceed what is necessary to cover all or part of the costs incurred in the discharge of the pso, taking into account the relevant receipts and a reasonable profit; and
4. where the undertaking is not chosen pursuant to a public procurement procedure which would allow for the selection of the bidder capable of providing those services at the least cost to the community, the level of compensation needed must be determined on the basis of an analysis of the costs of a typical, well run and adequately equipped undertaking.

Where the conditions are satisfied, the compensation is not considered to amount to State aid. As these are cumulative criteria, where only one condition is not met, the compensation constitutes State aid and is subject to the notification requirement and standstill obligation laid down in Article 108(3) TFEU. The aid measure can still be declared compatible under Articles 107(2), (3) TFEU (or 93 TFEU and secondary legislation where applicable). This extremely controversial judgment stimulated a substantial debate amongst commentators and has led to a spate of articles.[4]

With a view to further clarifying the application of the State aid rules to the financing of SGEI, the Commission in November 2005 adopted a Decision and a Framework on the application of Article 106(2) TFEU to State aid in the form of

---

[3] *Altmark Trans, supra* n 1, paras 89 et seq. For a detailed description of the judgment and an overview of the case law prior to *Altmark* see Klasse 2010a, p. 512, and Lübbig and Martin-Ehlers 2009, p. 66.

[4] See Klasse 2010a, p. 516 for further references.

public service compensation (known as the 'SGEI Package' or 'Monti-Kroes Package').[5] The SGEI Decision set out thresholds for certain small-scale State funding of public service missions. Where the conditions of the Decision were met, it conferred a block exemption and a derogation from the notification requirement to the State aid measures covered by it. Its legal basis was Article 86(3) of the Treaty, now Article 106(3) TFEU.

The Commission's SGEI Framework specifies under what conditions public service compensation can be considered compatible with the internal market under Article 106(2) TFEU for measures not covered by the SGEI Decision. The Framework made it clear that an exemption from Article 107(1) TFEU was possible on the basis of Article 106(2) TFEU, provided that the compensation was commensurate with the extra cost of providing the public service and subject to a number of conditions. The conditions of compatibility set out in the Framework by and large corresponded to the conditions of the Decision. Both measures replicated the first three criteria of the *Altmark* judgment, which did not deal with Article 106(2) but with 107(1) TFEU.

As a consequence, whenever the *Altmark* test is not satisfied, the test is to be repeated under Article 106(2) TFEU, with a slight relaxation as regards the fourth *Altmark* criterion. Where *Altmark* requires that the compensation be defined through a public tender procedure or a cost-benchmark based on the costs of a typical, well run and adequately equipped undertaking, it is sufficient under the SGEI Package that there is no overcompensation. This is established on the basis of a detailed estimate of the net-cost and a reasonable profit as specified in the Package.

The 2005 SGEI Package subsequently defined the Commission's approach towards SGEI compensation in numerous cases. Even where the set of rules was not applicable, such as in the area of land transport,[6] the Commission made recourse to the Framework and applied its rules *mutatis mutandis*.[7] In practice, the SGEI package clarified that the room for manoeuvre that had arguably been opened by the *Altmark* judgment for financing SGEI without the necessity for the Member States to notify the financing to the Commission under Article 108(3) TFEU was rather limited. With the SGEI Package, the Commission reclaimed control over the financing of public service obligations.

---

[5] See Klasse 2010a, p. 534 et seq. for a detailed description of the Package. The third measure in the Package was the revised Transparency Directive (Directive 2006/111/EC of 16 November 2006), see Klasse 2010c, p. 453.

[6] Cf. Regulation (EC) 1191/69 of the Council of 26 June 1969 on Action by Member States concerning the obligations inherent in the concept of a public service in transport by rail, road and inland waterway, *OJ* 1969 L 156/1, and Regulation (EC) 1370/2007 of 23 October 2007 on public passenger transport services by rail and by road and repealing Council Regulations 1191/69 and 1107/07 *OJ* 2007 L 315/1.

[7] Cf. e.g. Commission, 26 November 2008, State Aid C 16/2007 *Postbus Lienz OJ* 2009 L 306/26, paras 112, 113; Commission, 24 February 2010, State aid C 41/08 *Danske Statsbaner*, *OJ* 2011 L 7/1, para 352.

2.3 The Commission's Case Law

This part of the chapter deals with the Commission's decision-making practice in relation to each of the four *Altmark* criteria individually.

2.3.1 Clearly Defined PSO to Discharge

The first *Altmark* criterion is a procedural requirement. It seeks to ensure transparency and prevents Member States from establishing *ex-post* allegedly assigned public service missions. The notion of a pso, or more generally SGEI,[8] is not elaborated in the Treaty itself. The Commission has followed the jurisprudence of the CJEU that has emphasised that an activity is of general economic interest only if it exhibits special characteristics as compared with the general economic interest of other economic activities.[9] It is generally accepted by the Commission that Member States enjoy a wide margin of discretion when defining what they consider to be services of general economic interest. These definitions are only subject to control by the Commission for manifest errors or misjudgments. The main limiting factor for the Member States is the Union *acquis* in a particular sector. Where EU sector-specific rules exist on the concept of a universal service, such as in the telecoms sector or in the postal sector, these have to be taken into account and may limit the margin of discretion on the part of the Member State.

In its practice, post-*Altmark*, the criterion has not proven to be a major obstacle in the relevant cases, with the Commission generally rubber stamping the definitions provided by the Member States concerned.[10] There were ample examples of what services qualify as SGEI in the case law of the Courts and the Commission even prior to *Altmark*.[11] The Commission practice ranges from the operation of a public broadband communication network which allows for generalised access to broadband infrastructure for all of the population,[12] to regional passenger transport[13] and to universal banking services.[14]

---

[8] For a discussion of the development of the concept of SGEI, pso, and universal service obligations see Davies and Szyszczak 2011.

[9] Cf. for e.g. Commission, 25 April 2012, State aid SA.25051 *Germany—Aid to Zweckverband Tierkörperbeseitigung (association for disposal of dead animal bodies)*, para 160.

[10] Reference is also made to the case law set out in relation to the other *Altmark* criteria below.

[11] See the list provided by Grespan 2009, p. 1147.

[12] Commission, 16 November 2004, State Aid N 381/2004 *Broadband Infrastructure Project Pyrénées-Atlantiques*. The service in question did not entail the offering of a broad band service to the final consumer.

[13] See cases cited below.

[14] Commission, 6 April 2005, State aid N 244/2003 *Access to Basic Financial Services*, paras 59 et seq.; Commission, 21 October 2008, State Aid C 49/06 *Poste Italiane OJ* 2009 L 189/3.

However, in the recent decision in *Zweckverband Tierkörperbeseitigung* for instance, which concerned the financing of the disposal of dead animal carcasses and slaughterhouse waste, the Commission found that these services could not legitimately be considered as relating to an SGEI mission.[15] The question arose in relation to the obligation to retain spare operational capacity in case of an epidemic (for e.g. foot-and-mouth disease). Even though the Commission accepted that the services served to protect human health, it concluded that they would not be fundamentally different from other economic activities. The Commission did not stop here. In this case, it also interpreted a further criterion into the first *Altmark* requirement: it held that the first requirement would also imply assessing whether the compensation payments are indeed necessary for the provision of the SGEI. According to the Commission, even if the service in question was to constitute a service of general economic interest, the necessity of the compensation payment had to be examined, which it denied.[16] The Commission *inter alia* argued that elsewhere in Germany the service would be provided satisfactorily under normal market conditions.

What the Commission does here is to test whether the aid addresses a market failure, i.e. whether the services offered by existing market operators are insufficient to meet the public general interest. This clearly limits the Member States' discretion endorsed by the European Courts when defining public service missions, thereby expanding the Commission's scrutiny from a 'manifest error' test to a second-guessing of Member States' definitions. It appears questionable whether this is in line with the Courts' jurisprudence, such as, for example, the ruling of the General Court in *BUPA*. It may be argued that this is already a result of the new 2011 SGEI Package, dealt with in the subsequent chapters of this book.[17] However, this can also be found in previous Commission case law concerning the financing of broadband infrastructure (e.g. in the *Dorsal* case[18]) and of the digital terrestrial television transmission network (e.g. *DVB-T in North Rhine-Westphalia* and *DVB-T in Berlin-Brandenburg*[19]); in these cases, however, on the basis of more or less detailed Commission communications endorsing the principle. In the broadband sector, according to the Commission's guidelines, broadband network

---

[15] Commission, 25 April 2012, State aid SA.25051 *Germany—Aid to Zweckverband Tierkörperbeseitigung (association for disposal of dead animal bodies)*, paras 151–196.

[16] This was refused by the Commission. Ibid., at para 180.

[17] Indeed, in the 2011 SGEI Communication the Commission considers it would not be appropriate to attach specific pso to activities provided by undertakings operating under normal market conditions, cf. *Communication on the application of the European Union State aid rules to compensation granted for the provision of services of general economic interest, OJ* 2012 C 8/4, para 48.

[18] Commission, 3 May 2005, State aid N 382/2004 *Broadband Infrastructure Project Limousin (Dorsal)*, paras 45 et seq.

[19] Commission, 23 October 2007, State aid C 34/2006 *DVB-T in North Rhine-Westphalia*; Commission, 14 July 2004, State aid C 25/2004 *DVB-T in Berlin-Brandenburg*, upheld in CJEU, Case C-544/09 P *Germany* v. *Commission*, n.y.r.

infrastructure cannot be considered an SGEI where a competitive broadband infrastructure providing adequate coverage and established by private funding already exists.[20]

Other than these examples, the Commission has only made a few general reservations as to when it would find a manifest error of assessment by a Member State. For instance, as laid down in the Commission's broadcasting Communication, activities consisting of advertising, e-commerce, the use of premium rate telephone numbers in prize games and sponsoring or merchandising cannot be considered as SGEI, and including them in the ambit of a public service remit is a manifest error of assessment.[21] Another example cited by the Commission is the creation and retention of jobs in an undertaking because as such, this would lack the necessary service to the public.[22]

Finally, the requirement under the first *Altmark* criterion that the undertaking must have a pso to discharge has been understood to mean by the Commission that the operator must be entrusted with the SGEI mission, i.e. there must be an official act having binding legal force under national law in the sense that it creates an obligation on the operator to provide the services in question. The Commission has acknowledged that the requirements of an act of entrustment are rather basic.[23] However, this has not precluded the Commission from applying the minimum criteria to be satisfied in the act of entrustment as laid down in 2005 SGEI Package, in particular the content and duration of the pso, the undertaking and territory concerned, and the nature of any exclusive rights assigned to the undertaking.[24]

2.3.2 Objective Parameters

The second *Altmark* criterion requires that the parameters for calculating the compensation are established in advance and in an objective and transparent manner. This excludes the possibility of changing the parameters of the calculation of the compensation *ex post*. As can be inferred from the *Altmark* judgment, with this requirement, the CJEU seeks to avoid a situation whereby the undertaking accumulates losses and is subsequently compensated for its losses, irrespective of

---

[20] *Communication from the Commission Community Guidelines for the application of State aid rules in relation to rapid deployment of broadband networks, OJ* 2009 C 23/7.

[21] *Communication from the Commission on the application of State aid rules to public service broadcasting, OJ* 2009 C 257/1.

[22] *Commission staff working document, Guide to the Application of the European Union Rules on State Aid, Public Procurement and the Internal Market to Services of General Economic Interest, and in Particular to Social Services of General Interest,* SEC (2010) 1545 final of 7.12.2010, p. 19.

[23] Ibid., p. 38.

[24] Cf. para 12 of the 2005 SGEI Framework.

whether these actually relate to the operation of the SGEI. The rationale is that this would mean blunting any incentives for efficient provision of the service in question.[25] It should be noted, though, that the requirement refers to the *ex ante* establishment of parameters and does not necessarily encompass the establishment of the amount of compensation, even though this may well be the case.

Like the first *Altmark* criterion, the second criterion has not been the subject of much controversy in the Commission's case law. Relevant cases often relate to State measures that had been in place for some time at the time of the Commission Decision and predate the *Altmark* judgment. In the *Dorsal* case concerning the public co-funding of an open broadband infrastructure in Limousin, France, the Commission clarified that, as a matter of principle, any *ex post* discretion and room for manoeuvre on the part of the authority automatically indicates that the second criterion is not fulfilled, a principle endorsed by the Commission in a number of subsequent decisions.[26] Again, it appears difficult to reconcile this position with the General Court's judgment in *BUPA*. According to the Court, discretion is not in itself incompatible with the existence of objective and transparent parameters within the meaning of the second *Altmark* condition.[27]

In the Commission's case law, the criterion was found to be satisfied for e.g. in *Postbus Lienz*, *Southern Moravia Bus Companies* and other cases concerning public service compensation for regional passenger transport in which the compensation was calculated on the basis of a price per kilometre and the total number of kilometres provided for in the contract.[28] Similarly, a compensation based on the number of users meets the second requirement.[29] In *DSB*, concerning public service contracts for passenger transport relating to a major part of the Danish rail network, the Commission accepted that multi-annual forward budgets fulfil the second requirement where these budgets are based on data and hypotheses which are reasonable and sufficiently detailed.[30] Also, the Commission held that in the context of public transport service contracts which provide for a transport system composed of several interdependent lines, the Member State need not necessarily determine the amount of compensation for each line taken individually.[31]

---

[25] Santamato 2009, para 2.572.

[26] Commission, 3 May 2005, State aid N 382/2004 *Broadband Infrastructure Project Limousin (Dorsal)*, para 57; Commission, 23 February 2011, State aid C 58/06 *BSM, OJ* 2011 L 210/1, para 153.

[27] GC, Case T-289/03 *BUPA* [2008] *ECR* II-81, para 214.

[28] Cf. e.g. Commission, 26 November 2008, State Aid C 16/2007 *Postbus Lienz OJ* 2009 L 307/26, paras 72 et seq.; Commission, 26 November 2008, State aid C 3/08 *Southern Moravia Bus Companies OJ* 2009 L 97/14, para 56. For further details on the application of the *Altmark* criteria in land transport cases, see Kekelekis 2012, p. 73. See also the chapter by Rusche and Schmidt.

[29] Commission, 16 May 2006, State Aid N 604/2005 *Busverkehr Landkreis Wittenberg*, para 38 et. seq.

[30] Commission, 24 February 2010, State aid C 41/08 *DSB, OJ* 2011 L 7/1, para 281.

[31] Ibid., para 282.

On the other hand, in *Ustica Lines and NGI* concerning compensation for ferry services between Sicily and a number of smaller Islands, the Commission found that the second criterion was not fulfilled.[32] In this case, the parameters of the compensation were changed after the tender for the service. Participants in the tender had thus not been able to take the parameters into account when submitting their bids. In other cases, such as in *Poczta Polska* the Commission requested changes to the entrustment act in order to make the compensation compliant with the criterion.[33] In the *Zweckverband Tierkörperbeseitigung* case mentioned above, the Commission held that it was not sufficient to lay down the compensation for the reserve capacity *ex ante* in the annual business plan. It found that expected losses were not a sufficiently objective indicator of the cost of the epidemic reserve.[34] On a different note, however, the Commission concluded that Member States can define compensation in reference to the operating losses provided that overcompensation is excluded.[35]

2.3.3 Necessity Criterion

With the necessity criterion, the CJEU clarified that for any compensation to fall outside Article 107(1) TFEU the compensation may not only cover the costs of the public service mission but also a reasonable profit (without defining how such 'reasonable profit' should be determined). In the following section, the Commission's practice when checking for overcompensation over costs and the question of what constitutes a reasonable return will be dealt with separately. It should be borne in mind that the overcompensation criterion is in principle not related to the efficiency of the provider of the service. However, as can be concluded from the fourth *Altmark* criterion, in order to exclude State aid, it is not sufficient merely to rely on a negative balance of the compensation on the one hand and all the costs associated with the public service mission plus a reasonable profit. This nexus between the third and fourth criterion will be dealt with in Sect. 2.3.4 below.

2.3.3.1 Avoiding Overcompensation

In order to establish whether the compensation does not exceed the extra costs related to the public service mission, the Commission in its case law has relied on an *ex post* assessment/verification of the actual costs effectively borne by the

---

[32] Commission, 24 April 2007, State aid N 265/06 *Ustica Lines and NGI*, para 39. This case is mentioned by Santamato 2009, at para 2.573.

[33] Commission, 15 December 2009, State aid C 21/05 *Poczta Polska* OJ 2010 L 347/29.

[34] Commission, 25 April 2012, State aid SA.25051 *Germany—Aid to Zweckverband Tierkörperbeseitigung (association for disposal of dead animal bodies)*, para 200.

[35] Commission staff working document, supra n 22, p. 48.

SGEI. The Commission practice appears to be based on the premise that a full review of the actual costs by the public authorities as provided for in Article 6 of the 2005 SGEI Decision and para 20 of the 2005 SGEI Framework is the only means capable of proving that no overcompensation has occurred.[36] In the absence of *ex post* checks of the actual cost, it has excluded overcompensation where the public service mission was assigned to the undertaking requesting the lowest level of compensation on the basis of genuinely competitive tendering. Conversely, as will be discussed in more detail below, a tender procedure is not in itself sufficient to exclude overcompensation.

For instance, in *Busverkehr Wittenberg*, the Commission concluded that the lump-sum payment to a local passenger transport undertaking which had been selected on the basis of a competitive tender (on the basis of the lowest compensation) did not meet the third *Altmark* criterion.[37] The Commission criticised the fact that the amount of compensation to be paid had not been made dependent on the revenues earned from the service. The Commission took note of the fact that the contract provided for an incentive for the transport undertaking to win more passengers. At the same time, the undertaking also had to carry the risk that fewer passengers would use the service than expected. While the Commission accepted that, from an economic point of view, chances and risks under the contract were in balance (i.e. in was equally likely that the undertaking would generate less revenues from the contract than making more profit than expected), it came to the conclusion that under such a contract, overcompensation could not be ruled out as there was not sufficient correlation between the costs incurred and the compensation paid by the State.[38] Hence, the Commission held that the compensation to be paid would amount to State aid which, however, could be declared compatible with the common market on the basis of Article 107 (3) (c) TFEU.[39]

2.3.3.2 Reasonable Profit Benchmark

As mentioned before, there is little guidance from the Courts on how a reasonable profit should be determined. The Commission's case law on the subject is very case specific. The Commission has avoided any clear cut general statements as to what level of profit it would consider appropriate in light of the business risks, or absence of risks associated with the service. Rather, it appears that the Commission has been inclined to accept 'reasonable' proposals brought forward

---

[36] See, e.g. Commission, 15 December 2009, State aid C 21/05 *Poczta Polska*, OJ 2010 L 347/29. Commission, 29 October 2010, State aid N 178/2010 *Spain—Preferential dispatch of indigenous coal plants*.

[37] Commission, 16 May 2006, State Aid N 604/2005 *Busverkehr Landkreis Wittenberg*.

[38] Commission, ibid., para 60 (non-fulfilment of the third *Altmark* criterion). Cf. also the subsequent decision, which cleared the measure as State aid free: Commission, 15 September 2009, State Aid N 207/2009 *Busverkehr Landkreis Wittenberg*.

[39] Ibid., paras 78 et seq.

by the Member States. As a consequence, the few case-specific profit benchmarks publicised in the case law do not necessarily reflect the maximum profit the Commission would have accepted had the Member State set the benchmark at a higher level. The Commission has applied both capital-based (such as ROCE) as well as sales-based (such as EBITDA) profitability indicators, even though the 2005 SGEI Decision and Framework show a preference for assessing the profit on the basis of the return on own capital employed in the provision of the SGEI in question.

For instance, in the French broadband infrastructure case, *Pyrénées-Atlantiques* the Commission came to the conclusion that a ROCE of approx. 11 % was reasonable for the sector.[40] In *Southern Moravia Bus Companies*, the Commission considered a margin of close to 8 % as reasonable for the passenger transport in question,[41] while in the case of public passenger transport service compensation in *Anhalt-Bitterfeld,* the Commission held that the proposed margin cap of 5 % (turnover margin) over the costs of providing the service would allow for a reasonable margin.[42] In *DSB*, the Commission accepted that the reasonable profit would vary between 6 and 12 % (return on equity), with an annual cap set at 10 % over 3 years, to take account of efficiency gains and/or the improvement in the quality of the rail passenger services to be provided by DSB.[43] For the Spanish electricity sector, the Commission cleared a pre-tax rate of return of 7.86 %, corresponding to a post-tax rate of return of 5.5 %, as this was lower than the weighted average capital cost of the Spanish electricity sector as observed in the years preceding the decision.[44] Where available, as for instance in *DSB*, the Commission makes recourse to economic studies available to it in order to assess whether the level of profit is reasonable.

2.3.4 The Fourth Altmark Criterion

2.3.4.1 Competitive Tendering

It follows from the first limb of the fourth *Altmark* criterion that the CJEU believes that assignment of a public service mission by way of a tender procedure is the preferable solution with a view to establishing compensation in conformity with

---

[40] Commission, 16 November 2004, State Aid N 381/2004 *Broadband Infrastructure Project Pyrénées-Atlantiques*, paras 76 et seq., para 82.

[41] Commission, 26 November 2008, State aid C 3/08 *Southern Moravia Bus Companies, OJ* 2009 L 97/14, para 71.

[42] Commission, 15 September 2009, State aid N 206/2009 *Financing of the public transport services in district of Anhalt-Bitterfeld*, para 46.

[43] Commission, 24 February 2010, State aid C 41/08 *DSB OJ* 2011 L 7/1, paras 357, 359.

[44] Commission, 29 October 2010, State aid N 178/2010 *Spain—Preferential dispatch of indigenous coal plants*, para 145.

Article 107(1) TFEU. Where the service provider is chosen by virtue of a public tender procedure, there is a presumption that the transaction will necessitate the least cost for the State. This is clearly in line with the Commission's policy which has relied on competitive tendering in other State aid contexts, such as in the context of the private investor principle in relation to the privatisation of State-owned undertakings.[45] According to the Commission, where a tender procedure fulfils certain minimum criteria, it can be assumed that the compensation corresponds to the market price and does not include elements of excess compensation. For that to be the case, the Commission checks whether the relevant market is an effectively contestable market, whether the procedure has resulted in genuinely competitive tendering, and whether the SGEI is assigned to the undertaking requesting the lowest level of compensation. The latter requirement is reflected also in the fourth *Altmark* criterion (selection of the tenderer capable of providing the services 'at the least cost'). Where one of the elements of genuine competitive tendering is missing, the criterion will not be met. For instance, in *Southern Moravia Bus Companies*, the Commission concluded that it would not be sufficient to approach the known carriers already active in the region (in this case: 41) as this procedure ran counter to the possibility that carriers from other Member States could be taken into account.

In the aftermath of *Altmark,* the question arose whether 'qualitative' tenders would be acceptable, i.e. where the undertaking is selected on the basis of the most advantageous bid, or, in other words, where the highest quality of service for the lowest level of compensation is sought. The *Altmark* jurisprudence appears to suggest that while it is for the Member States to define the SGEI and the level of quality of the service, the authority has to award the SGEI to the undertaking requesting the lowest level of compensation in order for this compensation to be State aid free. Hence, the Member State has to choose the operator that fulfils the criteria set by the authority, irrespective of whether these criteria actually request a high or low level of quality of service (employment, or investments etc.).[46] This was confirmed by the Commission in its *CADA* (*Security of supply Ireland*) decision.[47] The decision concerned compensation payments to electricity network operators that invest in electricity reserve generation capacity in order to ensure the security of energy supplies in Ireland, including peak periods. The network generators that were granted the compensation were chosen by way of a competitive tender procedure equally open to Irish and foreign undertakings. The main criterion within the procurement decision was the amount of compensation requested by the undertaking, hence the procedure resulted in a 'lowest-price' tender. Here, the Commission concluded that this procedure complied with the

---

[45] See, for e.g., Commission staff working document, Guidance Paper on State aid-compliant financing, restructuring and privatisation of State-owned enterprises, SWD (2012) 14 final of 10 February 2012.

[46] See also *Santamato* 2009, para 2.578.

[47] Commission, 16 December 2003, State aid N 475/2003 *Security of supply Ireland (CADA)*.

fourth criterion and that the compensation payments granted would not constitute State aid. The Commission emphasised that in order to verify whether the procurement procedure would actually allow for the selection of the tenderer capable of providing those services at the least cost to the community it would need to undertake a 'material analysis' going beyond the mere consideration of the applicable public procurement rules.[48]

As a consequence, a competitive tender procedure, even when open, transparent and non-discriminatory, does not in itself provide a safe harbour from the State aid rules.[49] A material analysis may come to the conclusion that the tender does not suffice to meet the fourth criterion (first limb), or even where it does, the resulting compensation cannot *per se* be considered necessary (within the meaning of the third criterion). Examples of both scenarios can be found in the Commission's practice. In the *Busverkehr Wittenberg* case (mentioned above), the Commission came to the conclusion that the payments to finance public transport in the district of Wittenberg constituted State aid despite the fact that the service provider had been chosen by a public procurement procedure. In this case, the Commission found that the system adopted by the authority, namely aid commensurate with the number of passengers carried, while complying with the fourth *Altmark* criterion, could not exclude overcompensation and therefore did not meet the third *Altmark* criterion.[50] In the *Dorsal* case concerning public funding for a broadband network, the fact that the authorities undertook a public procurement procedure did not suffice as the service provider was not selected on the basis of the least cost, but on the most favourable conditions.[51]

It has been questioned whether a tender procedure always provides for the best results when assigning a SGEI. In many instances, such as in the case of the postal sector, the incumbent may be the only company which is suitable to provide the service universally. In complex cases, where it is particularly difficult to define the quality of service, it may be more efficient to negotiate appropriate quality standards directly with interested parties rather than the authority setting the standards itself and making the bidders compete purely on the price.[52]

2.3.4.2 Efficient Undertaking Comparator

Even though procurement is the main rule under *Altmark*, the CJEU has been reluctant to pose an obligation on the Member States to perform tenders every time. Instead, in *Altmark*, the CJEU created an alternative test based on efficiency

---

[48] Commission, ibid., para 57.

[49] Cf. also Rusche and Schmidt 2011, p. 257.

[50] Commission, 16 May 2006, State aid N 604/2005 *Busverkehr Landkreis Wittenberg.*

[51] Commission, 3 May 2005, State aid N 382/2004 *Broadband infrastructure project Limousin (Dorsal),* paras 66 et seq.

[52] See Opinion by the State Aid Group of EAGCP, Services of general economic interest, 29 June 2006, p. 7.

of the provider of the service and the least cost for the community. However, the *Altmark* judgment does not specify what constitutes a typical, well-run undertaking. The concept has been criticised for being virtually impossible to accomplish in practice because of a lack of comparable undertakings that could be used as benchmarks.[53]

The Commission's practice has not shed much light on the practical application of the criterion, either. For instance, in the *Dorsal* case, the condition was found to be met as the compensation was based on a comparative report analysis of the needs of the project and the offers of the candidates.[54] In the case of the postal bonds distributed by the Italian post in *Poste Italiane*, the Commission came to the conclusion that the criterion would be met.[55] The Commission undertook a 'highly complex economic assessment', and came to the conclusion that the remuneration for the distribution of the postal bonds was in line with the respective remuneration for the distribution of comparable financial products on the markets. The Commission found that the benchmark of market remuneration was an appropriate estimate of the level of costs, taking into account receipts and a reasonable profit that a typical efficiently run undertaking within the same sector would incur.

By contrast, in *Postbus Lienz* the Commission came to the conclusion that Austria had not been able to demonstrate that the cost of Postbus in discharging the pso corresponded to the cost of a typical well-run undertaking.[56] In this case, the Commission considered it appropriate to distinguish between the different aspects of the second limb of the fourth criterion. These are: (i) the cost of a typical undertaking and (ii) the cost of a well-run undertaking that is (iii) adequately provided with means of transport. Since the compensation in this case was based on standard parameters determined on average costs in the sector, the Commission found that Postbus constituted a typical undertaking. However, it held that these costs would not necessarily reflect an efficient undertaking and that Austria had failed to demonstrate that Postbus was such an efficient undertaking. However, the Commission indicated that Austria could have fulfilled the test by providing a cost-benchmark based on the average cost of undertakings that had been awarded

---

[53] See EAGCP Opinion, ibid., p. 7; Braun and Kühling 2008, p. 475.

[54] Commission, 3 May 2005, State aid N 382/2004 *Broadband infrastructure project Limousin (Dorsal)*, paras 66 et seq. In two cases concerning broadband services in Scotland and the East Midlands which appeared similar at the outset, the Commission held that the financing of these services amounted to State aid. The aid elements were declared compatible under Article 107(3) lit. c TFEU. The main difference to the French cases was that the compensation was not limited to the offset of the cost for the network operation, but also included the actual broadband services to end-customers. Commission, 16 November 2004, State Aid N 307/2004 *Broadband Project Scotland*; Commission, 16 November 2004, State Aid N 199/2004 *Broadband Project East Midlands*; cf. also Commission, 2 July 2008, State Aid N 250/2008 *Broadband Project South Tyrol*; see for a detailed overview of the cases concerning public funding of broadband networks Nicolaides and Kleis 2007, p. 627 et seq.

[55] Commission, 21 October 2008, State aid C 49/06 *Poste Italiane—Remuneration for distributing postal savings certificates OJ* 2009 L 189/3.

[56] Commission, 26 November 2008, State aid C 16/2007 *Postbus Lienz*.

contracts in the sector in previous years.[57] This position has been endorsed in other decisions. According to the Commission, statistical data based on the actual cost in a sector cannot be considered sufficient proof that an average of these costs represents the costs of an efficient undertaking, and hence does not suffice to meet the fourth criterion.[58] The benchmark for the Commission is the would-be price, had the public service been assigned by way of a competitive tender.[59]

In *DSB*, the Commission held that the public funding would not meet the fourth *Altmark* criterion, even though the Commission did not contest that DSB's financial requirements had been established on the basis of an in-depth economic analysis and steps to enhance the efficiency and productivity of the undertaking had been laid down in the forward business plan.[60] The Commission argued that the difficulties of drawing comparisons with the financial performances of national or European rail operators would not enable it to conclude that the compensation would indeed meet the efficiency standard. Furthermore, it pointed to the fact that a subsidiary of DSB had applied services at reduced costs when compared to those of DSB. This was seen as an indication by the Commission that DSB would have prospects of achieving similar productivity gains.

In *Energy Supply Slovenia*, the Commission deviated from the strict reading of the fourth *Altmark* criterion.[61] In its decision concerning the public support of certain power generators in Slovenia, the Commission held that the compensation payments in favour of the power plant Trbovlje were in line with the *Altmark* criteria and State aid free. Similar to the Irish scheme discussed above, the purpose of the public funding was to ensure national supply security. The compensation was affected by favourable feeding-in tariffs that were above market price for a particular percentage of the energy generated in the power plant. The Commission decision extensively deals with the fulfilment of the fourth *Altmark* criterion, questioning whether choosing the Trbovlje power plant, in the absence of a public procurement procedure, indeed guaranteed provision of the service at the least cost to the community. It appeared that, according to a literal reading of the second alternative of the fourth *Altmark* criterion, the criterion would not have been met. However, the Commission answered the question in the affirmative. It argued that there were no other power plants which had the capacity to fulfil the obligation. Furthermore, the power plant had been modernised and restructured, and there was no indication of bad management or obvious inefficiency. More significantly, the Commission found that the compensation did not include any profit element.[62] In fact, the Commission limited its analysis to the confirmation that by assigning the

---

[57] Commission, ibid., para 86.

[58] Commission, 26 November 2008, State aid C 3/08 *Southern Moravia Bus Companies OJ* 2009 L 97/14, paras 82, 83.

[59] Ibid., at para 83.

[60] Commission, 24 February 2011, State aid C 41/08 *DSB, OJ* 2011 L 7/1, paras 284 et seq.

[61] Commission, 24 May 2007 *Energy supply Slovenia, OJ* 2007 L 219/9, paras 111 et seq.

[62] Ibid.

task to the Trbovlje power plant Slovenia opted for the solution which would incur the least cost for the State.

Other than on the rare occasions mentioned above, the Commission has not accepted that a given service provider is a typical undertaking, well run and adequately equipped.

2.4 Conclusions

The analysis of the Commission's case law shows that the Commission has interpreted the *Altmark* test in a strict manner. As a consequence of the Commission's approach, the *Altmark* criteria are regularly considered *not* to be met. The Commission's point of view is comprehensible: while *Altmark* allows for a self-assessment by Member States of public service compensation, the assessment of whether compensation that qualifies as State aid meets the requirements for compatibility under Article 106(2) TFEU or other Treaty provision is a matter for exclusive competence of the Commission. In its practice, the Commission has had the tendency to find that the state-financing of public service missions does not comply with the *Altmark* criteria, thereby bringing it within the ambit of Article 107(1) TFEU, and then, subsequently, declaring it compatible with the common market on the basis of Article 106(2) or Article 107(3) TFEU. Hence, by its strict interpretation of the *Altmark* requirements, the Commission has seized control over Member States' spending in the context of what they consider to be a public service remit.

The main challenge has been the fourth *Altmark* criterion. In essence, the Commission's practice appears to be based on the premise that it can only be met in its first alternative, i.e. if the provider is chosen on the basis of a competitive tender. However, even in those cases where the choice of undertaking to be entrusted and the amount of compensation are affected by way of a procurement procedure perfectly in line with competition and public procurement rules, the compensation may fail the Commission's necessity test (or the 'least cost' criterion). The consequence of the *Altmark* test as interpreted by the Commission in these cases is that public service contracts that include incentives for the operator to increase its efforts, seek improvements in quality, attract more customers and retain additional revenues, require notification. The Commission thus has compelled the parties to agree on a more or less fixed margin that is not allowed to increase depending on the economic success of the service in question.

Where the Member States want to invoke the second alternative of the fourth criterion (typical, well-run undertaking comparator), the situation is even less clear. Absent additional guidance of what constitutes such an undertaking, the practical application of the test by the Commission has lacked foreseeability as to the results. As a consequence, there has been a considerable degree of legal uncertainty involved in the self-assessment of the Member States of whether the *Altmark* test would be fulfilled when assigning the SGEI. A sector benchmark is often not feasible and may well be considered meaningless where the market concerned does not afford suitable benchmarks for such an assessment. First, there may be no specific and objective references, for instance, where there are no private undertakings active in the sector. Second, differences in the public service task between the different Member States may not allow for cross-border comparisons. As a consequence, the benchmark may need to be based on a hypothetical (i.e. non-existent, fictitious) undertaking, making any finding on part of the Member State (or the Commission) in itself likely to be contestable.

It remains to be seen if, and to what extent, the Commission's approach can be reconciled with the more flexible stance taken by the General Court in *BUPA*.[63] Meanwhile, under the current practice of the Commission, the main problem for Member States and providers of public services is that in the absence of a Commission decision declaring compensation compatible with the common market, no legal certainty exists. Competitors may intervene and invoke these cases in national court proceedings. National courts may then stop further payments and/or order reimbursement, because they find a breach of the standstill obligation under Article 108(3) EC where the *Altmark* criteria are deemed not to be fulfilled. It is obvious that in such cases, the prospect of a subsequent approval of the payments by the Commission after months or years of a pending notification and (possible in-depth) investigation does not bring about sufficient relief.

References

Braun JD, Kühling J (2008) Article 87 EC and the community courts: from revolution to evolution. CML Rev 45(2):465

Davies J, Szyszczak E (2011) Universal service obligations: fulfilling new generations of services of general economic interest. In: Szyszczak E et al (eds) Developments in services of general interest, legal issues of services of general interest. TMC Asser Press, The Hague, p 155

Grespan D (2009) Services of general economic interest. In: Mederer W, Pesaresi N, van Hoof M (eds.), EU competition law, vol. 4, State Aid, Claeys & Casteels, Leuven, p 1123

Kekelekis M (2012) "Driving" Altmark in land transport EStAL p 73

Klasse M (2010a) Services of general economic interest. In: Heidenhain M (ed) European State aid law. C.H Beck, Hart, Munich, p 499

Klasse M (2010b) Sector specific rules In: Heidenhain M (ed) European State aid law, C.H. Beck, Hart, Munich, p 549

Klasse M (2010c) Transparency directive. In: Heidenhain M (ed) European State aid law. C.H Beck, Hart, Munich, p 453

Lübbig T, Martin-Ehlers A (2009) Beihilfenrecht der EU'[EU State aid rules]. C.H Beck, Munich

Nicolaides P, Kleis M (2007) Where is the advantage? The case of public funding of infrastructure and broadband networks EStAL, p 615

Maxian Rusche T, Schmidt S (2011) The post-*Altmark* era has started: 15 months of application of regulation (EC) No. 1370/2007 to public transport services EStAL p 249

Santamato S (2009), Advantage in the context of services of general economic interest under Altmark. In: Mederer W, Pesaresi N, van Hoof M (eds) EU competition law, vol. 4, State Aid, Claeys & Casteels, Leuven, p 369

---

[63] GC, T-289/03 *BUPA* v. *Commission* [2008] *ECR* II-81.

Chapter 3
The European Courts' Jurisprudence After *Altmark*; Evolution or Devolution?

Hans Vedder and Marijn Holwerda

Abstract [handwritten annotation obscures text] e of the ruling in
Altmark se[...] ing.

[handwritten note: The case law after Altmark seems to be less strict; specially flexible in the fourth criteria bc of its difficulty to interpret.]

Contents

H. Vedder (✉) · M. Holwerda
Department of European and Economic Law, Groningen Centre for Energy Law,
University of Groningen, Po Box 716, 9700 AS Groningen, The Netherlands
e-mail: h.h.b.vedder@rug.nl

M. Holwerda
e-mail: j.m.holwerda@rug.nl

E. Szyszczak and J.W. van de Gronden (eds.), *Financing Services of General Economic
Interest*, Legal Issues of Services of General Interest, DOI: 10.1007/978-90-6704-906-1_3,
© T.M.C. ASSER PRESS, The Hague, The Netherlands, and the authors 2013

3.1 Introduction

The judgment in *Altmark* was groundbreaking, but in many ways it can be seen in the light of its prequel, the judgment in *Ferring*. Many of the points that resulted in the critical reception of the latter judgment were addressed in *Altmark*. In this respect, the chronology coincides with an evolution and most of the cases since *Altmark* continue this evolutionary line.[1] However, there were also some cases that are rather more difficult to reconcile with *Altmark*. This chapter will review that jurisprudence since *Altmark*. Yet, in order to understand *Altmark*, we will first identify the genesis of that jurisprudence. In this regard, we will review both the pre- and post-*Altmark* case law from a constitutional and judicial protection perspective. This will expose the positions of the EU legislator, the Member States and Commission as well as that of national and the EU Courts in this area. Most importantly, it will also enable us to identify the role of private parties in the process of creating jurisprudence on this issue. Much like evolution, where (semi)external factors determine changes over generations leading to diversification, private parties with their widely differing backgrounds and reasons for starting actions can be seen as the natural environment that resulted in *Altmark*.[2] Evolution, however, has no purpose whereas its creationist counterpart devolution does presuppose such a motive. In this regard, reductions in complexity are often presented as evidence of devolution.[3] This chapter will identify whether or not there is a purpose to *Altmark* and if so, what it is, particularly in the light of law's objective of ensuring legal certainty in an increasingly complex world. Such a purpose could be the increase of efficiency in services of general economic interest or, on a more meta-legal level, the creation of an effective possibility to challenge the modalities governing such services or simply the creation of more legal certainty. Such legal certainty is all the more important in view of the importance of the services of general economic interest.

3.2 The Genesis of *Altmark*

In this section, we will study the genesis of the *Altmark* ruling from a constitutional and judicial protection perspective, as the substantive perspective, basically the jurisprudence from *ADBHU*, *FFSA* and *SIC* over *Ferring*, has been extensively

---

[1] See further to this evolutionary characteristic the opinion of A-G Stix Hackl in CJEU, Joined Cases C-34/01 to C-38/01 *Enirisorse SpA* [2003] *ECR* I-14243, para 157.

[2] There may be private parties interested in obtaining a more restrictive application of *Altmark*, whereas others may indeed ask for a more liberal reading, depending on their position concerning the service of general economic interest. Of course, the precise conditions attaching to the compensation scheme may differ between and even within the Member States.

[3] See, e.g. the article 'Creation, Devolution and wisdom teeth' available at http://www.jack cuozzo.com/.

documented.[4] In a nutshell, following *ADBHU*, the compensation of costs arising from a service of general economic interest was initially not regarded as State aid by the Commission. This compensation approach was rejected by the General Court in *FFSA* and *SIC*[5] in what has been dubbed the State aid approach.[6] The State aid approach entails a classification of the compensation as aid within the meaning of Article 107(1) TFEU. Such aid could then be justified on the basis of Article 106(2) TFEU. In the compensation approach, the government funding is considered outside the scope of Article 107(1), as that provision requires an advantage that does not exist if there is compensation of costs only. This line of jurisprudence was overturned by the Court in *Ferring* basically on the reasoning that mere compensation of costs does not confer the advantage that Article 107(1) TFEU requires for a presence of State aids.[7] This approach was then refined in *Altmark*.[8]

3.2.1 The Constitutional Framework for a Genesis

The relatively limited number of cases concerning services of general economic interest in the first four decades of European integration on the basis of the Treaty of Rome should not detract from the obvious importance attached to these services by the Member States. Such services have always featured prominently in the Treaties with a wide-ranging justification clause in the form of Article 106(2) TFEU. However, the simple reading of that provision as one that may justify the disapplication of the entire Treaty to services of general economic interest ignores the fact that the Treaty applies to myriad forms of state and private interventions in the market. Services of general economic interest may be connected to exclusive or special rights, as Article 106(1) TFEU indicates, but they may also involve financial compensation. In relation to the former Article 106(3), TFEU clearly puts the Commission in the driving seat insofar as enforcement is concerned. Moreover, in view of the fact that most if not all exclusive rights will automatically translate into dominant positions, the Commission's role in enforcing Article 102 TFEU means that it can effectively steer enforcement in this regard.[9] Concerning the

---

[4] See e.g., Sinnaeve 2003, p. 351, Thouvenin 2009; Winter 2004, p. 475.

[5] Respectively, GC Case T-46/97 *SIC* [2000] *ECR* II-2125, para 84 and GC, Case T-106/95 *FFSA* [1997] *ECR* II-229, paras 165–169.

[6] E.g. Opinion of AG Jacobs in CJEU, Case 126/01 *GEMO* [2003] *ECR* I-13769, para 94. In fact, Jacobs AG proposes a third approach, the *quid pro quo* approach.

[7] CJEU, Case C-53/00 *Ferring* [2001] *ECR* I-9067, para 27.

[8] The necessity of a substantive refinement of the compensation approach adopted in *Ferring* is clearly argued by Nicolaides 2002, pp. 313–319; Nicolaides 2003a, p. 572 and Nicolaides 2003b, pp. 183–209.

[9] Despite the decentralisation that has taken place as a result of Regulation 1/2003, *OJ* 2003 L1/1, the Commission is still very much the central authority. *Cf*. Case C-375/09 *Tele2 Polska*, Judgment of 3 May 2011, n.y.r., paras 27–29.

financing of services of general economic interest, the EU framework becomes considerably more complicated, as the Commission is the foremost enforcement body when transfers of state resources are involved insofar as such transfers amount to State aids and need to be declared compatible with the internal market on the basis of Article 107(3) TFEU. However, Article 108(2), third paragraph, TFEU allows the Council to declare State aid measures compatible with the internal market.[10]

The constitutional perspective on the genesis of Altmark can be seen in the opinion of Léger AG in *Altmark*, where he notes that the consequence of the compensation approach is to deprive Article 106(2) TFEU of a substantial part of its effect. This is problematic as it is exactly this provision that allows for a balancing of the Member States' and EU interests between the services of general economic interest, on the one hand, and undistorted competition and the creation of an internal market on the other.[11] Further to the constitutional perspective, Léger notes that the central position of the Commission in State aid supervision is undermined.[12] In a nutshell, the traditional antagonists involved in the tension between undistorted competition and the internal market, on the one hand, (the Commission) and the need to have national room for manoeuvre on the other (the Member States) both face constitutional issues in defining the exact legal framework for the financing of services of general economic interest.

3.2.2 The Judicial Protection Framework for a Genesis

Closely connected to the constitutional issues is the judicial protection aspect. This relates essentially to the influence on access to justice of the choice for the compensation or State aid approach. In view of the fact that both the Commission and the Member States have privileged standing under Article 263 TFEU, a choice for the State aid or compensation approach should not affect their possibilities of obtaining a judicial review of a decision. This is rather more different for the private parties involved. This element of the judicial protection perspective is noted by Jacobs AG in *GEMO*, where he reiterates that the standstill provision that attaches to State aids means that 'national courts must offer to individuals the certain prospect that all the appropriate conclusions will be drawn from the infringement of the last sentence of Article [108(3) TFEU]'.[13] This judicial perspective is particularly relevant in the light of the absence of a cost-effectiveness

---

[10] Nevertheless, the judgment in Case C-110/02 *Commission v. Council* (Portuguese Pig Farms) [2004] ECR I-6333, shows that this power can only be used in exceptional cases, reinforcing the Commissions central position.

[11] Opinion of AG Léger in CJEU, Case C-53/00 *Ferring* [2001] *ECR* I-9067, paras 79, 80.

[12] Ibid, para 93.

[13] Opinion of AG Jacobs in CJEU, Case 126/01 *GEMO* [2003] *ECR* I-13769, para 113.

test in *Ferring* and the effects of compensation on the position of competitors of the undertaking entrusted with the service of general economic interest.[14] Finally, the importance of the judicial protection aspect is evidenced by the fact that most post-*Altmark* cases were brought by competitors of the undertakings in charge of the service of general economic interest.[15]

3.2.3 *The* Altmark *Judgment*

Altmark clearly bears the signs of its own genesis, with the Court referring to *Ferring* to uphold the compensation approach and the interventions, following *Ferring* and the opinion of Jacobs AG in *GEMO*, arguing in favour of the State aid or the quid pro quo approach.[16]

In *Altmark*, the Court adopted a refined compensation approach according to which a state measure can be seen as compensation for public services, meaning that the undertakings providing those services do not enjoy a real financial advantage and the measure thus does not have the effect of putting them in a more favourable competitive position than the undertakings competing with them. Such a measure would fall outside the scope of Article 107(1) TFEU if four cumulative conditions are met.

First, the recipient undertaking is required to discharge public service obligations and those obligations have been clearly defined. Second, the parameters on the basis of which the compensation is calculated must have been established beforehand in an objective and transparent manner. Third, the compensation must not exceed what is necessary to cover all or part of the costs incurred in the discharge of public service obligations, taking into account the relevant receipts and a reasonable profit for discharging those obligations. Finally, where the undertaking which is to discharge public service obligations is not chosen in a public procurement procedure, the level of compensation needed must be determined on the basis of an analysis of the costs which a typical undertaking, well-run and adequately provided with means of transport so as to be able to meet the necessary public service requirements, would have incurred in discharging those obligations, taking into account the relevant receipts and a reasonable profit for discharging the obligations.

The refinement consists of the compromise or even hybrid character involving the compensation and State aid approaches.[17] This principally maintains the

---

[14] E.g. Vedder 2009, pp. 69 and 70.

[15] This is only logical in view of the incentives that the undertakings in charge of the services of general economic interests and their competitors have.

[16] This is explained in the Opinion of AG Jacobs in CJEU, Case 126/01 *GEMO* [2003] *ECR* I-13769, paras 119, 120.

[17] See, e.g. Thouvenin 2009, p. 107 and Santamato and Pesaresi 2004, p. 17.

compensation approach in *Ferring*, but complements it with two additional criteria to address concerns relating to the overly broad discretion for Member States in financing services of general economic interest, thus bringing it more in line with the limited discretion that Member States enjoy under the State aid rules.[18] This reduction of the Member State discretion to decide on the financing of services of general economic interest was a widely anticipated result of *Altmark*.[19] Moreover, the reduction in Member State discretion would effectively address the concerns identified above in relation to the judicial protection perspective, provided that the national and EU judiciary would apply a stringent test in this regard.

Moreover, addressing the constitutional issues, the parallel between the first and third *Altmark* criteria and Article 106(2) TFEU may be identified.[20] The first *Altmark* criterion, which requires the existence of a clearly defined framework for the entrustment of services of general economic interest, is consistent with Article 106(2) case law according to which there needs to be a clear public law framework entrusting the service of general economic interest. The third criterion according to which there must be no overcompensation compares to the proportionality test applied in Article 106(2).[21] This may be contrasted with the second and fourth *Altmark* conditions that introduce new standards compared to that prescribed by Article 106(2). The result of this appears to be a restriction of the Member State room for manoeuvre.[22]

By and large the result of *Altmark* is a strict framework within which the Member States can escape State aid scrutiny only under stringent conditions that may also be relied upon by private parties both before the national and the EU judiciary. The strictness of *Altmark*, however, also results in problems because the increasing complexity of societies requires ever more creativity on the part of the Member States. Connected to a need to increase efficiency in societies in general because of international competitiveness, the result is a drive to come to new mechanisms that will increase efficiency and competitiveness whilst protecting the interests underlying the service of general economic interest in an ever more fine-tuned balancing act between these interests.

3.3 Jurisprudence After *Altmark*

Following *Altmark*, almost 20 judgments have been handed down that apply the rule laid down in that judgment. The majority of these judgments contain what can be called a simple and straightforward application of *Altmark*. There are also a

---

[18] See, e.g., Sinnaeve 2003 p. 352 and Nicolaides 2003a, p. 572. See further on the restricted discretion as part of the State aid rules: Sauter and Vedder 2012, pp. 10–12.

[19] See Nicolaides 2003a, p. 572, and Hancher and Larouche 2011, p. 760.

[20] See Hancher and Larouche 2011, p 761.

[21] See Szyszczak 2004, p 989.

[22] See Hancher and Larouche 2011, p 760 and Szyszczak 2004, p 990.

number of judgments that point at the difficulties of applying *Altmark* in practice. This section will analyse these judgments from the perspective of the constitutional and judicial protection aspects identified above in order to determine the purpose of *Altmark*.

The first case to be mentioned in this regard is *Valmont*.[23] This essentially entails the appeal by a beneficiary of aid against the Commission's decision finding it to have received State aid for the construction of a car park that was incompatible with the internal market. One of Valmont's arguments was that in fact it was only compensated for the burden that resulted from a gentlemen's agreement with the municipality requiring it to also allow others to use the car park. The General Court read this in the light of the *Altmark* exception and dismissed the Commission's approach to qualify only 50 % of the financing by the municipality as State aids.[24] According to the General Court the Commission should have applied the *Altmark* test, even though the Commission argued that the first *Altmark* criterion was not met in this case.[25] This shows that the undertakings responsible for—albeit ill-defined—services of general economic interest may rely on *Altmark* in order to be shielded from the EU State aid rules and avoid, for example, having to repay illegally received aids.

A further example of this can be seen in *TV2/Danmark*.[26] Here, the Commission argued that Denmark had not conducted any analysis pertaining to the fourth *Altmark* criterion.[27] This, the General Court held, would only suffice if the Commission could show that Denmark had indeed done nothing that could be construed as complying with that criterion or when these measures would have been manifestly inadequate or inappropriate for that purpose.[28] This, however, was not the case and again the Commission was essentially ordered to investigate whether the *Altmark* conditions were met. The basic message from *TV2/Danmark* is that the Commission can confine itself to a statement that the *Altmark* conditions were not met in cases where these conditions are manifestly not met,[29] but in all other cases a serious scrutiny of the applicability of *Altmark* is required.

On a similar note, the appraisals of the applicability of *Altmark* will affect standing for competitors under the State aid rules in the Commission procedure. In this regard, the decision to open the Phase II (or Article 108(2) TFEU)

---

[23] GC, Case T-274/01 *Valmont* [2004] *ECR* II-3150.

[24] Ibid, paras 132, 133.

[25] GC, Case T-274/01 *Valmont* [2004] *ECR* II-3150, paras 135, 136. See further CJEU, Joined Cases C-34/01 to C-38/01 *Enirisorse* [2003] *ECR* I-14234, para 34 where the Court lays down a strict standard.

[26] GC, Joined Cases T-309/04, T-317/04, T-329/04 and T-336/04 *TV2/Danmark v. Commission* [2008] *ECR* II-2935.

[27] Commission decision 2005/127, *OJ* 2006 L 85/1, para 71.

[28] GC, Joined Cases T-309/04, T-317/04, T-329/04 and T-336/04 *TV2/Danmark v. Commission* [2008] *ECR* II-2935, para 232.

[29] It can be argued that this would apply to *Valmont*.

investigation turns on whether or not the compatibility with the internal market of the state measure presents serious difficulties. The message in *Deutsche Post* is that the appraisal of state measures in the light of *Altmark* will often entail a complex analysis that will not allow the Commission to come to a finding that a State aid measure presents no serious difficulties. As a result, a Phase II investigation on the basis of Article 108(2) will have to be opened.[30] This in turn offers competitors of the undertaking administering the service of general economic interest extra possibilities for judicial review of the Commission's decisions.

Such judicial review will then have to be sufficiently detailed to allow for an in-depth appraisal of the applicability of all four criteria. This is where the EU Courts have shown different degrees of deference. The first case to be discussed in this regard is *BUPA*.[31] This judgment resulted from the appeal by BUPA, a provider of medical insurance services, against a Commission decision declaring an Irish scheme for medical risk equalisation compatible with EU State aid law. Under the risk equalisation scheme, insurers with a better risk profile than the average market risk profile had to pay a charge to the Irish Health Insurance Authority. Corresponding payments were then made by the Health Insurance Authority to insurers with a risk profile worse than the average market risk profile. The aim of this scheme was to compensate the relatively bad risk profiles and thus level the playing field.[32] Interestingly, BUPA was the main competitor of the incumbent insurance company, VHI and as a newcomer to the market, BUPA had primarily young and healthy customers, whereas VHI insured mostly older people and thus had a correspondingly worse risk profile.[33]

BUPA argued that the Commission had misapplied Article 107(1) TFEU because the four *Altmark* conditions were not satisfied. In this regard, the General Court's approach to the Commission's application of the first and fourth criterion is particularly interesting.

Concerning the first criterion, BUPA argues essentially that there is a parallel between the service of general economic interest within the meaning of Article 106(2) TFEU and the public service obligation contained in the first *Altmark* criterion. From this, BUPA infers that the service must be universal and that its provision must be obligatory. Moreover, the obligation must be precise and limited and interpreted as a concept of EU law.[34] Relying on the Commission's Communication on SGEIs, earlier case law of the General Court and Article 14 TFEU, the General Court comes to the conclusion that its review of the first criterion is limited to manifest errors of appraisal.[35] The full and unrestricted review asked for

---

[30] GC, Case T-388/03 *Deutsche Post* [2009] *ECR* II-199.

[31] GC, Case T-289/03 *BUPA* [2008] *ECR* II-81.

[32] A relatively bad risk profile would translate into high insurance premiums and thus reduced competitiveness.

[33] Case T-289/03 *BUPA* [2008] *ECR* II-81, para 283.

[34] Ibid, paras 96–100.

[35] Ibid, paras 167, 168.

by BUPA was therefore not applicable. This deference on the part of the General Court is continued when the applicability of the first criterion to the Irish scheme is investigated.

Regarding the fourth criterion, BUPA argued that the absence of a comparison with an efficient operator ruled out the applicability of *Altmark*.[36] According to BUPA, the Commission did not compare VHI's costs in administering the service to those incurred by an efficient operator. Furthermore, the Irish scheme did provide a reference point for assessing the efficiency or a benchmark for comparing decisions with those of an efficient operator.

The General Court's answer was that the efficiency criterion could not be applied strictly in *BUPA*.[37] It based this on the neutrality of the compensation mechanism under the risk equalisation scheme by reference to the receipts and profits of the insurers and to the particular nature of the additional costs linked with a negative risk profile on the part of those insurers. The General Court noted that the payments under the Irish scheme were not determined solely by reference to the payments made by the insurer receiving compensation—which would correspond to the third and fourth *Altmark* criterion—but also by reference to the payments made by the contributing insurance company, which reflected the risk profile differentials of those two companies with the average market risk profile.[38] The level of compensation was determined by reference to the costs incurred by both the contributing and receiving company.

The General Court further held that the Commission was unable to identify the potential beneficiaries of payments under the Irish scheme and to compare these to an efficient operator because the risk equalisation scheme had not been activated when the contested decision was adopted.[39] At the time of the decision there was no undertaking whose efficiency could be judged against that of the benchmark.

The General Court then pointed to the purpose of the fourth *Altmark* criterion and held that the Commission was none the less required to satisfy itself that the compensation provided for by the Irish scheme did not entail the possibility of offsetting any costs that might result from inefficiency on the part of companies involved.[40] Here, the General Court stated that the Commission had found that the scheme allowed the insurers to keep the benefit of their own efficiencies. As the calculation of the compensation under the risk equalisation scheme depended solely on the costs not linked with the efficiency of the operators in question, that compensation was not capable of leading to the sharing of any costs resulting from their lack of efficiency.[41]

---

[36]   Ibid, para 124.
[37]   Ibid, para 246.
[38]   Ibid, para 247.
[39]   Ibid, para 248.
[40]   Ibid, para 249.
[41]   Ibid, para 250.

The judgment in *BUPA* can be seen as a modification of[42] and withdrawal from the strict efficiency approach taken in *Altmark*.[43] However, it has also been argued that *BUPA* must be seen as evidence of the flexibility offered by the *Altmark* exception to services of general economic interest.[44] Buendia Sierra, however, argues that the exceptional nature of the scheme at hand in *BUPA* made the efficiency test less relevant. This in turn means that for non-exceptional services of general economic interest, the *Altmark* criteria apply in full.[45]

This points to the fact that the biggest message coming from *BUPA* may well be that defining hard rules for services of general economic interest is well-nigh impossible in view of the diversity and complexity of services involved. Indeed, the distinction suggested by Buendia Sierra between special and normal services of general economic interest, only begs the next question: how to determine whether a specific service is normal or special? The approach by the General Court in *BUPA* looks at the purpose underlying the various *Altmark* criteria and what we can say is that this purpose functions as a teleological tool guiding the application of the *Altmark* test. In relation to the efficiency criterion, this shows that apart from competitive tendering and comparison to a benchmark efficient undertaking[46] there may also be other ways to ensure efficiency in the provision of services of general economic interest.

This idea of flexibility in the application of *Altmark* can also be found in the judgment in *Chronopost*.[47] The judgment in this case is the result of lengthy proceedings by UFEX et al., against the Commission decision declaring various measures undertaken by La Poste for the benefit of its daughter undertaking SFMI-Chronopost not to be State aid.[48]

In this regard, we must first look at the concept of 'normal market conditions' used in *SFEI*[49] to determine the circumstances in which the provision of logistical and commercial assistance by a public undertaking to its subsidiaries carrying on an activity open to competition constitutes State aid. UFEX et al., argued that the General Court, in referring to a private undertaking not operating in a reserved

---

[42] Bartosch 2008, p. 211; Hancher and Larouche 2011, p. 765.

[43] Hancher and Larouche 2011, p. 764. See also Sauter and van de Gronden 2011, p. 618. Sauter and van de Gronden state that the GC substantially amended the *Altmark* criteria and that it, by moderating the fourth criterion, called into question the strict efficiency approach that the Commission adopted in four healthcare decisions.

[44] Ross 2009, p. 138.

[45] Buendia Sierra 2008, p. 200.

[46] See, on the absence of a requirement to award the service of general economic interest by means of a competitive tendering procedure, GC, Case T-442/03 *SIC II* [2008] *ECR* II-1161, para 145.

[47] CJEU, Joined Cases C-341/06 P and C-342/06 P *Chronopost II* [2008] *ECR* I-4777.

[48] The contested decision, Decision 98/365, *OJ* 1998 L 164/37 was annulled by the judgment in GC, Case T-613/97 *Ufex and Others* v. *Commission* [2000] *ECR* II-4055. This judgment was in turn appealed by Chronopost, la Poste and France.

[49] CJEU, Case C-39/94 *SFEI* [1996] *ECR* I-3547.

sector, had erred in basing its comparison on an undertaking that was structurally different from La Poste, instead of comparing the conduct of the latter with that of an undertaking in the same position thus with a reserved sector at its disposal.[50]

The Court held that the General Court had failed to take account of the fact that an undertaking such as La Poste was in a situation very different from that of a private undertaking acting under normal market conditions.[51] In this regard, the Court referred to the fact that La Poste was entrusted with a service of general economic interest, and thus had at its disposal substantial infrastructures and resources.[52] In the absence of any possibility of comparing the situation of La Poste with that of a private group of undertakings not operating in a reserved sector, normal market conditions, which are necessarily hypothetical, had to be assessed by reference to the objective and verifiable elements which were available.[53] The Court stated that the costs borne by La Poste in respect of the provision to its subsidiary of logistical and commercial assistance could constitute such objective and verifiable elements.[54] There was no State aid to SFMI-Chronopost if, first, it was established that the price charged properly covered all the additional, variable costs incurred in providing the logistical and commercial assistance, an appropriate contribution to the fixed costs arising from use of the postal network and an adequate return on the capital investment in so far as it was used for SFMI-Chronopost's competitive activity and if, second, there was nothing to suggest that those elements had been underestimated or fixed in an arbitrary fashion.[55]

This effectively omits the efficiency test prescribed by the fourth *Altmark* criterion. Moreover, it was repeated in *Chronopost II*, where the Court held that the Commission should not, at first sight, be criticised for having based the contested decision on the only data available at the time, from which it was possible to reconstruct the costs incurred by La Poste.[56] The use of those data could be open to criticism only if it was established that they were based on manifestly incorrect considerations. The test laid down in Chronopost is very general in nature, prescribing the approach to be taken in order to assess whether the provision of commercial and logistical assistance involves State aid, without, however, specifying the economic, accounting or financial standards to be applied.[57] The exact definition of the variable costs to be included, as well as the 'appropriate contribution' and the 'adequate return on the capital investment' remain equally elusive. Apart from the discussion on the place of the *Chronopost* rulings in the grand

---

[50] Ibid, para 19.

[51] Ibid, para 33.

[52] Ibid, paras 34, 35.

[53] Ibid, para 38.

[54] Ibid, para 39.

[55] Ibid, para 40.

[56] Ibid, paras 148 and 149.

[57] CJEU, Joined Cases C-341/06 P and C-342/06 P *Chronopost II* [2008] *ECR* I-4777, Opinion of AG Sharpston, para 93.

scheme of *Altmark*,[58] this judgment points to the fact that cost-based standards are inherently complicated by the absence of precise cost allocation standards.

3.4 Financing and Costs of Services of General Economic Interest Outside the *Altmark* Context

The conclusion must be that an efficiency test like that prescribed in the fourth *Altmark* criterion may be difficult to implement in practice. Whereas a tendering procedure can be envisaged relatively easily in practice, the benchmark option appears to be a predominantly theoretical exercise. As a result, the underlying objective of ascertaining that services of general economic interest are provided at the least costs to society may also not be attained. Where, however, the public undertaking in charge of a service of general economic interest is accused of abusive practices in the meaning of Article 102 TFEU, the efficiency criterion is very much relevant again. This is because efficiencies derive from costs and costs are central to establishing many forms of abuse.

In this regard, we may point at the recent judgment in *Post Danmark*.[59] This is just one of a series of judgments dealing with undertakings delivering services of general economic interest in a reserved sector as well as being active in non-reserved sectors.[60] Basically, this concerned a decision by the Danish competition authority on exclusionary abuse undertaken by Post Danmark vis-à-vis its main competitor on the market for unaddressed mail, Forbruger-Kontakt.[61] The decision found that Post Danmark had abused its dominant position by engaging in price discrimination with regard to former customers of Forbruger-Kontakt. Whether or not such price discrimination amounts to abuse depends on the relation of the prices to the costs.

Setting the scene for its reasoning, the Court first reiterated the '*Michelin* special responsibility'. This refers to the Court's consistent case law that holds that dominance in itself is not a ground of criticism on the basis of Article 102 TFEU, but it does put upon that undertaking 'a special responsibility not to allow its

---

[58] Szyszczak 2004, pp. 990–991 and Sinnaeve 2003, p. 358, who argue that Chronopost is at odds with *Altmark*. See, on the other hand Bartosch 2003, p. 15, who argues that Chronopost is a lex specialis for the general rule laid down in *Altmark*.

[59] CJEU, Case C-209/10 *Post Danmark*, judgment of 27 March 2012, n.y.r.

[60] Further examples are CJEU, Case C-202/07 P *France Telecom* (Wanadoo) [2009] *ECR* I-2369; CJEU, Case C-280/08 P *Deutsche Telekom*, [2010] *ECR* I-9555 and CJEU, Case C-52/09 *TeliaSonera Sverige*, judgment of 17 February 2011, n.y.r.

[61] Exclusionary abuse is a category of abuse designed to or having as its effect the exclusion of competitors from a market, see CJEU, Case C-209/10 *Post Danmark*, judgment of 27 March 2012, n.y.r., para 20.

behaviour to impair genuine, undistorted competition on the internal market'.[62] As far as we can see, the Court has now for the first time stated that account must be taken of the fact that 'the existence of a dominant position has its origins in a former legal monopoly'.[63] The apparent meaning of this statement becomes clear only when we delve deeper into the cost allocation problems that arise. The Danish authority had used the incremental cost standard. This standard relates to those costs that would disappear in the next 3–5 years were Post Danmark to cease distributing unaddressed mail.[64] However, much like the situation in *Chronopost*, Post Danmark provided services in the non-reserved sector with the infrastructure and staff that it used in the reserved sector to meet the universal service obligation. This means that the costs of its universal service obligation activities would be reduced over a period of 3–5 years if Post Danmark would no longer distribute unaddressed mail. As a result, a portion of the common costs that related to both the reserved sector and commercial activities was included in the incremental costs.[65] This in turn is connected to the degree of efficiency with which a reserved activity is undertaken by the undertaking charged with the service of general economic interest. In relation to the fourth *Altmark* criterion, the effect is that a lack of efficiency in the reserved sector will translate into higher incremental costs because of the higher common costs. If, for example, Post Danmark would use the same postman to deliver both mails within the universal service remit and unaddressed mail, the lack of efficiency in delivering reserved mail would increase the costs that would need to be attributed to the delivery of non-addressed mail. As a rule, higher costs for a certain activity also mean that the price charged for that service needs to be higher. Given that whether or not a price is abusive depends on it exceeding, *inter alia*, average incremental costs, this would mean that Post Danmark would have to charge a relatively higher price if it wanted to avoid accusations of abusive conduct.

Efficiency again appears where the Court stated that only the exclusion of an 'as efficient competitor' would be abusive[66] and that exclusionary effects could be objectively justified on the basis of efficiencies that benefit consumers.[67] This again provides the public undertaking with an incentive to be efficient, as inefficiency on its part will make it easier for competitors to claim that they are 'as efficient' thus contributing to a finding of exclusionary abuse. On a similar note, it

---

[62] E.g. CJEU, Case C-209/10 *Post Danmark*, judgment of 27 March 2012, n.y.r., paras 21 and 23. For a critical discussion of this 'special responsibility' see: Allendesalazar 2008.

[63] CJEU, Case C-209/10 *Post Danmark*, judgment of 27 March 2012, n.y.r., para 23.

[64] Ibid, para 31. It may be noted that the Court appears to only endorse the incremental cost standard in this specific case, see, inter alia, the wording 'in the specific circumstances of the case in the main proceedings' in para 33. AG Mengozzi advocated a more general use of the incremental cost standard in cases involving a reserved sector, CJEU, Case C-209/10 *Post Danmark*, judgment of 27 March 2012, n.y.r. paras 33–35.

[65] CJEU, Case C-209/10 *Post Danmark*, judgment of 27 March 2012, n.y.r., paras 32 and 33.

[66] Ibid, paras 21, 22 and 38.

[67] Ibid, paras 41 and 42.

will be more difficult to argue that seemingly abusive behaviour is in fact objectively justified. The bottom line of Post Danmark is that an undertaking discharging a service of general economic interest whilst also providing commercial services is well-advised to be as efficient as possible.

3.5 Conclusions

Life after *Altmark* has not become any easier as far as the Courts' jurisprudence is concerned. There is no clear standard and apparently complex services of general economic interest warrant a more flexible approach to the *Altmark* criteria, and in particular the fourth criterion designed to ensure efficiency. Probably as a result of the constitutional perspective, the Member States were left relatively free under the *Altmark* criteria. The option of using a benchmark as an alternative for a tendering procedure clearly follows from the constitutional framework whereby the EU leaves the Member States free in their decisions to organise markets, and thus also services of general economic interest, themselves. This sovereignty, however, impacts the judicial protection perspective as it translates into significant leeway for the Member States and a limited review by the Courts.

Nonetheless, Member States treading the fine line between markets and public intervention are well-advised to ensure the efficiency of the provision of the service of general economic interest as competitors may not only have recourse to the protection offered to them by the State aid rules, but also the antitrust rules enshrined in the Treaty. It is in this regard that we come to our main conclusion that legal certainty and judicial protection do not appear to have been the prime purposes of *Altmark*. However, being firmly set in the competition rules, efficiency and its close corollary consumer welfare do appear to underlie *Altmark* and the other competition rules applied to services of general economic interest. Such efficiency reviews may well be triggered by competitors in judicial proceedings, and thus fit in the judicial protection perspective. As to the constitutional perspective, the deference in *BUPA* is clearly set in the Member States' wish to define and execute services of general economic interest in a sovereign manner. We see that much of the deference disappears where activities within the public service remit are undertaken together with commercial activities whilst entering the realm of the antitrust provisions. It is in relation to antitrust that the Treaty's efficiency paradigm was clear from 1958 onwards. Another way of looking at this would be to state that the Courts are deferent as regards the *ex ante* (creation) part of a service of general economic interest. Concerning the *ex post* (operation) of the service of general economic interest, the Courts are stricter. We find, to answer the question in the title, evolution, but not so much in relation to the *Altmark* exception itself.

References

Allendesalazar R (2008) Can we finally say farewell to the "special responsibility" of dominant companies? In: Ehlermann C-D, Marquis M (eds) (2007) European competition Law annual 2007: a reformed approach to Article 82 EC. Hart Pub, Oxford

Bartosch A (2003) Clarification or confusion? How to reconcile the ECJ's rulings in Altmark and chronopost? CLaSF working paper series Number 2, 2003, available at http://www.clasf.org/assets/CLaSF%20Working%20Paper%2002.pdf

Bartosch A (2008) The ruling in BUPA—clarification or modification of Altmark? EStAL 7:211

Buendia Sierra JL (2008) Finding the right balance: state aid and services of general economic interest. In Liber amicorum Francesco Santaolalla Gadea, EC State aid law, Alphen a/d Rijn. Kluwer Law International, The Hague

Hancher L, Larouche P (2011) The coming of age of EU regulation of network industries and services of general economic interest. In: Craig P, de Búrca G (eds) The evolution of EU Law. OUP, Oxford

Nicolaides P (2002) The distortive effects of compensatory aid measures: a note on the economics of the 'Ferring' judgement'. ECLR 23:313–319

Nicolaides P (2003a) Compensation for public service obligations: opening the floodgates of state aid? ECLR 24:561–573

Nicolaides P (2003b) Competition and services of general economic interest in the EU: reconciling economics and law. EStAL 3:183–209

Ross M (2009) A healthy approach to services of general economic interest? The BUPA judgment of the Court of first instance. ELRev 34:127–140

Santamato S, Pesaresi N (2004) Compensation for services of general economic interest: some thoughts on the Altmark ruling, CPL 17–21, available at: http://ec.europa.eu/competition/publications/cpn/2004_1_17.pdf

Sauter W, van de Gronden JW (2011) State aid, services of general economic interest and universal service in healthcare. ECLR 32:615–620

Sauter W, Vedder HHB (2012) State aid and selectivity in the context of emissions trading: an examination of the ECJ's 2011 NOx Case, ELRev 37:327–339 available also at: http://papers.ssrn.com/sol3/papers.cfm?abstract_id=2005755

Sinnaeve A (2003) State financing of public services: the Court's dilemma in the Altmark case. EstAL 3:351–364

Szyszczak E (2004) Financing services of general economic interest. MLR 67:982

Thouvenin JM (2009) The Altmark case and its consequences. In: Krajewski M, Neergaard U, van de Gronden J (eds) The changing legal framework for services of general economic interest in Europe—between competition and solidarity. TMC Asser Press, The Hague

Vedder HHB (2009) Of jurisdiction and justification; why competition is good for 'non-economic' goals, but may need to be restricted. CompLRev 6:51–75

Winter JA (2004) Re(de)fining the notion of state aid in Article 87(1) of the EC treaty. CMLRev 41:475, 504

Chapter 4
The Role of Procurement and SGEI After *Altmark*

Ian Clarke

Abstract This chapter examines the role of public procurement in the financing of Services of General Economic Interest (SGEI) following the *Altmark* judgment. The chapter explores the interplay between the application of State aid, service concessions and the use of procurement Directives in financing SGEI against a backdrop of public sector austerity measures and the privatisation of some public service obligations. The author charts how the Commission and the Courts have interpreted the landmark judgment both through case law and the application of soft law communications and Frameworks. The chapter focuses on the often complex issues that arise in interpreting the four *Altmark* conditions and the resulting stages in the evolution of the Commission's guidance on the financing of SGEI, culminating in the 2011 'Almunia Package'. The author argues that whilst the *Altmark* judgment was a step in the right direction, it also added a level of ambiguity, particularly in the interpretation of the fourth *Altmark* condition where the CJEU adopted a hybrid public procurement/compensation mechanism for determining whether the financing of SGEI was State aid. *Clarke* argues that there is a case for contracting authorities to apply a public procurement process as a default position for the financing of SGEI unless specific exemptions apply. He suggests that this would reduce the level of control currently being applied by the Commission and reporting would be by exception.

Contents

I. Clarke (✉)
School of Law, University of Leicester, Leicester LE1 7RH, UK
e-mail: iac6@le.ac.uk

E. Szyszczak and J.W. van de Gronden (eds.), *Financing Services of General Economic Interest*, Legal Issues of Services of General Interest, DOI: 10.1007/978-90-6704-906-1_4,
© T.M.C. ASSER PRESS, The Hague, The Netherlands, and the authors 2013

4.1 Introduction

The aim of this chapter is to explore the role of public procurement[1] and Services of General Economic Interest (SGEI)[2] following the landmark ruling in the *Altmark*[3] case. The reasons for doing this are twofold. Prior to the *Altmark* decision, the EC Commission had adopted an approach to the use of State aid by advising Member States that they must comply with the public procurement Directives where applicable or with the general principles of the Treaty notably as regards transparency, non-discrimination and competition. Where public procurement procedures were not used for awarding SGEI, the Commission advised the Council and European Parliament that the award had to be consistent with the common market principles and that any compensatory payments for the provision of those services should be of a limited amount in order not to distort trade and competition.[4] This approach led to situations where in some circumstances Member States could award contracts to providers of SGEIs, regardless of the economic sector they operated in, without the need to undertake normal EU procurement procedures. Prior to *Altmark,* case law had been inconsistent with conflicting legal opinions adding further complexity to an already unclear

---

[1] As defined in EU Directives 2004/17 EC, *OJ* 2004 L134/1 and 2004/18 EC, *OJ* 2004 L134/114. The Directives are currently under review by the Commission following the publication of the Green Paper on the modernisation of EU public procurement policy: Towards a more efficient European Procurement Market, COM 2011 15 Final.

[2] SGEI constitute a legal concept and are included in the wording of Article 106(2) TFEU, Article 14 TFEU, Protocol No 26 of the Treaty of Lisbon 2009 and Article 36 CFEU. Neergaard 2012 suggests there is an emerging typology in the definition of an SGEI and highlights the difficulties in defining the concept of SGEI as shown in GC, Case T-289/03 *BUPA and Other* v. *Commission* [2008] *ECR* II-81, para 165 and the Commission's expanded list of inclusions in the *Staff Working Paper, The Application of State Aid Rules on Services of General Economic Interest since 2005 and the Outcome of Public Consultation,* SEC(2011) 397.

[3] CJEU, Case C-280/00 *Altmark Trans GmbH* v *Nahverkehrsgesellschaft Altmark GmbH* [2003] *ECR* I-7747.

[4] Communication from the Commission to the Council and the European Parliament. The Reform of State-Owned Enterprises in Developing Countries with focus on public utilities: The Need to Assess All the Options COM (2003) 326 Final, para 50.

approach to the role of procurement and SGEI.[5] The anticipation was that the *Altmark* ruling would provide clarity on the circumstances under which Member States could grant amounts of State aid to finance SGEI without recourse to competition law. This chapter therefore looks at the impact on the legal relationship between SGEIs and public procurement rules following the *Altmark* decision.

The second reason for exploring the roles of public procurement and SGEI is to consider how case law has developed since the *Altmark* decision and how the introduction of new State aid rules may influence these roles in the future.[6] These new State aid rules have been introduced against a backdrop of economic uncertainty across Europe with many Member States implementing challenging austerity measures which include privatisation and restructuring public service delivery. This restructuring will lead to a mixed economy public services delivery environment where a range of providers from all sectors will deliver SGEI under some form of contractual arrangement. How these contracts are awarded depends to some extent on the robustness of the new State aid rules and their interpretation, particularly when deciding on whether a procurement process is required.

This chapter is organised as follows. Following this Introduction, Sect. 4.2 examines the aims and objectives of the State aid and public procurement rules and their importance to the internal market. Section 4.3 examines the outcomes of the *Altmark* ruling for procurement and SGEIs and Sect. 4.4 goes on to look at developments since *Altmark*. Finally, Sect. 4.5 draws some conclusions as to whether the roles of SGEI and public procurement are clearly defined or whether further improvements and clarity are needed.

4.2 The Aims and Objectives of State Aid and Public Procurement

In understanding the role of public procurement and SGEI, it is useful to consider the objectives of the State aid rules that apply to SGEI and the procurement Directives that are designed to facilitate Internal Market principles. Both sets of rules have a common aim which is to ensure fair competition in the internal market, but through different legal mechanisms. State aid rules aim at ensuring fair competition in order to avoid undue advantages to certain economic operators, which may distort competition. Articles 107 TFEU and 108 TFEU therefore

---

[5] See the Opinion of AG Tizzano in CJEU, Case 53/00 *Ferring* v *Agence Centrale des Organismes de Securite Sociale (ACOSS)* [2001] *ECR* I-9067 and the Opinion of AG Jacobs in CJEU, Case C-126/01 *Ministre de l'économie, des finances et de l'industrie* v *GEMO SA* [2003] *ECR* I-13769.

[6] Communication from the Commission on the application of the European Union State aid rules to compensation granted for the provision of services of general economic interest, *OJ* 2012 C 8/4.

provide the European Commission with the vehicle to prevent State aid being used as a mechanism to restrict trade within the internal market.

The Vice President of the Commission, Joaquín Almunia suggests that the Commission's policing role in this often complex area of EU law had 'kept governments from giving selective advantages to firms; and together with the other instruments of the competition policy it has prevented the erection of entry barriers; and has avoided that certain companies are given too much market power'.[7]

The importance of State aid control is such that the Commission considers it a mechanism that underpins the functioning of the Internal Market and supports economic integration. Even in difficult economic environments where lack of economic growth across Member States leads to both social and commercial tensions, it maintains that the application of these controls is important in ensuring that limited public funds are spent effectively and help to generate growth.[8] The aims and objectives of the Commission, by deploying State aid controls, are therefore to support the Member States' policies for growth whilst ensuring that the Internal Market remains open for consumers and suppliers.

Public procurement Directives have similar aims and objectives to the State aid rules and put in place procedures for the award of public contracts through a fair and transparent competitive process. They are designed to promote better value from the expenditure decisions of contracting authorities and to prevent the distortion of competition by eliminating discriminatory procurement practices.

The Directives are fundamental pieces of legislation that ensure the development of effective competition in the Internal Market and help eliminate the barriers to the free movement principles that underpin European integration. They protect the interests of economic operators wishing to offer goods or services to contracting authorities established in another Member State. This is achieved by ensuring that contracting authorities follow a procurement process that is designed to avoid those favouring national tenderers at the detriment to those from other Member States.

This analysis suggests that the relationship between State aid and public procurement rules are complimentary to wider competition policy aimed at avoiding distortion of competition in the internal market and ensuring compliance by public/contracting authorities. This is supported through case law where both State aid and public procurement rules are seen as integral to competition policy and the enforcement of competition rules. However, in 2002, Bartosch highlighted the potential conflict for contracting authorities in complying with public procurement procedures set out in secondary legislation and State aid law. He suggested that there were issues of interpretation between the suitability criteria used in the award of public service contracts other than those stipulated

---

[7] Modernising State aid control, Speech by Joaquín Almunia, Vice President of the European Commission responsible for Competition Policy to European Economic and Social Committee—plenary meeting, Brussels, 23 February 2012, SPEECH/12/117.

[8] Ibid.

in the Procurement Directives and the prohibition of State aid laid down in Article 87(1) EC.[9] Many of these interpretation issues still remain and are discussed later in the chapter.

> The public procurement and State aid rules, whilst having similar aims and objectives are less clear on their application in relation to SGEI and require clarity on whether these services should be tendered or financed.

The Courts have developed an approach to assessing whether the conditions are right for a SGEI to be directly financed by the State rather than procured through competition. This comprises of an assessment as to whether the aid being applied to the SGEI is prohibited under Article 107(1) TFEU or is compatible with the internal market under Article 106(2) TFEU. For an SGEI to be considered compatible with the internal market, all three of the following conditions must be fulfilled:

1. genuine services of general economic interest must be defined;
2. there must be an instrument specifying the public service obligations; and
3. there must be no overcompensation.

There are no similar tests that can be applied to public procurement because there is no explicit mention of SGEIs in the procurement Directives. However, the Directives do make reference to services concessions[10] which Article 1(4) of the Public Sector Directive defines as:

> a contract of the same type as a public service contract except for the fact that the consideration for the provision of services consists either solely in the right to exploit the service or in this right together with payment.[11]

Service concessions are explicitly excluded from the scope of the application of the public procurement Directives (Article 17 of the Public Sector Directive; Article 18 of the Utilities Directive). However, case law provides for the fundamental rules of the Treaty and the principle of non-discrimination on grounds of nationality and the principle of transparency to be applied to service concessions.[12]

This raises a number of questions of interpretation and suggests that although service concessions are explicitly excluded from the application of the public procurement Directives they (and accordingly SGEI) would need to be tendered to ensure there was an appropriate level of advertising of the opportunity to ensure compliance with the transparency principles of the Treaty.

Public procurement case law suggests that tendering processes should be undertaken prior to commencing the operation of an SGEI which further

---

[9] Bartosch 2002, p. 507.

[10] The Commission issued an interpretative communication on concessions under Community law in the *OJ* 2000 C 121/02.

[11] Article 1(4) of Directive 2004/18 EC.

[12] See CJEU, Case C-107/98 *Teckal Srl* v *Comune di Viano* [1999] *ECR* I-8121, para 51; CJEU, Case C-94/99 *ARGE Gewasserschutz* v *Bundesministerium fur Land- und Forstwirtschaft* [2000] *ECR* I-11037, para 40; CJEU, Case C-220/05 *Auroux* v *Commune de Roanne* [2007] *ECR* I-389, para 62.

complicates the interpretation of the State aid rules.[13] Add to this, the question of whether Article 106(2) TFEU allows derogation from the principle of non-discrimination and transparency to be applied and the complexities of legal interpretation become more challenging.

It is important to clarify at this point that where a public authority provides an SGEI directly or through an internal provider that is a legally distinct entity but wholly owned[14] by the public authority then procurement Directives and the principle of transparency do not apply.

Whilst there is no current case law to review on the issue of derogation to an SGEI under Article 106(2) TFEU, Hatzopoulos & Stergiou suggest that there is nothing to stop this derogation from being applied.[15]

4.3 The Effect of *Altmark* on the Role of SGEI and Public Procurement

Prior to the *Altmark* ruling, conflicting legal opinion on the application of SGEI financing and the application of the public procurement rules led to political debate between Member States on how SGEI should be treated.[16] The debate centred on whether these services should be subject to the competition rules or whether exemptions applied.

Following the *Altmark* ruling, and in particular the introduction of the Court's four criterion test the approach to the financing of SGEIs by Member States became more structured, providing clarity on the process for determining when financing without competition was appropriate.[17] However, the judgment failed to sufficiently clarify the interaction between the State aid and public procurement rules particularly in relation to the interpretation of the fourth *Altmark* criterion.

The fourth criterion states that:

> where the undertaking which is to discharge public service obligations is not chosen pursuant to a public procurement procedure which would allow for the selection of the tenderer capable of providing those services at the least cost to the community, the level of compensation needed must be determined on the basis of an analysis of the costs which a typical undertaking, well run and adequately provided with means of transport so as to be able to meet the necessary public service requirements, would have incurred in discharging

---

[13] Ibid.

[14] A minority share in the capital of the distinct entity by a private undertaking has been interpreted by the CJEU as the public authority not having full control over the entity and therefore the Procurement Directives and Transparency principle do apply. See Case C-26/03 *Stadt Halle* v *RPL Recyclingpark Lochau* [2005] *ECR* I-1, paras 49–50.

[15] Hatzopoulos and Stergiou 2011, p. 438.

[16] Nicolaides 2003.

[17] As defined in CJEU, Case C-280/00 *Altmark Trans GmbH* [2003] *ECR* I-7747 paras 88–93.

those obligations, taking into account the relevant receipts and a reasonable profit for discharging the obligations.[18]

This Court's inclusion of the need to implement the procurement Directives suggests that it would ensure compliance with this fourth condition. However, Santamato & Pesaresi suggested that whilst the judgment established principles of compensation in discharging public service obligations it linked 'some procedural requirements (ex-ante fixation of parameters, tender procedure, and analysis of the costs of a typical undertaking) to the notion of aid'.[19] They argued that whilst the judgment had the benefit of preserving Commission control, it also led to an assumption that all compensation not meeting the criterion was State aid and the application of a tendering process may in fact lead to higher costs to the community rather than the least possible cost.[20]

This argument challenges the first section of the fourth criterion of the *Altmark* judgment by suggesting that the selection of an undertaking to provide an SGEI following a procurement based on an evaluation criterion of 'least cost to the community' will not always deliver the best value for money for the community (as argued by Santamato and Pesaresi). It also raises questions as to how the Courts will interpret 'least cost for the community'. Most procurement practitioners operating within the public procurement environment would plan their procurements following careful consideration of three important procedural requirements:

(a) The nature of the award criteria, i.e. lowest price or most economically advantageous tender (MEAT)
(b) The type of procurement procedure used
(c) The extent to which the contract is covered by the procurement Directives

The first of these three procedural requirements, the award criteria, have different interpretations in terms of identifying the least cost to the community. In financial terms, the award of a contract for goods or services based on the lowest price would be likely to provide the best financial outcome for the community. This approach often drives a culture of delivering the bare minimum in terms of service quality which is proportionate to the price being paid. Whilst this is acceptable for some services, the importance of SGEI to the community is such that the services being procured will often need to consider and evaluate the wider quality, environmental and social consideration when assessing tenders. It is therefore now considered best practice in many Member States to adopt the 'most economically advantageous tender' criterion for the procurement of most public service requirements.

The second procedural requirement, the *type* of procurement procedure used, may also have an impact on the level of competition applied to the SGEI. The normal open, restricted competitive dialogue and negotiated procedures with publication of a tender notice in the Official Journal of the European Union

---

[18] Paragraph 86.
[19] Santamato and Pesaresi 2004.
[20] Ibid at 3.2.

(OJEU) should provide sufficient competition to meet the fourth *Altmark* criterion. However, employing a negotiated procedure to an SGEI without publication of a tender notice in the OJEU is unlikely to be sufficient to satisfy the fourth *Altmark* criterion.

The third procedural requirement is less contentious with regards to the application of the procurement Directives in the fourth *Altmark* criterion. Public contracts fully covered by the public procurement Directives will either apply to SGEIs or they will be considered out of scope (e.g. service concessions). However, as discussed earlier, procurement case law requires the general principles of the Treaty, and specifically transparency and non-discrimination, to be maintained even when the procurement Directives do not apply. It could therefore be argued that the second part of the fourth *Altmark* criterion allowing financing of an SGEI to be based on benchmarking data (e.g. an analysis of the costs of a typical undertaking, well run and adequately provided with means) does not only conflict with procurement principles but it could also be argued that they dilute the underlying non-discrimination and transparency principles of the Treaty.

The first element of the fourth *Altmark* criterion therefore introduced a level of flexibility in the financing of SGEIs but failed to clarify the interaction between public procurement and State aid rules. This means a number of questions still remain as to the role of the procurement process in ensuring compliance with the criterion, particularly where there is a lack of clarity on when a Member State is obliged to use a tendering process.

The second element of the fourth *Altmark* criterion provides for a Member State to prove compliance with the fourth *Altmark* criterion when financing an SGEI without undertaking a procurement process by using a benchmarking mechanism. Using this approach, contracting authorities are required to ensure that the level of compensation applied is no more than a 'typical undertaking, well run and adequately provided with means of transport so as to be able to meet the necessary public service requirements, would have incurred in discharging those obligations'. However, the application of this mechanism in more complex situations relies on a contracting authority's interpretation of a 'typical undertaking'. For example, many Member States as part of their austerity measures have privatised some public sector organisations that previously held a monopoly position. The lack of competition in the market suggests that by entrusting an SGEI to the new undertaking means that little or no benchmark data will be available to determine if they are well run and therefore if the level of compensation is appropriate. Further, problems may also arise where an undertaking may be involved in the delivery of a mixture of commercial and public services. There is a risk that the compensation it receives in delivering the SGEI could be used to support its commercial operations, providing it with a competitive advantage in the marketplace.[21]

---

[21] Szyszczak 2011.

The latter example is of particular importance because although state resources granted for the financing of an SGEI cannot be used to intervene in other markets outside the scope of the service being provided, an undertaking can use any reasonable profit gained from performing the SGEI in these markets.[22] This once again leads to the interpretation of 'reasonable profits' and how they influence the competitiveness of the undertaking, particularly where the level of compensation may have been determined against weak benchmarking data.

The financing of SGEIs by its very nature often conflict with the general competition principles that are not covered under the *Altmark* Criterion. For example, the contracting authority may require a level of familiarity of the local demographics to be included in the selection criteria in order to ensure the benefits from the service provided are maximised. They may also only want to engage the specific skills of the voluntary and community sectors which are in direct conflict with the procurement Directives because they do not allow contracts to be reserved for specific categories of undertakings. Separate case law in these situations has developed in parallel with the *Altmark* ruling to provide some clarity as to the restriction that apply to contracting authorities in these situations.[23]

The *Altmark* judgment was a seminal step in establishing tighter controls on the financing of SGEI but it also raised a number of issues that were tested through the European Courts and required the issuing of further guidance by the Commission. These are discussed in the next section.

4.4 Developments Since *Altmark*

Shortly after the *Altmark* judgment, the CJEU applied the *Altmark* criterion in *Enirisorse*[24] and found that the conditions were clearly not met. Thus, the Court did not provide any additional guidance on the interpretation of the criteria. However, in *Danske Busvognmænd*[25] the CFI rejected the Commission's position that Denmark had complied with the *Altmark* criterion on the grounds that both the Commission and the Danish Government failed to demonstrate that all the conditions for the application of derogation from the principle of prohibition of State aid were satisfied, and that the compensation did not fulfil the *Altmark* criterion.[26]

---

[22] The Transparency Directive 80/723/EEC (*OJ* 1980 L195/35) includes a requirement for internal accounts to show separately the costs and receipts associated with the SGEI and those of other services.

[23] For example, see CJEU Case C-234/03 *Contse SA* v. *Instituto Nacional de Gestion Sanitaria (INGESA) (formerly Instituto Nacional de la Salud (INSALUD))* [2005] *ECR* I-9315, para 79 and CJEU, Case C-70/95 *Sodemare SA* v. *Regione Lombardia* [1997] *ECR* I-3395.

[24] CJEU, Case C-34/01 *Enirisorse SpA* v. *Ministero delle Finanze* [2003] *ECR* I-14243.

[25] CJEU, Case T-157/01 *Danske Busvognmaend* v *Commission of the European Communities* [2004] *ECR* II-917.

[26] Paragraphs 96 and 97.

This later case provided early evidence that the interpretation and application of the *Altmark* conditions were likely to cause a problem in the future. The Commission added further confusion in its interpretation of the *Altmark* conditions in its Cumbrian Access decision.[27] In this decision, the Commission stated that by using a negotiated procedure, the public authority would not satisfy the requirements of *Altmark* even though the requirement was a technical and complex activity. The Commission's decision was controversial because the Court, in its ruling in *Altmark*, had not specified what formal procurement procedure must be carried out in meeting the condition. The Commission eventually exempt the requirement under the exemptions contained in what is now Article 107(3) TFEU which led some commentators to suggest that the 'interpretation of *Altmark* was indicative of an organisation that did not wish to relinquish control'.[28]

The second element of the fourth *Altmark* criterion requiring Public Authorities to ensure there is no over compensation to undertakings where the public procurement Directives are not applied and no competition takes place was tested in *Chronopost*.[29] In this decision, the CJEU recognised the difficulty in identifying relevant benchmarking data to determine if *Chronopost* had benefited from unlawful aid provided by the French postal service as a commercial subsidiary. The problem was that the postal network in France was designed to fulfil a universal obligation and not a commercial business operation, and therefore there were no commercial comparators to benchmark the level of compensation provided. The approach taken by the Court was that in the:

> absence of any possibility of comparing the situation of La Poste with that of a private group of undertakings not operating in a reserved sector, "normal market conditions", which are necessarily hypothetical, must be assessed by reference to the objective and verifiable elements which are available.[30]

This case clearly highlights the problems with interpreting the levels of compensation that should be applied under the second element of the fourth *Altmark* criterion, especially in complex SGEI where the undertaking is in a monopoly position.

---

[27] Commission Decision N 282/2003 Cumbria Broadband, Project Access, Advancing Communication for Cumbria and Enabling Sustainable Services, Brussels, 10 December 2003 C(2003)4480fin.

[28] Boyd and Teal 2004.

[29] CJEU, Joined Cases C-83/01 P, C-93/01 P and C-94/01 P *Chronopost* v *Ufex and Others* [2003] *ECR* I-6993.

[30] Paragraph 38.

4.4.1 Commission Guidance Material

Prior to *Altmark* Commission, guidance on the financing of SGEI was considered unreliable and it was hoped that the *Altmark* ruling would provide much needed clarity to this complex legal area. Following the ruling, the Commission adopted an approach which has seen the publication of various communications and frameworks which suggest that soft law mechanisms for controlling the interpretation and assessment of State aid and the financing of SGEI are the preferred option. The early Community Framework Paper[31] was useful in providing additional details on the requirements to satisfy the *Altmark* conditions in particular what was required when assigning State aid to SGEI financing under the first *Altmark* criteria. However, it did not provide any guidance on when a compliant public procurement exercise using a negotiated procedure was sufficient to avoid overcompensation in light of the decision taken by the Commission in Cumbrian Access.

The Commission also issued a number of additional publications including a draft amendment to Directive 80/723/EEC on the transparency of financial relations between Member States and public undertakings.[32] This draft amendment was helpful in bringing the Transparency Directive up to date by laying down minimum conditions for ensuring financial transparency between Member States and undertakings entrusted with SGEIs.

On 28 November 2005, the Commission introduced a series of measures aimed at taking more control over the interpretation and assessment of State aid for SGEI. The 'Monti-Kroes' Package consisted of a Commission Decision[33] and a Framework.[34] The Decision required Public Authorities to notify the Commission of any public service compensation which did not satisfy the *Altmark* criterion. This provided more detailed guidance than the earlier Community Framework but again lacked clarity on whether public procurement by itself could ensure that no overcompensation took place. The 'Monti-Kroes' Package also introduced a set of safe havens by excluding certain activities from the State aid rules and the *Altmark* ruling as well as creating a set of *de minimis* rules. The introduction of these *de minimis* rules suggested that the Commission had adopted a position where there was no cross border interest in trade below the *de minimis* threshold. This added further complexity to the interpretation of State aid rules and the relationship to public

---

[31] Community Framework for State aid in the form of public service compensation *OJ* 2005 C 297/04.

[32] *OJ* 1999 C 377/2.

[33] Commission Decision of 28 November 2005 on the application of Article 86(2) EEC to State aid in the form of public service compensation granted to certain undertakings entrusted with the operation of services of general economic interest, Document number C(2005) 2673, *OJ* L 2005 L312/67.

[34] Community Framework for State aid in the form of public service compensation, *OJ* 2005 C 297/4.

procurement because the CJEU had stated that *de minimis* did not apply to State aid.[35] The Framework addressed the application of Article 106(2) TFEU but the package as a whole failed to tackle whether the principles of proportionality would be satisfied where the *Altmark* conditions, the Decision or the Framework applied to the public service compensation.

In 2010, the Commission published staff working papers[36] which laid the foundation for the publication on 20 December 2011 of their revised package of measures designed to meet the challenges of a changing economic climate and Member State constitutional pressures.[37] This modernisation package looked to clarify 'key state aid principles and introduces a diversified and proportionate approach with simpler rules for SGEIs that are small, local in scope or pursue a social objective, while taking account of competition considerations for large cases.' The aim of the package was to put some regulation around the financing and operation of SGEIs and included a Communication, a revised Decision[38] and a Framework applicable from 31 January 2012.[39] A new *de minimis* Regulation for SGEI was delayed, but promised for Spring 2012, being finally adopted on 26 April 2012.[40]

The Commission has not limited its Communications and guidance activities to the provision of State aid and its application in financing SGEIs. On 9 May 2010, Professor Mario Monti presented a report to the President of the Commission on a new Strategy for the Single Market.[41] Part of the Report considers the role of social services and argues that the administrative burden that comes with the EU procurement rules are not consistent and do not align with small SGEI. This results in a lack of flexibility and a barrier to integration with wider social inclusion

---

[35] Szyszczak 2012.

[36] Commission Staff Working Document, Guide to the application of the European Union rules on State aid, public procurement and the internal market to services of general economic interest, and in particular to social services of general interest, SEC(2010) 1545 final.

[37] Communication from the Commission on the application of the European Union State aid rules to compensation granted for the provision of services of general economic interest, *OJ* 2012 C 8/4.

[38] Commission Decision of 20 December 2011 on the application of Article 106(2) TFEU to State aid in the form of public service compensation granted to certain undertakings entrusted with the operation of services of general economic interest, *OJ* 2012 L 7/3.

[39] Communication from the Commission, European Union framework for State aid in the form of public service compensation, *OJ* 2012 C 8/15.

[40] Draft Commission Regulation on the application of Articles 107 and 108 TFEU to *de minimis* aid granted to undertakings providing services of general economic interest, *OJ* 2012 1 C 8/23; Commission Regulation on the application of Articles 107 and 108 of the Treaty on the Functioning of the European Union to *de minimis* aid granted to undertakings providing services of general economic interest, *OJ* 2012 L 114/8.

[41] Report to the President of the Commission, Barroso on 9 May 2010: A New Strategy for the Single Market at the Service of Europe's Economy and Society. Available at http://ec.europa.eu/bepa/pdf/monti_report_final_10_05_2010_en.pdf (accessed 10 April 2012).

policy.[42] Following the Monti Report, the Commission undertook a period of consultation on the modernisation of EU procurement law.[43]

On 13 April 2011, the Commission issued a Communication outlining its 12 key priorities for re-launching the Single Market.[44] One of these priorities was the modernisation of the public procurement legislative framework which was supported by a press release issued by the Commission outlining its proposals.[45] The aim of the procurement modernisation agenda is to improve flexibility and simplify the procurement procedures for both contracting authorities and companies. Better use of negotiated procedures, the use of general notices, reduced documentation, better use of electronic procurement and shorter deadlines all feature in the modernisation process.

An important part of this modernisation programme is the implementation of the proposed Concessions Directive.[46] The aim of this Directive is to:

> establish a clear legal framework to ensure the necessary legal certainty for public authorities when performing their duties. They aim to guarantee effective access to the concessions market for all European businesses, including SMEs, and could thus help to stimulate the development of public-private partnerships, for which concessions constitute a tool of choice.[47]

The Commission has also recognised that wider use of concessions requires a level of governance to avoid abuse. It has therefore proposed the obligatory publication of concessions in the Official Journal of the European Union (OJEU) and the specification by the contracting authorities of selection and award criteria. Furthermore, it proposes to extend the benefits of the Remedies Directive[48] to any undertaking interested in obtaining a concession.

To avoid excessive administrative burden, the Commission proposes to only apply these publication requirements to large concessions that have a cross-border interest.[49] Identifying which concessions meet these publication criteria may

---

[42] Section 3.3.

[43] The Commission responded to the Monti Report 2010 with a consultation on modernising procurement law (which ended in April 2011). Available at http://ec.europa.eu/internal_market/publicprocurement/modernising_rules/consultations/index_en.htm (accessed 10 April 2012).

[44] The Single Market Act: Twelve levers to boost growth and confidence COM (2011) 206.

[45] Modernising European public procurement to support growth and employment, available at http://europa.eu/rapid/pressReleasesAction.do?reference=IP/11/1580&format=HTML&aged=0&language=EN&guiLanguage=en (accessed 10 April 2012).

[46] Ibid.

[47] Ibid.

[48] Directive 2007/66 amending Council Directives 89/665/EEC and 92/13/EEC with regard to improving the effectiveness of review procedures concerning the award of public contracts, OJ 2007 L335/31.

[49] Small value local services contracts would probably not have a cross-border interest, but value alone is not sufficient to indicate that there is no cross-border interest, see CJEU, Joined Cases C-147/06 *SECAP SpA* v *Comune di Torino* and C-148/06 *Santorso Soc. Coop. Arl* v. *Comune di Torino (Bresciani Bruno Srl and Others, intervening)* [2008] *ECR* I-3565, para 31.

become problematic especially where companies are accustomed to trading across borders. In a difficult economic climate, some may even argue that all concessions have a cross-border interest and that the value of even small concessions may be of commercial interest. The Court's interpretation of these criteria is also difficult to determine and by arming them with the provision of the Remedies Directive, the consequences of a contracting authority getting it wrong could be significant. The Commission will therefore need to issue clear guidance on the application of the Concessions Directive.

The proposed implementation of the Concessions Directive is further compli-cated by service concessions not being subject to Directive 2004/18/EC and in particular not being required to publish a notice in the Official Journal. However, the TFEU requirement to ensure that transparency and equal treatment are applied has led the CJEU to require contracting authorities to undertake a degree of advertising sufficient to allow competition and impartiality.[50] But the level of advertising is determined by the contracting authority, and therefore may not extend beyond a Member State's borders.

4.5 Concluding Remarks

The CJEU, in its judgment in *Altmark,* had a significant impact on the future financing of SGEI. By ruling that where State subsidies are applied to compensate an undertaking for discharging a pso, this does not constitute State aid as long as four conditions are satisfied. These conditions require a Member State to ensure that:

1. the recipient undertaking must have a public service obligation to discharge and then this obligation must be clearly defined;
2. the bases by which the compensation is calculated must be done in advance, in a fair and transparent manner to avoid the undertaking gaining a competitive advantage;
3. the compensation does not exceed what is required to cover all or part of the costs in discharging the public service obligation; and
4. where the undertaking is not chosen through a public procurement process, the level of compensation must be based on an analysis of the costs that a typical undertaking, well run and adequately provided with means to discharge the public obligation would incur.

The Court's judgment and approach to the financing of SGEI has generated a level of debate on the role of the state within the single market and how this applies to the application of compensation to service providers discharging pso.

---

[50] See CJEU, Case C-324/98 *Telaustria Verlags GmbH* v. *Telekom Austria AG* [2000] *ECR.* I-10745.

The Court's use of public procurement in the fourth *Altmark* condition highlights the link between State aid and public procurement but does raise a number of issues on interpretation. This is a particular problem for Member States who are implementing a privatisation programme or redesigning public services at a time of financial stress. The resulting pso may be more complex or new privatised providers may hold a monopoly position in the market. In these examples, the contracting authority will need to choose between implementing a public procurement exercise and adopting the more subjective compensation benchmarking mechanism when considering the financing of the pso.

The four *Altmark* conditions were a step in the right direction towards clarifying the financing of SGEIs but they also added a level of ambiguity that has required the Commission to issue further guidance on their application. The *Altmark* conditions have provided a link between a compensation approach and a *quid pro quo* approach to the financing mechanism. However, the judgement suggests that whilst a compensation approach is acceptable, there also needs to be a public procurement process to ensure competitiveness and transparency. This raises three potential areas of conflict. First, the objective and transparent selection of an undertaking to discharge a pso without the use of a procurement process could generate political and legal challenge by other Member States who feel there is cross-border interest in delivering the obligation. Second, determining a 'reasonable profit' when adopting the compensation benchmarking approach to the financing of a private sector undertaking delivering a pso is subjective and further complicates the selection process. Third, the application of a public procurement process in the selection of an undertaking to deliver a pso will often not offer up the least cost service provider.

The Commission has played an important role in attempting to clarify the financing of SGEI, first through the 2005 'Monti-Kroes' Package and more recently in the 2011 'Almunia' reforms. However, one fundamental question in relation to the role of procurement in the financing of SGEI still remains open ended: in the new Almunia package Framework, does tendering need to be applied to undertakings receiving State aid compensation for providing a pso? In not clarifying this important area of the reform package, the Commission has lost an opportunity to remove a level of subjective interpretation from the already complex area of SGEI financing. Furthermore, the new Framework suggests that a policy that increases the Commission's level of control in the application of SGEI financing is being applied.

It is important to put the *Altmark* ruling in perspective, especially when considering the overall aims and objectives of State aid and public procurement rules. By its nature, the subject of any public procurement is directly related to the provision of goods, works or services in the public interest with many being considered as SGEI. Therefore, by selecting the undertaking to deliver these services using a procurement process, State aid regulations would not apply because the contractual relationship and procedures mechanism used in the procurement Directives are sufficient to meet the competition principle that underpins the single market. This suggests that, in principle, the use of a public procurement when financing SGEI would be the most appropriate approach in ensuring that any compensation applied reflected true market value. There is an argument that public procurement does not always truly reflect the market conditions, especially where a specific SGEI market is immature or where there are few similarities to the service required in the private sector. However, there is also an argument for contracting authorities to adopt a public sector procurement process as the default position for the financing of SGEI unless there is demonstrable evidence that a procurement process is not appropriate.

Under this regime, the default position would reduce the level of control being applied by the Commission, limiting its involvement to only those SGEI where a contracting authority was seeking exemption or applying the compensation benchmarking approach.

References

Bartosch A (2002) The relationship of public procurement and state aid surveillance—the toughest standard applies? CML Rev 35:551–576

Boyd A, Teal J (2004) Interpreting the Altmark decision, the challenges from a private practitioner's perspective (McGrigors LLP)

Hatzopoulos V, Stergiou H (2011) Public procurement law and health care: from theory to practice. In: Van de Gronden J, Szyszczak E, Krajewski M, Neergaard U (eds) Healthcare and EU Law. TMC Asser Press, The Hague

Neergaard U (2012) The concept of SSGI and the asymmetries between free movement and competition law. In: Neergaard U, Szyszczak E, Van de Gronden J, Krajewski M (eds) Social services of general interest in the EU. TMC Asser Press, The Hague

Nicolaides P (2003) Compensation for public service obligations: the floodgates of state aid. ECLR 24(11):561–573

Santamato S, Pesaresi N (2004) Compensation for services of general economic interest: some thoughts on the *Altmark* ruling. Competition Policy Newsletter Number 1

Szyszczak E (2011) *Altmark* assessed. In: Szyszczak E (ed) Research handbook on European State Aid. Edward Elgar, Cheltenham

Szyszczak E (2012) Soft law and safe havens. In: Neergaard U, Szyszczak E, Van de Gronden J, Krajewski M (eds) Social services of general interest in the EU. TMC Asser Press, The Hague

Part II
Reform of the Altmark-Monti-Kroes Package

Chapter 5
The European Commission's Reform Strategy

Stéphane Rodrigues

Abstract The complementary link between EU competition rules and SGEI is clearly confirmed by the Treaty of Lisbon 2009 with the new Article 14 TFEU, Protocol No 26 on SGI and Article 36 CFREU. Among the competition rules, State aid rules play a very important role in order to ensure a sustainable financing of SG(E)I by the Member States. Such a balanced approach is the key milestone of the European Commission's strategy to reform the rules applicable to public service compensation, by giving them more clarification and more adaptability, in order to promote higher quality of service. The question remains whether such a strategy is sufficient to ensure an effective implementation of these rules by the public authorities, notably local entities.

Contents

Many thanks to Lara Thomes, LLM in European Law of the Free University of Brussels (ULB—European Law Institute), for her active collaboration in collecting and reviewing the most relevant EU documents referred to in this chapter.

S. Rodrigues (✉)
Sorbonne Research Institute for International and European Law (IREDIES),
Sorbonne Law School, University of Paris 1 Panthéon-Sorbonne, 12, Place du Panthéon
75005 Paris, France
e-mail: stephane.rodrigues-domingues@univ-paris1.fr

5.1 Introduction

As underlined by the Commission, 'the direct contribution of SGEIs to the GDP is of great importance'.[1] Pursuant to available statistics 'expenditure in health and social services accounts for as high as 9.4 % of GDP' and 'The sectors of infrastructure networks have a contribution of 4.8 % of GDP, while research and recruitment have a contribution of 0.9 % of GDP'.[2] In parallel, the total State aid represented more or less 10 % of the GDP of the EU 27 in 2010, including financial crisis aid, notably guarantee and liquidity measures.[3]

As stressed by the European Parliament, in times of crisis, SGEI, and notably social services of general interest (SSGI) play an important role as instrument of economic, social, and territorial cohesion.[4] On the other hand, control of State aid as laid down by Articles 107–109 TFEU is a key issue to financing SGEI and guaranteeing their existence for all EU citizens. Consequently, reforming the rules governing such a control, and known as the 'Monti-Kroes Package' adopted in November 2005[5] in order to clarify the *rationale* and scope of the 2003 *Altmark* ruling of the CJEU,[6] is a sensitive issue for both political and legal reasons.[7]

---

[1] See Commission Staff Working Paper—*Impact Assessment of the Reform of the EU Rules applicable to State aid in the form of public services compensation*: SEC(2011)1581 final of 20 December 2011, p. 12.

[2] Ibidem. See also Bauby and Similie 2010.

[3] See Commission Staff Working Paper—*Autumn 2011 Update*: SEC(2011)847 final of 1 December 2011, accompanying the *State Aid Scoreboard*: COM(2011) 848 final of 1 December 2011.

[4] See European Parliament resolution of 5 July 2011 on the future of social services of general interest; for a general comment on it by its own Rapporteur: see De Rossa 2011, pp. 18–21.

[5] See Commission Decision of 28 November 2005 on the application of Article 86(2) of the EC Treaty to State aid in the form of public service compensation granted to certain undertakings entrusted with the operation of services of general economic interest (notified under document number C(2005) 2673), *in OJ* L 2005 312/67 and Community framework for State aid in the form of public service compensation, in *OJ* 2005 C 297/4. See also: Commission Directive of 16 November 2006 on the transparency of financial relations between Member States and public undertakings as well as on financial transparency within certain undertakings (codified version), in *OJ* 2006 L 318/17.

[6] CJEU, Case C-280/00, *Altmark Trans GmbH and Regierungspräsidium Magdeburg* v *Nahverkehrsgesellschaft Altmark GmbH, and Oberbundesanwalt beim Bundesverwaltungsgericht* [2003] *ECR* I-7747.

[7] See Szyszczak 2004.

The aim of this chapter is to explain how this reform is part of a wider strategy of reform and modernization of EU State aid law and how the world economic crisis has an impact on the implementation of this strategy regarding the specific issue of financing SGEI by the Member States.

In order to analyze these developments, this chapter will start by recalling the links between competition policy and SGEI (Sect. 5.2) and the main reasons put forward by the Commission to modernize the EU State aid policy since 2005 (Sect. 5.3), before matching the Commission's own objectives pursued by the reform of the SGEI Package and checking whether such objectives have been achieved by the new texts adopted in 20 December 2011 and entered into force on 31 January 2012 (Sect. 5.4). The last section will draw some conclusions as to whether this reform is not missing another key objective, namely to ensure more effective enforcement of the State aid rules by the Member States and, notably, by local authorities (Sect. 5.5).

5.2 Competition Policy and SGEI

As stated by Article 3.3 TEU: 'The Union shall establish an internal market' and 'shall work for the sustainable development of Europe based on balanced economic growth and price stability, a highly competitive social market economy, aiming at full employment and social progress, and a high level of protection and improvement of the quality of the environment (...)'. No specific and direct reference is made to competition. This is a result of the Treaty of Lisbon signed on 13 December 2007. However, the same Treaty introduced a Protocol No 27 *'on the Internal Market and Competition'* explaining that 'the internal market as set out in Article 3 of the Treaty on European Union includes a system ensuring that competition is not distorted'. Without going into the details of a [maybe] sterile debate, it seems clear that competition must be considered as a tool to achieve the objectives of the EU, and not a goal in itself.[8] Hence, the EU rules related to aids granted by Member States, as laid down by Articles 107–109 TFEU which are part of the chapter related to rules on competition (see Chapter I of Title VII of Part III of the TFEU), must also be considered as a tool to satisfy the aims of the EU.

On the other hand, the Treaty of Lisbon 2009 offered an important contribution to the reinforcement of one of these aims we propose to name the sustainability of the SGEI. Given the place they occupy 'in the shared values of the Union as well as their role in promoting social and territorial cohesion', Article 14 TFEU imposes both to the EU and the Member States, 'each within their respective powers and within the scope of application of the Treaties', to 'take care that such services operate on the basis of principles and conditions, particularly economic and financial conditions, which enable them to fulfill their missions'. Such a

---

[8] Idot and Géradin 2008.

statement is developed from Article 16 EC, introduced by the Treaty of Amsterdam in 1997. The provision has been completed, with the Treaty of Lisbon 2009, by a new sentence:

> The European Parliament and the Council, acting by means of regulations in accordance with the ordinary legislative procedure, shall establish these principles and set these conditions without prejudice to the competence of Member States, in compliance with the Treaties, to provide, to commission and to fund such services.

It means that Article 14 TFEU is now a clear and unchallenged legal basis for EU secondary legislation with a horizontal perspective.[9] This new approach, from derogation to obligation,[10] is confirmed by the new Protocol No 26 on Services of General Interest (SGI) which introduces this concept in EU Primary Law for the first time and by the Charter of Fundamental Rights of the EU, which shall have now the same legal value as the Treaties (Article 6.1 TEU), and Article 36 CFREU is focused on the right of access to SGEI.[11] This latter provision confirms that, even in terms of competition policy, there is an evolution in the political and legal background 'from Single Market to Citizenship Rights'.[12]

Considering this new context, we are convinced that the relationship between SG(E)I and competition has to be revisited. There is no conflict anymore but complementarity, as the CJEU has always stressed by interpreting Article 86 (2) EC (now Article 106 (2) TFEU) as follows: the key issue is to reconcile the Member States' interest in using certain undertakings, in particular in the public sector, as an instrument of economic or fiscal policy with the [EU] interest in ensuring compliance with the rules on competition and the preservation of the unity of the common.[13] One may assume that Article 14 TFEU must be construed in the light of this assumption, the very beginning of this provision stating that it *is without prejudice* to Articles 106 and 107 TFEU.

The fact is, that such a balance is clearly pursued by the new reform of public aids to SGEI as far as it has been previously taken into consideration in the strategy of modernization for the EU State aid policy itself.

5.3 Which Strategy of Modernization for the EU State Aid Policy?

The strategy of modernization of the EU State Aid policy is a progressive and step-by-step process. It was initiated in 2005 with an Action Plan. Then the Monti

---

[9] Rodrigues 2009, pp. 255–266.

[10] Ross 2000, pp. 22–38.

[11] Bauby 2011, pp. 19–36 and Szyszczak 2011, pp. 13–16.

[12] Prosser 2005.

[13] CJEU, Case C-202/88 *France* v *Commission* [1991] *ECR* I-1223, para 12, and CJEU, Case C-159/04 *Commission* v *France* [1997] *ECR* I-5815, para 55.

Report issued in 2010 took a position on the necessity to go further in the area of the State aid rules applying to SGEI and partly influenced the proposal of the Commission to reform the *Altmark* Package in 2011.

5.3.1 The Action Plan for State Aids (2005)   Monti - Kroes Policy

The State Aid Action Plan submitted by the Commission was a roadmap for the reform of State aid policy that was supposed to cover a 5-year period (2005–2009).[14] The main objective of the reform was to encourage Member States to help achieve the objectives of the Lisbon Strategy by targeting State aid towards improving the competitiveness of European industry and creating sustainable jobs, and to contribute better to social and regional cohesion and environmental protection. Rationalization and simplification of the procedures were also pursued, in order to set up a clear and predictable framework in the area of State aid.

Regarding the specific issue of SGEI, one may stress that the Action Plan was based on a refined economic approach and the key concept of high quality SGEI.

As summarized by the Commission, a refined economic approach 'involves finding out why, without public intervention, the market does not achieve an optimum result, whether it is because there is a "market failure" or because it produces social or regional inequalities which must be corrected'.[15] It is therefore necessary to better evaluate whether State aid is justified, whether it represents the most appropriate solution, and how it can be implemented without distorting competition to an extent contrary to the common interest. This approach is supposed to facilitate and speed up authorization of the aid which least distorts competition and, at the same time, would focus attention on the aid likely to have the most serious distortive effect on competition. That will help us later to understand the *ratio legis* of the Almunia Reform regarding local and social public services (see *infra*).

In this context, the Commission considers that State aid measures will fulfill their public service aims by providing effective high-quality SGEI, implying that the Commission has to specify under which conditions public service compensation which constitutes State aid are compatible with the Treaty and to grant an exemption of notification for small-scale compensation. This link between *quality* of service and public aid is confirmed by the Commission in its communication of 20 December 2011 on a *Quality Framework for Services of General Interest in Europe*.[16] Recalling the aim 'to ensure that the EU regulatory framework which has an impact on the way SGEI are organised, financed and provided, enables them to accomplish their public service mission', the Commission underlines the fact

---

[14] See COM(2005) 107 final of 7 June 2005. On this Action Plan, see: Chérot 2005.

[15] See http://europa.eu/legislation_summaries/competition/state_aid/l26115_en.htm.

[16] See COM (2011) 900 final.

[17] See sect 1.1 of COM(2011)900.

that the 2005 Package of EU rules which apply to the public financing of SGEI can be made clearer, simpler, and more proportionate to ensure an easier application and, hence, 'to promote a more efficient delivery of high quality services, to the benefit of citizens'.[17] The same conclusion was reached by the Monti Report, released one year earlier.

5.3.2 The Monti Report (2010)

The former Commissioner for the Internal Market and then for Competition, Mario Monti, was charged by the President of the European Commission, José Manuel Durão Barroso, to draw up a 'new strategy for the Single Market,[18] Issued on 9 May 2010, the Monti Report addresses the issue of SI(E)G in Chapter 3 related to *Initiatives to build consensus on a stronger single market.* According to Mario Monti, the fundamental challenge for the provision of the social and local public services is to maintain their quality and scope in the context of increasing pressure on public finances. Consequently, the EU must assist the Member States in modernizing these services and adapting them to a changing environment and to the evolving needs of citizens regarding their scope and quality. In order to do so, the Report identified two key elements: legal certainty and inclusivity.

Legal certainty implies the predictability and flexibility of rules, in particular as regards the application of State aid rules, which are important for ensuring that SI(E)G can fulfill their missions. This is why the Monti Report invited the Commission to examine the possibilities to further increase the flexibility of the rules applicable to financial compensation, including through an increase of the thresholds and/or through expanding the list of activities for which compensation does not have to be notified irrespective of the amounts involved. Moreover, the Commission was also asked to review the procurement rules to align them with the rules on compensation in order to ensure a consistent approach concerning small SGEI.[19]

Regarding the issue of inclusivity, the main concern of the Monti Report was to ensure that all citizens could benefit from the Single Market. To achieve this, the Report considered that if the Commission should *not* present a proposal for a Framework Regulation based on Article 14 TFEU (because it would have limited added value), the Commission should consider proposing a Regulation ensuring that all citizens are entitled to a number of basic banking services, along with examining the case for extending the universal service obligation in electronic communications to the provision of broadband access.

---

[17]   See sect 1.1 of COM(2011)900.

[18]   On this report, see: Rodrigues 2010.

[19]   See the chapters by Clarke and Sánchez Graells on the procurement rules. See also: Bovis 2005 and Sánchez Graells 2011.

Thus, the way to reforming the *Altmark* Monti Kroes Package was clearly paved.

5.3.3 The Communication Proposal for Altmark Reform (2011)[20]

In its Communication on the Reform of the EU State Aid Rules on SGEI of 23 March 2011, the Commission underlines the overall objective to boost the contribution that SGEI can make to the wider EU economic recovery.[21] In the Commission's view, efficient and high quality public services support and underpin growth and jobs across the EU. To achieve this key objective, the Commission was considering basing the upcoming reform on two main principles: clarification and proportionality.

First, addressing a concern already identified, the Reform is supposed to clarify a number of key concepts relevant for the application of the State aid rules to SGEI (including the scope of the rules and conditions for the approval of SGEI aid by the Commission). This is not really new. The Commission services had already launched (in 2007) an Interactive Information Service (IIS) and published in 2007 a Frequently Asked Questions (FAQ) document which was up-to-dated in December 2010.[22] But the consultation process has nevertheless highlighted that uncertainties and misunderstandings may be among the reasons why the rules are sometimes applied incorrectly. The request for more clarity goes beyond the provisions of the *Altmark* Monti-Kroes Package and also relates to the nature of the activity and the question whether a measure falls under Article 107 TFEU at all. Particularly, the issues concern the distinction between economic and non-economic activities, the limits of the Member States under State aid rules when defining an economic activity as an SGEI, the conditions under which compensation for certain SGEI provided at local level affects trade between the Member States, the requirements which public authorities have to follow under State aid rules when they entrust an undertaking with the performance of an SGEI, the conditions under which compensation for SGEI does *not* involve State aid because the tender selects the provider at the least cost for the community or because the price charged is in line with that of an efficient and 'well-run' undertaking, how to increase convergence between the application of State aid and public procurement rules, and the interplay between the rules of the Package and other sector-specific SGEI rules.

On the other hand, the reform is intended to promote a more diversified and proportionate approach to the different types of SGEI depending on the extent to which State aid in these economic sectors poses a serious risk of creating

---

[20] For an overview of this proposal, see: Chérot 2011.

[21] See COM (2011) 146 final.

[22] See: SEC(2010) 1545 final of 7 December 2010; on this document: see Rodrigues 2011.

distortions of competition in the Internal Market. One way of adopting a more diversified approach could be to simplify the application of the State aid rules for certain types of services organized by local communities that are of a relatively limited scale and thus only have a minor impact on trade between the Member States.

To avoid distortions of competition in the Internal Market (ensued from the fact that some of the costs incurred by the provider of SGEI may be generated by low efficiency levels), the Commission seemed to be ready to consider to what extent greater account of both efficiency and quality should be taken when deciding on the approval of State aid measures in relation to SGEI (including measures aimed at achieving appropriate transparency in relation to public expenditure for SGEI, identification and definition of SGEI obligation and measures aimed at taking into account efficiency over the life of an entrustment with the provision of an SGEI).

5.4 Are the Objectives Pursued by the New SGEI Package Achieved?

Adopted by the College of the Commission on 20 December 2011 and published in the *Official Journal of the EU* on 11 January 2012,[23] the new SGEI Package (also called the 'Almunia Reform') is composed of three definitive texts and (at that time) a draft Regulation: a Communication from the Commission on the application of the European Union State aid rules to compensation granted for the provision of services of general economic interest (the Communication)[24]; a Commission Decision on the application of Article 106(2) TFEU to State aid in the form of public service compensation granted to certain undertakings entrusted with the operation of SGEI (the Decision)[25] and an EU framework for State aid in the form of public service compensation (the Framework).[26] The draft text was a proposal for a Commission Regulation on the application of Articles 107 and 108 TFEU to *de minimis* aid granted to undertakings providing SGEI.[27] Due to requests for further consultation by the Member States, this Regulation was expected to be adopted during Spring 2012 and was finally adopted on 25 April 2012.[28]

---

[23] See OJEU No. L-7 and No. C-8. Szyszczak 2012.

[24] See C (2011) 9404 final.

[25] See C (2011) 9380 final.

[26] See C (2011) 9406 final.

[27] See C (2011) 9381 draft.

[28] Commission Regulation on the application of Articles 107 and 108 of the Treaty on the Functioning of the European Union to *de minimis* aid granted to undertakings providing services of general economic interest, *OJ* 2012 L 114/8.

Entering into force on 31 January 2012, it is obviously difficult to assess whether the main general objective of the reform, i.e., boosting the economy in a context of crisis, is achieved; *a fortiori* considering that the economic crisis is still on-going with little sign of abatement. A long-term perspective is needed to adopt an objective and useful position on this question. However, regarding the two more specific objectives, i.e., clarification and adaptability/proportionality, a first assessment may be made on the basis of the texts themselves. Without making an in-depth legal analysis, our opinion, in terms of policy strategy, may be expressed as a 'half/half' achievement as far as if the reform implies more adaptability indeed for some SGEI, it entails also more complexity in other areas.

More adaptability: this looks to be real for two kinds of SGEI, i.e., for local public services and for social services. Indeed, the scope of the Decision, for the exemption from notification, includes compensation not exceeding an annual amount of EUR 15 million for the provision of an SGEI in areas other than transport and transport infrastructure (a threshold supposed to correspond to a large number of situations involving local entities) and compensation for the provision of SGEI 'meeting social needs as regards health and long term care, childcare, access to and reintegration into the labor market, social housing and the care and social inclusion of vulnerable groups' (which would address the most sensitive social services of general interest, but not necessarily all of them).[29]

More complexity: for public service compensation which constitutes State aid not covered by the Decision, it seems that new rules are imposed by the Framework, i.e., more complex requirements to be met. Three examples can be given: first, for the scope of application of the principles set out in the Framework, 'Member States should show that they have given proper consideration to the public service needs supported by way of a public consultation or other appropriate instruments to take the interests of users and providers into account'.[30] That would probably imply more red tape and maybe more national regulation to guarantee that such consultation process is objective and transparent. Does it mean simplification and less control? Let us be skeptical…

Secondly, the Framework refers to the obligation for Member States, when devising the method of compensation, to introduce 'incentives for the efficient provision of SGEI of a high standard, unless they can duly justify that it is not feasible or appropriate to do so'.[31] More efficiency is a good thing. Who would be against such a stimulating objective? But, does it mean that the European Commission is the right body to assess such efficiency, or that the EU is the relevant jurisdictional level to drive a test of 'efficient provision of SGEI of a high standard'? Does efficiency automatically imply more satisfaction for SGEI users? Must the welfare of the final consumer be considered as the main purpose of EU

---

[29] See Article 2.1 (a) and (c) of the Decision and the chapter by von de Gronden and Rusu.
[30] See para 14 of the Framework.
[31] See para 39 of the Framework.

competition law,[32] one may assume that it is not an efficiency objective in itself.[33] This is why the EU judge has insisted on the fact that:

> ...in the absence of any harmonized rules governing the matter, the [EU] institutions are not entitled to rule on the basis of the public service tasks assigned to the public operator (...), such as the level of costs linked to that service, or the expediency of the political choices made in this regard by the national authorities or... [the] economic efficiency of the undertaking.[34]

Thirdly, the Commission may decide additional requirements if they are considered as 'necessary to ensure that the development of trade is not affected to an extent contrary to the interests of the Union'.[35] Such additional requirements may be consisting on imposing a more limited entrustment in terms of duration or scope or on requiring amendments in the allocation of the aid, 'where it can reasonably show that it would be possible to provide the same SGEI at equivalent conditions for the users, in a less distortive manner and at lower cost for the State'.[36] Dealing with such additional requirements, as well as with the two other instruments (public consultation review and efficiency test) would not be easy for the Commission, considering what the Protocol No 26 refers to as 'the essential role and the wide discretion of national, regional and local authorities in providing, commissioning and organizing SGEI as closely as possible to the needs of the users'. This is not only a problem of subsidiarity, but also the expression of a collective responsibility to achieve a common goal: the existence of sustainable public services for every EU citizen.

5.5 Conclusion: Is Enforcement the Missing Objective?

The success of the reform will not be only focused on the achievement of the objectives of clarification and adaptability, but also on the way the rules on public compensations will be better understood by all the stakeholders and applied well by the public authorities, notably by the local authorities. Are such public bodies ready and 'adequately provided with means' (by reference to the 4th *Altmark* criteria) of legal support/assistance to implement the new SGEI Package?

It is well known that the main challenge for State aid rules is their appropriate enforcement. Information and training will be key issues to meet that challenge

---

[32] As stated in GC, Case T-168/01 *GlaxoSmithKline* [2006] *ECR*-II 2969, para 118.

[33] See: Odudu 2009.

[34] See Opinion of AG Tizzano delivered on 8 May 2001 in CJEU, Case C-53/00 *Ferring SA v Agence centrale des organismes de sécurité sociale (ACOSS)* [2001] *ECR* I-9067, para 51 and GC, *Métropole télévision (M6) and Télévision française 1 SA (TF1)* v *European Commission* nyr; GC Joined Cases T-568/08 and T-573/08, nyr, paras 139–140.

[35] See Sect 2.9 of the Framework.

[36] See para 56 of the Framework.

and the 2010 Guide of the Commission or its Interactive Information Service would probably not be sufficient. The role of national courts is also essential, as underpinned by the Commission in its 2009 Notice on the enforcement of State aid law by national courts.[37] But the challenge may be also an internal challenge for the Commission. Is there the necessary and adequately trained staff to proceed with the new procedural requirements laid down by the Reform? In a recent Special Report, the European Court of Auditors found that: if the Commission has made efforts to ensure that all relevant State aid cases are handled, 'its systems do not guarantee that all aid is captured'; the procedures for notified State aid take a long time; complaints continue to take a long time to resolve and the procedure is not transparent; and that the Commission does not assess the ex post impact of its State aid control in a comprehensive way.[38] These aims perhaps rely on a different issue, part of another strategy and of another debate...

References

Bauby P (2011) From Rome to Lisbon: SGIs in primary law. In: Szyszczak E, Davies J, Andenaes M, Bekkedal T (eds) Developments in services of general interest. TMC Asser Press, The Hague, pp 19–36

Bauby P, Similie P (eds) (2010) Public services in the European Union and in the 27 member states. Statistics, organization and regulations, study commissioned in the framework of the 'Mapping of the Public Services' project managed by CEEP. Available at: http://ftp. infoeuropa.eurocid.pt/database/000045001-000046000/000045742.pdf

Bovis C (2005) Financing services of general interest in the EU: how do public procurement and state aids interact to demarcate between market forces and protection? ELJ 11:79–109

Chérot J-Y (2005) State aid action plan: commission consultation paper on an exhaustive reform of state aid. Concurrences 3:104–106

Chérot J-Y (2011) The European Commission proposes new steps toward a reform of the Altmark package. Concurrences 2:165–166

De Rossa P (2011) The future of SSGI: an agenda for change. In Rodrigues S (ed), Vers un nouveau droit européen des services d'intérêt (économique) général? (Towards a new law on SGEI?). Concurrences Tendances 4:18–21

Idot L, Géradin D (ed) (2008) Competition law and the Lisbon Treaty: the place of competition law in the new legal Community order. Concurrences 1:78–109

Odudu O (2009) Competition: efficiency and other things. CLRev 6:1–4

Prosser T (2005) Competition law and public services: from single market to citizenship rights? EPL 11:543–563

Rodrigues S (2009) Towards a general EC framework instrument related to SGEI? Political considerations and legal constraints. In Krajewski M, Neergaard U, Van de Gronden J (eds) The changing legal framework for services of general interest in Europe. Between competition and solidarity. T.M.C. Asser Press, The Hague, pp 255–266

Rodrigues S (2010) Monti report: the former EU Internal Market and Competition commissioner issues a report insisting on refocusing EU institutions and policies on the single market by

---

[37] *OJ 2009* C 85/1, replacing a previous noticed published in 1995.

[38] See European Court of Auditors, Do the Commission's procedures ensure effective management of State aid control?, Special Report, No 15-2011.

reinforcing enforcement of the Internal Market rules and by revising them. Concurrences 3:170–171

Rodrigues S (2011) The application to services of general economic interest, notably to social services of general interest, of the EU rules related to state aids, public procurement and the internal market. One year after the Commission's Guide—SEC (2010) 1545 final. Eur J Social Law 4:254–267

Ross M (2000) Article 16 E.C. and services of general interest: from derogation to obligation? ELRev 25:22–38

Sánchez Graells A (2011) Public procurement and the EU competition rules. Hart Pub, Oxford

Szyszczak E (2004) Financing services of general economic interest. MLR 67:982–992

Szyszczak E (2011) The general debate on SGIs since the Treaty of Lisbon. In: Rodrigues S (ed), Vers un nouveau droit européen des services d'intérêt (économique) général? (Towards a new law on SG(E)I?), Concurrences. Tendances 4:13–16

Szyszczak E (2012) Soft law and safe havens. In Neergaard U, Szyszczak E, Von de Gronden J, Krajewski M (eds) Social services of general interest in the EU. TMC Asser Press, The Hague

Chapter 6
The Almunia Package: Legal Constraints, Policy Procedures, and Political Choices

Tim Maxian Rusche

- specially remarkable explaining the rise of Article 14 TFEU and its actual reach.

Abstract The entry into force of the Lisbon Treaty has, contrary to the view held by certain scholars, not changed the exclusive competence of the Commission for authorizing State aid for SGEI compensation. Article 14 TFEU, second sentence, does not provide a legal basis for legislating on the notion, the compatibility, or the notification exemption for State aid in the form of SGEI compensation. Under the legal constraints set by *Altmark* and its exclusive competence, the Commission has decided, first of all, to engage in a broad consultation and dialogue with the other Institutions and all stakeholders, including the legal community, prior to revising the Monti-Kroes package. With regard to the content of the Almunia package, it has opted for clarification (restatement of the case law and its decision practice); simplification (total notification exemption of social services) and proportionality (stricter rules for certain sectors and compensation above 15 million EUR). Whereas under the Monti-Kroes package, all SGEI were essentially treated the same way (verification for absence of overcompensation), the Almunia package tightens the rules for large SGEI. It excludes undertakings in difficulty from the benefit of SGEI compensations if they do not at the same time undergo in-depth restructuring (including usually compensatory measures in the form of disposals of assets and market share); requires award of the SGEI by tender (except for *in house* situations) and efficiency incentives in the compensation mechanism (so as to become *Altmark* compliant over time); and reserves the right for the Commission to ask for additional commitments in situations where there is particular risk of trade being affected to an extent contrary to the interest of the Union.

T. Maxian Rusche (✉)
European Commission, Legal Service, BERL 2/82 1049 Brussels, Belgium
e-mail: tim.rusche@ec.europa.eu

E. Szyszczak and J.W. van de Gronden (eds.), *Financing Services of General Economic Interest*, Legal Issues of Services of General Interest, DOI: 10.1007/978-90-6704-906-1_6, © T.M.C. ASSER PRESS, The Hague, The Netherlands, and the authors 2013

Contents

By adopting the Almunia Package, which provides this book with its raison d'être, the Commission has decided to reform the rules applicable to State aid in the form of compensation for services of general economic interest (SGEI) in a rather fundamental way. This chapter will set out the legal constraints the Commission was faced with (Sect. 6.1), the policy procedures it adopted (Sect. 6.2), and the political choices it made (Sect. 6.3).

6.1 Legal Constraints

There are two main legal constraints for the Commission in the field of compensation for SGEI: the interpretation of Article 107(1) TFEU given by the Court in *Altmark*, and the legal basis provided in the TFEU for its action. Whereas interpretation has remained unchanged since the Monti-Kroes package was adopted in 2005, the legislative basis may have been affected by the entry into force of the Lisbon Treaty.

6.1.1 The Altmark Ruling

In *Altmark*, the Court defined the conditions under which compensation for SGEI does not constitute State aid. By doing so, it limited the competence of the Commission, as certain payments financed from State resources now escape its scrutiny. At the same time, the ruling has set the bar relatively high, as only payments that meet four core conditions, in particular not to exceed the costs of an efficient undertaking, escape the Commission's control. All other payments require in principle *ex ante* Commission approval.

6.1.2 *The Legal Basis*

Prior to the entry into force of the Lisbon Treaty, the only legal basis for assessing compliance of SGEI with the rules of the Treaty, in particular the competition provisions, was Article 86 EC [now 106 TFEU]. It was directly applicable and could be invoked in national courts; furthermore, it was one of the rare instances where the Treaty conferred authority upon the Commission to adopt secondary legislation in the form of Directives and Decisions without any involvement of the other Institutions, most notably Parliament and Council.

The Lisbon Treaty maintained Article 86 EC unchanged as Article 106 TFEU. At the same time, it added to the former Article 16 EC (now Article 14 TFEU) a second sentence, which provides a legal basis for the adoption of regulations on SGEI by Parliament and Council through the ordinary legislative procedure. Article 16 EC itself was of relatively recent origin, as it had only been introduced by the Treaty of Amsterdam. Its current wording is as follows:

> Without prejudice to Article 4 of the Treaty on European Union or to Articles 93, 106 and 107 of this Treaty, and given the place occupied by services of general economic interest in the shared values of the Union as well as their role in promoting social and territorial cohesion, the Union and the Member States, each within their respective powers and within the scope of application of the Treaties, shall take care that such services operate on the basis of principles and conditions, particularly economic and financial conditions, which enable them to fulfill their missions. The European Parliament and the Council, acting by means of regulations in accordance with the ordinary legislative procedure, shall establish these principles and set these conditions without prejudice to the competence of Member States, in compliance with the Treaties, to provide, to commission and to fund such services.

This raises the question as to whether rules on State aid are part of the "principles and conditions, particularly economic and financial conditions, which enable services of general economic interest to fulfill their missions". If this was the case, then the Commission could have chosen either to adopt the Almunia package itself on the basis of Article 106 (3) TFEU, or it could instead have opted to submit a proposal for a Regulation to Parliament and Council.

In order to answer this question, it appears necessary to first look into the history of how the second sentence of Article 14 TFEU came into being (Sect. 6.1.2.1), and then to proceed with a classical legal interpretation (Sect. 6.1.2.2). On this basis, the question will be answered (Sect. 6.1.2.3).

6.1.2.1 The History of Article 14 TFEU

The introduction of Article 16 EC has to be seen in the context of the market opening, in particular in the network industries (telecommunications, postal services, energy, and transport), which started in the late 1980s and reached full speed in the 1990s in the context of the drive to complete the internal market. The transport sector played a special role as the Treaty included a special legal basis in

Articles 71 and 80 EC [now Articles 91 and 100 TFEU]. Outside transport, the Commission first relied on Article 86 EC (telecommunications).[1] Subsequently, the Court indicated that it would not necessarily be willing to accept Article 86 EC as legal basis[2] for energy which meant that the Commission had to rely on the general internal market competence of Article 95 EC.

Certain Member States (mainly Belgium and France) feared that this would lead to a one-sided approach to SGEI, favoring privatization. Therefore, Member States agreed to protect their say in SGEI by introducing Article 16 EC, which underlines the fact that SGEI are part of the "European model" and that Member States enjoy a wide margin of discretion in defining SGEI. Although Article 16 EC was of a symbolic, political, and programmatic nature and did not modify Article 86 EC,[3] it could be observed both in the actions of the Commission and in the case law of the Court that the balance between the principles of competition and the freedoms of the internal market on the one hand and the traditional prerogatives of the Member States for defining and financing SGEI on the other hand was readjusted.[4] The sitting Dutch judge at the Court spoke of a "first step in the constitutionalization of the services of general economic interest".[5]

Since the introduction of Article 16 EC, the Court appears not to have repeated its view on the strict interpretation of Article 86 EC which was first spelled out in *Belgische Radio en Televisie*[6]:

> As Article 90 (2) is a provision which permits, in certain circumstances, derogation from the rules of the Treaty, there must be a strict definition of those undertakings which can take advantage of it.

The Court of First Instance (now the General Court) did restate this interpretation after the introduction of Article 16 EC.[7] More recently, the General Court has, on the contrary, adopted a more lenient approach.[8]

---

[1] CJEU, Case C-202/88, *France v. Commission* [1991] *ECR* I-1223.

[2] CJEU, Case C-393/92 *Almelo* [1994] *ECR*-I 1477, para 50; CJEU, Case C-157/94 *Commission v. Netherlands*, [1997] *ECR*-I 5699, para 63; CJEU, Case C-158/94, *Commission v Italy*, [1997] *ECR*-I 5789, para 59; CJEU, Case C-159/94 *Commission v. France* [1997] *ECR*-I 5815, para 106. See also the standard monograph on this case law written by Buendía Sierra 1999.

[3] As here: Buendia Sierra 2008, p. 221. For the diverging view see authors quoted in the following footnote.

[4] See references in Prechal 2008; Radicati di Brozolo 1996, p. 9; Rodrigues 1998, 2009, pp. 256 et seq; Ross 2000; Wernicke 2011.

[5] Prechal 2008, p. 67.

[6] CJEU, Case 127/73 *BRT* v *Sabam* [1974] *ECR* 314, para 19. Bekkedal 2011 considers this case law to be still 'good law' and provides ample reasoning in this regard.

[7] GC, Case T-106/95 *FFSA a.o.* v *Commission* ECR [1997] *ECR* II-229, para 173; Case T-128/98 *Aéroports de Paris* v *Commission* ECR [2000] *ECR* II-3929, para 227.

[8] GC, Joined Cases T-568/08 and T-573/08 *M6 and TF1* v. *Commission* ECR [2010] *ECR* II-3397, paras 136–141.

Judge *Edward*[9] and, more recently and building on it, *Schweitzer*[10] have analyzed in-depth the case law, and found that the Court oscillates between a "limited sovereignty" and a "limited competition" approach, favoring the former in the application of the rules on competition and the latter in the application of the rules on free movement. *Wernicke* observed that the Court has over the last years (indeed, starting with *Altmark*) avoided to take a clear stance on the use of Article 86(2) EC (and now 106(2) TFEU) as justification for a restriction of the four freedoms or competition rules.[11] The latest judgment in that line is *Stadtreinigung Hamburg*: Germany expressly pleaded that the absence of a public procurement procedure for a waste disposal contract was justified on the basis of Article 86(2) EC. The Grand Chamber avoided taking a clear stance, combining elements of the *in house* doctrine with references to carrying out tasks in the public interest in order to conclude that the public procurement Directives did not apply to public–public partnerships.[12]

Despite discussions on the topic in the intergovernmental conference, the Nice Treaty did not modify Article 16 EC.[13]

In the Convention, the working group "Social Europe" discussed the need for amending Article 16, and could not agree on a common line. The relevant passage of their final report to the *Praesidium* reads as follows[14]:

> For various members, Article 16 TEC has an essentially declaratory value and cannot provide the basis for genuine European legislation on services of general interest, which would require a positive rather than an exceptional legal basis. These members therefore pleaded for the Constitutional Treaty to contain a legal basis allowing the Union to adopt framework legislation at European level, covering relevant aspects of the provision of such services e.g. universal access. Others considered the existing competences to be sufficient.

In particular following heavy lobbying from France,[15] the draft Constitutional Treaty included in its Article III-6 a legal basis for the adoption of regulations, which was similar, but not identical to the text that can be found now in Article 14 TFEU second sentence:

> European laws shall define these principles and conditions.

The proclaimed aim of France was to have a legal basis that would enable it to "export" its model of *service public* to the level of the Union. Germany, and in

---

[9] Edward 1996, pp. 8 et seq.

[10] Schweitzer 2011.

[11] Wernicke 2009, pp. 76–79.

[12] CJEU, Case C-480/06 *Commission* v. *Germany* [2009] *ECR* I-4747, paras 46–49. See for a diverging view Skovgaard Olykke 2011 who reads in this ruling "a renewed role for Article 106 (2) TFEU".

[13] Wernicke 2011; Rodrigues 1998.

[14] CONV 516/1/03 REV1, para 32 at the end.

[15] Council document 12029/01, French memorandum on services of general economic interest, 20 September 2001. On the genesis of Article 14 TFEU in the Convention see also Buendía Sierra 2012a, P. 363.

particular the *Länder* as well as the cities, municipalities, and counties had opposed this move, as they feared that they would lose part of their traditionally strong autonomy and self-governance.[16] In particular the German literature deplored in strong words the fact that this new competence had been created, and that it only foresaw the possibility of adopting Regulations, i.e. the most "intrusive" form of EU law making, whereas the principle of subsidiarity would have warranted the use of directives (including the sitting German judge at the ECJ, who spoke of a "*subsidiaritätsrechtlichen Missgriff*", which could be translated as 'a misconception of the principle of subsidiarity').[17]

6.1.2.2 The Legal Interpretation of Article 14 TFEU

The co-existence of two different legal bases for SGEI in Article 14 TFEU (in ordinary legislative procedure, i.e. adoption by Parliament and Council on the basis of a proposal by the Commission) and Article 106 (3) TFEU begs the question as to what their relationship is. For the present chapter, it is of particular importance to know whether all or at least part of the four texts which form the Almunia package could have been adopted on the basis of Article 14 TFEU.

Starting with a literal interpretation, the legal basis in Article 14 TFEU enables the Union legislator to establish the principles and set the conditions, particularly economic and financial conditions, which enable SGEI to fulfill their missions.

This wording remains relatively vague. In particular, it has to be taken into account that the Union legislator may not interfere with the competence of the Member States to provide, to commission, and to fund SGEI, which seems to exclude the possibility to oblige Member States to provide a certain type of service at certain conditions. It would then seem that any legislation will remain rather optional and programmatic. It could also be envisaged that the legislation foresees minimum requirements for SGEI in case the Member State decides to commission it. Another example, given by the Working Group on Social Europe of the Convention, is regulation of the principles governing universal access.

Nothing in the wording indicates that secondary legislation adopted on the basis of Article 14 TFEU could relate to the assessment of compensation payments for SGEI under State aid rules. On the contrary: Article 14 starts by stating that it is 'without prejudice' to Articles 93, 106 and 107 TFEU, which contain the rules on the assessment of compensation payments for SGEI under State aid rules. This would seem to entail two consequences[18]:

---

[16] Zimmermann 2008; Winterstein 2007.

[17] Von Danwitz 2004, p. 266; further examples include: Krajewski 2011, pp. 180 et seq.; Damjanovic and de Witte 2008, p. 29; Wuermeling 2008, p. 251.

[18] See in this sense also *Communication A Quality Framework for Services of General Economic Interest in Europe*, COM (2011) 900 final, p. 5, fn 9. See also in this sense Buendía Sierra 2012a, p. 365.

- Secondary legislation under Article 14 TFEU cannot interfere with the definition of State aid (and hence not with the interpretation of Article 107(1) TFEU which the Court has given in *Altmark*).
- Secondary legislation under Article 14 TFEU cannot cover the areas covered by the Commission's competence under Article 106(3) TFEU.

Article 14 does not mention Article 108 TFEU, which provides for the notification obligation for State aid, and Article 109 TFEU, which contains the legal basis for secondary legislation on the State aid procedure. However, as the notification obligation results from the qualification of a measure as State aid, it is indirectly covered by the reference to Article 107. With regard to Article 109 TFEU, it clearly constitutes a *lex specialis* with regard to the very broad scope of Article 14 TFEU.[19]

This reading of Article 14 TFEU, excluding any State aid competence, is confirmed by the following three systematic considerations. First, the control of State aid constitutes an exclusive competence of the Union. The first sentence of Article 14 recalls that the Union and the Member States shall act in the field of SGEI within their respective competences. It therefore does not intend to modify these competences. Therefore, the new legal basis cannot cover a field for which the TFEU has assigned an exclusive competence to the Union.

Second, Articles 106 and 108 TFEU provide for an exclusive competence for the Commission to adopt directives and decisions on the basis of Article 106 (3) TFEU and to authorize State aid on the basis of Article 107, 108 TFEU. This choice can be explained as the desire to put an "independent arbiter" in charge of decisions in an area where Member States may be tempted to foreclose markets or engage in subsidy races. If Article 14 TFEU was to enable the Union legislators to set out rules for State aid in secondary legislation, it would jeopardize the delicate balance between the institutions provided for in Articles 106–108.

The Court has expressly confirmed that parallelism between the Commission's competence under Articles 106(3) and 108(3) TFEU in *Netherlands* v *Commission*[20]:

> [The powers under Article 90 EEC (now Article 106 TFEU)] are also essential for the Commission so as to allow it to discharge the duty imposed upon it by Articles 85 to 93 of the Treaty to ensure the application of the rules on competition. [...] The powers which the Commission may exercise in respect of Member States by means of decisions under Article 90(3) of the Treaty are to be compared with the powers, conferred upon it by Article 93 of the Treaty, to find that a State aid which distorts or threatens to distort competition is not compatible with the common market.

Third, Article 14 TFEU provides only the possibility to adopt regulations, whereas Article 106 TFEU allows for Decisions and Directives. This also hints towards a complementary nature between the two legal bases, rather than a competing one.

---

[19] This conclusion is also reached by Bonkamp 2001 at p. 157.

[20] CJEU, Joined Cases C-48/90 and C-66/90, [1992] *ECR* I-565, paras 29 and 31; see in the same sense GC, Case T-266/97 *Vlaamse Televisie Maatschappij* v *Commission* [1999] *ECR* II-2329, point 34; GC Case T-53/01 R *Poste Italiane* v. *Commission* [2001] *ECR* II-1479, para 133.

Scholars have presented divergent views on this topic. *Wernicke* takes the view that a proposal establishing an exemption from the prior notification exemption could be based on a double legal basis of Articles 14 and 109 TFEU (which would be interesting for Parliament, as Article 109 TFEU only provides for a consultation of the Parliament). Going even further, he considers that a redefinition of the *Altmark*-criteria would be possible, using a circular logic by claiming that *Altmark*-compliant compensation payments do not fall in the scope of application of Article 107 TFEU.[21] This interpretation is shared by *Schweitzer*, who concludes that the scope of application of Article 106(2) TFEU is no longer a legal, but a political question, as in her view, the Union legislator could exempt all or parts of the SGEI from Article 106(2) TFEU altogether and rewrite the *Altmark* ruling.[22] A similar logic appears to be implicit in a recent contribution of *Von Danwitz*, where he states—without however entering into a detailed legal interpretation of Article 14 TFEU[23]:

> Once secondary legislation [based on Article 14 TFEU] has been enacted, [...] it remains to be seen to what extent the relevant jurisprudence of the Court, in particular *PreussenElektra*, *Stardust Marine*, *Chronopost* and *Altmark Trans*, will continue to play a crucial role in this field.

For *Rodrigues*, there can also be no doubt that Article 14 TFEU includes the competence to rewrite the State aid rules and define in secondary law what is considered as an economic activity (and therefore falls within the scope of the rules on competition). He bases his position on the fact that the application of State aid rules constitutes part of the 'economic and financial conditions'.[24] The same view, though without detailed legal reasoning, is also taken by *Bauby*.[25]

Krajewski claims that at the very least, the Commission needs to take into consideration the political signal that the authors of the Lisbon Treaty wanted to send, namely a 'protection' of SGEI against efforts of liberalization and a strengthening of 'social Europe'. He considers that Article 14 TFEU may shift the center of gravity of the debate and contribute to re-focus the secondary legislation.[26]

These arguments are, however, not convincing. As to *Wernicke*, *Schweitzer*, *Von Danwitz*, *Bauby* and *Rodrigues*, they all overlook the systematic arguments presented above. Furthermore, the use of a double legal basis for notification exemptions appears to go against the case law which says that the legal basis depends on the center of gravity of the secondary piece of legislation.[27] The position that a

---

[21] Wernicke 2011.

[22] Schweitzer 2004, pp. 293–312.

[23] Von Danwitz 2011, p. 104; Von Danwitz 2009, p. 117 (the two texts are very similar).

[24] Rodrigues 2009, pp. 262–265.

[25] Bauby 2001, p. 34.

[26] Krajewski 2011, p. 186.

[27] CJEU, Case C-155/07 *Commission* v. *Council* [2005] *ECR* I-7879, para 35. See for an extensive analysis of the case law on the question of a double legal basis Klamert 2010; Hoekstra 2011.

redefinition of *Altmark*, respectively, of the notion of economic activity was possible, because it does not fall in the scope of application of Article 107 (1) TFEU, is obviously wrong: If the conditions are formulated in a stricter way, the secondary legislation would extend the competences of the Union beyond the limits provided for by the treaties. If the conditions are rewritten in a more lenient way, the secondary legislation would reduce the competences of the Union. In both cases, such secondary legislation would violate Article 107 (1) TFEU, and therefore be illegal.

As to *Krajewski*, the introduction of a legal basis for SGEI is neutral as to the content which such secondary legislation may have. The rules on the substance of SGEI of the former Article 16 EC, however, have remained unchanged. Therefore, it is not clear why the introduction of the legal basis would be indicative of any shift whatsoever.

6.1.2.3 Conclusion: Article 14 TFEU Does Not Modify the Legal Basis for the Adoption on Rules on State Aid in the Form of Compensation Payments for SGEI

To sum up: contrary to the opinion of other scholars, Article 14 TFEU cannot be relied upon for the adoption of secondary legislation which regulates State aid in the form of compensation payments for SGEI. Any other interpretation would upset the institutional balance provided for by the treaty rules on competition and State aid, and be contrary to the systematic interpretation of Article 14 and 106(2) TFEU.

6.2 The Policy Procedures

The adoption of the Almunia package has to be seen against the political debates on SGEI (Sect. 6.2.1), which have been on-going ever since the *Altmark* ruling and gained new momentum with the entry into force of the Treaty of Lisbon, and in particular its changes to what is now Article 14 TFEU (Sect. 6.2.2). The first political choice, made by President nominated Barroso ahead of the confirmation vote in Parliament in his policy guidelines, was to abstain from making a legislative proposal on the basis of Article 14 TFEU during his mandate. Instead, he committed to the proposal of a "quality framework" (Sect. 6.2.3). Vice President Almunia made the preparation and adoption of the Almunia package his first policy priority in State aid; and opted for a very broad and inclusive consultation process (Sect. 6.2.4).

6.2.1 The Political Debate on SGEI

The political debate on SGEI has different facets. First of all, there is a clear divide between the right and the left in Parliament (Sect. 6.2.1.1). Secondly, a few

Member States (incidentally the six founding members) dominate the debate (Sect. 6.2.1.2). Thirdly, local and regional actors are of particular importance, as they fund the bulk of the services (Sect. 6.2.1.3). Absent from the general policy debate are the potential beneficiaries of stricter State aid control (Sect. 6.2.1.4).

6.2.1.1 The Divide in Parliament

In Parliament, there is a clear right-left divide when it comes to SGEI. The right has been broadly supportive of the initiatives taken by the Commission and the case law of the Court to open markets to competition, and to apply Article 86 EC in a way that favors the efficient provision of public services. The left, on the contrary, has criticized this as "neo-liberal" and "putting the European social model at risk". Therefore, in 2006, the Socialist group in Parliament has put forward a draft directive on SGEI.[28]

In Parliament, the most active voice on SGEI stems from the Intergroup 'Public Services'.[29] Intergroups can be formed of Members of Parliament from any political group and any committee, with a view to holding informal exchanges of views on particular subjects and promoting contact between Members and civil society. Intergroups are not Parliament bodies and therefore may not express Parliament's opinion. Intergroups are subject to internal rules adopted by the Conference of Presidents.[30]

This Intergroup is dominated by MEP from the left (i.e. besides the socialists, the Green group and the Left/Nordic Greens group). It also recruits the vast majority of its members from MEP which are from Member States with an SGEI "tradition", that is in particular the six founding Member States. It has been very active in the current legislature 2009–2014, in particular in the fields of public procurement and State aid.

6.2.1.2 The Positions of Member States

The Member States which are the most vocal in the debate on SGEI are Germany, France, Austria, Finland, the Netherlands, and Belgium. All of them aim at reducing the interference of the EU with their national SGEI to the minimum necessary. They use, however, very different strategies. This has come to the fore in a particularly prominent manner at the occasion of the debate on the new legal basis in Article 14 TFEU. Whereas France has lobbied hard for this new legal

---

[28] See Rodrigues 2009, pp. 256 et seq.; Neergaard 2011, pp. 44 et seq. for a detailed description of the political dynamics at work in Parliament and references to the different texts.

[29] http://services-publics-europe.eu/

[30] Rules governing the establishment of intergroups of on 16 December 1999 (last updated on 14 February 2008), available at http://www.europarl.europa.eu/pdf/intergroupes/Rule_Conference ofPresident_19991216_en.pdf.

basis, Germany (and in particular the *Länder*, cities, municipalities, and counties) fought hard against it. The motivation was identical: to limit interference. But whereas France considered that this would be best achieved by exporting its model at the EU level (for which it needed a legal basis), Germany played the subsidiarity card and opposed any new competences, hoping that the existing competences would not be sufficient to do any harm.

The strong interest in certain Member States in SGEI has also been reflected in the two rounds of public consultations which preceded the adoption of the Almunia Package. Most Member States replied; amongst the other stakeholders, there is a clear dominance of stakeholders from Austria, Belgium, Finland, France, Germany, Italy, the Netherlands, and Poland.[31]

6.2.1.3 The Particular Role Played by Local and Regional Authorities

SGEI are mainly procured and financed by local and regional authorities. They often also own the company providing the SGEI. They (respectively the associations which represent them) therefore play an important role in the debate on the State aid control of SGEI funding.

Given the limited administrative and legal capacities of (in particular) small municipalities and counties, local and regional authorities have pressed hard for broad exemptions from State aid control. This is often linked to the desire to preserve their rights of self-governance and/or autonomy.

6.2.1.4 The Absent Player: Private Competitors

Looking through the responses received by the Commission in its two rounds of consultation, it is striking that those who have the most to gain from strict State aid control are nearly absent from the debate: new entrants and private competitors.

At the same time, it becomes clear from individual State aid cases that these new entrants and private competitors exist. Indeed, most of the State aid cases where the Commission has opened formal investigation procedures are the result of complaints from competitors. But it would seem that they lack a coherent voice in the Brussels debate, which would go beyond the individual complaint.

---

[31] It has to be observed that in the first round of consultations, which was based on a questionnaire available in all official languages, a significant number of answers came from Poland and Italy. In the second round, which was based on a questionnaire in English, no contribution from those two countries was received.

6.2.2 Article 14 TFEU

The entry into force of the Lisbon Treaty, and with it of Article 14 TFEU sparked the debate on to what use that new legal basis could be put. The Left in the EP revived the idea of a Framework Directive (although it would now have to be a Framework Regulation), but was incapable of organizing a majority in Parliament for its position. At the same time, there was also a considerable amount of debate in academia.[32]

6.2.3 The Commitment for a 'Quality Framework'

When preparing for his confirmation by Parliament, President nominated Barroso faced the request of the Left in Parliament to commit to proposing a Framework Regulation on SGEI on the basis of Article 14 TFEU. He responded to that request by announcing a "quality framework for public and social services".[33]

This idea of a quality framework (avoiding any binding legislation) had for the first time been developed by the Commission in its 2007 Communication on SGI, which accompanied the Communication on "A single market for 21st century Europe".[34]

The quality framework was viewed by EPP and ALDE as the appropriate answer to the possibilities offered by Article 14. The Left did not have the necessary votes to force Barroso to go further. The Almunia package, together with the revision of the public procurement Directives, has been the main component of the quality framework, which was adopted as a Communication[35] the same day as the Almunia package and the proposals for the revision of the public procurement Directives.

---

[32] See references in the fns above in Sect. 6.1.2.2.

[33] Barroso 2009, p. 24.

[34] European Commission, *Services of general interest, including social services of general interest: a new European commitment* COM (2007) 725 final.

[35] *A Quality Framework for Services of General Economic Interest in Europe*, COM (2011) 900 final.

[36] Strictly speaking, Article 106(3) TFEU serves only as legal basis for the SGEI Decision. The SGEI Communication, as an interpretative communication, does not require any particular legal basis, as it does not have any legal effect. The SGEI Framework is based on the discretion the Commission enjoys under Article 106(2) TFEU; and the SGEI *de minimis* Regulation is based on Regulation No 994/98 on the application of Articles 92 and 93 of the Treaty establishing the European Community to certain categories of horizontal State aid (*OJ* L 142/1, hereafter: the Enabling Regulation), which in turn is based on Article 109 TFEU.

6.2.4 The Consultation Process of the Commission

Article 106(3) TFEU, the legal basis for the Almunia package,[36] does not require any prior consultations of other institutions or stakeholders. The Commission opted nevertheless for a broad consultation process in several steps (Sect. 6.2.4.1). This can be partly explained by general principles of Commission practice since the adoption of the governance White Paper[37] but also reflects a genuine choice with regard to the policy process (Sect. 6.2.4.2).

6.2.4.1 The Consultation Process Preceding the Adoption of the Almunia Package

The consultation process started in 2010, when the Commission invited Member States and stakeholders to comment on their experience with the application of the Monti-Kroes package. The Commission received a large number of replies. It summarized them in a staff working document, which was adopted on 23 March 2011.[38] On the same day, the Commission adopted a Communication in which it set out the broad lines it envisaged for the Almunia Package.[39] They are summarized under the headings clarification, simplification, and proportionality. These three policy goals constitute the *leitmotiv* of the Almunia Package. The Communication also sets out the architecture envisaged for the package: an interpretative Communication that clarified the notion of State aid, and in particular the precise meaning of the four Altmark conditions (a novelty; hereafter: the SGEI Communication); a Decision based on Article 106(3) TFEU exempting certain compensation payments from prior notification (as in Monti-Kroes; hereafter: the SGEI Decision); a Framework setting out the criteria for the compatibility of compensation payments which are not exempted from notification (as in Monti-Kroes; hereafter: the SGEI Framework); and a *de minimis* Regulation, stating that payments made to SGEI providers that do not exceed a threshold of 500,000 EUR over 3 years (which is higher than the general *de minimis* threshold of 200,000 EUR over 3 years) do not constitute State aid (a novelty, hereafter: the SGEI *de minimis* Regulation).

With the adoption of the Communication, the Commission launched a second round of consultations. It invited the other institutions, Member States, and stakeholders to react to the broad lines set out in its Communication. Parliament,[40]

---

[37] European Commission, *European Governance. A White Paper*. COM (2001) 428 final.

[38] *The Application of EU State Aid rules on Services of General Economic Interest since 2005 and the Outcome of the Public Consultation*, SEC (2011) 397.

[39] *Reform of the EU State Aid Rules on Services of General Economic Interest*, COM (2011) 146 final.

[40] Resolution A7 0371/2011 of 24 October 2011 (Draftsman: Peter Simon).

[41] Opinion COR/2011/150 (Draftsman: Karl-Heinz Lambertz), *OJ* 2011 C 259/40.

[42] Opinion EESC/2011/1008 (Draftsman: Raymond Hencks), *OJ* 2011 C 248/149.

Committee of the Regions[41] and Economic and Social Committee[42] responded with reports, which were adopted before the summer break. These reports were broadly supportive of the policy line proposed by the Commission, but requested more generous notification exemptions. One contentious point in all three bodies was the question of whether the Commission should make a proposal on the basis of Article 14 TFEU. In the Committee of the Regions and the Economic and Social Committee, a majority supported this idea, and invited the Commission to use this legal basis, rather than a Communication from the Commission, to clarify the notion of State aid and the precise meaning of the *Altmark* ruling.[43]

In September 2011, the Commission published the draft texts for the four instruments, and again invited comments from the other institutions, Member States, and stakeholders. The response was similar to the one that was given to the Communication: broad support, the wish for broader exceptions and notification exemptions, and calls from the left to use Article 14 TFEU. The only institution to formally adopt an opinion was the Committee of the Regions.[44]

In parallel to the outreach to the other institutions, Member States, and stakeholders, the Commission also engaged in a dialogue with the legal community. The initial consultation and the Communication were debated in the annual gatherings of the State aid community, in particular at the yearly conference of the European State Aid Law Institute (EStALI).[45] Vice President Almunia presented the draft texts at an academic conference at the College of Europe in Bruges.[46]

The results of these various consultations are reflected in the impact assessment accompanying the Almunia Package[47] as well as in the content of the final texts.

6.2.4.2 Broad and Repeated Consultation as a Conscious Policy Choice

With the exception of the Enabling Regulation, which constitutes the legal basis for the SGEI *de minimis* Regulation and requires two formal rounds of consultation of the Member States, the adoption of the texts comprising the Almunia Package does not, from a legal point of view, require any prior consultation of anyone.

The Commission could have simply adopted them: The SGEI Communication on the notion of State aid does not have any legal effects, as the Commission enjoys no discretion with regard to the objective notion of State aid. It therefore is not necessary to ground it on any legal basis. The SGEI Decision is based on

---

[43] Recital 4.11 of Opinion EESC/2011/1008; Recitals 12–14 of Opinion COR/2011/150.

[44] Opinion COR/2011/278 (Draftsman: Karl-Heinz Lambertz), *OJ* C 9 of 11 January 2012, p. 45.

[45] See for the written form of the contributions of Regner 2011; Jääskinen 2011.

[46] The conference proceedings have been edited by Messola 2011. Selected papers of the conference were also published in a supplement to EStAL 2/2012.

[47] SEC (2011) 1581.

[48] See out of the rich case law on this point in particular CJEU, Case C-313/90 *CIRFS* v *Commission* [1993] ECR I-1177, para 36; Case C-464/09 P *Holland Malt* v *Commission* [2010] *ECR* I-0000, para 47.

Article 106(3) TFEU, which grants regulatory powers to the Commission. The SGEI Framework is based on the discretion which the Commission enjoys under Article 106(2) TFEU for the assessment of the compatibility of compensation payments for SGEI. According to the case law, the Commission may auto-limit this discretion by adopting frameworks and guidelines. These texts then become binding for the Commission.[48]

What explains then, in the absence of any legal requirement, the policy choice of the Commission to consult broadly and repeatedly?

First of all, there is a political commitment of the Commission to *ex ante* consultation. This commitment results from the 'European Governance' White Paper.[49] Whereas prior to the adoption of this White Paper, certain Directorates General within the Commission (in particular DG Environment) had already developed a consultation culture, others acted without consulting.[50] The Commission has further strengthened the importance of consultations by rendering impact assessments, which rely in part on the results of consultations, mandatory in the internal process.[51] Finally and in parallel, there is a long tradition in State aid to consult Member states on draft guidelines.

But even compared to the by now firmly established 'consultation culture' of the Commission, the consultation process preceding the Almunia Package was strikingly broad and repeated. Partially, this policy style reflects certainly the personality of Vice President Almunia. In the concrete case of the Almunia Package, this choice appears particularly appropriate, for at least three reasons:

- First of all, certain actors (in particular in Parliament and the Committees) had disputed the very competence of the Commission. Although not majoritarian, they constituted a vocal and strong minority. A broad and repeated consultation, which took the form of a veritable dialogue, was the farthest the Commission could go legally and politically to accommodate their concern on process.
- Secondly, the rules on SGEI concern a vast number of regional and local bodies and (often small) undertakings. In order to design adequate rules centrally in Brussels, it is indispensable to have a profound understanding of their concerns. Consultation, together with the interactive question and answer online tool, is the best way of gathering this knowledge.

---

[49] European Commission, *European Governance. A White Paper*. COM (2001) 428 final.

[50] See for a more detailed analysis of this point Maxian Rusche 2010.

[51] The impact assessment system has been launched in 2002, see *Communication Impact Assessment*, COM (2002) 276 final. According to the most recent *Impact Assessment Guidelines* issued by the Commission (SEC (2009) 92, p. 6), an impact assessment is needed for all legislative proposals and for all non-legislative proposals which have clearly identifiable economic, social, and environmental impacts and for non-legislative initiatives which define future policies (such as white papers, action plans, expenditure programmes, negotiating guidelines for international agreements). Proposals in the area of State aid have been subject to impact assessments only since very recently, starting with the Community guidelines on State aid for railway undertakings (*OJ* 2008 C 184/13).

- Finally, the political choices made by the Commission are bold and courageous, as will be shown in the following section. Broad and repeated consultation is one means of increasing the likelihood that these choices will be accepted by all stakeholders, without the need for too much enforcement action based on complaints.

6.3 The Political Choices

The Monti-Kroes package consisted of two documents, namely a Decision exempting payments below 30 million EUR to undertakings with a turnover of less than 100 million EUR from the need of prior Commission approval, and a Framework auto-limiting the Commissions' discretion in assessing the compatibility of payments above that threshold to a simple check for the absence of overcompensation. In both instances, the Commission required the respect of the first to third *Altmark* conditions.[52] The Almunia package opted instead for a more diversified approach. First of all, it clearly spells out the Commissions' reading of the legal constraints deriving from the *Altmark* ruling in a new Communication on the notion of State aid in the context of SGEI (this corresponds to the goal of clarification, (Sect. 6.3.1). Secondly, it provides for simplification and less Commission control (and therefore administrative burden) for small compensation amounts and certain categories of SGEI (Sect. 6.3.2). This is counterbalanced by significantly stricter rules for larger (above 15 million EUR annually) payments for SGEI, applying the concept of proportionality (Sect. 6.3.3).

It would go beyond the scope of this chapter to provide a detailed legal analysis of all four texts (see for this Chap. 7 in this book).[53] Therefore, it will be limited to a presentation of the main political choices made by the Commission in comparison to the Monti-Kroes package and in the light of the expectations from stakeholders set out above.

The first choice—which came as no surprise in the light of the policy guidelines which President nominated Barroso had presented to Parliament, but was nevertheless qualified as "quite courageous in this time of centrifugal tendencies at the EU level"[54]—was not to heed to the chants of the sirens and to refrain from using Article

---

[52] To be precise, it would seem that the Monti-Kroes package, while requiring an entrustment act, is not as demanding as the second *Altmark* condition with regard to the content of the entrustment.

[53] See also the recent contributions of Geradin 2012; Jung and Deust 2012; Sauter 2012; Sinnaeve 2012; Lambertz and Hornung 2012.

[54] Buendía Sierra 2012b.

[55] Recital 3 of the SGEI Communication.

14 TFEU as legal basis. The fact that such a choice would have run into major legal obstacles certainly confirmed the College of Commissioners in this decision.

Following this implicit choice, it is time to turn to the explicit choices set out in the four texts of the Almunia Package.

6.3.1 Clarification: The SGEI Communication

The declared aim of the Communication is 'to clarify the key concepts underlying the application of the State aid rules to public service compensation'.[55] The interpretative Communication provides for a restatement of the case law of the Court. As the Commission is bound by the objective notion of State aid as it results from the case law,[56] there is, strictly speaking, no room for political choices. The most interesting aspects of such an interpretative Communication are fields where the case law is perceived as incomplete or open to interpretation.

In the political debate preceding the adoption of the Almunia Package, the following aspects received particular attention: the notion of economic activity; the assessment of in-house services; the potential of purely local services to affect trade; and the interpretation of the first, third, and fourth *Altmark* criteria.

There is extensive case law on the notion of economic activity, both in competition law and under the four freedoms.[57] Therefore, the Commission had no choice but to disappoint all those stakeholders that had called for an exemption from State aid rules by means of a reinterpretation of that notion: any such move of the Commission would simply have been illegal.[58]

The case law is equally well developed on the criteria 'impact on trade'. Indeed, in *Altmark* the Court also had the occasion to reconfirm that "there is no threshold or percentage below which trade between Member States can be regarded as not having been affected".[59] The Commission nevertheless also repeated its somewhat more generous decision practice, in which it has found that payments for purely local activities such as local swimming pools, hospitals, museums, and cultural events do not have the potential to affect trade, provided that all users/visitors live in the vicinity.[60] This line of decisions has never been tested in Court. There appears to be a certain tension between these decisions on the one hand and the

---

[56] CJEU, Case C-56/93 *Belgium* v. *Commission* [1996] *ECR* I-723, paras 10 and 11.

[57] It is important to note that the scope of application of the four freedoms is broader than the scope of application of the Treaty rules on competition. This has been explained in clear terms by the CJEU, Court in Case C-350/07 *Kattner Stahlbau* [2009] *ECR* I-1513, para 34 (compulsory insurance for accidents at work and occupational diseases is not an undertaking in the context of competition law) and 73–92 (rules on free movement of services are applicable to companies providing compulsory insurance for accidents at work and occupational diseases). See also recital 15 of the SGEI Communication with further references to the case law.

[58] See recital 15–30 of the SGEI Communication for the restatement of the case law.

[59] CJEU, Case C-280/00[2003] ECR I-7747, para 81.

[60] Recital 40 of the SGEI Communication.

facts and the reasoning in *Altmark* on the other hand. As to the facts, there is no indication that the bus service under assessment in *Altmark* would have been used by anybody but the local population. As to the reasoning, the Court in *Altmark* derived the potential impact on trade from the observation that opportunities for undertakings established in other Member States to offer their services were reduced by the subsidy. It did, in other words, not look at cross-border implications on the demand side (the users/visitors), but on the supply side (market open to service providers from other Member States).

If the Commission showed signs of pragmatic flexibility on the question of purely local services, it reaffirmed on the other hand its tough stance on the question of whether compensation payments to an *in house* provider were subject to State aid control. In this regard, Member State governments[61] and national judges[62] had expressed the view that such payments to *in house* providers somehow escaped State aid control. Different legal arguments were presented in this regard: the absence of an economic activity; the absence of an impact on trade; and, most recently and most surprisingly, the absence of the applicability of the fourth *Altmark* criterion.[63]

The Commission states in clear terms that "the fact that a particular service is provided in-house has no relevance for the economic nature of the activity".[64] As there is no case law on the question, the Commission bases its position on the conclusions of AG Geelhoed in *Asemfo*,[65] secondary legislation,[66] and its Decision in *Verkehrsverbund Rhein Ruhr*.[67]

The Commission also provides extensive reasoning as to why compensation payments to an *in-house* provider may distort competition. As this reasoning is not based on any case law or decision practice, it is worth quoting it in full:

---

[61] See for example the observations of Germany in Commission Decision 2011/501/EU implemented by Germany for Bahnen der Stadt Monheim (BSM) and Rheinische Bahngesellschaft (RBG) in the Verkehrsverbund Rhein-Ruhr, *OJ* 2011 210/1.

[62] Judgment of the *Bundesverwaltungsgericht* in Case BVerwG 3 C 44.09 of 16 December 2010, paras 38 and 39.

[63] Judgment of the *Bundesverwaltungsgericht* in Case BVerwG 3 C 44.09 of 16 December 2010, paras 38 and 39, (erroneously) referring to the judgment of the Court in CJEU, Case C-480/06 *Commission* v. *Germany* [2009] ECR I-4747, paras 46–49. This latter judgment of the CJEU concerned, as discussed above, public procurement, and not State aid and Article 106(2) TFEU.

[64] Interpretative SGEI Communication, recital 13.

[65] CJEU, Case C-295/05, [2007] *ECR* I-2999, paras 110–116.

[66] Regulation (EC) No 1370/2007 on public passenger transport services by rail and by road (*OJ* 2007 L 315/1), Articles 5(2) and 6(1).

[67] Commission Decision 2011/501/EU of 23 February 2011 on State aid implemented by Germany for Bahnen der Stadt Monheim (BSM) and Rheinische Bahngesellschaft (RBG) in the Verkehrsverbund Rhein-Ruhr, *OJ* 2011 L 210/1, paras 208–209.

[68] Commission Decision of 25 April 2012 on State aid implemented by Germany for Zweckverband Tierkoerperbeseitigung Rheinland-Pfalz, not yet published in the *OJ*, IP/12/308.

Where the market has been reserved for a single undertaking (including an in-house provider), the compensation granted to that undertaking is equally subject to State aid control. In fact, where economic activity has been opened up to competition, the decision to provide the SGEI by methods other than through a public procurement procedure that ensures the least cost to the community may lead to distortions in the form of preventing entry by competitors or making easier the expansion of the beneficiary in other markets.

This approach can be found in embryonic state in the decision in *Verkehrsverbund Rhein Ruhr*. However, it is for the first time developed in full in the SGEI Communication.

The SGEI Communication does not expressly address the reasoning developed by the *Bundesverwaltungsgericht*; however, the Commission has also rejected in no uncertain terms this reasoning in its decision on the same case.[68]

With regard to the *Altmark* criteria, the first issue on which stakeholders had sought clarification was the requirement of an 'entrustment' act, which results from the first *Altmark* criterion (*clearly defined public service obligations to discharge*). The SGEI Communication responds to the call for clarity with a list of five sets of information which constitute the minimum requirement for a valid entrustment; at the same time, there is flexibility as to the instrument chosen for the entrustment (legislative or regulatory act; contract; acceptance of application), and no requirement that the State has actually made use of powers as public authority.[69]

The second issue flagged by stakeholders was the interpretation to be given to the notion of 'reasonable profit', which is part of the third *Altmark* criterion. There is until today no case law that would elucidate the precise meaning of the word "reasonable". The Commission has presented in the SGEI Communication its take on the question. It takes as reference point the return on capital, and defines as benchmarks for defining a reasonable return on capital the level of risk and the return on capital achieved on similar contracts awarded under competitive conditions, preferably in the same Member State. Where the second benchmark does not exist, it accepts the use of data from other Member States and/or other sectors.[70]

The third issue concerns the question of which kind of competitive award constitutes a 'public procurement procedure which would allow for the selection of the tenderer capable of providing [... the SGEI] at the least cost to the community'. In the consultation, certain stakeholders had taken a maximalist position, pursuant to which any competitive procedure, including one respecting only the minimum requirements of transparency and non-discrimination established by the

---

[69] Recital 51–53 of the SGEI Communication.

[70] Recital 61 of the SGEI Communication.

[71] CJEU, Case C-324/98 *Telaustria Verlags GmbH and Telefonadress GmbH* v *Telekom Austria AG* [2000] *ECR* I-10745, para 60.

[72] *OJ* 2004 L 134/14.

[73] *OJ* 2004 L 134/1.

[74] SGEI Communication, Recital 66.

[75] SGEI Communication, Recital 67 and 68.

Court in *Telaustria*[71] would meet this test. In response to the request for clarification, the Commission presents its view on all four tender procedures foreseen by Directive 2004/17/EC coordinating the procurement procedures of entities operating in the water, energy, transport, and postal services sectors[72] and Directive 2004/18/EC on the coordination of procedures for the award of public works contracts, public supply contracts, and public service contracts.[73] The Commission explains that an "open" and, under certain circumstances, a 'restricted' procedure can meet the fourth *Altmark* criterion,[74] but qualifies this statement subsequently. Factors which may indicate that services are not procured 'at the least cost to the community' include: use of non-price-related award criteria; any 'particularities of the service in question'; and the presence of only one bidder.[75] It results *a fortiori* from these considerations that a competitive procedure complying only with the minimum requirements set by *Telaustria* is not capable of meeting the first alternative of the fourth *Altmark* criterion.

The fourth issue concerns the notion of a 'typical, well-run undertaking', which serves as benchmark for establishing compliance with the fourth *Altmark* criterion in the absence of a competitive award procedure. The Commission clarifies here in particular that it is not necessary to look at the average costs of undertakings operating in the sector; rather, it is necessary to establish the average cost structure of efficient and comparable undertakings in the sector under consideration.[76]

Overall, the interpretative guidance given by the Commission on the most contentious issues can be described as a mix of pragmatism and firmness. Pragmatic, so as to make the criteria operational; firm, so that no loopholes are opened for circumventing State aid control. At the same time, the Commission sticks to the case law where a broad body of case law exists, but does not hesitate to give its own view on issues that are not yet clearly decided.

This political choice is likely to disappoint all those who had hoped that the Commission would exclude certain activities from State aid control by means of a creative (one may also say revolutionary) interpretation of the notion of State aid (and thereby attack frontally the case law of the Court). But the SGEI Communication fully respects the absence of discretion of the Commission when it comes to the notion of State aid, and adheres to the case law. At the same time, it provides the clarification and guidance sought by stakeholders.

6.3.2 Simplification and Less ex ante Control for Small Amounts and Certain Categories of Aid

The aim of simplification (and less *ex ante* control) is pursued by two different instruments, namely the SGEI *de minimis* Regulation for aid to undertakings entrusted with an SGEI and the SGEI Decision.

---

[76] Interpretative SGEI Communication, recital 75.

The SGEI *de minimis* Regulation only requires two things: that the aid does not exceed the *de minimis* amount of 500,000 EUR in 3 years, and that the aid beneficiary is entrusted with an SGEI (the first *Altmark* criterion). It is, on the contrary, not necessary to verify the respect of the second to fourth *Altmark* criteria. The theoretical justification for an increase of the *de minimis* amount is that contrary to normal *de minimis* aid, which is a grant without any strings attached, the beneficiary of the SGEI *de minimis* aid is entrusted with an SGEI, the provision of which will consume most, if not the entirety of the aid. Therefore, the risk of distortions of competition is lower.

As the bulk of SGEI is procured by small local authorities, the *de minimis* Regulation should lead to a considerable simplification for those public authorities that do not necessarily have the administrative know-how to comply with the *Altmark* ruling. At the same time, this is unlikely to result in distortions of competition.

The new SGEI Decision has two different objectives: on the one hand, simplification, on the other, proportionality (on this aspect, see Sect. 6.3.3).

With regard to simplification, it extends the exemption of the notification obligation to all compensation payments to hospitals and social services. Social services are defined as 'services [...] meeting social needs as regards health and long-term care, childcare, access to and reintegration into the labor market, social housing, and the care and social inclusion of vulnerable groups' (Article 2(1) letter c).[77]

It also provides simplification in three further aspects: First of all, the limitation to undertakings with a turnover of less than 100 million EUR disappears. The new rule foresees that the threshold is 15 million EUR compensation per SGEI; the undertaking is entrusted with (Article 2(1) letter a). This is both stricter and more generous than the old rule: where an undertaking is entrusted with only one SGEI, the compensation amount that is exempted has been halved. Where, on the contrary, the undertaking is entrusted with more than one SGEI, this is more generous than the previous SGEI decision. Secondly, the SGEI decision contains a "safe haven" with regard to the rate of reasonable profit. It is set at the relevant swap rate plus 100 basis points (Article 5(7)). Thirdly, it clarifies that the maximal length of the entrustment is 10 years, except where significant investment has to be carried out by the undertaking entrusted, which is amortized according to generally accepted accounting principles over a period of more than 10 years (Article 2(2)).

---

[77] See Chap. 10 by *van de Gronden and Rusu*.

6.3.3 Proportionality: The SGEI Decision and the SGEI Framework

The SGEI Decision and the SGEI Framework differentiate more between different categories of services and the amount of compensation, by applying stricter rules to certain sectors and aid above a certain amount.

The SGEI Decision has a lower threshold of 15 million EUR (but this threshold is per SGEI, and no longer subject to a second threshold linked to the turnover of the undertaking providing that service, see above in Sect. 6.3.2). Furthermore, it contains special (and no longer alternative) thresholds for air and maritime transport (Article 2 (1) letter d and e; see on this in more detail in Chap. 11 on Transport). Finally, it requires compliance with the requirements flowing from the Treaty or from sectoral Union legislation (Article 3), whereas the old SGEI Decision applied without prejudice to these requirements. This means, for instance, that where an SGEI is awarded in violation of the *Telaustria* case law or of the public procurement Directives, or violates a condition for SGEI foreseen in the regulatory framework for energy, postal services or telecommunications, it is not exempted from notification, even if all the other conditions are met. As a result, certain compensation payments that were exempt from notification now fall within the SGEI Framework.

The SGEI Framework contains a number of conditions for compatibility which go beyond what was required under the old SGEI Framework. To start with, it does not apply to undertakings in difficulty.[78] Secondly, the SGEI Framework requires compliance with the Union rules on public procurement, including the *Telaustria* case law.[79] It does, however, apply only without prejudice to sectoral regulation, so that non-compliance for example with the regulatory framework on energy, postal services, or telecommunication is not *per se* a reason for declaring the compensation incompatible with the internal market.[80] Thirdly, the method for calculating compensation payments has to include so-called efficiency incentives, which set the entrusted undertaking on course towards compliance with the fourth *Altmark* criterion.[81] Finally, the SGEI Framework stipulates that the Commission may impose additional requirements which may be necessary to ensure that the development of trade is not affected to an extent contrary to the interests of the Union.[82]

---

[78] Recital 9 of the SGEI Framework.

[79] Recital 19 of the SGEI Framework.

[80] Recital 10d of the SGEI Framework.

[81] Recital 39–43 of the SGEI Framework.

[82] Recital 51–59 of the SGEI Framework.

[83] See for a comprehensive summary of the discussion Buendía Sierra 2008, pp. 214–218.

[84] GC, Joined Cases T-568/08 and T-573/08 *M6 and TF1* v. *Commission* [2010] *ECR* II-3397, paras 136–141.

In the immediate aftermath of the *Altmark* judgment, there was considerable discussion on whether the Commission could still declare aid compatible if one of the *Altmark* criteria, in particular the fourth one, was not met.[83] The question has been answered in the affirmative by the Commission, when adopting the Monti-Kroes package; and it appears to have been accepted by the legal community.

Following the adoption of the Almunia package, the Commission will be faced with another question: How much discretion does it actually enjoy when assessing under Article 106(2) TFEU the compatibility of an SGEI compensation with the internal market? The General Court stated recently in an *obiter dictum* its view that the Commission's powers under Article 106(2) TFEU are limited to verifying whether the SGEI compensation does not go beyond the additional net costs of the SGEI.[84] This position appears, however, not very convincing. It would deprive the second sentence of Article 106(2) TFEU of any *effet utile*. The first sentence of Article 106(2) TFEU is in itself sufficient to limit the allowable amount of compensation to the net additional costs of the service. The recovery of any over-compensation is not capable of obstructing the performance of the SGEI, as it is *per definitionem* not necessary for the performance of the SGEI. The second sentence of Article 106(2) TFEU adds to the condition of necessity a proportionality test, by stating:

> The development of trade must not be affected to such an extent as would be contrary to the interests of the Union.

This language is reminiscent of the language of Article 107(3) letter c TFEU (*not adversely affect trading conditions to an extent contrary to the common interest*). The assessment of whether the development of trade is affected to such an extent necessarily involves a complex economic assessment by the Commission; it therefore would appear that the Commission does enjoy at least a certain degree of discretion when authorizing SGEI compensation on the basis of Article 106(2) TFEU.

6.4 Conclusion

This chapter has first clarified that the entry into force of the Lisbon Treaty has, contrary to the view held by certain scholars, not changed the exclusive competence of the Commission for authorizing State aid for SGEI compensation. Article 14 TFEU second sentence, does not provide a legal basis for legislating on the notion, the compatibility or the notification exemption for State aid in the form of SGEI compensation.

Under the legal constraints set by *Altmark* and its exclusive competence, the Commission has decided, first of all, to engage in a broad consultation and dialogue with the other Institutions and all stakeholders, including the legal community, prior to revising the Monti-Kroes package.

With regard to the content of the Almunia package, it has opted for clarification (restatement of the case law and its decision practice); simplification (total notification exemption of social services), and proportionality (stricter rules for certain sectors and compensation above 15 million EUR). Whereas under the Monti-Kroes package, all SGEI were essentially treated the same way (verification for absence of overcompensation), the Almunia package tightens the rules for large SGEI. It excludes undertakings in difficulty from the benefit of SGEI compensations if they do not at the same time undergo in-depth restructuring (including usually compensatory measures in the form of disposals of assets and market share); requires award of the SGEI by tender (except for *in house* situations) and efficiency incentives in the compensation mechanism (so as to become *Altmark* compliant over time); and reserves the right for the Commission to ask for additional commitments in situations where there is particular risk of trade being affected to an extent contrary to the interest of the Union.

References

Barroso JM (2009) Political guidelines for the next Commission. European Commission, Brussels

Bauby P (2001) L'européanisation des services publics. Les Presses Sciences Po, Paris

Bekkedal T (2011) Article 106 TFEU is dead. Long live Article 106 TFEU! In: Szyszczak E et al (eds) Developments in services of general economic interest. TMC Asser Press, The Hague, p 61

Bonkamp J (2001) Die Bedeutung des gemeinschaftsrechtlichen Beihilfeverbotes für die Beteiligung der öffentlichen Hand an einer Kapitalgesellschaft (The implications of the EU prohibition of state aid for the state's ability to participate in a capital company). Duncker und Humboldt, Berlin

Buendía Sierra JL (1999) Exclusive rights and state monopolies under EC law. OUP, Oxford

Buendía Sierra JL (2008) State aid and services of general economic interest. In: Flett J et al (ed) EC state aid law. Liber Amicorum Santaolalla. Kluwer Law International, Alphen aan den Rijn, p 191

Buendía Sierra JL (2012a) Writing straight with crooked lines: competition policy and services of general economic interest in the Treaty of Lisbon. In: Biondi A, Eeckhout P and Ripley S (eds) EU Law after Lisbon, p 347

Buendía Sierra JL (2012b) A turn of the screw, comment on the Almunia package on the blog 'chilling competition. http://chillingcompetition.com/2012/03/14/a-turn-of-the-screw-jl-buendia-on-sgeis/

Damjanovic D, de Witte B (2008) Welfare integration through EU law: the overall picture in the light of the Lisbon Treaty. EUI working papers law 2008/34

Edward D (1996) Article 90 EC Treaty and the deregulation, liberalization and privatization of public enterprise and public monopoly. Universität zu Bonn, Bonn

Geradin D (2012) Public compensation for services of general economic interest: an analysis of the 2011 European Commission framework. Available at SSRN: http://ssrn.com/abstract=2031564

Hoekstra T (2011) Double legal basis—identical procedures versus compatible procedures. In: The institutional functioning of the EU. Maastricht University, Maastricht, p 47

Jääskinen N (2011) The new rules on SGEI, EStAL, p 599

Jung C, Deuster J (2012) Einfacher, klarer, verhältnismäßiger? Das neue EU-Beihilfen-Paket für Dienstleistungen von allgemeinem wirtschaftlichem Interesse (Simpler, clearer, more proportionate? The new EU package for SGEI) BRZ, p 24

Klamert M (2010) Conflicts of legal basis: no legality and no basis but a bright future under the Lisbon Treaty? EL Rev, p 497

Krajewski M (2011) Grundstrukturen des Rechts öffentlicher Dienstleistungen (Fundamental principles of the law of public services). Springer, Heidelberg

Lambertz KH and Hornung M (2012) State aid rules on services of general economic interest: For the committee of the regions the glass is half-full, EStAL, p 329

Maxian Rusche T (2010) The European climate change program: an evaluation of stakeholder involvement and policy achievements. Energy Policy 38:6349

Messola M (ed) (2011) The reform of state aid rules on services of general economic interest: From the 2005 Monti-Kroes package to the 2011 Almunia package. College of Europe, Bruges

Neergaard U (2011) The Commission's soft law in the area of services of general economic interest. In: Szyszczak et al (eds), Developments in services of general economic interest. TMC Asser Press, The Hague, p 37

Prechal S (2008) Fundamental rights as limits to the liberalisation of service markets. In: van de Gronden J (ed) The EU and WTO law on services. Kluwer Law International, The Hague, p 55

Radicati di Brozolo L (1996) La nuova disposizione sui servizi di interesse economico generale, Il diritto dell'Unione europea (The new provision on SGEI), p 9

Regner E (2011) Reform of the legal framework for services of general interest: where do we stand? What should a reform look like? EStAL, p 597

Rodrigues S (1998) Les services publics et le traite d'Amsterdam (Public services and the treaty of Amsterdam) RMCUE, p 37

Rodrigues S (2009) Towards a general EC framework instrument related to SGEI? In: Krajewski M, Neergard U, Van de Gronden J (eds), The changing legal framework for services of general interest in Europe. TMC Asser Press, The Hague, p 255

Ross M (2000) Article 16 E.C. and services of general economic interest: from derogation to obligation? ELRev, p 22

Sauter W (2012) The *Altmark* Package Mark II: New rules for State aid and the compensation of services of general economic interest, ECLR, p 307

Schweitzer H (2004) Die Daseinsvorsorge im Verfassungsentwurf des Europaeischen Konvents—Ein europaeischer Service Public? (The general interest in the draft constitution of the European Convention—a European public service?). In: Schwarze (ed) Der Verfassungsentwurf des Europaeischen Konvents (The draft constitution in the European convention). Nomos, Baden–Baden, p 269

Schweitzer H (2011) Services of general economic interest: European Law's impact on the role of markets and of member states. In: Cremona M (ed), Market integration and public services in the European Union. OUP, Oxford, p 11

Sinnaeve A (2012) What's new in SGEI in 2012? An overview of the Commission's SGEI package, EStAL, p 347

Skovgaard Olykke G (2011) The definition of a 'contract' under Article 106 TFEU. In: Szyszczak E et al (eds), Developments in services of general economic interest. TMC Asser Press, The Hague, p 103

Von Danwitz T (2004) Die Rolle der Unternehmen der Daseinsvorsorge im Verfassungsentwurf. In: Schwarze J (ed.), Der Verfassungsentwurf des Europäischen Konvents. Nomos, Baden–Baden, p 251 (The role of undertakings providing services of general interest in the draft constitution, in Schwarze J (ed.), The European convention's draft constitution)

Von Danwitz T (2009) State aid control over public services: a view from the court. In: Krajewski M, Neergard U, Van de Gronden J (eds), The changing legal framework for services of general interest in Europe. TMC Asser Press, The Hague, p 117

Von Danwitz T (2011) State aid in liberalized sectors. In: Cremona M (ed) Market integration and public services in the European Union. OUP, Oxford, p 103

Wernicke S (2011) Artikel 14 AEUV. In: Grabitz E, Hilf M, Nettesheim M (eds), Das Recht der Europäischen Union (loose leaf) (Article 14 TFEU, in: Grabitz/Hilf/Nettesheim, The law of the European Union)

Wernicke S (2009) Taking stock: the EU institutions and SGEI. In: Krajewski M et al (eds), The changing legal framework for services of general economic interest in Europe. TMC Asser Press, The Hague, p 69

Winterstein A (2007) The internal market and services of general economic interest. In: Amato G, Bribois H, De Witte B (eds), Genesis and destinies of the European constitution. Bruylant, Brussels, p 645

Wuermeling J (2008) Auswirkungen des Lissabonner Vertrags auf die Daseinsvorsorge (The implications of the Treaty of Lisbon for services of general interest). Wirtschaft und Verwaltung, p 247

Zimmermann D (2008) Von der EU-Verfassung zum Vertrag von Lissabon—zu den kommunalen Rechten im EU-Reformvertrag (From the EU constitution to the Treaty of Lisbon—on municipal rights in the EU reform treaty). KommJur, p 41

Chapter 7
The Almunia Package: State Aid and Services of General Economic Interest

José Luís Buendía Sierra and José Manuel Panero Rivas

Abstract This chapter sets the Almunia reform package in its historical context and analyses the thinking of the Commission behind the new measures. The analysis argues that the Commission has made an attempt to introduce flexibility into the rules for small-scale SGEI and created a practical framework for assessing larger scale SGEI. Combined with the application of the EU competition and procurement rules, the new package would appear to have substantially limited the Member States' discretion to organise larger SGEI. The new rules are complex, with some overlaps and it is concluded that the Commission must exercise its discretion in applying the rules in a consistent and predictable manner if the Commission's objectives of clarifying and simplifying the rules relating to SGEI financing are to be achieved.

Contents

J. L. Buendía Sierra (✉) · J. M. Panero Rivas (✉)
Garrigues, Avenue d'Auderghem 22-28, 1000 Brussels, Belgium
e-mail: jose.luis.buendia@garrigues.com

J. M. Panero Rivas
e-mail: jose.manuel.panero@garrigues.com

E. Szyszczak and J.W. van de Gronden (eds.), *Financing Services of General Economic Interest*, Legal Issues of Services of General Interest, DOI: 10.1007/978-90-6704-906-1_7, © T.M.C. ASSER PRESS, The Hague, The Netherlands, and the authors 2013

7.1 Introduction

After a complex review process, in December 2011, the Commission unveiled its eagerly anticipated new package for the assessment of state support granted to providers of Services of General Economic Interest (SGEI).

The new set of rules, named after Competition Commissioner Joaquin Almunia, replaces the 'post-*Altmark* package', also known as the 'Monti package' or the 'Monti-Kroes package'. The objectives of the Almunia package were defined in the following terms: (i) clarifying the rules, (ii) reducing the administrative burden on local and small SGEIs (concentrating the Commission's scrutiny activity on large-scale commercial services with a clear impact on the internal market) and (iii) taking into account the range of ways of organising public services throughout the EU.[1]

Irrespective of its objectives, the new package was adopted in a unique context that, like the red threads that were an integral part of old Royal Navy ropes,[2] cannot be separated from the final result and, almost inevitably, has influenced the new rules.

From a macroeconomic point of view, the economic crisis, which has afflicted the Union since 2008, has imposed the need for greater efficiency and austerity in the use of public funds. EU citizens are being asked to endorse significant austerity programmes due to tough fiscal discipline. As a result, Member States are being requested to reign in public spending while ensuring the provision of public services, or at least the most essential ones.

From a political-institutional point of view, the package has been adopted at a time of strong centrifugal tendencies in the EU. However, these trends are not precisely new in this specific area of EU law. Thus, certain Member States have traditionally attempted to protect their public services as much as possible from the

---

[1] Joaquín Almunia, Vice President of the European Commission, responsible for Competition Policy Reform of the State aid rules for Services of General Economic Interest (SGEI). SPEECH/11/901. Joaquín Almunia Vice President of the European Commission responsible for Competition Policy Reforming EU State aid rules on public services: The way forward EPC policy Dialogue, Brussels Brussels, 2 May 2011 SPEECH/11/300.

[2] Goethe's *Elective affinities* (1809) mentions the fact that the ropes used in the British Navy, from the largest to the smallest, were twisted in such a way that a red thread ran through them from end to end, which could not be extracted without undoing the whole. Apparently, the reason for the inclusion of the red thread was that if any rope was lost or stolen, it would be obvious who the owner was.

application of the rules contained in the EU/EC treaties. Proof of this 'traditional' pressure was the introduction of Article 16 EC by the Treaty of Amsterdam 1997, subsequently amended to become Article 14 TFEU. Against these attempts by certain Member States to increase their discretion to organise and fund SGEI, the Commission has traditionally held its ground and rigorously defended the application of the rules contained in the Treaties.[3]

The first impression from reading the new package is that the Commission has, courageously, also continued this approach in the new package and exercised a centripetal force which is at least strong enough to counterbalance both the traditional claims of certain Member States as well as more contemporary centrifugal trends.

On re-reading the new texts some nuances become apparent. First, it is clear that the Commission has not adopted a general approach of making more flexible the application of State aid rules to public support provided to SGEI providers. On the contrary, there are new additional specific conditions which must be met in order for certain state support to be considered as compatible with the internal market under Article 106(2) TFEU. Second, there are several points where, despite its prescriptive and detailed language, the new package contains a number of ambiguous statements whose effects on the assessment of state support to SGEI providers will largely depend on how rigorously—or generously—the Commission decides to apply its own rules.

In terms of complexity, it appears that the Commission has made the general structure created by the post-*Altmark* package more complex. However, whether or not this will lead to a simplification of the rules for a given operator will largely depend on the kind of operator and the SGEI in question. Thus, while there is more flexibility for small operators entrusted with certain SGEI (in particular, there is an exemption for some social services and a new *de minimis* Regulation specially designed for SGEI), the story is quite different for bigger operators subject to individual notification to be assessed under the new Framework.

In this chapter, we will: (i) briefly recall the origins of the new package, which go back to the *Altmark* judgment[4] and the Commission's post-*Altmark* package (Sect. 7.2); (ii) provide a brief overview of the new package and discuss some of its general features (Sect. 7.3); (iii) discuss certain issues relating to each of the rules making up the package (Sect. 7.4); and (iv) give our conclusions (Sect. 7.5).

---

[3] For a more detailed explanation of how the different positions interact, see Buendía Sierra 2008.

[4] CJEU, Case C-280/00, *Altmark Trans GmbH and Regierungspräsidium Magdeburg v Nahverkehrsgesellschaft Altmark GmbH, and Oberbundesanwalt beim Bundesverwaltungsgericht* [2003] *ECR* I-7747.

7.2 A Little History: The Post-*Altmark* Package

In July 2003, the CJEU issued its landmark judgment in *Altmark*.[5] This judgment adopted a 'third way' in the debate existing at that time between the 'aid approach' (support granted should be considered State aid which is compatible in so far as it does not exceed the costs incurred in the provision of the SGEI in question) and the 'non-aid approach' (the mere compensation of the extra costs incurred due to the provision of the SGEI excludes the existence of an advantage and, thus, of State aid) to the compensation to SGEI that preceded the judgment.[6] As is well known, in its judgment, the Court considered that state support for the provision of an SGEI by an undertaking could not be classified as State aid if four well-defined conditions were fulfilled.[7]

---

[5] Ibidem.

[6] A general overview of the situation can be found at paras 34 et seq. of the Opinion of AG Jääskinen delivered on 24 March 2010 in CJEU, Case C-399/08 *Commission v Deutsche Post AG*. [n.y.r]. For the non-aid approach, see CJEU, Case 240/83 *Procureur de la République v ADBHU* [1985] *ECR* 531 and CJEU, Case C-53/00 *Ferring* [2001] *ECR* I-9067. For the 'aid approach', see CJEU, Case C-387/92 *Banco Exterior de España v Ayuntamiento de Valencia* [1994] *ECR* I-877 and CJEU, Case C-332/98, *France v Commission* [2000] *ECR* I-4833.

[7] These conditions are set out in paras 89–93 of the *Altmark* judgment (n 4 above):

First, the recipient undertaking must actually have public service obligations to discharge, and the obligations must be clearly defined. In the main proceedings, the national court will therefore have to examine whether the public service obligations which were imposed on Altmark Trans are clear from the national legislation and/or the licences at issue in the main proceedings.

Second, the parameters on the basis of which the compensation is calculated must be established in advance in an objective and transparent manner, to avoid it conferring an economic advantage which may favour the recipient undertaking over competing undertakings.

Payment by a Member State of compensation for the loss incurred by an undertaking without the parameters of such compensation having been established beforehand, where it turns out after the event that the operation of certain services in connection with the discharge of public service obligations was not economically viable, therefore constitutes a financial measure which falls within the concept of State aid within the meaning of Article [107] (1) of the Treaty.

Third, the compensation cannot exceed what is necessary to cover all or part of the costs incurred in the discharge of public service obligations, taking into account the relevant receipts and a reasonable profit for discharging those obligations. Compliance with such a condition is essential to ensure that the recipient undertaking is not given any advantage which distorts or threatens to distort competition by strengthening that undertaking's competitive position.

Fourth, where the undertaking which is to discharge public service obligations, in a specific case, is not chosen pursuant to a public procurement procedure which would allow for the selection of the tenderer capable of providing those services at the least cost to the community, the level of compensation needed must be determined on the basis of an analysis of the costs which a typical undertaking, well run and adequately provided with means of transport so as to be able to meet the necessary public service requirements,

On the contrary, if the support does not fulfil the strict conditions laid down by the Court, it is classified as State aid, a separate issue being whether it could be considered as compatible State aid under Article 106(2) TFEU.

However, the conditions laid down by the Court in *Altmark*—particularly the fourth one—are rather difficult to fulfil. As a result, the vast majority of cases of public support to the provision of SGEI were assessed on compatibility grounds.[8]

But what factors should be taken into account in carrying out an assessment of compatibility? The large number of cases that were not eligible for a post-*Altmark* non-aid outcome required legal certainty. As a result, the Commission took the initiative and set out those matters to be taken into account in the assessment of the compatibility of these cases with the Treaties. Thus, in response to the situation, in 2005 the Commission issued the 'post-*Altmark* Package', composed of the closely interrelated legal instruments described below.

Perhaps the most important rule was the 'horizontal' Commission Decision 2005/842/EC,[9] which conferred an *ex ante* block exemption on the aid granted to undertakings performing certain activities and on aid to SGEI providers for amounts below certain thresholds, subject to certain conditions being fulfilled. Its legal basis was former Article 86(3) EC, now Article 106(3) TFEU.

Specifically, the Decision covered—under certain circumstances—compensation of less than €30 million per year, provided that its beneficiaries had an annual turnover of less than €100 million. Besides this general threshold, the providers of the following services were also exempted, irrespective of the aid amount provided: hospitals and social housing and air and sea transport to islands. In addition, airports and ports below specific thresholds defined in passenger volumes were also covered. However, in all of the above cases, certain conditions had to be fulfilled to qualify for the exemption, particularly with regard to the act of entrustment, the manner in which the compensation had to be calculated— including a reference to the relevant costs to be considered—and the existence of controls on overcompensation and the availability of information.

In the cases covered by the Decision, State aid was *ex ante* declared to be compatible without the need for notification to the Commission pursuant to Article 106(2) TFEU. If compensation did not qualify for an exemption under the Decision, it had another opportunity under the second of the instruments making up the Package.

(Footnote 7 continued)

would have incurred in discharging those obligations, taking into account the relevant receipts and a reasonable profit for discharging the obligations.

[8] Szyszczak 2011.

[9] Commission Decision 2005/842/EC on the application of Article 86(2) of the EC Treaty to State aid in the form of public service compensation granted to certain undertakings entrusted with the operation of services of general economic interest *OJ* 2005 L 312/67.

The second legal instrument was the Community Framework for State aid in the form of public service compensation.[10] The aim of the Framework, which was a soft law instrument, was to serve as a compatibility benchmark for all cases of aid to SGEI providers that could not benefit from the *ex ante* exemption under the Commission Decision. For these purposes, the Framework established a similar substantive test to the one laid down in the Decision.

The third legal text in the Package was a Directive, whose purpose was to amend the Transparency Directive in order to increase the quality of the accounting information to be kept by SGEI providers. From this moment onwards, SGEI providers are included in the scope of the Transparency Directive, irrespective of their ownership, and when performing activities unrelated to the SGEI, are required to maintain separate accounts.[11]

Apart from being a useful reminder of our immediate past,[12] this brief introduction to the solution provided by the Commission after *Altmark* provides the background to the new package, which to a great extent replicates the functioning of the previous rules.

7.3 The New Package (Overview)

7.3.1 Formal Structure of the New Package

The new package is composed of four instruments, as briefly described in the following paragraphs.

First, there is a new Commission Communication[13] ('the Communication'). This essentially provides: (i) an extensive overview of key concepts of the application of State aid rules to SGEI compensation and (ii) a detailed explanation of the Commission's approach to how the *Altmark* criteria should be fulfilled in order for a measure not to be classified as State aid. This is an innovative instrument, whose importance for the assessment of compensation to SGEI providers should not be underestimated. The Communication is soft law and therefore not legally binding on third parties, and certainly not on the EU Courts. However, it gives a good idea of the Commission's thinking and its interpretation of the European Courts' case law in this field.

---

[10] Community Framework for State aid in the form of public service compensation, *OJ* 2005 C 297/4.

[11] Commission Directive 2005/81/EC amending Directive 80/73EEC on the transparency of financial relations between Member States and their public undertakings as well as on financial transparency within certain undertakings, *OJ* 2005 L 312/47.

[12] For further details see Buendía Sierra 2008.

[13] Communication from the Commission on the application of the European Union State aid rules to compensation granted for the provision of services of general economic interest, *OJ* 2012 C 8/15.

Second, there is a new 'horizontal' Commission Decision[14] ('the Decision'), issued on the basis of Article 106(3) TFEU, which allows certain types of State aid to SGEI providers to be assessed as *ex ante* compatible, without the need for notification to the Commission. Compared to the previous Decision, it extends the scope of the block exemption to cover sectors not formerly covered, including additional social services beside the hospitals and social housing services included in the original decision (Article 2(1) c) and recital 11 of the Decision),[15] while also altering the thresholds which generally apply to SGEIs, that is halved to compensation not exceeding €15 million (Article 2(1) a) of the Decision). As regards this general threshold, it is also worth noting that the former turnover threshold of €100 million during the two previous financial years to the one in which the provision of the SGEI is entrusted has been removed.[16]

As in the previous Decision, the fact that a given measure could, in principle, come within Article 2(1) does not mean that it will automatically benefit from the *ex ante* exemption. On the contrary, the measure must also fulfil all other conditions stated in the Decision, not least the length of the period of entrustment that, according to Article 2(2) thereof, should in general be limited to ten years.[17]

The third instrument is a new Framework[18] ('the Framework') for the assessment of the compatibility of State aid granted in the form of public service compensation. As with its predecessor, this new Framework provides the compatibility conditions for any State aid that may not benefit from the Decision. These conditions are fairly similar to those established in the Decision. However, there are some remarkable differences that lead to an asymmetric treatment between those SGEI that could benefit from the Decision and those that should be assessed under the Framework, the latter being treated more strictly by the Commission.

---

[14] Commission Decision of 20 December 2011 on the application of Article 106(2) of the Treaty on the Functioning of the European Union to State aid in the form of public service compensation granted to certain undertakings entrusted with the operation of services of general economic interest, *OJ* 2012 L7/3.

[15] However, contrary to what the Commission stated in its press release, it is not clear from Article 2 of the Decision that all social services could be included therein.

[16] The cases in which specific aid to the provision of SGEIs to airports can benefit from the Decision have also been amended and reduced to those cases in which '(...) average annual traffic during the 2 financial years preceding that in which the service of general economic interest was assigned does not exceed 200,000 passengers (...)' (Article 2(1) e). The previous threshold was one million passengers for the same period of time. Compensation for the provision of services of general economic interest as regards air or maritime links to islands has remained unchanged. Support can be provided when average annual traffic during the two financial years preceding that in which the service of general economic interest was assigned does not exceed 300,000 passengers.

[17] With the exception, according to Article 2(2) of the Decision, of those cases in which 'a significant investment is required from the service provider that needs to be amortised over a longer period in accordance with generally accepted accounting principles.'

[18] *Communication from the Commission, European Union framework for State aid in the form of public service compensation OJ* 2011 C 8/15.

Finally, the Commission issued a proposal for a *de minimis* Commission Regulation[19] as regards State support to undertakings providing SGEIs. The Regulation was adopted on 25 April 2012[20] and establishes a general threshold of support of €500,000 over three years.

Both the Decision and the Framework replace the previous rules. The only rule of the former Package that remains in force is the amendment introduced by Directive 2005/81/EC on the Transparency Directive. The purpose of that Directive was to serve an ancillary role to the other rules in order to properly identify the amounts of compensation granted to SGEI providers. This goal will be equally served under the new Package.

7.3.2 *Suggested Analytical Approach Under the New Rules*

In general, it is not obvious how the different instruments interact with each other either under the original post-*Altmark* package or the new package. Accordingly, to facilitate the task of those who are less familiar with these rules, we would suggest the following procedure when assessing a given measure under the new package:

(a) **First step**: Is the measure covered by the *de minimis* Regulation? If so, the measure does not constitute State aid.

(b) **Second step**: If the answer to the first question is 'no', the next question would be: can the measure benefit from the *Altmark* criteria—as specified by the Commission in the new Communication? If so, the measure would not be State aid either.

(c) **Third step**: If the answer to the second question is 'no', the next question would be: can the measure be covered by the Decision—in particular because of the amount of compensation provided? And could it thus be considered as *ex ante* compatible State aid?

(d) **Fourth step**: If the answer to all of the above questions is 'no', state support should be assessed under the new Framework, and notified to the Commission for its evaluation.

---

[19] Draft Commission Regulation on the application of Articles 107 and 108 of the Treaty on the Functioning of the European Union to *de minimis* aid granted to undertakings providing services of general economic interest, *OJ* 2012 C 8/23.

[20] Commission Regulation of 25 April on the application of Articles 107 and 108 of the Treaty on the Functioning of the European Union to *de minimis* aid granted to undertakings providing services of general economic interest *OJ* 2012 L 114/8.

7.3.3 Political-Institutional Remarks: The Issue of the Legal Basis

The application of the rules contained in the EC/EU Treaties (including those regarding State aid, public procurement and freedom to provide services and establishment) to SGEI has always been a battleground between the Commission and certain groups and Member States. On the one hand, are those who consider that EU law and the Commission's decision-making practice are biased against SGEIs and need to be rebalanced, while on the other hand are those who consider that the treatment of SGEIs is fair and balanced.[21] This has been a constant subject of debate at the successive Intergovernmental Conferences on the amendment of the Treaties.

In this context, while discussions on the EU Constitutional Treaty were taking place, the supporters of a Treaty modification on the rules governing SGEIs, while avoiding an open debate on the issue, managed to slip in an amendment of the former Article 16 EC at the very last minute of the works of the European Convention.[22] The change was made to Article III-122 of the Draft Constitutional Treaty and provided an additional legal basis for establishing principles and conditions for the provisions of such services.

Although the provision was one of the casualties of the rejection of the failed Constitutional Treaty, its content was recycled into what is now Article 14 TFEU. This Article goes beyond the rather rhetorical formulation of former Article 16 EC by including a new legal basis—which is subsidiary as regards Article 106(3) TFEU—for legislating in the field of SGEI. In its current wording, Article 14 TFEU reads as follows:

> [W]ithout prejudice to Article 4 of the Treaty on the European Union or to Articles 93, 106 and 107 of this Treaty and given the place occupied by services of general economic interest in the shared values of the Union as well as their role in promoting social and territorial cohesion, The Union and the Member States, each within their respective powers on the basis of principles and conditions, particularly economic and financial conditions, which enable them to fulfil their missions. The European Parliament and the Council, acting by means of regulations in accordance with the ordinary legislative procedure, shall establish these principles and set these conditions without prejudice to the competence of Member States, in compliance with the Treaties, to provide, to commission and to fund such services.

The convoluted grammar of this Article, full of caveats [*without prejudice of Article 4 or Article 93, 106 and 107(...)*] is not at all easy to understand.[23]

---

[21] Buendía Sierra 2008.

[22] See the minutes of the penultimate plenary session of the European Convention held in Brussels on 4 July 2003, CONV 849/03, according to which the initiative for the adoption of this provision came from the Presidium of the Convention. In the last session, certain members of the Convention stated their disagreement with the introduction of this amendment, on the basis that it was not of a technical nature. See the minutes of the last plenary session of the European Convention held in Brussels on 9 and 10 July 2003, CONV 853/03.

[23] Buendía Sierra 2011.

However, what is clear is that in the new package the Commission has decided not to make use of the hypothetical—and still untried—legal basis under Article 14 TFEU and chosen instead to rely on the one already tested in the post-*Altmark* package and it was probably right to do so.

7.4 Selected Issues Regarding Each of the Instruments Making Up the Package

7.4.1 The Communication (Redefining the Boundaries of Altmark)

The Communication is a completely new instrument. According to the Commission, the only goal of the new text is *'to clarify the key concepts underlying the application of the State aid rules to public service compensation'*.[24] However, it seems to go well beyond that. In the paragraphs below, we will comment on some of the theories put forward by the Commission regarding the new text.[25]

The first question is whether a given activity should be considered as an economic activity and, therefore, within the scope of the Treaties. Particularly interesting in this regard are paras 12 and 14 of the Communication, according to which it appears that national decisions could influence whether a given activity should be considered as 'economic' or not.[26] However, these provisions, which conflict with the existence of an objective definition of what constitutes an economic activity, are contradicted by the content of paras 13 and 37 of the Communication. In our view, there is some confusion here between what constitutes an economic activity and the separate question of how the market is affected by the measure. This issue is clarified in paras 13 and 37. Paragraph 13 states as follows:

---

[24] Paragraph 3 of the Communication.

[25] For a more detailed description of the content of the Communication, in particular as regards the engagement of public funds Buendía Sierra and Muñoz de Juan 2012.

[26] Paragraph 12 of the Communication reads: 'The question whether a market exists for certain services may depend on the way those services are organised in the Member State concerned. The State aid rules only apply where a certain activity is provided in a market environment. The economic nature of certain services can therefore differ from one Member State to another. Moreover, due to political choice or economic developments, the classification of a given service can change over time. What is not a market activity today may turn into one in the future, and vice versa.'

Paragraph 14 of the Communication states: 'Since the distinction between economic and non-economic services depends on political and economic specificities in a given Member State, it is not possible to draw up an exhaustive list of activities that a priori would never be economic. Such a list would not provide genuine legal certainty and would thus be of little use. The following paragraphs instead seek to clarify the distinction with respect to a number of important areas.'

The decision of an authority not to allow third parties to provide a certain service (for example, because it wishes to provide the service in-house) does not rule out the existence of an economic activity. In spite of such market closure, an economic activity can exist where other operators would be willing and able to provide the service in the market concerned. More generally, the fact that a particular service is provided in-house has no relevance for the economic nature of the activity.

This is complemented by para 37, which provides that:

In order to be caught by Article 107 of the Treaty, public service compensation must affect or threaten to affect trade between Member States. Such an effect generally presupposes the existence of a market open to competition. Therefore, where markets have been opened up to competition either by Union or national legislation or de facto by economic development, State aid rules apply. In such situations Member States retain their discretion as to how to define, organise and finance SGEIs, subject to State aid control where compensation is granted to the SGEI provider, be it private or public (including in-house). Where the market has been reserved for a single undertaking (including an in-house provider), the compensation granted to that undertaking is equally subject to State aid control. In fact, where economic activity has been opened up to competition, the decision to provide the SGEI by methods other than through a public procurement procedure that ensures the least cost to the community may lead to distortions in the form of preventing entry by competitors or making easier the expansion of the beneficiary in other markets. Distortions may also occur in the input markets. Aid granted to an undertaking operating on a non-liberalised market may affect trade if the recipient undertaking is also active on liberalised markets.

A second interesting question is the theory put forward by the Commission in the Communication according to which '[t]he granting, without tendering, of licences to occupy or use public domain, or of other special or exclusive rights having an economic value, may imply a waiver of State resources and create an advantage for the beneficiaries'.[27] Even if it is doubtful whether this principle derives from the case law mentioned by the Commission in the Communication, the idea has its appeal, at least intellectually. However, as the Commission implicitly recognises, not every case in which there is an exclusive right—even if this is granted without a tender—automatically means a waiver of State resources. It may well be that the protection granted through the exclusive right would correspond to what it is strictly necessary to reduce the compensation granted to the SGEI operator. In any event, the Commission puts forward a principle that it should nevertheless explore with care. One of the reasons for this note of caution is that the new idea blurs the traditional dividing line between Articles 106(1) and 107(1) TFEU and might be seen as an attempt by the Commission to use a specific policy instrument (State aid control) to achieve a goal that is only partially connected with it (liberalisation).

Another issue of note in the new package is how the Commission has introduced some kind of new limits as regards what is and what is not capable of constituting a 'true' SGEI. The Commission starts by recalling that Member States have a great degree of discretion to decide what is an SGEI and the limits of the

---

[27] Paragraph 33 of the Communication.

Commission's assessment in this regard, namely checking Member States' possible manifest errors.[28] However, at paras 48–50 of the Communication, the Commission seems to suggest two new conditions, specifically: (i) 'The Commission (…) considers that it would not be appropriate to attach specific public service obligations to an activity which is already provided or can be provided satisfactorily and under conditions, such as price, objective quality characteristics, continuity and access to the service, consistent with the public interest, as defined by the state, by undertakings operating under normal market conditions' and (ii) 'The Commission also considers that the services to be classified as SGEIs must be addressed to citizens or be in the interest of society as a whole.'[29]

It would appear that the Commission is widening—or at least threatening to widen—the traditional scope of the assessment of what constitutes a 'true' SGEI. A broad interpretation of this condition could lead to the conclusion that the Commission would be able to exercise a considerable degree of control. In practice, it is difficult for Member States to argue that a service that is already available in the market is not provided on conditions consistent with the public interest or socially acceptable. Similar problems could arise when a service is provided in two Member States on similar conditions but in one of those Member States the government decides that a public service obligation should be imposed.

Taking this restrictive line, the Commission mentions its decision-making practice in the broadband sector, where in only a few cases it has seemed ready to accept the provision of internet access as an SGEI. In particular, according with the Commission, this would never be the case for standard broadband commercial speeds or where there is already a parallel network to the one seeking to be declared as an SGEI.[30]

As regard the costs that can be compensated, in the Communication the Commission seems to be ready to accept all net costs (revenues less costs) incurred as a result of the provision of the SGEI. No details are provided as to how to assign common or joint costs related to both the provision of the SGEI subject to compensation and other possible services provided by the undertaking operating the SGEI.

In relation to the fourth *Altmark* condition, the Communication also has something interesting to say. Thus, it details the condition that a possible tender should fulfil, stating that: (i) a negotiated procedure or a competitive dialogue would not be sufficient, in principle, for the purposes of the fourth *Altmark* condition[31] and (ii) public procurement procedures where only one bid is submitted cannot be deemed as sufficient for the same purposes.[32] Neither would it be

---

[28] Paragraph 45 of the Communication.

[29] Paragraph 50 of the Communication.

[30] Community Guidelines for the application of State aid rules in relation to rapid deployment of broadband networks, *OJ* 2009 C 235/7.

[31] Paragraph 66 of the Communication.

[32] Paragraph 68 of the Communication.

sufficient for this purpose a procurement procedure where 'the particularities of the service in question, existing intellectual property rights or necessary infrastructure [were] owned by a particular service provider.'[33]

These strict principles seem to make stricter the conditions for a measure to escape its classification as State aid by fulfilling the fourth *Altmark* condition. However, in exchange the Commission seems to be ready to accept tender award criteria other than the lowest price. Specifically, it mentions that this could be 'the most economically advantageous tender, provided that the award criteria, including environmental or social ones, are closely related to the subject-matter of the service provided and allow for the most economically advantageous offer to match the value of the market'. Although the Commission clarifies that these criteria will only be acceptable if they are 'closely related to the subject-matter of the services provided and allow for the most economically advantageous offer to match the value of the market', its willingness to accept award criteria other than those that are purely economic is somewhat surprising given the strict economic criteria that underpin the whole package.

In addition, it is worth recalling that when a public procurement procedure has not been carried out, it is possible—at least in theory—to fulfil the fourth *Altmark* criteria when the amount of compensation is determined on the basis of an analysis of the costs that a typical undertaking, that is well run and adequately provided with the material means to be able to meet the necessary public service require-ments, would have incurred in discharging those obligations, taking into account the relevant receipts and a reasonable profit for the same.[34] In this regard, the Communication contains several points which help explain what is meant by a 'well-run undertaking',[35] a 'typical undertaking',[36] an 'adequately provided undertaking'[37] and 'reasonable profit'.[38] It appears that these elements will be assessed on a case-by-case basis and it is difficult to anticipate how much dis-cretion the Commission will allow Member States in this regard.

7.4.2 The Decision (Conditions for State Aid to an SGEI Provider to be Ex Ante Exempted)

The new Decision makes several changes to the system. First, Article 2 modifies the range of undertakings and SGEI that can benefit from *ex ante* compatibility. The reduction of the general threshold for benefitting from the block exemption

---

[33] Idem.

[34] See n 7 above.

[35] Paragraphs 70–72 of the Communication.

[36] Paragraphs 73–75 of the Communication.

[37] Paragraph 76 of the Communication.

[38] Paragraph 77 of the Communication.

from €30 to €15 million of annual compensation in principle reduces the number of potential undertakings that could benefit from the exemption. However, this should be counterbalanced by the elimination of the turnover threshold of €100 million during the two previous years.

The elimination of the former turnover thresholds is in line with the philosophy of the Package. The objective is to scrutinise the compensation of large-scale SGEIs with a clear impact on the internal market, but to leave on one side small SGEIs—thus eliminating the administrative burdens placed on them—regardless of the operator providing them. In other words, the emphasis is placed on the amount of compensation for SGEIs, not the size of the SGEI provider.

While in theory this makes sense, the new method is likely to allow very large undertakings which operate networks of similar SGEIs to escape the control of the Commission. Thus, for example, there will be differences in the treatment of SGEIs which are operated locally where compensation is less than €15 million but entrusted to one and the same undertaking (covered by the Decision) and cases involving the same services which are operated nationally and the total compensation is above €15 million (not covered by the Decision and therefore assessed under the Framework). Apart from these services, where the possibility of being covered by the Decision depends in the first place on the amount of compensation provided, there are other services that, irrespective of this amount, could in principle be covered by the Decision. Here the new Decision extends its scope to social services beyond those included in the original decision to all sorts of 'services of general economic interest meeting social needs as regards health and long term care, childcare, access to and reintegration into the labour market, social housing and the care and social inclusion of vulnerable groups'.[39]

Another remarkable change in the scope of the Decision is that, in principle, only SGEI whose period of entrustment are not longer than 10 years could benefit from the Decision.[40] However, there is an exception to this rule for those cases in which 'a significant investment is required from the service provider that needs to be amortised over a longer period in accordance with generally accepted accounting principles.'[41]

We now turn to analyse the new rules on compensation. As in the post-*Altmark* package, these rules are largely common to both the Decision and the Framework. Therefore, for the sake of simplicity, we will examine them largely together in the following paragraphs, although specific features of the Framework will be examined in the next section.

The first point to note as regards compensation is that, unlike the situation with those cases to be assessed under the *Altmark* test (no aid), under both the Decision and the Framework all costs actually incurred by the undertaking can be compensated. Therefore, the compensation is composed of two parts: (i) that which

---

[39] Article 2(1) c of the Decision.

[40] Article 2(2) of the Decision.

[41] Idem.

covers the net costs actually incurred by the undertaking for the provision of the services and (ii) a reasonable profit.

Regarding the first of these elements, the new Decision introduces the possibility of using the so called Net Avoided Cost Methodology ('NACM') and obtaining such amount directly from the comparison between 'the net cost for the undertaking of operating with the public service obligation and the net cost or profit of the same undertaking operating without the public service obligation'.[42]

Thus, when such methodology could be applied:

$$NC^s = \pi - \pi^s$$

where:

NC^s Net Cost of the SGEI provision.[43]

π Profit or loss of the firm prior to the entrustment of the SGEI.[44]

π^s Profit or loss of the firm after the entrustment of the SGEI.

However, this methodology cannot be used in all cases. Alternatively, both the Decision and the Framework allow the use of other methodologies based on cost allocation for the determination of NC^s.[45]

According to this methodology:

(a) The costs to be taken into account would be all those necessary to operate the SGEI. However, two scenarios must be distinguished:

- When the undertaking limits itself exclusively to the provision of the SGEI entrusted, all existing costs may be computed.[46]
- When the undertaking carries out any activity outside the scope of the SGEI, direct costs necessary for its provision as well as an appropriate part of the common costs should be taken into account.[47]

(b) The revenues to be taken into account should, at least, include the entire revenue earned from the SGEI and the excess profits generated from special or exclusive rights even if linked to other activities regardless of whether those excessive profits are classified as State aid.[48]

This methodology creates uncertainty, particularly as regards the allocation of costs that are truly common or joint for SGEI activities and non-SGEI activities. One would have expected greater certainty on this point from the Commission.

---

[42] Article 5(2) of the Decision.

[43] We have assumed that this value is always positive as normally the provision of SGEI entails net losses for undertakings entrusted with running them.

[44] The value will be positive in the case of profit and negative in the case of loss.

[45] Articles 5(3) and 5(4) of the Decision and paras 28–32 of the Framework.

[46] Paragraph 30 of the Framework and para 5.3 a of the Decision.

[47] Paragraph 31 of the Framework and para 5.3 b and c of the Decision.

[48] Article 5.4 of the Decision and para 32 of the Framework.

However, this could be due to the fact that, as certain authors have pointed out, 'there is no sound economic logic that would lead one to prefer one allocation of common costs over any other. As a result, any rule for allocating common costs between products is essentially arbitrary'.[49]

On the revenue side, the idea of including extra revenue arising from possible special or exclusive rights merits at least a brief comment. Even if this seems right in theory, in principle it may prove difficult to quantify the extra revenue generated by the exclusive rights themselves. Indeed, it does not appear clear which benchmark can be used in these cases to calculate the extra profit. It is not simply a case of comparing a model of perfect competition with a hypothetical monopolist (where output is restricted to the point where MC = MR and price increases as a consequence) because, *inter alia*, of the following reasons:

(a) Perfect competition models are rarely found outside of textbooks, and therefore would not seem to be a good comparison. In any event, if an open tender exists, it seems that 'extra revenue' expected from the exclusive rights would have been discounted from its offer by the winner bidder. In this case, competition might be better described as competition *for* the market (the possible extra revenue arising from the exclusive rights already having been discounted) than competition *in* the market.
(b) SGEI are generally regulated in terms of price or quantity and therefore the effect of the exclusive right is not that obvious (as the monopolist cannot adjust its output to the point where MR = MC).
(c) Most SGEI are in markets where there are strong economies of scale and therefore tend to be natural monopolies. In these markets, the granting of an exclusive right would have less effect than in more fragmented markets, as the counterfactual could well be the existence of a sole provider. Therefore, the task of quantifying the advantage granted by the special or exclusive right would not be an easy one.

Once the net cost incurred because of the provision of the SGEI has been determined, the reasonable profit (RP) to be awarded to the SGEI provider is equalled by the Commission with the Internal Rate of Return (IRR) that would be required by a typical company considering whether or not to provide the SGEI for the period of entrustment, taking into account the level of risk.[50]

Apart from that, the Decision introduces a 'safe harbour' which is a rate of return that should be considered reasonable in any event. This 'safe harbour' consists in a return on capital (ROC) not higher than the relevant swap rate plus 100 basis points. The relevant swap rate for the purposes is the one whose maturity and currency corresponds to the duration and currency of the entrustment. This

---

[49] Bishop and Walker 2010, p. 345. For some proposals on how to allocate these costs see the contribution of Kavanagh to this book.

[50] Article 5.5 of the Decision and para 33 of the Framework.

safe harbour could, in the opposite sense, serve as a 'cap' when the provision of the SGEI is not connected with a substantial commercial or contractual risk.[51]

Notwithstanding the above, the Decision leaves open the possibility of using profit indicators other than the ROC, such as the average return on equity (ROE) over the entrustment period, the return on capital employed (ROCE), the return on assets (ROA) or the return on sales (ROS).[52] The Commission gives no guidance on when one or other indicator will be preferred.

Another novel issue is that both the Decision and the Framework suggest the introduction of incentive criteria relating to possible gains in productive efficiency that can be achieved by the entrusted undertaking once the SGEI is operating.[53]

The idea is that if additional efficiencies can be achieved, the resulting extra profit must be fairly shared between the public administration and the undertaking entrusted with the provision of the SGEI. The claw-back mechanisms to be established provide undertakings with an incentive to reduce their costs and therefore obtain more profit. They also benefit the public body in question by reducing the amount spent on compensating the provision of the SGEI.

The question is how to ensure that this type of mechanism will not affect the quality of the services. In this regard, the Commission clarifies that the reduction of costs cannot be due to—or lead to—a lower quality service.[54]

It is difficult to imagine how to measure effectively whether quality is reduced during the period in which the services are provided. This is particularly true when, in difficult economic circumstances, there are powerful incentives for both undertakings and Member States to reduce an undertaking's costs once it has already been granted an SGEI. The Commission gives little guidance about claw-back mechanisms, but their design would therefore be of the utmost importance so as not to create incentives that would hamper the provision of high quality public services.[55]

Moreover, there is the separate issue of whether or not these claw-back mechanisms are appropriate when the provider has been selected through a competitive public procurement process. In theory, if the selection is carried out correctly it should guarantee that the most efficient option is selected (both in terms of price and quality). Therefore, a claw-back mechanism should normally be unnecessary in such cases. One might even argue that the possible 'extra profit' would have been foreseen by the undertakings when submitting their offers and included as a reduction of the compensation. If this 'extra profit' is subsequently partially 'confiscated' by the State, then the final effect could well be that the initial bids of the different undertakings would be less favourable to the State.

---

[51] Article 5.7 of the Decision. See also paras 33 et seq of the Framework.

[52] Article 5.8 of the Decision.

[53] Article 5.6 of the Decision and paras 39–43 of the Framework.

[54] Article 5(6) of the Decision and para 53 of the Framework.

[55] See paras 40 and 41 of the Framework.

But even when a tender has not taken place, these efficiency incentives should be put in context. In this regard, neither under the old nor under the new package is there any prohibition on Member States compensating the costs of SGEIs that are above the level that an efficient operator would request. On this point, as previously noted, the new package introduces the new efficiency incentives while maintaining the possibility of covering the costs incurred in the provision of the SGEI (plus a reasonable profit). This is so irrespective of whether the undertaking selected is considered *ex ante* to be efficient. Arguably, there may be a certain contradiction here between the fact that *ex post* efficiency incentives are required while no control of efficiency is *ex ante* required.

On this point, the new framework's impact on the assessment of the support granted to SGEI providers will once again largely depend on how rigorously the Commission enforces its own rules.

7.4.3 *The Framework (Compatibility Benchmark)*

The Framework is the third legal instrument in the package. It provides the benchmark for the compatibility of State support to SGEI that cannot be declared to be *ex ante* compatible and therefore should be notified for assessment to the Commission.

Its basis is similar to that of the Decision; there are also some striking differences which we will describe below.

First, para 13 is worthy of note. Closely related to the statements made about the Communication, the service to be compensated must be a 'true' SGEI. In this regard, the Framework provides that:

> Member States cannot attach specific public service obligations to services that are already provided or can be provided satisfactorily and under conditions, such as price, objective quality characteristics, continuity and access to the service, consistent with the public interest, as defined by the State, by undertakings operating under normal market conditions. As for the question of whether a service can be provided by the market, the Commission's assessment is limited to checking whether the Member State's definition is vitiated by a manifest error, unless provisions of Union law provide a stricter standard.[56]

The comments made above in relation to the Communication also apply here. It remains to be seen whether the Commission will allow Member States to retain—as the case law requires—a genuine degree of discretion to declare a given service as an SGEI or if the Commission will adopt a more restrictive approach—as, for instance, was the case of State support in the deployment of broadband networks.

Another interesting issue is the requirement that Member States 'should show that they have given proper consideration to the public service needs supported by way of a public consultation or other appropriate instruments to take the interests

---

[56] Paragraph 13 of the Framework.

of users and providers into account.'[57] In our opinion, following the Commission's practice as regard broadband services, it is possible that the existence of a consultation for users and providers will become a standard condition for the compatibility of support to SGEI providers that should be assessed under the Framework. This is probably excessive. After all, the definition of an SGEI is supposed to be within the area of competence of the Member State. It is, therefore, for the Member State to decide whether or not it needs a specific consultation. After all, elections are also types of public consultation, probably the most obvious one. On this point—as on many others—only time will tell what the Commission's position will be.

Paragraph 19 of the Framework expressly describes an interesting link between State aid and public procurement rules. The provision suggests that for State support to SGEI to be considered compatible with the internal market, the responsible authority, when entrusting the provision of the services, should comply with EU rules in the area of public procurement. This includes any requirements regarding transparency, equal treatment and non-discrimination deriving directly from the Treaty as well as, when applicable, from secondary EU law. The consequence of breaching any of these rules will be that the Commission will declare any method of selection that does not comply with these principles to be incompatible aid. Therefore, this provision is, in principle, of utmost importance, introducing a link between State aid rules and public procurement rules that gives greater force to the latter.[58]

This is a very delicate point. Until now, Member States have had no clear obligation to choose SGEI operators through competitive tenders. The *Altmark* judgment simply provided an incentive to use this mechanism by stating that a competitive tender may exclude the presence of aid. However, under the old package, the absence of such a tender did not prevent the aid received by the SGEI from being declared compatible.

This appears to have changed with the Almunia package, which now seems to require a competitive tender for the entrustment of bigger SGEI, to be assessed under the Framework, as a condition for approving the aid. In other words, if an SGEI has been entrusted without a tender, the EC should, in principle, not authorise any State aid for its financing.

This requirement seems to be in line with the need to achieve a more efficient use of public money and, in this regard, it appears to be both logical and positive. However, it is perhaps over ambitious if one looks at how the real world works. Thus, the vast majority of SGEI have been entrusted by the authorities without any tender and the situation is unlikely to change overnight as a consequence of the

---

[57] Paragraph 14 of the Framework.

[58] For a detailed analysis of the interface between State aid, public procurement and financing to SGEI, including a critique of the approach taken by the Commission, see the contribution of Sanchez Graells to this book.

entry into force of the package.[59] Does this mean that a large number of SGEIs in Europe are now incompatible as a consequence of the new package? In our view, the normative force of facts is likely to lead to a more flexible interpretation of the package. The text itself already suggests a reasonable degree of flexibility by accepting that, instead of having already used the tender, the Member State may simply promise to use one in the future.

A similar provision, but this time regarding the fulfilment of the Transparency Directive rules, precedes this provision,[60] according to which the Commission will not declare state support to SGEI provided by undertakings that do not comply with the Transparency Directive to be compatible State aid. Again, the consequences of this, which are very different from those deriving from the fact that a given Member State has not correctly implemented the Directive or that a specific undertaking has not complied with it, will give Member States and undertakings entrusted with the operation of SGEI a renewed incentive to comply with other provisions of EU law.

As regards the rule on the calculation of compensation, the Framework lays down similar rules to those contained in the Decision. Here the Commission states its preference for the net avoided cost methodology (NACM) when the latter can be applied. However, it also allows the cost allocation methodology to be used when the NACM cannot be applied. The principles established in this regard are similar to those mentioned above in the Decision. However, unlike in the Decision, where the criteria for defining the contribution of the common cost that should be allocated to the SGEI was left open, in the Framework the Commission suggests that '[t]o determine the appropriate contribution to the common costs, market prices for the use of the resources, where available, can be taken as a benchmark.' It is unclear how this provision should be interpreted. If the Commission is referring to the prices at which the services are offered as the criterion for allocating common costs between the SGEIs and the other activities, it possibly risks a certain degree of circular reasoning. If, on the other hand, this provision means that the Commission is ready to accept that common costs should be allocated on the basis of the hypothetical prices which an undertaking placed in the conditions of the one in question would be ready to accept for the costs incurred in providing the SGEI and (particularly) non-SGEI services, this would seem a more sensible approach. A 'second best' option in this regard that is mentioned by the Commission is the allocation of the common costs on the basis of the profit which the

---

[59] For an explanation of the transitional provisions contained in the Decision and the Framework see Buendía Sierra and Muñoz de Juan 2012.

[60] Paragraph 18 of the Framework provides as follows: 'Aid will be considered compatible with the internal market on the basis of Article 106(2) of the Treaty only where the undertaking complies, where applicable, with Directive 2006/111/EC. Aid that does not comply with that Directive is considered to affect the development of trade to an extent that would be contrary to the interest of the Union within the meaning of Article 106(2) of the Treaty.'

undertaking is expected to make on the activities falling outside of the scope of the SGEI.[61] The risks would be, once more, a certain degree of circular reasoning.

Another new issue raised by the Commission in the Framework is that it reserves the right to examine more closely compensation to SGEI providers when certain circumstances exist, such as: (i) a longer duration than is objectively necessary[62]; (ii) a series of tasks which are bundled together[63]; (iii) where similar services to those of the SGEI are provided or can be expected to be provided in the near future in the absence of the SGEI[64]; (iv) where there are special or exclusive rights that seriously restrict competition within the internal market[65]; (v) where the aid allows the undertaking to finance the creation of an essential facility[66]; or (vi) 'If distortions of competition are a consequence of the entrustment hindering effective implementation or enforcement of Union legislation aimed at safe-guarding the proper functioning of the internal market'. In each of these cases, the Commission reserves the right to require 'commitments' from the Member State in order to solve the problems created by the aid granted to the SGEI provider. In our view, this is very closely related to the Commission's powers as regards the enforcement of Article 106(1) TFEU. Therefore, on this point the Commission also appears to have created a link between State aid rules and Article 106(1) that it can use in order to foster the liberalisation of markets. The obvious risk here is that legal certainty will be damaged, since if certain compatibility conditions may be traded against certain alternative commitments it would be difficult to know what the law actually requires.

7.4.4 The New de Minimis Regulation

The last instrument in the package is the Regulation, which establishes a specific *de minimis* threshold for compensation payable to SGEI.

Specifically, aid granted to undertakings providing an SGEI is deemed not to affect trade between Member States and/or not to distort or threaten to distort competition (and therefore does not constitute State aid) provided that the total

---

[61] Paragraph 31 of the Framework.

[62] Paragraph 55 of the Framework.

[63] Idem.

[64] Paragraph 56 of the Framework.

[65] Paragraph 57 of the Framework. Here the Commission recognises that the main means of challenging such rights would be under Article 106(1) TFEU. However, State aid cannot be declared compatible with the internal market when the exclusive or special rights provide an advantage that cannot be quantified and therefore the compensation cannot be properly assessed. This should be put into context with the difficulties of quantifying the extra revenue arising from the grant of special or exclusive rights mentioned in section IV (b) above.

[66] Paragraph 58 of the Framework.

amount of aid granted for the provision of SGEIs received by the beneficiary undertaking does not exceed €500,000 over any period of three fiscal years.

Two issues arise here in relation to the *de minimis* Regulation. The first is that one might ask whether the new Regulation is truly necessary given the existence of the general *de minimis* Regulation and the general block exemption granted by the Decision to SGEI compensation of less than €15 million. In any event, whatever the answer to that question, what is clear is that this alleviates the Commission's burden, allowing it to focus on the more relevant cases. This therefore fulfils one of the declared essential goals of the new package, i.e. that of concentrating the Commission's scrutiny only on the compensation of large-scale SGEI.

A second issue is that the new Regulation breaks the *status quo* on non-transparent aid in the form of guarantees as regards the general thresholds established in relation thereto in the *de minimis* rules.

Commission Regulation (EC) No 1998/2006 excludes non-transparent aid from its scope. Thus, Article 2(4) of the Regulation provides as follows:

> This Regulation shall apply only to aid in respect of which it is possible to calculate precisely the gross grant equivalent of the aid ex ante without need to undertake a risk assessment ('transparent aid').

There are certain exceptions to this principle for capital injections or public guarantees. With respect to the latter, Regulation 1998/2006 establishes that the *de minimis* rules apply to guarantees as long as the guaranteed part of the underlying loan provided under such a scheme does not exceed €1,500,000.

The new *de minimis* Regulation departs from this general treatment of aid in the form of guarantees. According to Article 3.2 of the draft Regulation:

> Where aid takes forms other than a grant, such as loans or capital injections, it can benefit from this Regulation only if the amount paid out to the undertaking does not exceed the ceiling laid down in paragraph 2. Where aid takes the form of a guarantee, the guaranteed part of the underlying loan shall not exceed that ceiling.

Therefore, there is a difference between the general treatment of guarantees as *de minimis* aid in the Regulation and in the general *de minimis* rules laid down in Regulation 1998/2006. Moreover, as the general *de minimis* Regulation may be applied to compensation to SGEI providers,[67] the larger amount allowed by that rule makes inoperative the provision on guarantees contained in the new Regulation. There does not appear to be any good reason for such treatment.

---

[67] Paragraph 13 of the Regulation provides as follows: 'This Regulation should not restrict the application of Regulation (EC) No 1998/2006 to undertakings providing services of general economic interest. Member States should remain free to rely either on this Regulation or on Regulation (EC) No 1998/2006 as regards aid granted for the provision of services of general economic interest.'

7.5 Conclusions

As stated in the introduction, the objectives of the new package were defined by the Commission as: (i) clarifying the rules, (ii) reducing the administrative burden on local and small SGEIs (concentrating the Commission's scrutiny on large-scale commercial services with a clear impact on the internal market) and (iii) taking into account the range of ways of organising public services throughout the EU.

In the new package, even at the risk of creating a largely asymmetrical system, the Commission has made a laudable attempt to make more flexible the rules for small SGEI while creating a new framework for assessing their large-scale counterparts. In that second group of services, the Commission has made a considerable effort to search for solutions that makes the provision of high-level SGEIs at a reasonable price compatible with the creation of the lowest possible degree of distortion on competition within the internal market.

This difficult task has been fulfilled by the Commission while resisting pressure from Member States who sought a greater degree of discretion to organise and fund their SGEI. For this reason alone the Commission should be applauded.

In substance, the new package is like a very ambitious painting. However, the Commission seems to have been affected by a certain *horror vacui*[68] which caused it to try to fill every possible space on the canvass. Thus, the detailed regulation of an extraordinary number of fields for large SGEI and the establishment of close links with other EU rules—such as Article 106(1) TFEU or the EU rules on public procurement contained in primary and secondary EU law—seems, in principle, to have substantially limited the degree of discretion of Member States to organise such large-scale SGEI.

On the other hand, there are details in the painting which are not totally clear to an external observer. As mentioned above, some of the conditions in the new rules—particularly the Framework—are drafted in a rather ambiguous manner, giving the Commission a degree of discretion. Depending on how the Commission interprets the principles contained in the new rules, the rigour referred to above could be much less than is first supposed.

It is to be hoped that these details and uncertainties will be resolved by the Commission's future decision-making practice. Only by observing how the Commission and Member States behave under the new rules will we be truly able to evaluate the impact of the new package on the provision of SGEI.

It is nevertheless important that, irrespective of how they are ultimately interpreted, the Commission applies the rules in a consistent and predictable way. After all, the Commission's main objective regarding SGEI has traditionally been to provide legal certainty, equal treatment and a reasonable balance for Member States, SGEI and the undertakings entrusted with their operation. This objective

---

[68] In visual art, the Latin expression *horror vacui* ('fear of empty space') means filling the entire surface of a work of art with detail.

seems even more important now given the current euro-scepticism of many national authorities and citizens.

There can be no doubt that the Commission has already taken an important step forward by adopting the package. Now, it faces an even more important challenge: to implement it in a reasonable and consistent manner.

References

Bishop S, Walker M (2010) The economics of EC competition law: concepts, applications and measurement. Sweet and Maxwell, London

Buendía Sierra JL (2008) Finding the right balance: state aid and services of general economic interest. In: EC State Aid Law: Liber Amicorum Francisco Santaolalla. Kluwer, The Hague

Buendía Sierra JL (2011) Writing straight with crooked lines: competition policy and services of general economic Interest in the Treaty of Lisbon. In: Biondi A, Eeckhout P (eds) European Union law after the Treaty of Lisbon. OUP, Oxford

Buendía Sierra JL, Muñoz de Juan M (2012) Some legal reflections on the Almunia package. In: Proceedings of the conference The reform of state aid rules on services of general economic interest from the 2005 Monti-Kroes package to the 2011 Almunia reform, Lexxion, Berlin

Szyszczak E (2011) Altmark assessed. In: Szyszczak E (ed) Research handbook on European state aid law. Edward Elgar, Cheltenham

Chapter 8
Financing Services of General Economic Interest: The European Commission's Economic Tests

James Kavanagh

Abstract The object of the revised SGEI package is to specify the conditions under which State aid for such services can be found to be compatible with Article 106(2) TFEU. Within the package, the revised SGEI Framework establishes a more prescriptive methodology for determining the compensation to the undertaking entrusted with offering the SGEI, as well as enhanced efficiency incentives. This chapter surveys the revised financial and economic tests for determining appropriate SGEI compensation, commenting on the theoretical basis and practical implementation of these tests.

Contents

The views expressed in this chapter are personal.

J. Kavanagh (✉)
Oxera Consulting Ltd, Park Central, 40/41 Park End St Oxford, Oxford OX1 1JD, UK
e-mail: James.Kavanagh@oxera.com

E. Szyszczak and J.W. van de Gronden (eds.), *Financing Services of General Economic Interest*, Legal Issues of Services of General Interest, DOI: 10.1007/978-90-6704-906-1_8, © T.M.C. ASSER PRESS, The Hague, The Netherlands, and the authors 2013

8.1 The Commission's Revised Economic Approach

In December 2011, the European Commission adopted a revised package of EU State aid rules for the assessment of public compensation for services of general economic interest (SGEI). The new SGEI package included a 'Communication',[1] which clarified basic concepts of State aid that are relevant for SGEI, a 'Decision'[2] and a 'Framework'.[3,4] SGEI have been defined by Member States in many sectors, including obligations on airlines to operate routes that are not commercially viable, an obligation to distribute post across a national territory at a uniform tariff, and the provision of private medical insurance at an affordable price. Other SGEI are found in areas such as gas, electricity and telecoms, all of which provide services that are considered 'essential' to consumers.

The objective of the revised SGEI package is to specify the conditions under which State aid for such services can be found to be compatible with Article 106(2) TFEU. The revised SGEI package exempts governments from the obligation to notify compensation for the running of social services, and for services receiving public compensation of less than €15 m a year.[5] In some of the relevant sectors, such as transport, SGEI compensation is also addressed in separate sector-specific rules.[6] The main focus of the revised SGEI Framework is to establish a more prescriptive methodology for determining the compensation to the undertaking 'entrusted' with offering the service on behalf of the public sector, as well as enhanced efficiency incentives. By exempting smaller amounts of SGEI compensation, and strengthening the assessment of larger awards of compensation, the overall package leads to a change in the way that the Commission will handle these cases. As the Vice President of the European Commission, Joaquín Almunia, has noted:

---

[1] European Commission, *Communication from the Commission on the application of the European Union State aid rules to compensation granted for the provision of services of general economic interest OJ* 2012 C 8/4.

[2] European Commission, *Commission Decision of 20 December 2011 on the application of Article 106(2) of the Treaty on the Functioning of the European Union to State aid in the form of public service compensation granted to certain undertakings entrusted with the operation of services of general economic interest, OJ* 2012 L7/3.

[3] European Commission, *Communication from the Commission, European Union framework for State aid in the form of public service compensation, OJ* 2012 C8/15.

[4] European Commission, 'State aid: Commission adopts new rules on services of general economic interest (SGEI)', Press Release IP/11/1571, 20 December 2012.

[5] Almunia, J. 'Reform of the State aid rules for Services of General Economic Interest (SGEI) and decisions on WestLB, Bank of Ireland and France Telecom', speech to Brussels press conference, 20 December 2011.

[6] Regulation (EC) No 1370/2007 of the European Parliament and of the Council of 23 October 2007 on public passenger transport services by rail and by road and repealing Council Regulations (EEC) Nos 1191/69 and 1107/70, *OJ* 2007 L 315/1. See the chapter by Maxian Rusche and Schmidt in this volume.

The new SGEI package follows three objectives: clarification, simplification, and a focus on services that receive big amounts of money and have a greater potential to distort the conditions of competition in the single market...my experience to date shows that the Commission is all too often asked to decide or arbitrate on small cases with little or no impact in the internal market. I believe there is a need to set priorities and use our resources to control the subsidies that have a real potential to distort competition in Europe.[7]

The controls on compensation to be adopted by the Commission (as with other mechanisms in State aid, such as Regulation 1370/2007, which provides similar rules in the public transport sector[8]) will require considerable economic analysis, such as:

– determining the costs and revenues of the undertaking with and without the obligation to provide the service;
– the allocation of costs between commercial and entrusted (subsidised) activities;
– establishing a benchmark rate of return ('reasonable profit'), against which the profitability of the entrusted party can be measured; and
– establishing how to incentivise and measure efficiency in service provision.

This chapter describes the approach that the Commission has determined in its revised SGEI Framework to each of the above areas. It is structured as follows: Section 8.2 describes the economic rationale for controlling SGEI compensation; Sect. 8.3 sets out the financial tests for appropriate compensation; Sect. 8.4 outlines the enhanced efficiency incentives to be included in SGEI contracts; Sect. 8.5 concludes.

8.2 The Rationale for Controlling SGEI Compensation

Governments require SGEI to be provided in order to fulfil certain policy objectives. One such objective might be the provision of a universal postal service, whereby sending a letter has the same price regardless of the distance it travels. Other SGEI examples include public service broadcasting, health insurance provision for the chronically sick, and ferry and air routes to remote islands.

The need for governments to define SGEI arises when the required services would not be provided by the market, which might be for two main reasons. First, the cost of provision exceeds the revenues. Second, the market does not provide such services at a socially acceptable (e.g. uniform) price. A 'reverse definition' of SGEI is given by the Commission in its SGEI Framework:

---

[7] Supra n 5.

[8] Supra n 6.

Member States cannot attach specific public service obligations to services that are already provided or can be provided satisfactorily and under conditions, such as price, objective quality characteristics, continuity and access to the service, consistent with the public interest, as defined by the State, by undertakings operating under normal market conditions.[9]

In other words, if the service can be provided by the market at a price and level of access that are compatible with the public interest, it is *not* an SGEI.

Having defined a service as being of general economic interest, the public sector needs to establish who is going to provide the service: itself, or a private sector party. Since, by definition, such services will be loss-making, if the government wants them to be provided by another party, it will need to subsidise the provider.

The purpose of then controlling SGEI compensation, or subsidy, is twofold. The first purpose is to avoid SGEI cross-subsidising commercial activities, which could distort competition in adjacent, non-SGEI markets. The second is to avoid overcompensation of the SGEI activity, which could waste taxpayers' money and implicitly is not the outcome expected under competitive conditions for the provision of SGEI (e.g., if SGEI contracts were systematically put out to competitive tender).

8.3 Financial Tests in the New SGEI Framework

As set out in the new SGEI Framework, the appropriate financial tests should ensure that the compensation method meets two objectives: first, 'the amount of compensation must not exceed what is necessary to cover the net cost of discharging the public service obligations, including a reasonable profit' (para 21); second, the method of compensation 'must introduce incentives for the efficient provision of SGEI of a high standard, unless [the Member States] can duly justify that it is not feasible or appropriate to do so' (para 39).

Ensuring these objectives requires a calculation of the appropriate net cost of provision of the SGEI and the level of reasonable profit. In calculating the costs and revenues, the Commission is open to using cost and revenues actually incurred, or those that are expected to be incurred, or a combination of the two; the choice depends on the efficiency incentives that the Member State wants to provide. Where expected costs are used, the cost estimates should incorporate the expected efficiencies over the lifetime of the entrustment (para 23).

---

[9] Supra n 3, para 13.

8.3.1 Calculating the Net Cost of Provision of the SGEI

The Commission's preference is that a 'net avoided cost methodology' be applied in order to determine the extent of compensation required under an entrustment, and that the methodology be based on a forward-looking assessment covering the lifetime of the contract between the state and the provider, which is described in the contract (the 'entrustment act' in the Commission's terminology).

The methodology envisaged is similar to Directives in the communications sector, and amounts to calculating ex ante 'the difference between the net cost for the provider of operating with the public service obligation and the net cost or profit for the same provider of operating without that obligation' (para 25).[10] In theory this involves envisaging the costs and revenues of a business operating purely in a competitive market without SGEI obligations, and comparing that hypothetical business with the actual one, which provides the SGEI envisaged under the entrustment act. For example, a ferry service operating to a holiday island might operate only during the summer months without government support, but is obliged by the government to operate all year to serve islanders. The new SGEI Framework would, in principle, require the government to compare the 'summer only' business plan with the 'year round' business plan. The net avoided cost is then the difference between net costs in the two business plans.

Applying this logic may require an element of judgement. While the Commission may reasonably expect that a business will understand which parts of its activities make certain levels of contribution to overheads, it is a difficult line to draw between what would, and what would not, be provided without an entrustment act. This is particularly the case where the obligations placed on an SGEI provider change over time, which is likely when government policy, or economic conditions, evolve to a significant extent. It is also problematic when a business runs a complex network, such as a national railway service, where it is difficult to envisage the counterfactual of that business operating without SGEI obligations.

Where it is not feasible or appropriate to apply the net avoided cost methodology, an alternative approach suggested by the Commission is what it calls the 'cost allocation methodology'. Under this approach, the net cost of provision is calculated as 'the difference between the costs and the revenues for a designated provider of fulfilling the public service obligations' (para 28). In calculating the costs, all costs necessary to operate the SGEI should be taken into account. This includes any investment cost (for e.g., infrastructure costs) and other direct costs necessary for the operation of the SGEI, as well as 'an appropriate contribution' to any indirect costs common to both the SGEI and to other activities of the entity being entrusted.

While the Commission suggests that the appropriate allocation of common costs is determined by reference to market prices for the use of the resources or the

---

[10] The net cost calculation should take into account the costs that the service provider is expected to avoid as well as the revenues it is expected not to receive, in the absence of the pso.

expected profits of the non-SGEI activity, it is open to other methodologies, as appropriate (para 31). In addition, where an undertaking is providing activities other than those required simply to deliver the SGEI, its accounts must show costs and revenues arising from the SGEI separately from those relating to the other activities.

8.3.2 Calculation of Reasonable Profit

The Commission requires that 'the amount of compensation must not exceed what is necessary to cover the net cost of discharging the public service obligations, including a reasonable profit' (para 21). In order to establish what is a 'reasonable' level of profit, two main issues need to be considered: how to measure profitability; and how to assess the appropriate benchmark against which to compare profitability.

The approach advocated by the Commission is to assess reasonable profits from an ex ante perspective (i.e based on forecasts), in order to provide appropriate efficiency incentives. The Commission's preference is to measure profitability using an internal rate of return (IRR) approach, in which the IRR is calculated over the lifetime of the entrustment. This is consistent with appropriate methods to assess economic profitability in competition cases more generally.[11] Alternative measures to assess profitability—return on equity (ROE), return on capital employed (ROCE), return on assets (ROA) or return on sales (ROS)—should only be used if 'duly justified' (para 34).

The advantage of these alternative measures is that they are based on more readily available accounting data. Hence they are often used in profitability measurement, despite their drawbacks.[12] The ROCE is calculated by dividing earnings before interest and taxes (EBIT) by total capital (i.e., debt and equity). The ROE employs the same data, but is calculated by dividing net earnings after tax by equity-funded capital employed. Figure 8.1 shows these accounting relationships.

Both the ROE and the ROCE involve measuring equity capital, either in isolation or as a component of total capital (equity plus debt). Where a business does not have equity capital, which is likely in the case of a state-owned entity, there are two options. First, a proxy for equity capital can be estimated from various items on the balance sheet, depending on which of the items are akin to equity capital and total capital in a privately owned company. Alternatively, a proxy for equity capital can be estimated by first considering the capital structure of comparator companies, and then applying this hypothetical capital structure to the SGEI undertaking.

---

[11] Oxera (2003).

[12] The drawbacks are described in Niels et al. 2011, p. 156.

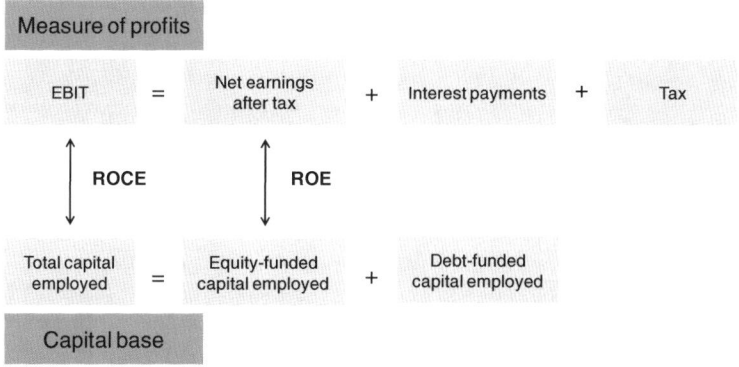

Fig. 8.1 ROCE and ROE. *Source* Oxera

8.3.3 Benchmarks for Profitability

8.3.3.1 Safe Harbour

In assessing the appropriate benchmark against which to compare observed profitability, the Commission draws on regulatory and financial economics. It notes that benchmarking reasonable profit under the SGEI entrustment should take into account the level of risk, which 'depends on the sector concerned, the type of service and the characteristics of the compensation mechanism' (para 33). However, it also provides a 'safe harbour' rate of return, which does not account for risk:

> A rate of return on capital that does not exceed the relevant swap rate plus a premium of 100 basis points is regarded as reasonable in any event (para 36)

The relevant swap rate is viewed by the Commission as an appropriate rate of return for a non-risky investment.[13] By providing this safe harbour, the Commission seems to be aiming to balance the need to ensure an economically robust benchmark with the practical considerations of providing clear guidance.

Since the swap rate safe harbour takes no account of risk, a more robust approach for a benchmark is to measure the cost of capital for the entity providing an SGEI, or to draw a benchmark rate of return from evidence on returns achieved by comparator firms providing similar services. Given the general scarcity of evidence on the financial performance of SGEI contracts awarded in competitive tenders, there are practical problems with applying the comparator firms approach. In some cases it may be more transparent and robust to rely on an estimate of the cost of capital as the competitive benchmark. This fits naturally with the standard approach to assessing profitability in competition cases, where it is normal to compare a rate of profit earned against a cost of capital benchmark.[14]

---

[13] Supra n 2, para 19.

[14] Oxera (2003).

8.3.3.2 Cost of Capital as a Benchmark

The cost of capital is an estimate of the price a company must pay to raise the capital that it has employed—i.e. it is the return that private investors would require if they invested in the company. The standard measure of this is the weighted average cost of capital (WACC). This is the average of expected rates of return to debt and equity, weighted by the relative proportions of debt and equity in a company's capital structure.

WACC is straightforward to calculate for a company listed on a stock market and with debt that is publicly traded. For a non-listed company—such as one that is state-owned—the approach is to find a suitable set of listed comparators. For example, if the alleged aid beneficiary is a television broadcaster, it is possible to estimate the average rate of return on equity that investors require for listed European broadcasters. Although this exercise depends on finding comparators, and is therefore subject to the same practical problem of identifying suitable comparator firms, the measurement issue is less acute since the cost of capital takes data on comparators as only one input among several.

Table 8.1 shows how a cost of capital calculation is performed. In this example a comparison is made between the cost of capital for a relatively low-risk firm, a power generator, and for a higher risk firm, an airline. Inputs for this calculation are shown in the shaded boxes, and outputs in un-shaded boxes. Some of the detail behind the calculation is given in the text below the table. The cost of capital for the airline is considerably higher than for the utility, a result that is driven by the differences in the debt premium (i.e. the return demanded by creditors to the company over a risk-free rate), and by differences in the equity beta (which is a measure of the extent to which the company's returns follow the stock market). For a utility business, returns will tend to be fairly stable through time, yielding a low equity beta; for an airline, returns will tend to be more sensitive to wider trends in the economy, yielding a higher equity beta.

The risk-free rate represents the cost of 'risk-free' borrowing, which is usually approximated by redemption yields on government bonds (which normally, but not always, have very limited risk). The debt premium and the equity beta capture the riskiness of the company's activities, while the equity risk premium (ERP) captures a premium that investors, on average, require from investing in equities as opposed to risk-free assets. A multiple of the equity beta and the ERP captures the market risk premium of a particular company.

For state-owned and most other non-listed companies, the risk inherent in equity cannot be estimated directly. Instead, the approach is to identify relevant publicly listed comparator companies, and to estimate the equity beta for these as an approximation of the equity beta of the company in question. Similarly, the cost of debt can be obtained from yields on outstanding debt or credit default swaps of comparator companies. All of this information is entered into the WACC formula, which is worked out as follows:

Table 8.1 Example of a cost of capital calculation

INPUT		
OUTPUT		
	'Less risky' eg, power generator	'More risky' eg, airline
Cost of debt		
Risk-free rate (%)	3.00	3.00
Debt premium (%)	2.00	4.00
Cost of debt (%)	5.00	7.00
Cost of equity		
Risk-free rate (%)	3.00	3.00
Asset beta	0.30	1.00
Gearing (%)	60.0	60.0
Equity beta	0.75	2.50
Equity risk premium	4.50	4.50
Corporate tax rate (%)	28.0	28.0
Cost of equity (%)	6.38	14.25
WACC		
Pre-tax WACC (%)	6.54	12.12

Source Oxera

cost of debt = risk-free rate + debt premium
equity beta = asset beta/(1−gearing)
cost of equity = risk-free rate + (equity beta × equity risk premium)
pre-tax cost of equity = cost of equity/(1−corporate tax rate)
pre-tax weighted average cost of capital = cost of debt × gearing + ((1−gearing) × pre-tax cost of equity)

For the airline's cost of capital, we therefore have the following calculation:

cost of debt = 3 % risk-free rate + 4 % debt premium = 7 %
equity beta = 1.00 asset beta/(1 − 0.60 gearing) = 2.50
cost of equity = 3 % risk-free rate + (2.50 equity beta × 4.5 % equity risk premium) = 14.25 %
pre-tax cost of equity = 14.25 % cost of equity/(1−corporate tax rate of 28 %) = 19.79 %
pre-tax weighted average cost of capital = 7 % cost of debt × 0.60 gearing + 19.79 % pre-tax cost of equity × (1 − 0.60 gearing) = 12.12 %

If the state is a pure equity investor, the appropriate required rate of return is the cost of equity, rather than the WACC. Conversely, if the state provides only guaranteed debt, the appropriate rate of return is the cost of debt.

8.4 Efficiency Incentives

In paras 37 and 38 of the SGEI Framework, the Commission expects that the nature of the compensation mechanism will have a considerable bearing on the rate of return that the service provider will earn over the lifetime of the entrustment. It contrasts instances where 'compensation takes the form of a fixed lump sum payment covering expected net costs and a reasonable profit' (para 37) with a situation where 'the *ex post* net costs are essentially compensated in full' (para 38). In the former, the Commission clearly expects risk to be higher, and for this risk to be rewarded with a higher return (i.e. greater compensation, and a higher level of 'reasonable profit'). The choice of compensation mechanism also affects efficiency incentives on the SGEI provider during the entrustment, to which we now turn.

The Commission requires that in devising a method of compensation, Member States must introduce incentives 'for the efficient provision of SGEI of a high standard, unless they can duly justify that it is not feasible or appropriate to do so'.[15] The Commission discourages the ex post provision of compensation, as this does not create efficiency incentives for an undertaking providing an SGEI. Specifically, the Commission expects that the ex post provision of compensation should be 'strictly limited to cases where the Member State is able to justify that it is not feasible or appropriate to take into account productive efficiency and to have a contract design which gives incentives to achieve efficiency gains'.[16]

The Commission does allow Member States some discretion in the design of efficiency incentives to suit the specificity of each case or sector, and provides examples of how efficiency gains can be incorporated in the entrustment act:

...Member States can define upfront a fixed compensation level which anticipates and incorporates the efficiency gains that the undertaking can be expected to make over the lifetime of the entrustment act.

... Alternatively, Member States can define productive efficiency targets in the entrustment act whereby the level of compensation is made dependent upon the extent to which the targets have been met. If the undertaking does not meet the objectives, the compensation should be reduced following a calculation method specified in the entrustment act. In contrast, if the undertaking exceeds the objectives, the compensation should be increased following a method specified in the entrustment act. Rewards linked to productive efficiency gains are to be set at a level such as to allow balanced sharing of those gains between the undertaking and the Member State and/or the users.[17]

The 'fixed compensation' option outlined by the Commission has the economic characteristics (and, therefore, incentive properties) of a price cap. Such an arrangement would provide incentives for the SGEI provider to find more efficient ways of delivering the required level of service over the course of the entrustment.

---

[15] Supra n 3, para 39.

[16] Supra n 3, para 38.

[17] Supra n 3, paras 40–41.

The Commission requires at the same time that efficiency delivered during the entrustment should not come at the expense of quality of service.[18]

The second option, using 'productive efficiency targets', implies some variability in remuneration depending on the extent of outperformance relative to expectations. Depending on the method of compensation, there is a risk that, as the end of an entrustment approaches, the SGEI provider has limited incentives to improve efficiency, since the rewards will be considerably diminished. The Commission's suggestion of linking compensation more explicitly to the delivery of efficiency targets (if efficiency performance can be measured objectively) might go some way towards the aim of maintaining the strength of incentives throughout the entrustment period.

8.5 Conclusion

The discussion above has highlighted that the Commission's revised Framework employs a strengthened set of economic tests with the purpose of ensuring that SGEI providers earn only a reasonable profit and have strong incentives to deliver efficiency and innovation. The reform brings a greater degree of European Commission control over SGEI compensation, and with it an increased obligation on Member States to justify the financial terms of large SGEI contracts.

The new SGEI Framework will require competent authorities making major entrustments to ensure that SGEI provision is characterised by reasonable profitability, incentives for efficiency and transparent accounting. To a certain extent the Commission is encouraging a form of economic regulation in relation to SGEI provision—indeed, the Commission refers to compensation assessment relying 'where appropriate, on the expertise of sector regulators' (para 23). It remains to be seen whether the relationship between contracting parties in all Member States can easily comply with this more sophisticated model for SGEI compensation. Potentially the compliance obligation will encourage more Member States to use competitive tenders for SGEI contracts, with the result that those contracts may be deemed to fall under the *Altmark* criteria (no State aid) rather than the SGEI Framework (compatible State aid).[19]

References

Niels G, Jenkins H, Kavanagh J (2011) Economics for competition lawyers. OUP, Oxford
Oxera (2003) Assessing profitability in competition policy analysis. OFT Economic discussion paper 6 July

---

[18] Supra n 3, para 43.

[19] CJEU, Case C-280/00 *Altmark Trans GmbH and Regierungspräsidium Magdeburg v Nahverkehrsgesellschaft Altmark GmbH ('Altmark')* [2003] *ECR* I-7747.

Chapter 9
The Commission's Modernisation Agenda for Procurement and SGEI

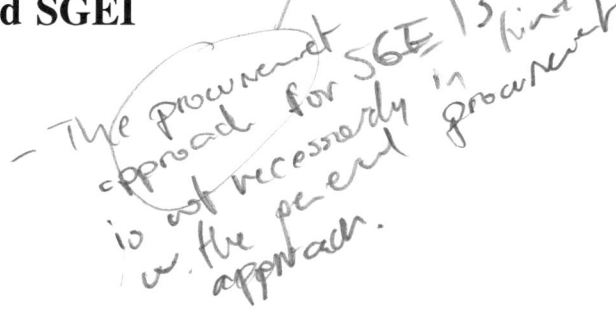

Albert Sanchez Graells

Abstract This chapter focuses on the recent novelties introduced by the 'Almunia' Package in the regulation of activities at the intersection of the EU rules on State aid, public procurement and the financing of SGEI. Taking the uncertainties left by the fourth *Altmark* condition as the point of departure, this chapter describes and critically appraises the position of the European Commission regarding the use of procurement procedures as a device to exclude the existence of State aid or, in case it exists, to contribute to its compatibility with the internal market and, at any rate, as a mechanism of control of contracting entities' 'market' behaviour. This chapter also stresses that there may be a disconnection between the two legs of the modernisation agenda, in that the reform of public procurement rules currently underway may diminish the effectiveness of the recent SGEI 'Almunia' reform or, in some instances, even be in frontal clash with some of its basic assumptions—which may call for a major revision of a system of oversight of public expenditure that is in crisis.

Contents

A. Sanchez Graells (✉)
Law School, University of Hull, Hull HU6 7RX, UK
e-mail: A.Sanchez-Graells@hull.ac.uk

E. Szyszczak and J.W. van de Gronden (eds.), *Financing Services of General Economic Interest*, Legal Issues of Services of General Interest, DOI: 10.1007/978-90-6704-906-1_9,
© T.M.C. Asser Press, The Hague, The Netherlands, and the authors 2013

9.1 Introduction

The aim of this chapter is to critically appraise the Commission's modernisation agenda for public procurement and services of general economic interest (SGEI) in view of the still unresolved questions that the interplay of State aid control, the award of public contracts for the provision of SGEI and the financing of SGEI raises—which were only partially tackled and insufficiently answered by the European Court of Justice in the *Altmark*[1] case,[2] and which have now been at the spotlight of the reforms introduced by the European Commission through the 'Almunia Package'.[3]

---

[1] Case C-280/00 *Altmark Trans GmbH* v *Nahverkehrsgesellschaft Altmark GmbH* [2003] *ECR* I-7747.

[2] For further commentary on the relevance of *Altmark* from a public procurement perspective, see the rest of the contributions to this book and, particularly, Clarke's. See also Schnelle 2002; Chérot 2007, pp. 196–202; Dethlefsen 2007; Szyszczak 2007, pp. 193–194. See also Arrowsmith 2005, p. 224; Bartosch 2002; Bovis 2005; Buendía Sierra 2008, pp. 210–214 and Karayigit 2009. With reference to a broader analytical framework, see also Sauter and Schepel 2009, pp. 189–191, 207–209. More recently, see Szyszczak 2011 and Szyszczak 2013.

[3] The expression 'Almunia Package' refers to the instruments adopted by the European Commission between December 2011 and April 2012 for the modernisation of SGEI rules. These are: (1) Communication from the Commission to the European Parliament, the Council, the European Economic and Social Committee and the Committee of the Regions, *A Quality Framework for Services of General Interest in Europe*, Brussels, 20.12.2011, COM(2011) 900 final (the 'SGEI Quality Framework'); (2) the Commission Decision of 20 December 2011 on the application of Article 106(2) of the Treaty on the Functioning of the European Union to State aid in the form of public service compensation granted to certain undertakings entrusted with the operation of services of general economic interest [*OJ* 2012/21/EU] (the 'SGEI Compensation Decision'); (3) Communication from the Commission on the application of the European Union State aid rules to compensation granted for the provision of services of general economic interest [*OJ* 2012/C 8/02] (the 'SGEI Compensation Communication'); (4) Communication from the Commission— *European Union framework for State aid in the form of public service compensation (2011)* [*OJ* 2012/C 8/03] ('2011 SGEI Framework'); and (5) Commission Regulation (EU) No 360/2012 of 25 April 2012 on the application of Articles 107 and 108 of the Treaty on the Functioning of the European Union to *de minimis* aid granted to undertakings providing services of general economic interest [*OJ* 2012/L 114/8] (the 'SGEI de minimis Regulation').

As indicated by the Commission, the *SGEI Compensation Communication* clarifies key concepts related to State aid for SGEIs, while the *SGEI Compensation Decision* and the *2011 SGEI*

The main objective in this chapter is to adopt a 'public procurement perspective' and to see whether the logic behind the ECJ and the Commission's use of procurement procedures as a device to exclude the existence of State aid or, in case it exists, to contribute to its compatibility with the internal market is consistent with current trends in public procurement reform.[4] To that aim, the open issues that the so-called fourth *Altmark* condition left unanswered will be shortly revisited (Sect. 9.2) and will be followed by a critical review of the procurement-related rules and criteria included in the 'Almunia Package' (Sect. 9.3). The analysis will also include the potential inconsistencies between the new SGEI rules and the proposed amendments to the EU public procurement Directives (Sect. 9.4). Finally, as a conclusion, it will be of interest to critically appraise the consequences of trying to use public procurement as a mechanism of control of contracting entities' 'market' behaviour—i.e as a device to unburden the Commission in its monitoring tasks of SGEI financing (Sect. 9.5).

9.2 The Unfinished Business of Supervising SGEI Procurement and Financing After *Altmark*

Even if the *Altmark* case was a significant development in the clarification of the relevance of public procurement procedures in the selection of SGEI providers and, more particularly, in the determination of the amount of their compensation that was covered by the 'public mission exception' in Article 106(2) TFEU[5]; the laconic and diverging references that the ECJ made to the use of procurement procedures left some questions unanswered[6] (some of which have still not been expressly addressed, either in subsequent case law or in the 'Almunia Package').

Amongst the several requirements for the inexistence of State aid in any scheme for SGEI compensation, the ECJ made reference to public procurement procedures in the fourth *Altmark* condition, in the following terms:

(Footnote 3 continued)

Framework specify the conditions under which State aid in the form of public service compensation is compatible with the TFEU. The *de minimis* Regulation establishes a threshold below which compensation is deemed no aid.

[4] EU public procurement rules are currently under reform. The European Commission published proposals for new substantive public procurement Directives in December 2011, which are currently being negotiated and should be adopted before the end of 2012. All information regarding reform proposals is at http://ec.europa.eu/internal_market/publicprocurement/modernising_rules/reform_proposals_en.htm (last accessed 28 May 2012).

[5] On the scope of this exception, see Buendía Sierra 1999, pp. 271–360; Maillo 2007, pp. 604–612; Prosser 2005, pp. 132–141; and Sauter and Schepel 2009, 164–192. *Cf.* Baquero Cruz 2005, pp. 209 and 212.

[6] For some additional discussion on the lack of clarity of the *Altmark* conditions and the connection with public procurement rules, see Hervey 2011, pp. 204–210; and Schweitzer 2011, pp. 28–42.

... where the undertaking which is to discharge public service obligations, in a specific case, is not chosen *pursuant to a public procurement procedure which would allow for the selection of the tenderer capable of providing those services at the least cost to the community...*[7]

However, in its final drafting of the conditions and in the operative part of the *Altmark* judgment, the ECJ dropped (or *rectius*, left implicit) the requirement for the procurement procedure to '*allow for the selection of the tenderer capable of providing those services at the least cost to the community*'. Indeed, in the final drafting, the 'lowest cost for the community' (or, indirectly, the minimisation of public expense, or maximisation of value for money) is not an express requirement:

... where the undertaking which is to discharge public service obligations is not chosen in a public procurement procedure, the level of compensation needed [must be] determined on the basis of an analysis of the costs which a typical undertaking, well run and adequately provided with [material] means [...] so as to be able to meet the necessary public service requirements, would have incurred in discharging those obligations, taking into account the relevant receipts and a reasonable profit for discharging the obligations.[8]

Therefore, even if there is a relatively clear hint that the main purpose for the use of public procurement procedures in the selection of the undertaking entrusted with the SGEI is to achieve competitive cost advantages, the requirement seems to be oriented towards excluding the existence of excessive compensation because the consideration/compensation that will be paid by the contracting entity has been *competed for* in the tender—hence, not necessarily oriented towards ensuring absolute minimum (ideal) costs, but rather the selection of the most efficient option actually available in the market. Such 'most efficient actual option' must not necessarily involve 'least cost to the community' in absolute terms (i.e if compared against a theoretical, ideal standard), but 'lowest available competitive cost to the community'.[9]

This seemed to be (implicitly) supported by the European General Court in the subsequent *BUPA* case, where it interpreted that:

---

[7] Case C-280/00 *Altmark* at para 93, emphasis added. This is the wording chosen by the Commission in its design of the 'Modernisation Package', and as such is presented in the *SGEI Compensation Decision*, at recital (4) and in the *2011 SGEI Framework* at fn 2.

[8] Case C-280/00 *Altmark* at para 95, emphasis added. See also operative part of the Judgment.

[9] Along the same lines, see the contribution by Buendía Sierra and Panero Rivas to this book, where they indicate clearly that the purpose is not necessarily to achieve a result derived from a perfect competition model but rather that '*if the selection is carried out correctly it should guarantee that the most efficient option is selected (both in terms of price and quality)*' (emphasis added). Such most efficient option must not necessarily involve 'least cost to the community' in absolute terms (ie if compared against a theoretical, ideal standard), but 'lowest available competitive cost to the community'. That is particularly true, at least, in certain sectors such as public service broadcasting, where the Commission found that '*it was possible for an undertaking to receive State aid which exceeded the costs of an ideal, efficient undertaking, without there being overcompensation to invoke the State aid rules*' Decision N46/2007 – *BBC Digital Curriculum*, of 1 October 2003; see the comment by Szyszczak 2011, p. 307.

... the purpose of the fourth *Altmark* condition [is to ensure] *that the compensation provided for [... does] not entail the possibility of offsetting any costs that might result from inefficiency.*[10]

In my opinion, this understanding of the fourth *Altmark* condition would be consistent with the basic foundations of public procurement rules, which are oriented towards ensuring that contracting authorities benefit from efficient market conditions set through effective competition, but not necessarily obtain absolute (ideal) best contract conditions—since value for money is a goal or aspiration of public procurement rules, but not a *conditio sine qua non*, nor a guarantee.[11]

Consequently, reading an absolute requirement for 'lowest cost' in the fourth *Altmark* condition seems highly contentious and at odds with the purpose and reality of public procurement rules.[12] In my opinion, therefore, it seems clear that a less restrictive approach, with a looser link to (absolute) 'least cost' implications can be extracted from the final findings of the ECJ in its reply to the preliminary questions put in *Altmark*, where *the only requirement is that the undertaking which is going to discharge public service obligations is chosen in a properly designed and adequately run public procurement procedure aimed at avoiding economic inefficiency through competition* (or, alternatively where that is at all possible, that the remuneration for the discharge of the public service obligations is determined against the benchmark of an efficient typical undertaking, well run and adequately provided with the relevant material means).

Therefore, the interpretation of the breadth of the reference to procurement in the fourth *Altmark* condition is not a trivial issue, for the array of public procurement procedures and decisions that allow for an effective, undistorted competition for the contract goes well beyond the public procurement instruments specifically or

---

[10] Case T-289/03 *British United Provident Association Ltd (BUPA) and Others v Commission of the European Communities* [2008] *ECR* II-81, at para 249 (emphasis added). Along those lines, with an emphasis on the efficiency of the SGEI provider, see Santamato and Pesaresi 2004. In my view, however, the condition should be better understood in the terms of Opinion of Advocate General Jacobs of 30 April 2002 in Case C-126/01, *GEMO* at para 122, where he clearly explained that the purpose is basically to ensure that, by running adequate procurement procedures, the terms of the contract reflect normal market conditions.

[11] In this regard, it is important to stress that 'value for money' is not even seen as one of the main goals of the EU public procurement rules by main academic commentators. See Arrowsmith 2002, who clearly holds '*that it is not an objective of the directives to ensure value for money in procurement*'—as reiterated recently in Arrowsmith 2012, p. 74. Without going that far, I have personally indicated that competition (ie value for money) and efficiency of the procurement processes are key goals of public procurement regulations, and that even if '*public procurement is not designed to prevent distortions of competition between undertakings*', '*the attainment of the competition goal requires developing a pro-competitive public procurement system that avoids publicly-generated distortions of competition*'—which, however, do not require an intervention in the market of a quasi-regulatory nature to impose perfect competition, since it would result in artificially created, unsustainable competition. For discussion on the goals of procurement, and further references, see Sanchez Graells 2011, pp. 97–110.

[12] Again, in substantially coincidental terms, see the contribution by Buendía Sierra and Panero Rivas.

narrowly designed to achieve minimum or lowest cost.[13] Therefore, a strict reading of the fourth *Altmark* condition would exclude many public procurement tools from the generally available options for contracting entities looking to outsource SGEIs.

Such ambiguities and scope for interpretation of the *Altmark* ruling generated significant legal uncertainty, nonetheless because the European Commission has tended to apply changing standards, depending on the specific circumstances of the case and on the economic sector concerned. Indeed, the analysis of the 'public procurement requirement' moved rather quickly from a detailed, overall material assessment of whether procurement procedures actually allowed for the selection of the tenderer capable of providing those services at the least cost to the community (and, hence, excluded the existence of State aid);[14] towards a more formalistic, box-ticking approach to the control of procurement procedures, where (formal) compliance with procurement legislation was considered to set a (hard to rebut) presumption of inexistence of State aid.[15] In this regard, the further development of the Commission's policy regarding the interplay of public procurement and SGEIs in the 'Almunia Package' was impatiently awaited.

9.3 The Commission's Modernisation Agenda for Procurement and SGEI

In order to provide legal certainty and to clarify the applicable rules to the financing of SGEI and, in particular, its procurement-related dimension, the European Commission has recently adopted a number of hard and soft law instruments (the 'Almunia Package') and is pushing for the further modernisation of public procurement rules. As indicated in the *SGEI Quality Framework*—which sets the architecture of the modernisation agenda for procurement and SGEI—it encompasses:

---

[13] Indeed, if properly designed, all public procurement devices can even be made pro-competitive and ensure effective competition for the contracts, as discussed at length in Sanchez Graells 2011, pp. 227–369.

[14] See Decision N 475/2003—*Ireland, Public Service Obligation in respect of new electricity generation capacity for security of supply*, of 16 December 2003 at para 57, where it was stressed that '*the Commission has to verify whether the characteristics of the procurement procedure at stake are such as to actually "allow for the selection of the tenderer capable of providing those services at the least cost to the community". This is a material analysis which is different and goes beyond the mere respect of the applicable public procurement rules*' (emphasis in the original).

[15] See Decision N 46/2007—*Welsh Public Sector Network Scheme*, of 30 May 2007 at para 18, where the Commission changes approach and is satisfied that '*The procurement procedure is compliant with the public procurement directives and suitable for achieving best value for money* [because] *the award is made in line with the national legislation transposing the EU procurement directives*'. See also Tosics and Gaál 2008, p. 18: '*… in the case of pure procurement transactions, the use of a competitive procurement procedure which is in line with the EU public procurement rules and thus suitable to achieve best value for money, i.e. fair market price for the goods, services or infrastructure purchased, creates a presumption that no State aid will be involved to the economic operator concerned.*'.

... reforms of two key sets of rules - for State aid for services of general economic interest and for public procurement - both of which will increase flexibility and simplification for Member States when providing these services. These reforms also aim at increasing consistency between both policies and *to deliver greater assurance to stakeholders who fully comply with the public procurement rules that, under certain conditions, they also fulfil the relevant State aid requirement under the Altmark judgment*. This should provide more legal certainty and simplification to public authorities and undertakings.[16]

Such a modernisation agenda is clearly driven by the understanding of the fourth *Altmark* condition by the European Commission, which permeates all documents in the 'Almunia Package'. In short, its understanding of the procurement requirement in *Altmark* has been clearly spelled out:

Based on the case law of the Court of Justice, *a public procurement procedure only excludes* the existence of State aid where it allows for the selection of the tenderer capable of providing the service at "the least cost to the community".[17]

And, in even more detailed terms, the European Commission has generally indicated that:

... full compliance with *open or restricted public procurement procedures awarded on the basis of either the lowest price or, under certain conditions, the most economically advantageous tender* means that the contract is awarded at the "least cost to the community" as required by the Court as one of the conditions for excluding the existence of State aid.[18]

In my opinion, confronting the fourth *Altmark* condition with the Commission's reading, two main areas of concern can be readily identified. Firstly and for the reasons given above (*supra* Sect. 9.2), in such literal terms this reading seems unnecessarily restrictive regarding the requirement of 'least cost to the community' and the acceptable award criteria, since the Commission seems to be putting a strong emphasis on cost-related aspects of the provision of SGEIs and restricting the potential for taking other dimensions of SGEI provision into consideration in the award of contracts (*infra* Sect. 9.3.3).[19]

---

[16] *SGEI Quality Framework*, p. 3 (emphasis added).

[17] *SGEI Compensation Communication*, at para 65 (emphasis added).

[18] *SGEI Quality Framework*, p. 6 (emphasis added). However, I tend to agree with the scepticism shown by Buendía Sierra and Panero Rivas in this book, where they clearly state that '*willingness to accept award criteria other than those that are purely economic is somewhat surprising given the strict economic criteria that underpin the whole package*'. My impression is that the European Commission retains significant discretion to interpret the 'certain conditions' under which the most economically advantageous tender award criterion is acceptable.

[19] Which seems to imply that cost factors should control the award of public contracts in this area (over quality concerns)—whereas in other parts of the 'Almunia Package', non-cost concerns are claimed to be encouraged. *Cf. SGEI Quality Framework*, p. 7, where it is expressly emphasised that the reform of the rules on public procurement and concessions try to '*encourage a quality approach*', or that the reform '*will also help to ensure that contracts are not awarded on the basis of the lowest price only but adequately reflect increased environmental and societal considerations*'.

Secondly, even if initially the Commission's position does not necessarily exclude that public procurement procedures other than open and restricted can be considered suitable to ensure that the contract is awarded at the 'least cost to the community'; it can easily be argued that, with no explanation and for no good reason, the Commission's position would be (actually and implicitly) excluding the possibility to comply with the fourth *Altmark* condition in cases of procurement below EU thresholds (where no specific procedure is mandated at all and, therefore, represents procurement potentially unregulated, depending on the applicable national rules);[20] or in cases where procedures other than open or restricted are lawfully available to (and functionally preferable for) contracting entities, such as the competitive dialogue (on this, see more *infra* Sect. 9.3.2).

Further than that, at the same time, such orientation would perpetuate the highly formalistic, box-ticking approach adopted by the Commission concerning the actual conditions of the contracts awarded (particularly their 'consideration') and their potential implications in terms of (disguised) State aid.[21] By focusing (solely) on the choice of procedure and award criteria, the Commission is concentrating on very specific characteristics of the procurement process that do not necessarily ensure actual competition for the contract (which could be prevented or distorted by rules on past experience, biased technical specifications, excessive financial standing requirements, or a large number of other factors). Moreover, it is signalling a preferred tender design choice that implies a very rigid procedure and evaluation and award processes—which is not necessarily consistent (or, rather, is in clear contrast) with the basic objectives of public procurement reform: namely, simplification and flexibility (on this, see *infra* Sect. 9.4).

As we will briefly analyse in the following sections, the position of the European Commission in the more specific guidance offered in the *SGEI Compensation Communication* offers further reasons for concern and makes it doubtful that its orientation can either help to ensure that the entrustment and financing of SGEIs is conducted in a practical and efficient manner, or guarantee consistency with public procurement reform (as we shall see *infra* Sect. 9.4).[22] The *SGEI Compensation Communication* is the *clef de voûte* of the 'Almunia Package', as it serves the purpose of specifying the operational requirements that the Commission has set for an SGEI scheme that exceeds the *de minimis*

---

[20] On the issue of below-thresholds procurement, see Risvig Hansen 2012 and, for a comparative perspective, the collective book on the same topic edited by Caranta and Dragos (eds) 2012.

[21] For a critique, and a claim for a more substantive, material appraisal of procurement procedures to exclude the existence of State aid, see Sanchez Graells 2012.

[22] Similarly, Merola 2011; Sauter 2012; Sinnaeve 2012 and Buendía Sierra and Muñoz de Juan 2012.

thresholds to directly benefit from the *Altmark exemption*.[23] Therefore, understanding its shortcomings and rigidities seems highly relevant from a practical point of view, and may help anticipate areas of future litigation where the Commission may not be supported by the EU Courts.

9.3.1 The Discharge of Public Procurement Obligations as a Misunderstood Requirement

Even if all documents in the 'Almunia Package' are careful to indicate that they do not alter in any manner the general obligations derived from the EU public procurement rules—i.e, that they apply without prejudice of the requirements imposed by Union law in the field of procurement—one can wonder whether that is the case. A critical reading of the documents shows how *there is a significant push for an 'expanded application' of public procurement rules in full* (even when they are not directly applicable), *particularly in view of the 'preferred route' approach to procurement that the 'Almunia Package' shows* vis-à-vis the alternative means of compliance with the fourth *Altmark* condition (that is, a benchmark appraisal against a theoretical efficient SGEI supplier). This can clearly be seen in the *SGEI Compensation Communication*, where it is stated that:

> The *simplest way* for public authorities to meet the fourth Altmark criterion is to conduct an open, transparent and non-discriminatory public procurement procedure in line with [Directives 2004/17 and 2004/18 ... Moreover,] the conduct of such a public procurement procedure is often a mandatoy requirement under existing Union rules. [...] Also in cases where it is not a legal requirement, an open, transparent and non-discriminatory public procurement procedure is an appropriate method to compare different potential offers and set the compensation so as to exclude the presence of aid.[24]

Such an approach to the use of public procurement as a device to exclude State aid can be misleading, since it presents the discharge of public procurement obligations as an advantage that contracting entities can benefit from (at their discretion)—whereas the conduct of procurement procedures that ensure the effectiveness of the Treaty principles is not optional, but a mandatory requirement under EU law even when the EU procurement Directives are not, or are only

---

[23] Buendía Sierra and Panero Rivas advance a coincidental analytical approach under the new rules, where they suggest evaluating whether non *de minimis* measures can benefit from the *Altmark* criteria as specified by the Commission in the new Communication before proceeding to their analysis under the *SGEI Compensation Decision* and the *2011 SGEI Framework*.

[24] *SGEI Compensation Communication*, at paras 63 and 64.

partially applicable.[25] Therefore, it is not the easiest way to meet the fourth *Altmark* condition, but the only way that contracting entities can meet their general obligations under EU public procurement law. Moreover, it suggests that the European Commission favours the full subjection of SGEI tendering to the rules of the EU public procurement Directives and the national rules that transpose them, but only in the specific terms of the *SGEI Compensation Communication* (which the Commission intends to amend once new Union rules on public procurement have been adopted, in order to clarify the relevance for State aid purposes of the use of the procedures foreseen in those new rules, *infra* 9.4).[26] Therefore, not any type of procurement-compliant procedure will suffice to (simply) benefit from the *Altmark* exemption, but only those tailored to the very restrictive guidelines of the *SGEI Compensation Communication* (that we will review *infra* Sects. 9.3.2– 9.3.4).

In my view, the position of the Commission in the *2011 SGEI Framework* for those cases where SGEI compensation does not meet the criteria in the *SGEI Compensation Communication* has a similar defect in the way it conceptualises the relationship between public procurement compliance and the existence of State aid.[27] The *2011 SGEI Framework* states:

> Aid will be considered compatible with the internal market on the basis of Article 106(2) of the Treaty *only where the responsible authority*, when entrusting the provision of the service to the undertaking in question, *has complied or commits to comply with the applicable Union rules in the area of public procurement. This includes any requirements of transparency, equal treatment and non-discrimination resulting directly from the Treaty and, where applicable, secondary Union law.* Aid that does not comply with such rules and requirements is considered to affect the development of trade to an extent that would be contrary to the interests of the Union within the meaning of Article 106(2) of the Treaty.[28]

Even if the wording of the *2011 SGEI Framework* is clearer in presenting the non-discretionary obligation to comply with primary and secondary EU procurement law, the consequences that it attaches to non-compliance can create a circular test. If compliance with EU procurement rules ensures meeting the fourth *Altmark* criterion (i.e, no State aid) and non-compliance with EU procurement rules (primary and/or secondary, where applicable) determines that the SGEI scheme cannot benefit from Article 106(2) TFUE; then, the analysis seems limited to

---

[25] Again, on the mandatory application of the general principles of TFEU to all procurement activities and the positive obligations that it implies, see Risvig Hansen 2012 *in totum*. Regarding the type of arrangements that must be considered a 'contract' and, therefore, subjected to procurement rules, see Skovgaard Ølykke 2011. *Cf.* with Clarke's concluding remarks in his contribution to this book, where he considers that '*the contracting authority will need to choose between implementing a public procurement exercise and adopting the more subjective compensation benchmarking mechanism when considering the financing of the* [SGEI]'. In my view, in most cases, it will not be optional at all.

[26] *SGEI Compensation Communication*, at para 63 and fn 88.

[27] For a similar criticism, see Geradin 2012, pp. 5–7.

[28] *2011 SGEI Framework* at para 19 (emphasis added).

whether procurement rules where complied with or not. Non-compliance will imply the double, simultaneous breach of procurement and SGEI rules, while compliance with EU public procurement rules would be a safeguard for the application of the SGEI rules—as long as the other *Altmark* conditions are met, which seems relatively easy (inasmuch as the terms of the tender and the contract are clear regarding the definition of the SGEI as the contractual object, the conditions of the entrustment and the design of the compensation mechanism).

As already mentioned in passing, this tends to perpetuate the very formalistic approach adopted by the European Commission in the analysis of public procurement as a tool to grant disguised State aid.[29] According to the Commission's practice, compliance with the EU public procurement rules in the tendering of a contract that would otherwise raise *prima facie* concerns about its compatibility with the State aid rules establishes a rebuttable presumption of compliance with the State aid regime (*rectius*, of the inexistence of illegal State aid).[30] To rebut such a presumption, it would be necessary to determine that, despite having complied with mandatory (primary and secondary) public procurement rules, the public contractor entrusted with the SGEI actually received an economic advantage because the terms of the contract did not reflect normal market conditions.[31] As was properly stressed by Advocate General Jacobs,

> ... bilateral arrangements or more complex transactions involving mutual rights and obligations are to be analysed as a whole. Where for example the State purchases goods or services from an undertaking, there will be aid *only if and to the extent that the price paid exceeds the market price*.[32]

It follows that, in the absence of a clear disproportion between the obligations imposed on the public contractor (in this case, the undertaking entrusted with the SGEI, such as the ensuing universal service obligations) and the consideration or SGEI compensation paid by the public buyer (which needs to be assessed in light of such complex criteria as the risks assumed by the contractor, technical difficulty, delay for implementation, prevailing market conditions, etc.);[33] State aid rules applied in accordance with the *SGEI Compensation Communication* and the *2011*

---

[29] With similar concerns, see Heuninckx 2009.

[30] Such an approach is consistent with the understanding that these rules hold a common control device, ie that competition for a public contract is an indication of fair and equal market access in accordance with the procurement rules and, likewise, as regards State aid, of a fair balance of the obligations imposed and the economic advantages granted to the public contractor. However, a less formalistic approach to the analysis of procurement is desirable; see Buendía Sierra 2008, p. 211.

[31] As regards the importance of the analysis of '*consideration*' in public contracts to exclude the existence of a gratuitous advantage to the government contractor, see Winter 2004, pp. 487–501.

[32] Opinion of AG Jacobs in case C-126/01 *GEMO* at para 122 (emphasis added). See also Opinion of Advocate General Fennelly of 26 November 1998 in case C-251/97 *France v Commission* at para 19.

[33] In similar terms, Doern 2004, p. 117; Arrowsmith 2005, pp. 224–227.

SGEI Framework impose a very limited constraint on the development of public procurement that results in inappropriate SGEI compensation. That is, determining whether an award was (formally) properly made according to the public procurement rules will generally be the acid test to decide whether State aid has been granted, which results in a circular test to establish in the first place whether the award of the public contract constitutes State aid in and by itself.[34]

Therefore, this restriction of the scope of the State aid rules to (only) cases where public contractors obtain an undue economic advantage through excessive SGEI compensation (which should be proven directly and in full by the Commission, and which would face the hurdle of the difficult interpretation of the fourth *Altmark* condition, see *supra* Sect. 9.1) significantly restricts their effectiveness—unless the conduct of competition-distorting public procurement is itself considered to generate a situation that excludes 'normal market conditions' and, as a result, the award of the public contract for the SGEI scheme under those circumstances is considered an undue economic advantage *per se* (which, in my view, is a highly unforeseeable development of EU State aid law).

9.3.2 Excessively Limited Choice of Procurement Procedure

One of the main distortions that the *SGEI Compensation Communication* introduces in the interplay between public procurement and SGEI rules is the exclusion of an important number of public procurement tools from the alternatives that would ensure compliance with the fourth *Altmark* condition. Regarding the selection of procurement procedures, as already anticipated (*supra* Sect. 9.3), the *SGEI Compensation Communication* almost rejects the use of public procurement procedures other than the open and restricted (although with an important caveat), in a reductionist approach to the design of public procurement procedures that can promote effective competition[35]:

> Concerning the characteristics of the tender, an open procedure in line with the requirement of the public procurement rules is certainly acceptable, but also a restricted procedure can satisfy the fourth Altmark criterion, unless interested operators are prevented to

---

[34] Again, for criticism and a claim for a more substantive analysis, see Sanchez Graells 2012.

[35] For further discussion on how to choose a procurement procedure to prevent restrictions of competition, see Sanchez Graells 2011, pp. 234–246, where I adopted a less aggressive approach to the choice of procedure than the one included in the *SGEI Compensation Communication*, and submitted that '*contracting authorities are under an obligation to avoid restrictions of competition derived from the choice of procurement procedures. This obligation should be discharged by having recourse to open or restricted procedures when not doing so would be disproportionate if compared to the administrative complications or the increased costs implied by the imposition of a more competitive procurement procedure—ie, when the negative effects of the restriction of competition associated with the conduct of the tender by procedures other than open or restricted ones are larger than the additional costs associated to such competitive procedures*'.

tender without valid reasons. On the other hand, a competitive dialogue or a negotiated procedure with prior publication confer a wide discretion upon the adjudicating authority and may restrict the participation of interested operators. Therefore, they can only be deemed sufficient to satisfy the fourth Altmark criterion in exceptional cases. The negotiated procedure without publication of a contract notice cannot ensure that the procedure leads to the selection of the tenderer capable of providing those services at the least cost to the community.[36]

The position of the Commission boils down to require unlimited participation possibilities for potentially interested tenderers in a procedure that excludes (or substantially restricts) the discretion of the contracting entity in the choice of the undertaking to be entrusted with the SGEI. In my opinion, this is at odds with the general trend towards increased flexibility in the current revision of the procurement rules (*infra* Sect. 9.4) and creates a shadow of suspicion in the use of the competitive dialogue or a negotiated procedure with prior publication (which are procedures that may be particularly useful in the case of SGEI, where the scheme envisaged by the contracting entity may require specific technical or financial negotiations with interested tenderers, as well as the possibility to accept alternative methods to deliver the services concerned). Tendering SGEI through open procedures requires a very detailed set of technical and economic specifications that may be difficult to draft by the contracting entity and that may, in any case, stifle innovation in the discharge of the SGEI by innovative undertakings that cannot meet them (particularly in cases where variant tenders are not accepted). In short, this position seems excessively rigid,[37] and a more permissive approach where the Commission required that the procedure chosen (whichever it was) promoted and allowed for sufficient competition for the SGEI entrustment contract would have been preferable—which would not have been at odds with a recommendation to choose open or restricted procedures where feasible and not excessively burdensome in economic and technical terms.

9.3.3 Cost-Biased Choice of Award Criteria

A similarly restrictive approach can be seen in the position of the *SGEI Compensation Communication* regarding the choice of award criteria, which indicates that:

> … the 'lowest price' obviously satisfies the fourth Altmark criterion. Also the 'most economically advantageous tender' is deemed sufficient, provided that the award criteria, including environmental or social ones, are closely related to the subject-matter of the service provided *and allow for the most economically advantageous offer to match the*

---

[36] *SGEI Compensation Communication*, at para 66 (footnotes omitted).

[37] Buendía Sierra & Panero Rivas also consider that the Commission '*seems to make stricter the conditions for a measure to escape its classification as State aid by fulfilling the fourth* Altmark *condition*'.

value of the market (sic). Where such circumstances occur, a claw-back mechanism may be appropriate to minimise the risk of overcompensation *ex ante*. The awarding authority is not prevented from setting qualitative standards to be met by all economic operators or from taking qualitative aspects related to the different proposals into account in its award decision.[38]

In general terms, the Commission seems to adopt a position substantially in line with the rules in the EU public procurement Directives and their interpreting case law, which require that the inclusion of non-cost related criteria in the determination of the most economically advantageous tender (MEAT) is limited to those that are closely linked to the specific characteristics of SGEI to be entrusted (regardless of the environmental, social or different nature of the specific award criteria).

Nonetheless, the caveat that the use of the MEAT allows for the most economically advantageous offer 'to match the value of the market' seems to indicate that non-cost criteria can only be used as award preferences or devices to undo ties between equally priced offers (which are a rare occurrence and, in some instances, could deserve scrutiny to exclude that they are the result of bidder collusion). Therefore, it is clear to see that the Commission has a clear 'pure (lowest) cost' approach to the appraisal of the choice of award criteria that generates an unjustified restriction of the scope of the fourth *Altmark* condition (*supra* Sect. 9.2).[39]

9.3.4 Distrustful Assessment of Particular Circumstances

The Commission also maintains the restrictive approach in the assessment of particular (and rather infrequent) circumstances that could concur in the tendering of SGEIs and that, under the EU public procurement rules, would justify the conduct of a less than full-open procurement process. In the terms of the *SGEI Compensation Communication*:

---

[38] *SGEI Compensation Communication*, at para 67 (emphasis added).

[39] This also generates uncertainty regarding the use of competitively tendered SGEI contracts' conditions as a benchmark to appraise the potential existence of excessive compensation. More specifically, the *2011 SGEI Framework* indicates that: '*Where the provision of the SGEI is connected with a substantial commercial or contractual risk, for instance because the compensation takes the form of a fixed lump sum payment covering expected net costs and a reasonable profit and the undertaking operates in a competitive environment, the reasonable profit may not exceed the level that corresponds to a rate of return on capital that is commensurate with the level of risk. That rate should be determined where possible by reference to the rate of return on capital that is achieved on similar types of public service contracts awarded under competitive conditions (for example, contracts awarded under a tender)*', *2011 SGEI Framework* at para 37. However, if not all tenders are actually acceptable for the Commission (depending on choice of procedure, awarding criteria, etc.) it may be difficult to find valid benchmarks to be used with a sufficient degree of certainty.

> ... there can be circumstances where a procurement procedure cannot allow for the least cost to the community as it does not give rise to a sufficient open and genuine competition. This could be the case, for example, due to the particularities of the service in question, existing intellectual property rights or necessary infrastructure owned by a particular service provider. Similarly, in the case of procedures where only one bid is submitted, the tender cannot be deemed sufficient to ensure that the procedure leads to the least cost for the community.[40]

Even if there can actually be circumstances where the procurement procedure does not give rise to a (theoretically) sufficient open and genuine competition, the two circumstances identified by the Commission seem to be clearly at odds with the purpose of public procurement of SGEI—which is to allow for their outsourcing (first) in the most efficient possible conditions (second).

On the one hand, regarding the existence of intellectual property rights or necessary infrastructure owned by a particular service provider, it is difficult to see how the contracting out of the SGEI would be possible (in legal form) without resorting to the undertaking that owns the IP or infrastructure. In this case, the position of the Commission simply seems to block the possibility to procure the SGEI in compliance with Article 106(2) TFEU in those cases, which clearly cannot be the proper interpretation of the situation—and, at any rate, is fundamentally unsatisfactory.

On the other hand, the Commission fails to take into account that, in some circumstances (basically, as long as the tenderer did not know that it would be the only one submitting a bid) and in the absence of bid challenges that would show unjustified exclusion of other potential tenderers, one single offer is enough to reflect competitive market conditions.[41] Therefore, also in the appraisal of such particular or exceptional circumstances in the tendering of SGEI entrustment contracts, the Commission seems to have adopted an exceedingly formal and narrow approach that might not allow for the best results (and therefore, this guidance can be self-defeating).

9.3.5 Additional Procurement-Related Incentives in the Appraisal of SGEI Financing

Finally, and in line with the above-mentioned 'preferred route' approach to procurement shown by the Commission in the 'Almunia Package', the *2011 SGEI Framework* offers additional incentives to use procurement procedures even in those cases where State aid exists and needs to be declared compatible with TFEU rules. More specifically, the *2011 SGEI Framework* flexibilises the oversight obligations of contracting entities when they have used procurement procedures with publication:

---

[40] *SGEI Compensation Communication*, at para 68.

[41] For discussion of the possibility of obtaining competitive results with only one contractor, see Keisler and Buehring 2005. See also Sanchez Graells 2011, pp. 341–342.

Member States must ensure [...] that undertakings are not receiving compensation in excess of the amount determined in accordance with the requirements set out in this section. They must provide evidence upon request from the Commission. They must carry out regular checks, or ensure that such checks are carried out, at the end of the period of entrustment and, in any event, at intervals of not more than three years. *For aid granted by means other than a public procurement procedure with publication*, checks should normally be made at least every two years.[42]

As we can see, this is yet an additional procurement-related incentive in the appraisal of SGEI financing schemes that do qualify as State aid—and, however, it is hard to understand the logic to draw such a difference in *ex post* oversight duties, regardless of the method of selection of the undertaking entrusted with the SGEI *ab initio*.

9.4 The Likely Impact of New Procurement Rules on the Control of SGEI Financing

As has evaporated from the analysis in the prior sections, in my opinion, the procurement-related rules and guidelines of the 'Almunia Package' clearly point towards the use of relatively inflexible, cost-oriented procurement procedures where the contracting entity retains the minimum possible room for discretion—so that procurement is basically understood as a *deus ex machina* that excludes the existence of State aid, either due to a lack of selectivity of the measure or, most likely, given that the *competition for the contract* excludes any undue economic advantage.[43] However, this blunt exclusion of State aid control in the field of public procurement (which has not been free from criticism) may be about to require re-examination if the push for more flexibility and increased scope for negotiations in the 2011 Commission's proposal for new procurement Directives gets approved.[44]

Indeed, the 2011 European Commission Proposal for new EU public procurement Directives strongly relies on three main principles: simplification, modernisation and increased flexibility of the public procurement rules, with the fundamental goal of promoting increased efficiency of the procurement system and, ultimately, economic growth—as part of the Europe 2020 Growth Strategy. Throughout the process of modernisation and simplification of the procurement Directives, the Commission stresses the relevance of preventing distortions of

---

[42] *2011 SGEI Framework* at para 49 (footnote omitted, emphasis added).

[43] However, it is to be stressed that the absence of a tendering procedure does not preclude a finding that State aid and other competition rules have not been violated; see Case T-17/02 *Olsen v Commission* [2005] *ECR* II-2031 at paras 237–239, confirmed on appeal by the ECJ, Case C-320/05 P *Olsen v Commission and Spain* [2007] *ECR* I-131.

[44] Nonetheless, the actual potential for simplification and flexibility of the Commission's proposal has been rightly criticised by Arrowsmith 2012 *passim*.

competition. Given that public procurement strongly relies on competitive markets, there is a strong need to ensure that the design of public procurement rules and administrative practices, while fit and appropriate to promote competition in a narrow sense (i.e competition within the specific tender or procurement process), do not generate unnecessary distortions to competition in its broader sense (i.e, competition in the market where public procurement activities take place). This has been recently emphasised in the framework of the revision of the current EU public procurement rules, which stresses that:

> [t]he first objective [...] is to increase the efficiency of public spending. This includes on the one hand, the search for best possible procurement outcomes (best value for money). To reach this aim, it is vital to generate the strongest possible competition for public contracts awarded in the internal market. Bidders must be given the opportunity to compete on a level-playing field and distortions of competition must be avoided. At the same time, it is crucial to increase the efficiency of procurement procedures as such.[45]

Therefore, it seems clear to me that the revision of the current EU public procurement rules have a clear orientation towards promoting (or, at least, safeguarding) competitive neutrality as a booster for enhanced competition and, in the end, achieve value for money through increased procurement efficiency— including in the field of SGEIs. In this regard, it is interesting to stress that the Commission has itself identified (new) competition risks associated with the simplification of the procurement rules and the increased room they aim to create for negotiations between contracting authorities or entities and tenderers. More specifically, the Commission has acknowledged the risks that increased flexibility in the choice of procedures, the possibility to conduct negotiations in almost all procurements, and the possibility to introduce (or give greater importance) to considerations unrelated or only tenuously connected with the subject matter of the contract (to name only a few of the relevant proposals) can generate in terms of State aid control—which, at the same time, '*may present certain opportunities to increase convergence between the application of the EU public procurement and State aid rules*'.[46]

On the one hand, as stressed in the *Green Paper*, the increased flexibility for contracting authorities to use the competitive procedure with negotiations generates significant (new) risks:

> The possible advantages of more flexibility and potential simplification must be weighed against the increased risks of favouritism and, more generally, of overly subjective decisions arising from the greater discretion enjoyed by contracting authorities in the

---

[45] Commission, *Green Paper on the modernisation of EU public procurement policy—Towards a more efficient European Procurement Market.* COM(2011) 15 final, http://eur-lex.europa.eu/LexUriServ/LexUriServ.do?uri=CELEX:DKEY=556316:EN:NOT (last accessed 28 May 2012).

[46] *Green Paper on the modernisation of EU public procurement policy*, p. 5. See also *Communication from the Commission on the Application of the EU State aid rules to compensation granted for the provision of services of general economic interest* [2012] C8/4, paras 63–68.

negotiated procedure. Such subjectivity would in turn make it harder to show that the resulting contract did not involve State aid.[47]

Along the same lines, but in relation with the integration of environmental and social considerations in the array of award criteria, the *Green Paper* also emphasised that:

> ... public procurement policy must ensure the most efficient use of public funds. At the same time, this guarantee of purchases at the best price ensures a measure of consistency between EU public procurement policy and the rules in the field of State aid, as it makes sure that no undue economic advantage is conferred on economic operators through the award of public contracts. Loosening the link with the subject matter of the contract might therefore entail a risk of distancing the application of EU public procurement rules from that of the State aid rules, and may eventually run counter to the objective of more convergence between State aid rules and public procurement rules.[48]

Finally, the *Green Paper* identified concerns about the use of State aid in innovation-promoting mechanisms; although the approach has been rather optimistic and the European Commission has indicated that the use of "pre-commercial" procurement:

> enables public authorities to share the risks and benefits of designing, prototyping and testing a limited volume of new products and services with suppliers, without involving State aid.[49]

In my opinion (and substantially in line with the European Commission's except in relation with pre-commercial and innovative procurement), the main sources of increased risks in connection with State aid are the increased scope for negotiations that broaden the discretion of the contracting authority or entity, and the public finance of R&D projects by means of the new 'innovative partnership'—which goes further in flexibility than the current 'competitive dialogue'.[50]

As already follows from this short discussion, the feeble justification for the current position of the Commission that compliance with EU public procurement rules excludes the risk of disguised State aid—because current procurement rules prevent the granting of contracts that imply an (undue) economic advantage for the public contractor—is in crisis, particularly in view of the proposal for new EU public procurement Directives and the significantly expanded room for discretion and for the use of procurement procedures other than open and restricted. The introduction of increased flexibility and the broadening of the scope for negotiations require guidance as to the limits within which contractual conditions must remain for them to comply with EU State aid law (and, therefore, potentially outdates significant parts of the 'Almunia Package').

---

[47] Ibid, para 15.

[48] Ibid, para 39.

[49] Ibid, paras 45–46.

[50] For a more detailed analysis, see Sanchez Graells 2012.

Therefore, it looks like the two legs of the Modernisation Agenda for Procurement and SGEIs promoted by the European Commission are trying to move in opposite directions and, in that respect, it is difficult to envisage an scenario where the numerous questions that the interplay between State aid, public procurement and SGEI financing pose can be answered in a consistent and legally predictable manner, or that allows for the required adoption of lasting guidance criteria that help overcome the state of constant flux (or permanent crisis) in which this area of EU law has been immersed already for too long a period.

9.5 Concluding Remarks

As a conclusion, I personally think that the system of control of public expenditure is in crisis—which has been slightly slowed down by the financial downturn but that, more than ever, requires an effective solution to ensure the wise and efficient expenditure of public funds and their appropriate control. Regarding the competition implications of public expenditure, I think that there is a fundamental gap in competition policy and enforcement that concerns the development and adoption of a reliable 'market economy buyer' test that helps appraise procurement decisions and their outcomes—both in the field of SGEIs, and more generally. Otherwise, trying to discharge State aid control on public procurement rules and their enforcement only generates legal uncertainty. If EU public procurement rules finally move towards increased flexibility and expanded discretion for contracting authorities, it is foreseeable that there will be a retreat by the Commission from reliance in public procurement procedures (or a further narrowing down of those considered acceptable)—which, in turn, will generate a negative pressure against the use of more innovative and flexible procurement procedures if there can be State aid implications. A more fundamental revision of the system seems, then, necessary—but probably it must wait until public procurement rules are modernised and there is time to regain a broader perspective on this area of EU law and policy.

References

Arrowsmith S (2002) The EC procurement directives, national procurement policies and better governance: the case for a new approach. Eur Law Rev 27:3

Arrowsmith S (2005) The law of public and utilities procurement, 2nd edn. Sweet and Maxwell, London

Arrowsmith S (2012) Modernising the EU's public procurement regime: a blueprint for real simplicity and flexibility. Public Procure Law Rev 21:74

Baquero CJ (2005) Beyond competition: services of general interest and European community law. In: De Búrca G (ed.) EU law and the welfare state: in search of solidarity. OUP, Oxford p 169

Bartosch A (2002) The relationship of public procurement and state aid surveillance: the toughest standard applies? Common Mark Law Rev 35:551

Bovis C (2005) Financing services of general interest, public procurement and state aid: the delineation between market forces and protection in the European common market. J Bus Law 1

Buendía Sierra JL (1999) Exclusive rights and state monopolies under EC law. OUP, Oxford

Buendía Sierra JL (2008) Finding the right balance: state aid and services of general economic interest. In: Rodríguez Iglesias GC et al (eds), EC state aid law. Liber Amicorum Francisco Santaolalla Gadea, international competition law series (Alphen aan den Rijn, Kluwer Law International) 191

Buendía Sierra JL, Muñoz de Juan M (2012) Some legal reflections on the Almunia package. Eur State Aid Law Q (forthcoming)

Caranta R, Dragos D (eds) (2012) Public procurement outside the EU directives. Eur Procure Law Series n 4. DJØF, Copenhagen (forthcoming)

Chérot J–Y (2007) Droit public économique, 2nd edn. Economica, Paris

Dethlefsen P (2007) Public services in the EU—between state aid and public procurement. Public Procure Law Rev 16

Doern A (2004) The interaction between EC rules on public procurement and state aid. Public Procure Law Rev 13:97

Geradin D (2012) Public compensation for services of general economic interest: an analysis of the 2011 European commission framework. TILEC working paper, available at SSRN: http://ssrn.com/abstract=2031564

Hervey TK (2011) If only it were so simple: public health services and EU law. In: Cremona M (ed.) Market integration and public services in the European Union. OUP, Oxford p 179

Heuninckx B (2009) Defence procurement: the most effective way to grant illegal state aid and get away with it … or is it? Comm Mark Law Rev 46:191

Karayigit MT (2009) Under the triangle rules of competition, state aid and public procurement: public undertakings entrusted with the operation of services of general economic interest. Eur Compet Law Rev 11:542

Keisler JM, Buehring WA (2005) How many vendors does it take to screw down a price? A primer on competition. J Public Procure 5:291

Maillo J (2007) Article 86—services of general interest and competition law. In: Amato G, Ehlermann CD (eds.) Competition law. A critical assessment. Hart Publishing, Oxford p. 591

Merola M (ed) (2011) The reform of state aid rules on services of general economic interest—from the 2005 Monti-Kroes package to the 2011 Almunia reform. Conference proceedings—GCLC college of Europe Bruges, available at http://www.coleurop.be/content/gclc/documents/GCLC%20-%20SGEI%20Conference%20Booklet.pdf

Prosser T (2005) The limits of competition law. Markets and public services, OUP, Oxford

Risvig Hansen C (2012) Contracts not covered, or not fully covered, by the public sector directive. DJØF, Copenhagen (forthcoming)

Sanchez Graells A (2011) Public procurement and the EU competition rules. Hart Publishing, Oxford

Sanchez Graells A (2012) Public procurement and state aid: reopening the debate?' Public Procure Law Rev, (forthcoming)

Santamato S, Pesaresi N (2004) Compensation for services of general economic interest: some thoughts on the Altmark ruling. Compet Policy Newslett 1:17

Sauter W (2012) The commission's new SGEI package: the rules for state aid and the compensation of services of general economic interest. TILEC discussion paper No. 2012-018, Available at SSRN: http://ssrn.com/abstract=2044680

Sauter W, Schepel H (2009) State and market in European union law. The public and private spheres of the internal market before the EU courts. CUP, Cambridge

Sinnaeve A (2012) What's new in SGEI in 2012? An overview of the commission's SGEI package. Eur State Aid Law Q 2:347

Schnelle U (2002) Unconditional and non–discriminatory bidding procedures in EC state aid surveillance over public services. Eur State Aid Law Q 2:195

Schweitzer H (2011) Services of general economic interest: european law's impact on the role of markets and of member states. In: Cremona M (ed.) Market integration and public services in the European Union. OUP, Oxford, p 11

Skovgaard Ølykke G (2011) The definition of a "Contract" under article 106 TFEU. In: Szyszczak E et al. (eds), Developments in services of general interest, TMC Asser Press, The Hague, p 103

Szyszczak E (2007) The regulation of the state in competitive markets in the EU. Hart Publishing, Oxford

Szyszczak E (2011) *Altmark* assessed. In: Szyszczak E (ed.) Research handbook on European state aid. Edward Elgar, Cheltenham, p 293

Szyszczak E (2013) Soft law and safe Havens. In: Neergaard U, Szyszczak E, Von de Gronden J, Krajewski M (eds.) Social services of general interest in the EU. TMC Asser Press, The Hague

Tosics N, Gaál N (2008) Public procurement and state aid control—the ISSUE of Economic advantage. EC Compet Policy Newslett 3:15

Winter JA (2004) Re(de)fining the notion of state aid in Article 87(1) of the EC Treaty. Comm Mark Law Rev 41:475

Part III
Exclusions from the Package

- Act of entrustment
↳ (Rot.?)

Chapter 10
The *Altmark* Update and Social Services: Toward a European Approach

Johan W. van de Gronden and Catalin Stefan Rusu

- The approach of Social Service of the Commission decision doesn't coincide w. the approach in other cases.

Abstract The 2011 updated *Altmark* package exempts only particular social services from the notification requirement embedded in Article 108 (3) TFEU. This means that Member States must bring the financing of social services in line with the conditions set out in the 2011 Commission Decision (by changing some key features of the measures governing social services), in order to benefit from the carve out. This may be a rather sensitive matter, given that Member States regard social services as important elements of their domestic policies, whereas the Commission may be inclined to follow a European agenda in this context. This contribution aims to examine whether the Commission compels Member States to adopt a specific (European) model for social services. Furthermore, the contribution dwells upon the intricacies of the latest developments brought about by the 2011 *Altmark* package by investigating the implications for social services in the EU. This is done by analyzing *inter alia* the relevant case law and decisional practice, the applicable soft law documents and the relationship between SSGI and competition and free movement rules; furthermore, the 2011 Commission Decision is explored in great detail, the focus being directed at the Decision's main provisions on matters relating to definitions, act of entrustment, compensation and overcompensation, transparency, and information, as well as the role of Article 106 (2) TFEU in the context of social services. Hard law with a bearing on social services is scarce in EU law. Therefore, the 2011 Commission Decision is of great interest for social services and, as a result, for the national social welfare states, especially since, it may be argued that the Decision provides for some significant

J. W. van de Gronden (✉) · C. S. Rusu (✉)
Department of International and European Law, Radboud University Nijmegen,
P.O. Box 9049, 6500 KK Nijmegen, The Netherlands
e-mail: j.vandegronden@jur.ru.nl

C. S. Rusu
e-mail: C.Rusu@jur.ru.nl

E. Szyszczak and J.W. van de Gronden (eds.), *Financing Services of General Economic
Interest*, Legal Issues of Services of General Interest, DOI: 10.1007/978-90-6704-906-1_10,
© T.M.C. ASSER PRESS, The Hague, The Netherlands, and the authors 2013

185

bits and pieces of a comprehensive model for the delivery of social services. Thus, the adoption of the updated *Altmark* package constitutes a significant step toward an EU approach to social services. Last but not least, one may argue that the path has been paved for more binding EU measures meant to further build an EU model for social services based on a balance between State involvement and social needs, on the one hand and considerations of efficiency and competition, on the other hand.

Contents

10.1 Introduction

In its 2011 updated *Altmark* package the European Commission has decided not to carve out all kinds of social services from the notification requirement embedded in Article 108(3) TFEU, but to limit this exemption to particular social services. The Commission's measures suggest that yet another safe haven is created for certain social services, in addition to the already existing ones, such as the Services Directive.[1] However, Member States must bring the financing of social services in

---

[1]   Directive 2006/123/EC of the European Parliament and of the Council of 12 December 2006 on services in the internal market, *OJ* 2006 L376/36.

line with the conditions set out in the 2011 Commission Decision, in order to benefit from the carve out.[2] From the outset, it cannot be excluded that Member States, therefore, have to change some key features of the measures governing social services, particularly when it comes to issues such as the avoidance of overcompensation and transparency of the PSO entrustment process. This may prove to be a rather sensitive matter between the Member States and the Commission, given that Member States continue to regard social services as important elements of their domestic policies, whereas the Commission may be inclined to follow a European agenda in this context.

This chapter aims to examine whether the Commission compels Member States to adopt a specific model for social services, especially since the Commission has lately manifested itself as the driving force in stimulating a process of Europeanization with regard to these services. Furthermore, this contribution will dwell upon the intricacies of the latest developments brought about by the recent modernization process of the 2005 *Monti-Kroes* package by investigating the implications for social services in the EU.

This chapter approaches these topics as follows: Sect. 10.2 explores the basic concepts relating to social services in the context of the Commission's (soft) law documents, as well as in the context of the application of the EU competition and Internal Market rules to these services. Section 10.3 reveals how both the European Courts and the Commission have applied the State aid rules to social services. Section 10.4 discusses the main features of the 2011 updated *Altmark* package, with a focus on the Commission Decision's main provisions on matters relating to definitions, act of entrustment, issues regarding compensation and overcompensation, transparency and information, as well as the role of Article 106(2) TFEU in the context of social services. This chapter ends with some conclusion in Sect. 10.5.

10.2 What are Social Services?

This section explores the concept social services. It examines what these services encompass in EU law and whether the EU competition and Internal Market rules apply to them.

---

[2] Commission Decision on the application of Article 106(2) of the Treaty on the Functioning of the European Union to State aid in the form of public service compensation granted to certain undertakings entrusted with the operation of services of general economic interest, *OJ* 2012 L7/3.

10.2.1 Definitional Issues: From Social Services to Social Services of General Interest

As early as 2004, soft law documents of the European Commission acknowledged the special features that social services possess.[3] The Commission referred to them as Social Services of General Interest (SSGI), which indicated that these services could be part of the category of Services of General Economic Interest (SGEI). In this respect, it was recognized that although SSGI belong to the competences of the Member States, EU law plays an important role regarding their delivery and financing. As it will be detailed below, in the absence of competences to legislate in the area of SSGI, the Commission has made use of safe havens and soft law measures to move the modernization of SSGI away from the Member States' autonomous policy making to a Europeanization process.[4]

Generally speaking, SSGI have a specific role to play as an integral part of the European model of society and the European economy, as a result of their contribution to several essential values and objectives of the EU, such as achieving a high level of employment and social protection, a high level of human health protection, equality between men and women, and economic, social, and territorial cohesion. These issues were clearly admitted in the Commission's first Communication on SSGI from 2006.[5] Here, the specific character of SSGI is reiterated by emphasizing that they operate on the basis of the solidarity principle, they respond to differing needs in order to guarantee fundamental human rights and protect the most vulnerable, they are not for profit and in particular address the most difficult situations, they are often part of a historical legacy, while being strongly rooted in local cultural traditions, etc.[6]

SSGI have emerged as a special form of SGEI, to the extent that Member States use the protection of the SGEI concept to shield the economic activities of an undertaking performing an SSGI from the full force of the Treaty rules. Still, no unitary definition of SSGI exists for them to emerge as a special legal category in EU law.[7] Therefore, from the outset, it should be stressed that under EU law, SSGI are not a legally distinct category of services within SGI, as this concept appears

---

[3] White Paper on Services of General Interest, COM (2004) 374 final. This was not the first time the concept of SSGI was mentioned; one can recall the 2001 Commission's Report to the Laeken European Council on SGI, COM (2001) 598 final.

[4] See Szyszczak 2012, pp. 27–28.

[5] Communication from the Commission—Implementing the Community Lisbon Programme—Social services of general interest in the European Union, SEC (2006) 516, COM/2006/0177 final, p. 4.

[6] Ibid, pp. 4–5.

[7] Szyszczak 2012, p. 3. Indeed Neergaard 2012 argues that even within SSGI there may be subcategories recognized by different treatment in Commission policy or European Courts' case law.

only in policy documents of the Commission and not in EU primary or secondary law or acknowledged in the European Courts' case law.[8]

In its Communications, the Commission presents a straightforward categorization of SSGI, in that two main categories of social services may exist: statutory and complementary social security schemes, organized in various ways and covering the main risks of life such as those related to aging and unemployment and other essential services provided directly to the person, which aim at facilitating social inclusion and safeguarding fundamental rights.[9] Furthermore, the 2007 Commission Communication[10] highlights the objectives and the organizational principles which characterize SSGI: they are person oriented, they play a preventive and socially cohesive role, which is addressed to the whole population, independently of wealth or income, they contribute to non-discrimination, etc.

In its soft law documents, the Commission has framed social services as SSGI and, on top of that, it has construed this concept broadly. The creation of the concept of SSGI has enabled the Commission to stimulate a process of Europeanization with regard to social services.

10.2.2 The Application of the Free Movement and Competition Rules

Is this process, which the Commission attempts to further in its soft law approach, also reflected in the case law on the Treaty provisions on free movement and competition law? This question will be addressed below.

10.2.2.1 Preliminary Issues and Soft Law References

A clear distinction should be made, depending on the activity under consideration, between the services of an economic nature, namely SSGI which constitute economic activities and those of a noneconomic nature, namely SSGI which do not constitute economic activities. The Commission Guide to the application of the EU rules on State aid, public procurement and the Internal Market to SGEI, and in particular to SSGI[11] states that the fact that the activity in question is termed 'social' is not of itself enough for it to avoid being regarded as an economic

---

[8] Van de Gronden 2011, p. 125.

[9] See the Commission Communication Implementing the Community Lisbon programme: Social services of general interest in the European Union, COM/2006/0177 final, p 4 and the Commission Communication A Quality Framework for Services of General Interest in Europe, COM (2011) 900 final, pp. 3 and 4.

[10] Commission Communication—Services of general interest, including social services of general interest: a new European commitment, COM (2007) 725 final, p. 7.

[11] Commission Staff Working Document, SEC (2010) 1545 final, p. 17.

activity within the meaning of the Court's case law. It should be noted that SSGI that are economic in nature could also be labeled as SGEI, if they concern special tasks entrusted by the State. This finding is important as far as the application of the EU competition law and free movement rules is concerned. Last, but not least, a similar distinction using economic criteria is to be found in Protocol No. 26 to the Treaty of Lisbon 2009 on SGI, which, besides stressing the importance of SGI, confirms that SGI is an overarching concept that should be divided into two categories: SGEI and noneconomic SGI.[12]

In deciding whether SSGI fall under the application of the EU competition and free movement rules it is important to properly assess the concepts of undertaking and economic activity. First, as far as undertakings are concerned, the CJEU[13] defines them as entities engaged in economic activities, regardless of the legal status or the manner of financing. This definition is crucial because competition law traditionally applies to undertakings.[14] With regard to the concept of economic activity, according to the judgment in *Pavlov*,[15] an economic activity is described as any activity consisting in offering goods and services on a given market, in particular if this occurs in return for remuneration and, if the provider of services assumes the economic risk involved. It is no surprise that in its Communication on the application of the EU State aid rules to compensation granted for the provision of SGEI, which is part of the updated *Altmark* package, the Commission refers to this important definition.[16] However, the 2001 Commission Communication on SGI[17] acknowledges that it is not always easy to distinguish between what should and should not be regarded as economic activity. The Commission argues that a straightforward answer cannot be given a priori and a case-by-case analysis is required.

10.2.2.2 SSGI and the Free Movement Rules

This section approaches the discussion on the applicability of the EU free movement rules to SSGI from the angle of the two-prong definition given by the Commission: social security schemes and social services provided directly to the person. In this regard, it has to be recalled that according to Articles 56 and 57 TFEU services are to be regarded as such as long as they are provided for remuneration.

---

[12] Van de Gronden and Rusu 2012, p. 435.

[13] Case C-41/90 *Höfner and Elser v Macrotron GmbH* [1991] *ECR* I-1979, para 21.

[14] Graham 2010, p. 301.

[15] CJEU, Joined Cases C-180/98—C-184/98 *Pavlov v Stichting Profesioenfonds Medische Specialisten* [2000] *ECR* I-6451, para 73.

[16] *OJ* 2012 C8/4.

[17] 2001/C 17/04.

Social security schemes amount to economic activities if they meet the requirements set by the CJEU.[18] Thus, the application of the TFEU free movement rules is warranted.[19] To exemplify, the CJEU gave a broad reading to the application of the free movement rules in *Freskot*,[20]while confirming that when a Member State introduces a social scheme that covers insurable risk, that particular scheme must comply with the Treaty rules on free movement. Of course, the express derogation embedded in the Treaty and the rule of reason are available means for Member States when attempting to justify their measures in such contexts. Consequently, it seems that the CJEU is prepared to assess social security schemes in the light of the Treaty provisions on free movement, if they cover insurable risks.[21] On different occasions, the European Citizenship concept also appeared to be of relevance, however the CJEU drew a sharp distinction between these free movement provisions and the free movement provisions that have an economic dimension. In *Von Chamier-Glisczinski*[22] the CJEU held that disparities between the various social security systems of the Member States do not infringe Article 21 TFEU thus sending the message that the European Citizenship provisions are not capable of breaking open national security schemes.[23] Admittedly, in *Ruiz Zambrano*[24] the CJEU held that the Treaty provisions on European Citizenship preclude any national measure that deprives Union citizens of the genuine enjoyment of their rights. However, in *McCarthy*[25] and *Dereci*[26] the CJEU stressed that these provisions cannot be applied to purely internal situations; rather they impose a ban on national measures that force Union citizens to leave the territory of the EU and have, as a result, a 'cross-border element'. Consequently, the CJEU seems to endorse a cautious approach toward European Citizenship and extending this concept is not high on its agenda.[27] In the same vein, it may be assumed that CJEU will not be prepared to derive far-reaching consequences from Article 21 TFEU for national social security systems.

---

[18]   See also Van de Gronden 2011, 125.

[19]   See also Commission Communication—Services of general interest, including social services of general interest: a new European commitment, COM (2007) 725 final.

[20]   CJEU, Case C-355/00, *Freskot* [2003] *ECR* I-5263.

[21]   See also CJEU, Case C-350/07, *Kattner Stahlbau* v *Maschinenbau- und Metall- Berufsgenossenschaft* [2009] *ECR* I-1513.

[22]   Case C-208/08 *Petra von Chamier–Glisczinski* v. *Deutsche Angestellten-Krankenkasse* [2009] *ECR* I-6095.

[23]   Van de Gronden 2011, p. 129.

[24]   Case C-34/09, *Gerardo Ruiz Zambrano v Office national de l'emploi (ONEm)*, 8 March 2011, n.y.r.

[25]   Case C-434/09, *Shirley McCarthy v Secretary of State for the Home Department*, 5 May 2011, n.y.r.

[26]   Case 256/11, *Murat Dereci, Vishaka Heiml, Alban Kokollari, Izunna Emmanuel Maduike and Dragica Stevic v Bundesministerium für Inneres*, 15 November 2011, n.y.r.

[27]   Adam and Van Elsuwege 2012, p. 182.

With regard to the category of services directly provided to the person, the discussion regarding the applicability of Articles 56 and 57 TFEU applies *mutatis mutandis*. The case law is diverse and is not confined only to the freedom to provide services and the freedom of establishment, as it was the case in *Sodemare*,[28] where the CJEU found that social care services provided for the elderly are caught by the Treaty provisions of free movement. In the relevant case law of the Court, the free movement of capital has also been present. In *Sint Servatius*[29] the Court analyzed the Dutch social housing scheme only in the context of this freedom and found that a prior authorization scheme for cross-border investment projects constitutes a restriction on free movement of capital, which may be justified using the rule of reason.[30]

10.2.2.3 SSGI and EU Competition Law

Regarding the applicability of the Treaty rules on competition the discussion may follow a similar twofold pattern: social security schemes and social services provided directly to the person.

With regard to the former category, the case law of the Courts[31] shows that whereas the majority of statutory social security schemes, which are predominantly based on the principle of solidarity and subject to substantial State control, are not seen as economic activities, complementary schemes will, in contrast, be usually caught by the competition rules. The principle of solidarity plays a key role in the CJEU's case law, as shown in *Freskot* and *Kattner Stahlbau*. In the latter case, the Court found that the managing bodies concerned were not engaged in economic activities and therefore competition law did not apply, however the free movement rules were applicable in this particular case. As a consequence, one could argue that the scope of free movement rules is broader than the scope of the rules on competition,[32] a conclusion also drawn by the Commission in its Communication on the application of the EU State aid rules to compensation granted

---

[28] CJEU, Case C-70/95 *Sodemare* [1997] *ECR* I-3395.

[29] CJEU, Case C-567/07 *Sint Servatius* [2009] *ECR* I-9021.

[30] See Szyszczak 2011, pp. 9–11.

[31] CJEU, Case C-160/91 *Poucet et Pistre* [1993] *ECR* I-637; CJEU, Case C-67/96 *Albany* [1999] *ECR* I-5751; CJEU, Joined Cases C-115/97, Case C-219/97 *Drijvende bokken* [1999] *ECR* I-6121 and CJEU, Case C-437/09, *AG2R Prévoyance v Beaudout Père et Fils SARL*, judgment of 3 March 2011 (n.y.r.). In *AG2R* the Court adopted a remarkable standard in evaluating the relevant factors and despite the fact that the scheme under review was characterized by a high degree of solidarity and although the managing body was held to be non-profit-making and under a certain level of state control (even if monitoring the functioning of the scheme had been devolved to representatives of the parties), it was considered to be an undertaking engaged in an economic activity, since the level of State control was not substantial. See also Kerstin 2011, pp. 474–475.

[32] Szyszczak 2009, 210.

for the provision of SGEI.[33] One of the latest trends that may be observed in practice is the introduction by Member States of competition elements in statutory schemes. This approach is regarded as a sign of modernisation of social policy. In such a situation the Commission will not hesitate to find the existence of an economic activity opening the door for the application of competition rules.[34] A similar outcome (namely applicability of EU competition rules) will be noticed in cases[35] where the national legislator in designing a complementary social security scheme has opted for a mix between competition and solidarity.[36]

If this is the case, the salvation comes from the SGEI concept (subject to whether the SSGI in question is of an economic nature) as embedded in Article 106 (2) TFEU, which may justify possible restrictions of free competition. Such competition issue could also arise under EU State aid law, as, for example, the rights and tasks conferred on managing bodies of (complementary) social security schemes which are also supported by transfers of financial resources, State aid problems may occur under the application of Article 107 TFEU. Going beyond the issue of financial resources transfers, in *Freskot* the Court argued that other State aid issues may also occur in relation to the possibility of compulsory social security schemes conferring benefits on the companies that are covered thereunder.[37]

With regard to social services provided directly to the person the CJEU decided in *Höfner, Job Centre*[38] and in the Irish case on social housing[39] that organizations providing this kind of services are engaged in economic activities, since such services are market oriented regardless of the public or private law type of designation performed by member States. The Court does not pay much attention to the principle of solidarity in such cases and therefore a large diversity of social services provided directly to the person fall under the incidence of EU competition rules. Consequently, since many such social services are financed by public means the discussion on the applicability of the State aid rules may be brought in the picture in a similar fashion as with regard to social security schemes. Thus, the SGEI concept can play an important role in this respect, which is confirmed by the case law in this field. Member States that model the relevant activities pertaining to social services provided directly to the person (especially funding of social housing activities) in the form of SGEI missions have the option to invoke justifications related to these missions.[40]

---

[33] *OJ* 2012 C8/4.

[34] See for example the *Zorgverzekeringswet* case, Decision of the Commission of 22 December 2005 on the introduction of a risk equalization system in the Dutch Health Insurance, N541/2004 and N542/2004—C(2005) 1329 fin.

[35] Such as CJEU, Case C-116/97 and C-117/97 *Brentjens* [1999] *ECR* I-6025.

[36] Van de Gronden 2011, p. 139.

[37] Paragraph 82 of the *Freskot* ruling.

[38] CJEU, Case C-55/96 *Job Centre* [1997] *ECR* I-7119.

[39] Decision of the Commission in case State aid N 209/2001—Ireland, Guarantee for borrowings of the Housing Finance Agency, 3 July 2001.

[40] See Van de Gronden 2011, p. 146.

10.3 Case Law and Decisional Practice on State aid and SSGI

The previous section has shown that many SSGI are not immune from EU competition and internal market law. As a consequence, Member States must observe the Treaty provisions on State aid, when financing the provision of these services. Below, the case law and decisional practice regarding State aid and SSGI will be outlined, but first, the most significant rulings on the main principles of SGEI will be discussed.

10.3.1 The Case Law on the Conceptual Issues

As already outline in other chapters of this volume, in its case law, the CJEU developed a special approach to State aid and issues of general interest. The opportunity arose in the context of the *Altmark* case.[41] In this case, the Court held that compensatory measures for the execution of public service obligations (PSO) do not constitute State aid, provided that the four conditions listed in paras 88–93 of the judgment are met: the undertaking is charged with the execution of a PSO, the parameters of the amount of the compensation are established in an objective and transparent manner, the compensation does not exceed what is necessary, and in the case of absence of public procurement for the contract concerned, the amount of the compensation is determined on the basis of the expenses a well-run undertaking would have incurred. The importance of the *Altmark* ruling is emphasized by certain remarkable elements: first, PSO and SGEI are similar concepts,[42] in that they both relate to certain special tasks that state bodies impose on undertakings. Second, a major advantage of the approach developed in *Altmark* is that compensation measures do not need to be notified to the Commission and they are not subject to the standstill provision (which may have led to recovery of illegal aid).[43] Thus, it may be argued that by delivering its judgment in *Altmark* the CJEU has developed a jurisdictional approach to State aid.[44] Third, without giving Member States *carte blanche*, the *Altmark* ruling extended their powers to finance PSO.[45] Last but not least, as it will be detailed below, the judgment in *Altmark* judgment seems to have inspired the European courts in furthering the SSGI concept in State aid cases. However, inconsistencies regarding the interpretation of

---

[41] CJEU, Case C-280/00 *Altmark* [2003] *ECR* I-7747.

[42] As detailed below, this view is consistent with the GC's approach in *BUPA* (paras 161 and 162).

[43] See Nistor 2011, p. 262.

[44] See Van de Gronden 2009, p. 11.

[45] See Van de Gronden 2011, p. 140 and Fiedziuk 2010, p. 280.

the *Altmark* criteria in the case law of the Courts and in the Commission's decisional practice and (soft) law documents are certainly present.

At the heart of the *Altmark* approach is the entrustment of SGEI missions. With regard to this issue, the recent case *AG2R Prévoyance* is of great importance.[46] This case concerned a supplementary health care scheme, set up by representative organizations of employers and trade unions in the bakeries sector, the management of which was assigned to an insurer (AG2R). In this case, the CJEU had to decide whether a task to preform SGEI was allotted to the insurer concerned. It is striking that not much was made of the need for a formal act of entrustment.[47] The Court following the approach in *BUPA*[48] and *TV2/Danmark*,[49] accepted that the designation of the task to provide SGEI may be construed on the basis of semi-collective actors (of a private nature) entrusting special operators with this task[50]: provident operations may be entrusted not only to provident societies and mutual insurance associations, but also to insurance companies.[51] Therefore, the CJEU found that AG2R was entrusted with the provision of SGEI. All in all, this recent case law of the CJEU seems to convey the message that the European judiciary seems to adopt a more relaxed approach regarding the requirement of entrustment. If, until recently, the Court required an explicit act of entrustment by a public body,[52] lately 'implicit acts of entrustment' may also be inferred from general obligations and conditions laid down in national legislation. As it will be detailed below, this stance seems to be at odds with the Commission's approach as embedded in (soft) law documents and its decisional practice.

10.3.2 Social Security Services

As already outlined in Sect. 10.2, various social security services, most notably supplementary schemes, are caught by the Treaty provisions on competition, including those on State aid. As a result, Article 107 TFEU was applied by both

---

[46] Supra note 31.

[47] Paragraph 73 of the ruling states that it still remains to be determined whether AG2R is entrusted with the operation of services of general economic interest within the meaning of Article 106(2) TFEU. See also Sauter 2011a, p. 6.

[48] GC, Case T-289/03 *British United Provident Association* [2008] *ECR* II-81.

[49] Joined Cases T-309/04, T-317/04, T-329/04 and T-336/04 *TV2/Danmark* v *Commission*, [2008] *ECR* II-02935.

[50] See also Van de Gronden and Rusu 2012, pp. 421–422.

[51] Also, according to para 65 of the ruling, as an undertaking engaged in an economic activity, AG2R was chosen by the social partners, on the basis of financial and economic considerations, from among other undertakings with which it is in competition on the market in the provident services which it offers.

[52] See for example CJEU, Case C-159/94 *Commission* v *France (energy monopolies)* [1997] *ECR* I-5851.

the European judiciary and the Commission to these services. In *Freskot*, for example, the CJEU was called upon to consider the transfer of financial sources to a body managing a social security scheme. The CJEU held that the managing body concerned was not engaged in economic activities, as the compulsory scheme at issue was predominately based on the principle of solidarity. The CJEU moved on by pointing out that Article 107(1) TFEU could nevertheless be violated, as the beneficiaries were undertakings. The cover provided was related to damages suffered by agricultural undertaking from natural risks. As a result, it had to be examined whether the compulsory scheme at issue constituted an economic advantage for the operators covered thereunder. The main question was whether, in the absence of a compulsory scheme, it had been possible to have obtained insurance cover against natural risks at contribution rates corresponding to those due under this compulsory scheme. However, the CJEU was not sufficiently appraised by the relevant points of fact and law in order to answer this question. It was therefore left to the referring domestic court to settle this matter. Admittedly, the *Freskot* case is not representative for the issues that are at play in social security matters, because in this case the beneficiaries were undertakings. Then again, the CJEU took an important decision by holding that social benefits can constitute State aid, if undertakings belong to the group of beneficiaries.

A lot of attention was drawn to the *BUPA* case.[53] This case concerned a supplementary health care scheme and therefore the institutions administering it were undertakings for the purposes of EU competition law. As these bodies were engaged in a system of risk equalization, financial resources were transferred to one of these bodies, which raised a State aid issue. The Commission decision to approve the Irish system concerned was challenged before the General Court. This court examined whether the Irish measures under review were justifiable in the light of the *Altmark* conditions. In finding that these conditions were met the General Court took two remarkable decisions. In the first place, it derived an SGEI mission from the general obligations (such as open enrollment and community rating) laid down in the Irish health legislation. In line with the approach adopted by CJEU in *AG2R* the General Court does not require an explicit act of entrustment. In this regard, it should be noted that in *BUPA* it was contended that SGEI and PSO are identical concepts. Furthermore, the fourth *Altmark* condition, that takes the expenses of a well-run company as a benchmark, was moderated.[54] It was believed that in a health insurance case this condition cannot strictly be complied with. What mattered the most in the General Court's view was that the Irish system of risk equalization did not amount to offsetting costs resulting from inefficiency.[55] As there is a gray area between the costs of an efficient firm and the costs of a firm operating inefficiently, in *BUPA* the General Court adhered to a

---

[53] Supra note 48.

[54] See also Schweitzer 2011, p. 30.

[55] Sauter 2009, p. 279.

flexible approach to *Altmark* and, by doing so, left a considerable margin of appreciation to Member States in matters of financing health insurance.[56]

Strikingly, in contrast with the approach adopted by the General Court in *BUPA*, the Commission departed from a strict reading of the fourth *Altmark* condition in the *Zorgverzekeringswet* case.[57] At issue was the Dutch system of risk equalization, which was set up in order to guarantee access for all to private health insurance cover. In the Netherlands, private insurers administer the basic health care schemes. The Commission was of the opinion that Dutch health insurance companies were engaged in economic activities and that therefore, the flow of funds, which is at the heart of the operation of a risk equalization scheme, should be assessed under the EU State aid rules. Its most significant finding was that the Dutch system did not aim at compensating costs; rather it is concerned with tackling problems of risk. Consequently, the fourth *Altmark* condition was not fulfilled in the view of the Commission. Eventually, the Commission approved the Dutch system on the basis of Article 106 (2) TFEU, by arguing that compensation of the costs, incurred by insurers due to patients with high-risk profiles, is necessary in order to guarantee open enrollment. It is clear from the outset that in *Zorgverzekeringswet* the Commission applied the *Altmark* conditions stricter than the General Court did in BUPA. However, the approaches of these two institutions had one thing in common: like the General Court the Commission derived an SGEI mission from general obligations, which were laid down in the Dutch Act on Health Insurance.

To date, *Zorverzekeringswet* is the most important case decided by the Commission. In other cases, the Commission was also confronted with issues of financing social security services. For example, in *Arctia Shipping*[58] the Commission approved financing given by the Finnish government to a specific company that took over employees of a former State enterprise. The aim of this financing was to compensate for the costs caused by the fact that these employees had lost their rights of the supplementary government pension. As the company concerned was not entrusted with the operation of an SGEI, the Commission cleared the transfer of money on the basis of Article 107(3)(c)TFEU. By levelling out the differences in pension costs caused by the transfer of workers from a State enterprise to a private company the Finnish government restored the level playing field. It is apparent from this case that the Commission is sensitive to arguments related to the special features of pension rights.

In the case on the *Reform of the organization of the supplementary pension regime in the banking sector*[59] the Commission had to examine whether the

---

[56]   See De Vries 2011, pp. 302–305 and Van de Gronden 2009, p. 18.

[57]   Supra note 34.

[58]   Decision of the Commission of 6 July 2010 in case N152/2010-Compensation to Arctia Shipping Oy with respect to supplementary pension rights of its employees, C(2010) 4505 Final.

[59]   Decision of the Commission of 10 October 2007 in case N 597/2006—Reform of the organization of the supplementary pension regime in the banking sector, *OJ* 2007 C308/9.

measures that changed the contributions due by the banks constituted State aid. As the reform did not release the banks from financial charges resulting from the general system of social security, the Commission concluded that the entire operation did not amount to State aid and, therefore, Article 107(1) TFEU was not violated.[60] The nonapplicability of the State aid rules relieved the Commission of the task to examine whether the pension scheme concerned could be regarded as SGEI (or PSO).

10.3.3 Social Services Provided Directly to the Person

An important case for State aid and social services provided directly to the person is the *Dutch Social Housing* case.[61] At issue in this case was the financing of the organization of the Dutch social housing sector. The Dutch government was forced to review its system of financing this sector after the Commission had posed some critical questions about the transfer of financial resources to housing companies.[62] It was decided to improve the financial transparency of the measures concerned and to oblige the social housing companies to introduce a system of separate accounts.[63] What is even more important is that these companies must rent 90 % of their dwellings to less advantaged persons. This target group was defined as households having an income below 33.000 euro per year.[64] In the view of the Commission the precise definition of the target group led to a clear delineation of an SGEI mission. Furthermore, the Commission was not opposed to renting out 10 % to higher income groups, since this practice would stimulate social mixity and social cohesion in urban areas in the Netherlands. Consequently, the Commission approved the Dutch social housing system on the basis of Article 106 (2) TFEU. It is striking, however, that the Commission refused to clear the financial measures concerned in the light of the *Altmark* approach. It claimed that in particular the fourth condition of this approach was not fulfilled.[65] In other words, the Commission continues to depart from a strict reading of this condition. It should be noted that the Commission decision was challenged as it was claimed that the Commission does not have the authority to intervene in national policies on social

---

[60] See Boeshertz and Frederick 2008, p. 34.

[61] Commission Decision of 15 December 2009 in cases No E 2/2005 and N 642/2009 (The Netherlands, Existing and special project aid to housing corporations).

[62] Cf. also Lavrijssen and De Vries 2009, p. 408.

[63] See e.g. the letter of the Minister of Housing of 13 September 2005, Woningcorporaties, Kamerstukken II (Dutch Official Parliamentary Documents), 29 453, no. 20.

[64] This threshold was recently raised up to EUR 34.850,00. See http://www.europadecentraal.nl/europesester/643/2123/.

[65] See para 14 of the Commission Decision of 15 December 2009 in cases No E 2/2005 and N 642/2009 (The Netherlands, Existing and special project aid to housing corporations).

housing and Services of General (Economic) Interest.[66] At the writing of this chapter, the General Court had not handed down its judgment in this case yet.

Another important case is the Irish case on social housing.[67] In Ireland, the Housing Finance Agency (HFA) raised funds at the finest rates on the capital market and it then advanced these funds to the institutions providing social housing services to the most socially disadvantaged households. As in the Dutch case, the Irish system was approved, because these institutions were entrusted with a clearly defined SGEI mission. The Commission clearance was based on Article 106(2) TFEU and, apparently, it was believed that the *Altmark* conditions were not met.

It is apparent from the analysis above that Article 106(2) TFEU plays a large role in the Decisions on social housing, as the Commission based the compatibility of the national systems under review with the EU rules on State aid on this Treaty provision. Great importance was assigned to the clear definition of a particular SGEI mission. From an EFTA case it is apparent what will happen if a clear mission is absent. In *Icelandic Housing Financing Fund* the EFTA surveillance authority contended that the Icelandic competent authorities had failed to designate an SGEI mission and, as a result, the State aid measures were not justifiable in the light of Article 106(2) TFEU.[68]

10.3.4 Evaluation

In social housing cases a consistent approach, which departs from a strict reading of the fourth *Altmark* condition and the need of a well-defined SGEI mission, is developed by the Commission. However, these two features of the Commission approach are at odds with recent case law of both the CJEU and the GC. It should be pointed out that these two EU Courts seem to prefer to interpret the condition of the expenses of a well-run company in a flexible way and to derive SGEI entrustments from general obligations. The strict views of the Commission seem not to match with an important development emerging from the case law of the European judiciary, which has increasingly a more flexible take on SGEI and State aid.

10.4 The 2011 Commission Decision

The 2011 Commission Decision assigns great value to social services. It creates a safe haven for a considerable amount of these services. It goes without saying that the special position of social services is clearly an added value of the recent update

---

[66] This appeal is registered as GC, Case T-201/10, Case T-202/10 and Case T-203/10.

[67] Supra note 39.

[68] See the decision of the EFTA surveillance authority in case No 406/08/COL to initiate the formal investigation procedure with regard to the relief of the Icelandic Housing Financing Fund from payment of a State guarantee premium, 27 June 2008.

of the *Altmark* package. The 2011 Commission Decision puts forward that services provided by operators such as hospitals and other enterprises in charge of social services have special characteristics that need to be taken into account.[69] These special characteristics explain that aid given to the providers of social services does not necessarily lead to competition distortions. Therefore, the transfer of a relatively great amount of financial resources to these providers does not meet with insuperable difficulties. In contrast with the general exemption, which is lowered from compensation not exceeding the amount of EUR 30 million to compensations below EUR 15 million, all social services are exempted from the Treaty provisions on State aid. In other words, the Commission has introduced a generous regime for social services. This does not mean, however, that no conditions apply to national compensatory measures taken with regard to social services. Below the conditions of the 2011 Commission Decision will be discussed in relation to social services. In this regard, it should, however, be noted that the 2011 Commission Decision is only relevant in so far as one or more conditions set out in *Altmark* are not fulfilled.[70] In the event that all these conditions are met, the national measure concerned does not constitute State aid for the purposes of Article 107 TFEU and no assessment under the 2011 Commission Decision needs to be carried out.

10.4.1 Social Services Covered

The first question that should be addressed is which social services are covered by the 2011 Commission Decision. Article 2 sets out how social services are defined. By drafting this provision, the Commission did not take any elements from its soft law documents on SSGI. The definition of SSGI, which is repeatedly given in the Commission Communications, is absent in Article 2. Consequently, the Commission has decided not to carve out all kinds of SSGI but to limit this exemption to particular social services. The first section of Article 2 identifies these services, which will be discussed below.

10.4.1.1 Hospital Services

The first section under (b) of this provision identifies medical care services provided by hospitals, including emergency services, as social services. The concept of 'hospital' is not defined in the Decision or in any other document of the updated *Altmark* package. Yet, it is clear from the wording of the section 1 under (b) that the

---

[69] See recital 11 of the Commission Decision on the application of Article 106 (2) TFEU to State aid in the form of public service compensation granted to certain undertakings entrusted with the operation of services of general economic interest, 2012/21/EU.

[70] Cf also Thouvenin 2009, pp. 114 and 115.

entity concerned should provide 'medical care'. For the rest, the Decision is silent on what is meant by a hospital. As a result it may be assumed that both aid granted to public and private hospitals could benefit from the generous exemption of the Commission Decision. It is striking that no guidance is given on how to determine whether a particular entity qualifies as a hospital. Therefore, considerable room for maneuver is left to the Member States. Nevertheless, it may be assumed that from the perspective of EU law the claim of a Member State that a particular operator is a hospital will be subject to some review and, if necessary, will be rejected when the line of reasoning of the Member State concerned is not adequate. In order to verify whether a particular provider should be regarded as a hospital, Union Institutions, such as the Commission and the CJEU, could take definitions used in other areas of EU law. For example, it is apparent from the Services Directive, which also contains an important carve-out for health care, that services provided '…to patients to assess, maintain or restore their state of health where those activities are reserved to a regulated health profession..'[71] are regarded as health care services. Furthermore, it can be derived from the Directive on patients' rights in cross-border health care that a hospital presupposes the presence of medical infrastructure, equipment and accommodation facilities.[72]

In this regard, mention should be made of an important indication given in Article 2 section 1 under (b). The pursuit of activities ancillary to hospital services, such as research, does not prevent the exemption from being applicable. It is, of course, reasonable to allow for investments in research (which could lead to ground-breaking results for the treatment of patients) or for engagement in other activities closely related to care. In our view, the test to be carried out in this respect should be whether the ancillary activities are concerned with curing patients and are necessary in order to contribute to the process of diagnosing and treating.

In this regard, it should be noted that the concept of a 'hospital' is increasingly used as a safe haven. Pursuant to Article 8 of the Directive on patients' rights in cross-border health care it is permitted to restrict the free movement of patients, if this is necessary for the purposes of the planning of hospital care. The 2011 Commission Decision assigns a similar role to the term hospital. In the long run, therefore, it will be inevitable to give a clear and transparent definition of this term at EU level.

10.4.1.2 Other Social Services

Article 2 under (c) exempts a wide range of social services from the State aid rules. In this provision, these activities are described as '…services of general economic interest meeting social needs as regards health and long term care, childcare,

---

[71] See recital 22 of Directive 2006/123/EC of the European Parliament and the Council of 12 December 2006 on Services in the Internal Market, *OJ* 2006 L376/page number missing.

[72] See recitals 12, 40 and 41, and Article 8 section 2 of Directive 2011/24/EU of the European Parliament and of the Council on the application of patients' rights in cross-border healthcare, *OJ* 2011 L88/45.

202 J. W. van de Gronden and C. S. Rusu

access to and reintegration into the labor market, social housing and the care and social inclusion of vulnerable group...'.

It cannot be ruled out that the specific social services mentioned by Article 2 section 1 under (c) will be subject to questions of interpretation. The organization and delivery of social services varies from Member State to Member State and, as a result, the interpretation of what constitutes health and long-term care, childcare, access to (and reintegration into) the labor market, social housing and the care and social inclusion of vulnerable groups, is dependent on the differing legal and social traditions of the EU Member States. Yet, the outcome of this debate is crucial, as the financing of these services falls entirely outside of the scope of the Treaty provisions on State aid (provided that the other relevant conditions are met as well). By listing specific social services the Commission has given to the Member States a great incentive to label all kinds of services as one of the social services mentioned in Article 2 section 1 under (c). It may be expected that, as a result, a lot of interpretation questions will arise under this provision and, therefore, the Commission will be forced to give guidance, which would come down to defining the services listed.

Like medical care, social services are carved out from the scope of the Services Directive. It should be noted that the 2011 Commission Decision adopts an approach different from the Services Directive in this respect. In contrast with Article 2(2)(j) of the Services Directive, which exempts specific social services in so far as these services are provided by the State or by bodies mandated or recognized by the state, Article 2 of the 2011 Commission Decision does not refer to any state role. It should nevertheless be noted that state involvement is a key element in Article 4 of this Decision, which sets out the criteria for the entrustment of an SGEI mission. But provision by the state or mandates and recognitions given by the state do not completely overlap with entrustments by the state. As a consequence, Member States designing the provision of social services should pay close attention to subtleties of social services exemptions of both EU measures. Another remarkable difference is that labor market integration activities benefit from the exemption of the 2011 Commission Decision, whereas these services are absent in the social services exemption of the Services Directive. Furthermore, the 2011 Commission Decision speaks of 'the care and social inclusion of vulnerable groups', while the Services Directive refers to the 'support of families and persons permanently or temporally in need'. One cannot help thinking that these services largely overlap but, as long as no clear guidance is given in this respect, it cannot be excluded that differences may exist between these two categories. All in all, no coherent approach to the definitions of the various social services is adopted (yet) leading to a fragmentation of EU policy.[73]

---

[73] Szyszczak 2012.

10.4.1.3 Evaluation: From SSGI Back to Social Services

From the foregoing, it is apparent that no general definition of the concept social services has been given. Rather, the Commission has preferred to enumerate *particular* services. This approach is not a surprise, as it is very difficult to formulate a definition of social services that fits every Member State. Nevertheless, the enumeration of the services in Article 2 under (c) seems to contain at least one element of such a definition, because it refers to services '…meeting social needs…'. This suggests that such needs are at the heart of the provision of social services. In any event, it may be assumed that a comprehensive definition of social services could interfere with the Member States' view of what services deem to have a social character and, a as a result, would meet fierce opposition from these States. Therefore, the Commission took the safe route by simply listing a couple of social services and to exempt these services from the scope of the Treaty provisions on State aid.

It is striking that this list does not match well with the definition of the concept SSGI given by the Commission in its Communications. From this definition, it is apparent that not only services directly provided to the person but also social security services are of a social character. Furthermore, the analysis of the case law in Sect. 10.3 shows that several social security schemes fall within the ambit of the Treaty provisions on competition, including those on State aid. Moreover, in its Communication on the application of the EU State aid rules to compensation granted for the provision of services of general economic interest,[74] which is part of the updated *Altmark* package, the Commission also contends that some social security schemes have economic features, which prompts the applicability of the Treaty provisions on State aid. It is, therefore, a pity that the 2011 Commission Decision fails to exempt these schemes from the scope of these provisions. The lessons that could be learned from the *BUPA* and *Zorgverzekeringswet* cases[75] are that EU State aid rules are capable of putting under pressure the operation of social security schemes that play a key role in the welfare states of the Member States. It is hard to understand why a safe haven should be created for social housing and for what reason social security services are not caught by a generous exemption. Both social services are of eminent significance for all EU Member States. By not including social security schemes in the exemption of Article 2 section 1 under (c) the Commission has—we assume unintentionally—given priority to social services directly provided to the person (such as social housing) over social security services (that have economic features).

---

[74] *OJ* 2012 C8/4.
[75] Supra notes 34 and 48.

10.4.2 Act of Entrustment

A very important condition for invoking the exemption of the 2011 Commission Decision is related to the issue of entrustment. The Decision sets out a couple of criteria that are considerably strict and, on top of that, stresses the importance of administrative requirements.

To start with, Article 2 section 2 of the 2011 Commission Decision provides that the exemption only applies if the period for which the undertaking is entrusted with the operation of the SGEI mission does not exceed 10 years. The rationale behind this requirement is clear: by limiting the duration of a particular SGEI mission, the Commission has made possible that the right to provide SGEI will be given to other enterprises. This would stimulate competition and market access from operators coming from other Member States. Missions granted for a longer period than 10 years are only allowed, if a significant investment that needs to be amortised over a period in excess of 10 years is required. The 2011 Commission Decision acknowledges that, for example, in social housing such investments should be made in order to provide accommodation for low-income groups. Yet, also in these circumstances the duration of the mission concerned should be limited in time. Permanent entrustments of SGEI mission do not seem to be acceptable under the 2011 Commission Decision.

Of great importance is Article 4 of the 2011 Commission Decision. This Article requires that the operation of an SGEI is entrusted to an undertaking '...by way of one or more acts...'. On first sight this requirement seems to be drafted in a flexible way, as it accepts that an SGEI mission can be derived from various acts. However, by setting out which elements must be included in the act(s) of entrustment Article 4 makes it impossible to derive such a mission from general obligations as the GC and the CJEU did in recent case law, and which, in fact, the Commission itself did in *Zorgverzekeringswet*.[76] It is simply not possible that general obligations address all issues listed in this provision of the 2011 Commission Decision.

The first paragraph of Article 4 points out that the form of the act(s) of entrustment may be determined by the Member States, but the list of requirements applicable to such an act or acts limits the room of maneuver considerably. To start with, the entrustment act must specify the content and duration of the PSO (SGEI mission). As already stated, in principle the duration ought not to exceed 10 years. Furthermore, it should be clear to which undertaking the special tasks are assigned and, where applicable, also on which territory it will provide its services. Moreover, the nature of the exclusive or special rights granted should be specified. On top of that, the compensation mechanism and the parameters for calculating, controlling and reviewing the compensation concerned should be outlined in the act(s) of entrustment. The 2011 Commission Decision is very much concerned with the issue of overcompensation. Therefore, arrangements for avoiding and

---

[76] Supra note 34.

recovering any overcompensation should be included in the act(s) of entrustment. A remarkable requirement applicable to the act(s) of entrustment is the last one mentioned in Article 4. Pursuant to this requirement reference to the 2011 Commission Decision must be made.

It is clear from the outset that the approach adopted by the Commission is largely different from the recent case law of the GC and the CJEU on social services; in this case law, SGEI missions were derived from general obligations.[77] Strikingly, it does not even match with its own decision taken in the *Zorgverzekeringswet* case, where the Commission cleared a Dutch system of risk equalization, which is one of the pillars of the statutory health care scheme in the Netherlands, on the basis of a flexible interpretation of the requirement of entrustment.

The tensions between the recent case law and the 2011 Commission Decision lead to the finding that a public service obligation within the meaning of the *Altmark* judgment is construed more easily in State aid cases on social services, than the existence of an act of entrustment for the purposes of the 2011 Commission Decision can be proven. Consequently, the finding that no public service obligation is present and that, therefore, the *Altmark* approach does not apply, leads automatically to the conclusion that the conditions of the 2011 Commission Decision are also not met.

In any event, the drafting of Article 4 has important consequences for national social service policies. This provision obliges Member States to introduce several mechanisms for cost control in the provision and organization of social services. One of the most important issues is avoiding overcompensation. In other words, Member States should oblige their social service providers to live up to efficiency standards. Furthermore, the tasks of these providers must be described with great precision. On top of that, the entrustment of the task to provide the services concerned should be limited in time. This requirement could lead to important changes in the national tradition of social services provision.

10.4.3 Issues Relating to Compensation/No Overcompensation

The 2011 Decision, Communication and Framework forming the updated *Altmark* package contain extensive provisions with regard to compensation for discharging PSO. This stresses the importance that the Commission attaches to correctly calculating the amount of the compensation and also to avoiding situations of overcompensation, which are prone to have disruptive effects on the competitiveness of the markets concerned. The fact that the Commission is highly concerned with compensation/overcompensation issues is also emphasized by the depth of the relevant provisions of the 2011 Decision, in comparison with its 2005

---

[77] See Sauter 2011b, p. 229.

predecessor Decision. In this respect, one may notice that the Commission chose to qualify its approach to the compensation issue by providing more concrete guidelines as to how compensations should be evaluated.

To start off, the amount of compensation shall not exceed what is necessary to cover the net cost incurred in discharging the public service obligations, including a reasonable profit.[78] The natural continuation of this provision is that Member States shall require the undertaking concerned to repay any overcompensation received. The language used in Article 5 of the 2011 Decision seems to be more exact than the one preferred in the 2005 Decision. While the provisions regarding the calculation of costs and revenues remained mainly untouched, the 2011 Decision seems to insist on the notion of net costs. This is probably because the Commission acknowledged the technical challenges that such calculation may pose in practice. In this respect, the Commission provides alternative methods of calculation of these net costs: either as the difference between costs and revenues as defined in paras 3 and 4 of Article 5, either as the difference between the net cost for the undertaking of operating with the public service obligation and the net cost or profit of the same undertaking operating without the public service obligation. The 2011 Framework furthers the net costs discussion by providing that the preferred method of calculation should be performed according to the net avoided cost methodology, this being regarded as the most accurate method of calculation, however, not always feasible or appropriate. Should this be the case, the Commission will also accept the cost allocation methodology.[79] One may notice that by allocating extensive attention to the net cost calculation discussion and by providing stricter and more economically grounded criteria, the Commission aims to cover any possible gaps that the 2005 package may have had in this respect. However, it may be the case that postulating clearer guidelines regarding the calculation of net costs will result in lower compensation in practice. In any case, further practical developments will clarify if this assumption may be verified.

In the same vein, the 2011 Decision thoroughly defines the concept of 'reasonable profit' as a part of the concept of compensation. This is important because the notion of 'reasonable profit' clearly relates to situations that in practice may lead to cases of overcompensation, depending on the correctness of assessing the profit level, which is (or is not) reasonable. Thus, it is crucial not only to set clear criteria on how to define profitability, but also to define the benchmark against which profitability should be judged. In this respect, the Commission seems to be drawing on concepts of financial economics when stating that level of risk (which is dependent of the sector concerned), the type of service, and the characteristics of compensation should be taken into account when defining this benchmark.[80] The relevant provisions of the 2011 Decision are considerably more forceful than the provisions of the 2005 Decision, allowing less room for interpretation when the

---

[78] See Article 5, para 1 of the 2011 Decision.

[79] See paras 25–31 of the 2011 Framework.

[80] See Article 5, para 5 of the 2011 Decision.

reasonableness of the profit is assessed. This is a reflection of the Commission's response to the stakeholders' concerns regarding the lack of a clear benchmark for the calculation of 'reasonable profit' in the 2005 package. In this respect, the comparative approach regarding the rate of return of other undertakings in the sector, undertakings situated in other Member States, or if necessary, undertakings in other sectors has been partly abandoned. This move is meant to enhance legal certainty while avoiding situations that allow for overextensive and inappropriate interpretations of the rather loose term 'reasonable profit', the features of which may vary from sector to sector and from Member State to Member State. Furthermore, the Commission chose to complete the discussion on 'reasonable profit' by drawing concrete guidelines on how to determine the rate of return on capital or, if the specific circumstances do not allow for such an assessment, what other proxies may be used to determine profit level indicators. Surprisingly, in para 8 of Article 5 the Commission returns to the comparative approach by providing that whatever indicator is chosen in establishing the reasonableness of the profit, Member States shall be able to prove that the profit does not exceed what would be required of a typical undertaking considering whether or not to provide the service, for instance by providing references to returns achieved on similar types of contracts awarded under competitive conditions. All in all, one may argue that the changes brought about by the 2011 reforms are likely to result in a reduction in the level or 'reasonable profit' due to the move from an appropriate (comparative) rate of return on capital (given the risk incurred) approach (in the 2005 package) to a reference rate pertaining to the internal rate of return or to the return on capital employed, equity or assets benchmark (in the 2011 package).[81]

In any case, according to the 2011 Framework, the 'reasonable profit' will be assessed from an *ex ante* perspective (based on expected profits rather than on realized profits) in order not to remove the incentives for the undertaking to make efficiency gains when operating activities outside the SGEI. Speaking of efficiency gains, the Commission seems to place a great deal of attention on this particular issue. Article 5, para 6 of the 2011 Decision states that in determining what constitutes a 'reasonable profit', Member States may introduce incentive criteria relating, in particular, to the quality of service provided and gains in productive efficiency, which shall not reduce the quality of the service provided. The 2011 Framework seems to be using a stronger formulation, by providing that in devising the method of compensation, Member States must introduce incentives for the efficient provision of SGEI of a high standard, unless they can duly justify that it is not feasible or appropriate to do so.[82] The following paragraphs of the Framework provide concrete guidelines as to the different ways in which efficiency incentives can be designed. Regardless of the approach chosen, both the Decision and the Framework provide that due attention should be given to the quality of the service provided, which should not be offset by any efficiencies realized. Furthermore,

---

[81]   See Coppi 2011.

[82]   See para 39 of the 2011 Framework.

efficiency gains should be in line with the standards laid down in the Union legislation, thus emphasizing the fact that the Commission is unlikely to compromise on the quality standards that market operators and Member States should abide to. This approach is consistent with the Commission's general endeavor relating to welfare enhancement. After all, one could easily argue that a great deal of welfare enhancement stems from stimulating economic efficiency and maintaining high-quality standards for services provided, especially given the current economic crisis conditions the EU is facing.

Last but not least, Member States should make sure that undertakings are not receiving compensation in excess of the amount determined in accordance with Article 5 of the 2011 Decision. Of course, since overcompensation is not necessary for the operation of the SGEI, it constitutes incompatible State aid. In this respect, repayment of the excess compensation amounts is necessary. What is remarkable with regard to the control of overcompensation provisions in the 2011 Decision is the fact that the paragraph regarding the social housing sector has been deleted. This is probably connected to the new categorization (hospital services and other social services) that the Decision adheres to, as described in Sect. 4.1 of this chapter. In any event, where the amount of overcompensation does not exceed 10 % of the amount of the average annual compensation, such overcompensation may be carried forward to the next period and deducted from the amount of compensation payable in respect of that period.[83]

What are the compensation/overcompensation implications for social services? First, it must be acknowledged that this discussion has to be related to the efficiency concerns that the Commission is exhibiting lately. And this is so, not only because efficiencies may lead to societal welfare enhancement, as already discussed above, but also because efficiency gains in the context of social services may also be prone to lead to overcompensation. In this respect, a careful framework needs to be designed at Member States' level in order to insure a correct and economically sensible use of the benefits stemming from such gains. Generally speaking, by providing extensive discussions on efficiency issues both in the 2011 Decision and in the 2011 framework, the Commission clearly sends the message that it is preoccupied with stimulating the efficient delivery of (social) services. As far as the Member States are concerned, this may lead to a certain change of policy, at least for those Member States that had in place systems of delivery of social services which were not necessarily guided by efficiency considerations. As things currently stand, these Member States must provide incentives for efficient delivery of quality services, and also stimulants and rewards for achieving productive efficiency gains. On top of this, according to Article 5, para 6 of the 2011 Decision and para 41 of the 2011 Framework these gains should be shared in a balanced manner between the undertaking, on one hand and the Member States and/or users, on the other hand. What are the consequences for these actors in the context of the delivery of social services? As far as the undertakings are

---

[83] Article 6, para 2 of the 2011 Decision.

concerned, the realization of these efficiency gains, or on the contrary, failing to meet the projected gains will result in increases or decreases of the level of compensation received. Consequently, as far as Member States are concerned, this may result in public savings. Last but not least, the users/consumers may be affected in direct or indirect ways. For example, in the context of social housing, the realization of efficiency gains may result in lower rents. Also, in Member States that instituted social services based on contributions, achieving efficiency gains may result in lower contributions being paid by the users. In a more indirect manner, consumers may also benefit from such efficiency gains in lower taxation levels that they may be subjected to.

10.4.4 Information and Transparency

The 2011 Decision contains provisions[84] on the availability of information necessary to determine whether the compensation granted is compatible with the Decision, just like the 2005 Decision did. The Member States must comply with the Commission's investigative requests with regard to compatibility of the compensations awarded. The novelty introduced by the 2011 Decision relates to the period that Member States must keep the information available. According to the 2011 developments, this period extends over the whole duration of the entrustment, as embedded in the act of entrustment, according to Article 4 (a) of the 2011 Decision, and over of period of 10 years from the end of the period of entrustment. This amounts to an extension of the timeframe that this information should be kept available, since the 2005 Decision required member States to maintain the relevant information for a period of 10 years, without any mention of the duration of the entrustment. It is imaginable that in practice this extended obligation will not pose considerably more severe burdens on the Member States; however, the new provision is likely to improve legal certainty and transparency relating to the appropriateness of the compensation granted.

Another novelty brought about by the 2011 Decision is contained in Article 7 on transparency. What is striking is that this Article made its way into the text of the Decision after the consultation procedure relating to the adoption of the 2011 package ended. The provisions of Article 7 are clearly transparency enhancing and are rather straightforward in setting clear obligations for the Member States to appropriately publish information relating to the contents of the entrustment act and to the amounts of the aid granted on a yearly basis. This provision pertains only to undertakings which have additional commercial activities outside the scope of the SGEI. This is even more important having in mind the practical problems that might occur in connection to establishing the correct proportion of costs and revenues pertaining to the activities relating to the SGEI on one hand, and the

---

[84] Article 8 of the 2011 Decision.

other activities performed by the undertaking concerned on the other hand. In this respect, Article 5, para 5 of the 2011 Decision, and para 44 of the 2011 Framework both require beneficiaries to keep separate accounts for activities falling inside and outside the scope of the SGEI they perform. Also, according to Article 5, para 9 of the 2011 Decision, no compensation shall be granted in respects of the costs pertaining to the activities falling outside the scope of the SGEI. The practical difficulties mentioned above are conceivable if one also takes into account the generous choice of calculation methods that the Commission has put forward in para 31 of the 2011 Framework. Concluding, one may argue that while Article 8 of the 2011 Decision insures a basic level of transparency with regard to all situations covered by the Decision, in Article 7 the Commission chose to specifically insure that transparency is provided for in practical situations which may be particularly prone to opaque transactions.

An increased level of transparency is important as far as social services are concerned and one may argue that Articles 7 and 8 of the 2011 Decision indeed afford this basic level of transparency. What this means is that Member States must observe the transparency requirement when they design this type of service. In other words, if the Commission took the first step in affording increased transparency in the field of social services, it is now up to the Member States to comply with this requirement and also further the degree of transparency conferred. The Commission's concern with regard to a transparent functioning of social services is even more emphasized by the strict requirements regarding the entrustment act, as embedded in the 2011 package. Instituting such stringent criteria when it comes to the entrustment act sends the message that the Commission is careful in avoiding any lack of transparency that may stem from a more relaxed approach of finding the existence of entrustment from less exact, or more general legal provisions. Furthermore, since overcompensation is prone to occur also in the context of delivery of social services, the Commission seems to be paying close attention to the transparency relating to these aspects as well, by setting clear rules of calculating the net costs, the revenues and the 'reasonable profit' elements of the compensatory amounts. In this respect as well, going beyond the basic level of transparency afforded by the Commission in Articles 7 and 8 of the 2011 Decision, it is up to the Member States to further the level of transparency with regard to possible issues of overcompensation that may occur in connection to the delivery of social services.

10.4.5 The Role of Article 106(2) TFEU

The 2011 Commission Decision comes into play, if the *Altmark* conditions do not apply. It is apparent from the analysis above that the European Courts' readings of these conditions are less strict than the requirements set out by the Commission in its Decision. Nevertheless, it cannot be ruled out that compensatory measures taken by a Member State will not pass the flexible *Altmark* test or the criteria of the 2011 Commission Decision. In that case, Article 106(2) TFEU comes into play.

In its Communication, European Framework for State aid in the form of public service obligation,[85] the Commission contends that Article 106(2) TFEU is relevant, only in so far as the national compensatory measure at hand is subject to the prior notification requirement.[86] From this statement, it should be derived that a Member State cannot invoke this Treaty provision in order to justify State aid without prior permission from the Commission. Although on this point—strikingly—no case law is available, the position of the Commission seems fully in line with the system introduced by the CJEU in *Altmark*. Meeting the conditions of this ruling leads to lifting of the obligation to notify, whereas, in contrast, the application of Article 106(2) TFEU to State aid measures should be verified by the Commission.

A very important point of departure of the Communication European Framework for State aid in the form of public service obligation is that it is only permitted to invoke Article 106(2) TFEU if the service concerned is not provided on the market and cannot satisfactorily be supplied on the marketplace as well.[87] In examining whether services cannot be offered in a market environment the Commission will confine its assessment as to whether the Member States have not made a manifest error. Yet, this approach of the Commission has considerable consequences for the Member States, as Article 106(2) TFEU will only be applied if no other means are available. Supporting services that are in the interest of society is not possible, if commercial operators already provide them adequately. In the view of the Commission State aid is a policy instrument of last resort. So, under a review based on Article 106(2) TFEU, not only the presence of acts of entrustment matters but also the level of market failure is of interest.

In this respect, it should be noted, however, that for many social services it could be argued that the services offered on the market place do not meet the social needs of society. It may be assumed that in many cases access for all to a particular service is an issue that is hard to solve. To a certain extent, a political debate on what is the necessary level of provision of social services in society seems inevitable.[88] After all, these services are at the heart of the social welfares states. But it should be awaited how these things play out, as the Commission will only engage in an assessment based on the test of manifest error. On top of that many compensatory measures will benefit from the *Altmark* approach and the 2011 Commission Decision.

---

[85] *OJ* 2012 C8/15.

[86] See para 7 of this communication. See also para 48 of the Communication on the application of the European Union State aid rules to compensation granted for the provision of services of general economic interest.

[87] See para 13 of this Communication.

[88] Neergaard rightly noted that the claim that SGEI is a concept of EU law seems to be in conflict with the point of departure that the competence to define SGEI missions is vested with the Member States. See Neergaard 2011, p. 41. Debates between the EU institutions and the Member States on the exact contours of SGEI are, therefore, inherent in the EU approach to these services.

In its Communication European Framework for State aid in the form of public service obligation, the Commission points to the importance of the act of entrustment. This act should meet the same requirements as set out in the 2011 Commission Decision. As a result, national compensatory measures that are not in line with this Commission Decision for reasons of failing to meet the strict requirements for entrustment are not justifiable on the basis of Article 106 (2) TFEU either.

Therefore, Article 106(2) TFEU is only of any help, if other conditions of the 2011 Commission are not met, which do not apply (similarly) under Article 106(2) TFEU. For example, the Commission puts forward that the duration of the period of entrustment should be justified on the basis of objective criteria, such as the need to amortise nontransferable fixed assets. In contrast with the 2011 Commission Decision, it is not required that in principle the duration of the SGEI mission should not exceed a period of 10 years. On this point Article 106(2) TFEU seems to allow for more flexibility.

The 2011 Communication, which explains how the Commission will use its powers under Article 106 TFEU, also clarifies the preferred approach relating to the parameters for calculating the compensation. Paragraphs 54 and 55 of the Communication state that these parameters should be established in advance in an objective and transparent manner (without necessarily using a rigid formula) in order to ensure that they do not confer an economic advantage that could favor the recipient undertaking over competing undertakings. Should the undertaking at hand carry out activities falling both inside and outside the scope of the SGEI, the provisions of the Communication are in keeping with those of the 2011 Decision, in the sense that only the costs directly associated with the provision of the SGEI can be taken into account when calculating the compensation.[89] This assertion is also valid when talking about incentive criteria relating to the quality of services provided and productive efficiency gains in the context of establishing 'reasonable profit'.[90] Speaking of this, the Communication pays due attention to the 'reasonable profit' discussion. If 'reasonable profit' is part of the compensation, the entrustment act must clearly establish the criteria for its calculation. This may pose problems given the tensions between the recent case law and the 2011 Commission Decision which emphasize differences in flexibility regarding the approach of the Commission and the CJEU concerning the constitutive elements of the entrustment act. Also, one striking fact when talking about the calculation of the 'reasonable profit' is that the Communication seems to allow comparisons regarding the rate of return of other undertakings in the sector, undertakings situated in other Member States, or if necessary, undertakings in other sectors, whereas the 2011 Decision seems to have abandoned this approach in favor of a more pragmatic reading of the features that would make profit reasonable.

---

[89] See para 56 of the 2011 Communication and Article 5, para 9 of the 2011 Decision.

[90] See para 61 of the 2011 Communication and Article 5, para 6 of the 2011 Decision.

As compensatory measures could be justifiable both in the light of the *Altmark* approach and the 2011 Commission Decision, the added value of Article 106 (2) TFEU is limited. Yet, the Commission has given a clear statement, which is of great importance for social services. State aid given in order to compensate for the costs of an SGEI mission is justified, in so far as the services concerned cannot be provided on the market place adequately. In other words, the Commission has a clear and political view on how the provision of social services should be organized. The point of departure is the market forces and competition, whereas State intervention by means of subsidies and similar financial advantages serves as a means of last resort.

10.5 Conclusions and Evaluation

The Commission has created a generous exemption for financial compensation measures for social services. The 2011 Commission Decision is not the first action taken on the EU level in order to address issues related to these services. In contrast with many communications, this Decision is of a binding nature. Hard law with a bearing on social services is scarce in EU law. Therefore, the 2011 Commission Decision is of great interest for social services and, as a result, for the national social welfare states.

As this Decision exempts various social services from its scope, it identifies which services are supposed to meet the social needs of the population of the Member States. By doing so, it has influenced the priority setting in the delivery of social services. It is remarkable that by identifying the social services covered by the Decision the Commission did not draw any inspiration from its own definition of SSGI. As a result, no social security scheme (having an economic character) such as supplementary pension and health care schemes benefit from the exemption of the 2011 Commission Decision. It is apparent from the case law and decisional practices that these social services have given rise to more litigation than other social services. Yet, the generous exemption of the updated *Altmark* package applies solely to other social services, such as social housing and, by so doing, gives—possibly unintentionally—priority to these services. In our view, it seems inevitable that in the long run the Commission will be forced to pay due consideration to its own soft law approach to SSGI by setting out under which circumstances the provision of (economic) social security services ought to be financed.

In its present form, the 2011 Commission Decision does not define the social services covered. However, it may be assumed that interpretation problems will arise as to what hospital services, social housing, etc. constitute. As a result, the Commission and also the European Courts will be called upon to define these services. The need to give definitions is likely to have spillover effects: these definitions will lead to the Europeanization of social services and as a result to a European approach to important features of the social welfare states. At EU level, the main characteristics of social housing, hospital services, health and long-term care, childcare, access to and reintegration into the labor market, etc. will be outlined.

Although many issues are not settled (yet), the analysis of the updated *Altmark* package, as it stands now, already reveals some features, which are regarded as important elements of social services. To start with, the services offered should meet the social needs of society. This requirement is explicitly mentioned in Article 2 of the 2011 Commission Decision.

Furthermore, of great importance is a clear act of entrustment. It should be outlined with great precision what social task is entrusted to a particular operator. In contrast with important case law, such as *AG2R*[91] and *BUPA*,[92] the Commission continues to adhere to an explicit act of entrustment. This has significant consequences for social services. In order to avoid State aid problems, Member States must clearly delineate the social services that are of general interest in their national laws and decisions. Transparency on which services are financed and for what reason compensation was given is a key issue.

Another important element is the introduction of efficiency mechanisms. The Commission requires that the Member States take these mechanisms as point of departure, when financing SGEI missions. This implies that Member States verify whether the social services providers operate in an efficient way. As it is not permitted to compensate costs resulting from inefficiencies, Member States are forced to oblige their social services' providers to live up to efficiency standards. In other words, the distortion of competition resulting from the State aid given is partly 'compensated' by efficiency mechanisms.

In this regard, it is also important to note that the duration of an SGEI mission should be limited and, in principle, should not exceed a time period of 10 years. This means that other operators than the incumbents the public authorities of a Member State usually do business with should be given the opportunity to supply the services concerned. Competition should not entirely be eliminated. In this regard, it should be noted that State aid control is concerned with use and abuse of State resources in a competitive environment.[93]

It would go too far to argue that the Commission has introduced a comprehensive model for the social services delivery. Nevertheless, the 2011 Commission Decision provides for some significant bits and pieces of such a model: the organization and provision of social services should be based on clear State involvement (act of entrustment), the aim to meet particular social needs, transparency principle, efficiency considerations and a certain degree of competition.

For the Europeanization process of social services, the adoption of the updated *Altmark* package was an important development. A significant step toward an EU approach to social services is taken. In our view, the path is paved for more

---

[91] Supra note 31.

[92] Supra note 48.

[93] Von Danwitz 2011, p. 115.

binding EU measures in order to further build an EU model for social services based on a balance between State involvement and social needs, on the one hand and considerations of efficiency and competition, on the other hand.

References

Adam S, Van Elsuwege P (2012) Citizenship rights and the federal balance between the European Union and its Member States: comment on Dereci. Eur Law Rev 37(2):176–190

Boeshertz D, Frederick B (2008) The notion of economic advantage in the context of reforms to pension schemes. Comp Policy Newsletter 1:31–35

Coppi L (2011) The reform of state aid rules and SGEI—an economic perspective on compensation. In: The reform of state aid rules on SGEI: from the 2005 Monti-Kroes Package to the 2011 Almunia reform conference, Bruges, 30 Sept 2011

De Vries SA (2011) BUPA; a healthy case, in the light of a changing constitutional setting in Europe? In: van de Gronden JW, Szyszczak E, Neergaard U, Krajewski M (eds) Health care and EU law. TMC Asser Press, The Hague

Fiedziuk N (2010) Towards a more defined economic approach to services of general interest. Eur Public Law 16:280

Graham C (2010) EU and UK competition law. Pearson, Harlow

Kerstin C (2011) Social security and competition law—ECJ focuses on Art. 106(2) TFEU. J Eur Compét Law Pract 2(5):473–476

Lavrijssen S, De Vries SA (2009), Country report on SGI in The Netherlands. In: Krajewski M, Neergaard U, van de Gronden JW (eds) The changing legal framework for services of general interest in Europe—between competition and solidarity. TMC Asser Press, The Hague

Neergaard U (2011) EU health care law in a constitutional light: distribution of competences, notions of 'solidarity', and 'social Europe'? In: van de Gronden JW, Szyszczak E, Neergaard U, Krajewski M (eds) Health care and EU law. TMC Asser Press, The Hague

Nistor L (2011) Public services and the European Union. TMC Asser Press, The Hague

Sauter W (2009) Case comment on Case T-289/03, British United Provident Association Ltd (BUPA) BUPA Insurance Ltd, BUPA Ireland Ltd v Commission of the European Communities. Common Mark Law Rev 46(1):269–286

Sauter W (2011a) Health insurance and EU law, available as: TILEC DP 2011-034. http://ssrn.com/abstract=1876304

Sauter W (2011b) De herziening van het Altmark-pakket (The review of the Altmark package. Markt en Mededinging (Market Compét) 6:224–230

Schweitzer H (2011) Services of general economic interest: European law's impact on the role of markets and of Member States. In: Cremona M (ed) Market integration and public services in the European Union. Oxford University Press, Oxford

Szyszczak E (2009) Modernising healthcare: pilgrimage for the Holy Grail? In: Krajewski M, Neergaard U, van de Gronden JW (eds) The changing legal framework for services of general interest in Europe—between competition and solidarity. TMC Asser Press, The Hague

Szyszczak E (2011) Why do public services challenge the European Union? In: Szyszczak E, Davies J, Andenæs M, Bekkedal T (eds) Developments in services of general interest, legal issues of services of general interest. TMC Asser Press, The Hague, pp 1–18

Szyszczak E (2012) Soft law and safe havens. In: Neergaard U, Szyszczak E, Von de Gronden J, Krajewski M (eds) Social services of general interest and EU law. TMC Asser Press, The Hague (forthcoming)

Thouvenin J-M (2009) The Altmark case and its consequences, ? In: Krajewski M, Neergaard U, van de Gronden JW (eds) The changing legal framework for services of general interest in Europe—between competition and solidarity. TMC Asser Press, The Hague

Van de Gronden JW (2009) Financing health care in EU law: do the European State aid rules write out an effective prescription for integrating competition law with health care. Compét Law Rev 6(1):5–29

Van de Gronden JW (2011) Social services of general interest and EU law. In: Szyszczak E, Davies J, Andenæs M, Bekkedal T (eds) Developments in services of general interest, legal issues of services of general interest. TMC Asser Press, Springer, The Hague, pp 123–153

Van de Gronden JW, Rusu CS (2012) Services of general (economic) interest post-Lisbon. In: Trybus M, Rubini L (eds) The Treaty of Lisbon and the future of European law and policy. Edward Elgar, Cheltenham

Von Danwitz T (2011) The concept of State aid in liberalized sectors. In: Cremona M (ed) Market integration and public services in the European Union. Oxford University Press, Oxford

Chapter 11
Transport

Tim Maxian Rusche and Silvia Schmidt

Abstract This chapter explores the complexities of the transport sector and the way it has been influenced by recent legislative developments on Services of General Economic Interest (SGEI). Starting on the different legal bases, the authors examine Article 93 TFEU which applies to land transport and Article 106 TFEU which applies to air and maritime transport. It is argued that Article 93 TFEU takes a more permissible view on State aid. Given the diversity of legal bases in the transport sector, the remainder of the chapter is divided between an initial discussion on the applicable rules and case law in land transport and, lastly, air and maritime transport. With regard to land transport, it is argued that while the Commission is restricted by Articles 93, 91 and 109 TFEU, there are indications that the Commission has started taking a more assertive role here. This part of the chapter focuses on the applicable secondary legislation, including the new *de minimis* Regulation which exempts small local transport undertakings from notification under certain circumstances. The last part of the chapter examines air and maritime transport with particular focus on the new SGEI Decision which has lowered the notification thresholds and this is felt particularly with regard to airports. The new SGEI Framework applies, other than the 2005 framework, to air and maritime transport. The possible effects of the new rules are assessed on the basis of available figures from the transport sector as well as Commission Decisions and case law.

The views expressed in this chapter are strictly personal to the authors, and can in no way engage the Institution they are working for.

T. Maxian Rusche (✉)
European Commission, Legal Service, BERL 2/82 1049 Brussels, Belgium
e-mail: Tim.RUSCHE@ec.europa.eu

S. Schmidt (✉)
Clifford Chance LLP, 10 Upper Bank Street, London E145JJ, UK
e-mail: sschmid@tcd.ie

E. Szyszczak and J.W. van de Gronden (eds.), *Financing Services of General Economic Interest*, Legal Issues of Services of General Interest, DOI: 10.1007/978-90-6704-906-1_11, © T.M.C. ASSER PRESS, The Hague, The Netherlands, and the authors 2013

Contents

11.1 Introduction

The aim of this chapter is to explore the rules applicable to public services and to SGEI in the field of transport following the adoption of the 2012 SGEI package (see for the references to the measures of this package Chap. 1 above, footnotes 1–4). Transport has in many regards always had a special place in EU law. In this diverse sector, the Union's powers are constraint and wide-ranging at the same time. On the one hand, the freedom to provide services only applies to transport if the Union legislators have adopted secondary legislation on market opening (see Article 58(1) TFEU[1]). On the other hand, the Court has emphasised on several occasions that the Treaty chapter on Transport, Title VI, confers wide-ranging competences on the Union, enabling it to develop a common transport policy.[2]

Within this, the powers of the Union with regard to State aid have steadily been growing in significance. The Transport chapter contains a special provision for State aid in Article 93 TFEU (ex Article 73 EC), and until the Barroso II Commission took office in 2010, State aid for transport was one of the competences of the Commissioner for transport. Since then it has become a competence of the Commissioner for competition; currently Vice President Almunia. This, as well as the trend of streamlining and harmonising the various State aid procedures in the different subsectors is symbolic of the growing significance of State aid control in transport.

The transport sector is not only 'special' when it comes to its place within EU law and State aid law in general, but also with regard to its place in SGEI. To start

---

[1] Article 58 (1) TFEU provides: 'Freedom to provide services in the field of transport shall be governed by the provisions of the Title relating to transport'.

[2] Standing case law since CJEU, Case 97/78 *Schumalla* [1978] *ECR* 2311, para 4.

with, SGEI are called 'public services' in transport. Very early on, in 1969, specific secondary legislation covering State aid for public services in land transport[3] was adopted (Regulations (EEC) No. 1191/1969 and 1192/1969[4]). It comes as no surprise that a substantive amount of case law, including the *Altmark* judgment, was given in the context of public transport services. Finally, Union regulation in transport has, to an important degree, harmonised rules on SGEI in sectoral legislation.[5] This restricts the otherwise very broad discretion that the Member States enjoy in defining and imposing SGEI. According to the case law, Article 106(2) TFEU cannot be relied on in a field which is the subject of harmonisation, in the context of which the Union legislature has taken account of the general interests, in contradiction to the rules of that harmonisation.[6]

In addition to taking a special place within general Union law, State aid law and SGEI, the transport sector 'offers' the further complication that it is split into several different subsectors. In spite of the recent attempts to streamline State aid rules, the transport sector remains complex and is, in and of itself, far away from being harmonised. This chapter will explore the differences and similarities within the transport sector, and the relationship to the general rules on SGEI. It aims to give a concise overview of the rules currently in force in the transport sector.

The chapter will proceed as follows: an initial examination of Articles 93 and 106 TFEU explains the differences with regard to the legal bases (Sect. 11.2). This is followed by an examination of the applicable rules, the case law and the case practice of the Commission in land transport (Sect. 11.3) and in air and maritime transport (Sect. 11.4).

11.2 Different Legal Bases: Article 93 TFEU (Land) Versus Article 106 TFEU (Air and Maritime)

Article 93 TFEU constitutes a *lex specialis* to Article 106(2) TFEU. Therefore, State aid for public services in the area of land transport has to be assessed on the basis of the former. Article 93 TFEU states:

> *Aids* shall be compatible with the Treaties *if* they meet the needs of coordination of transport *or if* they represent reimbursement for the discharge of certain obligations inherent in the concept of a *public service* [emphasis added].

---

[3] 'Land transport' is commonly used as a short hand for transport by rail, road and inland waterway, as defined in Article 100 (1) TFEU.

[4] *OJ* 1969 L 156/1 respectively 8. The former has been repealed by Regulation (EC) No. 1370/2007, the latter is still in force. See detailed discussion in Sect. 11.2.

[5] Regulation (EC) No. 1370/2007 (land transport), Regulation (EC) No. 1008/2008 (air services) and Regulation (EC) No. 3577/92 (maritime services). These Regulations are discussed in more detail below.

[6] CJEU, Case C-206/98 *Belgium* v *Commission* [2000] *ECR* I-3509, para 45.

Comparing this to 106(2) TFEU, we note important differences:

Undertakings entrusted with the operation of *services of general economic interest* or having the character of a revenue-producing monopoly shall be subject to the rules contained in the Treaties, in particular to the rules on competition, *in so far as* the application of such rules does not obstruct the performance, in law or in fact, of the particular tasks assigned to them. *The development of trade must not be affected to such an extent as would be contrary to the interests of the Union.* [emphasis added].

Looking at the wording and scope of these two Articles it becomes clear that Article 93 TFEU takes a more permissible view on State aid in the land transport sector than on State aid for SGEI in general: Article 93 TFEU explicitly refers to 'aids' whereas Article 106(2) TFEU only implies their existence. They also approach aids from a different angle: Article 93 TFEU starts from the premise that aids *are* compatible, if they meet one of two broadly worded exceptions. In contrast, Article 106(2) TFEU starts with the opposite premise that SGEI are subject to the general *prohibition* of State aid contained 'in the Treaties', and are only exempt from control if the prohibition would obstruct their performance.

This difference in attitude is exacerbated by the fact that the exemptions in Article 106(2) TFEU for the performance of SGEI are limited by the second sentence which finds no equivalent in Article 93 TFEU: exemptions from the general prohibition for the benefit of SGEI are only permissible in so far as they do not affect trade to such an extent as would be contrary to the (potentially wide-ranging) 'interests of the Union'.

Finally, Article 106(3) TFEU grants exclusive competence to the Commission for adopting Directives and Decisions. There is no such provision with regard to land transport in Article 93 TFEU. When proposing Regulations (EEC) No. 1191/1969 and 1192/1969, the Commission based itself on what are today Articles 91 and 109 TFEU (at the time Articles 75 and 94 EEC).

In 2005, the Commission decided to adopt secondary legislation on SGEI (the 2005 SGEI Decision) on the basis of (the then) Article 86(3) EC. This raises the question as to whether it could also have adopted Regulations (EEC) No. 1191/1969 and 1192/1969 on the basis of Article 90(3) EEC. In 1969, the Commission had not yet 'discovered' that Article 90 EEC (today Article 106 TFEU) also applied to State aid. Furthermore, the Court had not yet handed down its judgment in *Nouvelles Frontières*, which clarified that 'rules in the Treaty on competition, in particular Articles 85–90, are applicable to transport'.[7] But the Commission stuck to its old habit of basing itself on Articles 71 and 89 EC when proposing in 2000 to Parliament and Council what has finally been adopted, after seven years of protracted negotiations, as Regulation (EC) No. 1370/2007.[8]

Could it have opted instead for Article 86(3) EC (now 106(3) TFEU)? At first sight, Article 93 TFEU is *lex specialis* only to Article 106(2) TFEU, but—as it does not foresee a legal basis by—*not* to Article 106(3) TFEU. On the basis of

---

[7] CJEU Joined Cases 209- 214/84 *Nouvelles Frontières* [1986] *ECR* 1457, para 42.

[8] Regulation EC 1370/2007 *OJ* 2007 L 315/1.

Nouvelles Frontières, Article 106(3) TFEU would thus be available as a legal basis for Directives and Decisions which concern public land transport services. However, the legal basis provided for in Article 106(3) TFEU is limited to Directives and Decisions for 'the application of the provisions of this article'. In State aid, the provision of Article 106(2) TFEU cannot be applied to public services in land transport, because Article 93 TFEU is *lex specialis*. This means that Article 106(3) TFEU can be relied upon for Directives and Decisions concerning, for example, the application of Articles 101 and 102 TFEU to undertakings entrusted with public land transport services. However, it cannot be relied upon for the application of State aid rules to these undertakings.

11.3 Land Transport

As outlined in the previous section, public services in the land transport sector occupy a special position in the SGEI field. The Commission's role is limited, not only by the restrictions deriving directly from Article 93 TFEU, but also by Articles 91 and 109 TFEU which give the last say to the Union legislator, rather than to the Commission as is the situation under Article 106(3) TFEU.

However, there may be room for the Commission to take a more assertive role in the field of land transport, as it has done recently in the air and maritime transport sector (see following section). In the second half of the 2000s, following the *Altmark* judgment, the Commission has opened eight formal investigation procedures[9] into public land transport services; thus far, it has closed four of them with positive decisions.[10] The remaining four investigations are, however, still pending. This year, it has launched another investigation concerning Italy.[11]

---

[9] See the openings in State aid cases: C 58/2006 *Verkehrsverbund Rhein-Ruhr, OJ* 2006 C 74/18; C 16/2007, *Postbus AG, OJ* 2007 C 162/19; C 31/2007 *Córas Iompair Éireann Bus Companies, OJ* 2007 C 217/44; C 47/2007 *Deutsche Bahn Regio, OJ* 2008 C 35/13; C 54/07 *Emsländische Eisenbahn GmbH, OJ* 2008 C 174/13; C 3/2008 *Bus transport CAS services, OJ* 2008 C 43/19; C 17/2008 *Bus transport in Usti Region, OJ* 2008 C 187/14; C 41/2008 *Danske Statsbaner, OJ* 2008 C 309/14; the opening of the EFTA surveillance authority concerning bus transport in Oslo, nyr in the *OJ*, press release PR/12/18, following the annulment of a no objection decision by the EFTA Court in Case E-14/10 *Konkurrenten.no AS* v *EFTA Surveillance Authority*, EFTA Court Report 2011, p. 266.

[10] Commission Decision 2009/845/EC of 26 November 2008 on State aid granted by Austria to the company Postbus in the Lienz district, *OJ* 2009 L 306/26; Commission Decision 2009/325/EC of 26 November 2008 on State aid concerning public service compensations for Southern Moravia Bus Companies, *OJ* 2009 L 97/14; Commission Decision 2011/3/EU of 24 February 2010 concerning public transport service contracts between the Danish Ministry of Transport and Danske Statsbaner, *OJ* 2011 L 7/1; Commission Decision 2011/501/EU of 23 February 2011 on Aid for the Bahnen der Stadt Monheim (BSM) and Rheinische Bahngesellschaft (RBM) companies in the Verkehrsverbund Rhein Ruhr, *OJ* 2011 L 210/1.

[11] SA.33037, SIMET, nyr, see IP/12/518.

Land transport remains excluded, for the legal reasons set out above, from the scope of application of the 2012 SGEI decision[12] and the 2012 SGEI framework.[13] On the other hand, the new Communication on the notion of State aid and the *de minimis* Regulation also apply to public land transport services. With regard to the former, this follows from the fact that the notion of State aid is identical across all sectors. However, the *de minimis* Regulation could indicate that the Commission is moving towards a more unified approach to SGEI in general.

The remainder of this section will discuss the rules of secondary law, the Commission notices and guidelines, the principles the Commission has developed for the direct application of Article 93 TFEU and compare them to the general rules applicable to other sectors pursuant to the 2012 SGEI package.

11.3.1 Secondary Law in Land Transport: Regulations (EC) No. 1370/2007 and 1192/1969

11.3.1.1 Regulation (EC) 1370/2007 on Public Passenger Transport Services by Rail and by Road

The Regulation entered into force on 3 December 2009 and has been widely discussed in the academic literature[14]; therefore only a short summary of the Regulation will be given here. Secondly, while the Regulation is also of significance for public procurement of land transport service contracts and concessions, only its significance for State aid will be dealt with here.

The Regulation clarified the situations in which State aid in the land transport sector is exempted from prior notification to the Commission, and corresponds therefore in its function to the 2012 SGEI decision. According to its Article 9(1), aids, here called 'public service compensation', do not need to be notified to the Commission under Article 108(3) TFEU if they comply with the Regulation. It reads:

---

[12] Commission Decision of 20 December on the application of Article 106(2) TFEU to State aid in the form of public service compensation granted to certain undertakings entrusted with the operation of services of general economic interest, *OJ* L7, C(2011) 9380, Article 2.4.

[13] Recital 8.

[14] See for example Skovgaard Oelykke 2008; Kekelekis and Rusu 2010; Maxian Rusche and Schmidt 2011; Schröder 2010; Polster 2009, 2010; Pünder 2010a, b, c; Schmitz and Winkelhüsener 2009; Nettesheim 2009; Linke 2010; Saxinger 2010a, b; Scheps and Otting 2008; Ziekow 2009; Olgemöller and Otting 2009; Schön 2009; Wittig and Schimanek 2008; Schröder 2008; Winnes 2009; Bayreuther 2009; Röbke and Rechten 2010; Deuster 2010, p. 591; Kramer 2010; Deuster 2009; Haats and Richter 2010; Hübner 2009; Tegner and Wachinger 2010; Stickler and Feske 2010; Jasper et al. 2008; Winnes et al. 2009; Kaufmann et al. 2010.

Public service compensation for the operation of public passenger transport services or for complying with tariff obligations established through general rules paid in accordance with this Regulation shall be compatible with the common market.

The situation of public land transport services is to a certain extent comparable to social services under the 2012 SGEI decision, insofar as they are exempted from notification independently of the amount of compensation paid. However, the conditions for being exempt are far more demanding for public land transport services.

The precise conditions for complying with the Regulation can be found in Articles 4–7. Article 4 specifies the mandatory content of such 'public service contracts'. In particular, the public service obligation has to be clearly defined, establishing the parameters for compensation and nature of exclusive rights granted in advance. Article 5 sets out the principle that public service contracts have to be awarded on the basis of the public procurement Directives 2004/17/EC and 2004/18/EC and that public service concessions have to be awarded on the basis of a competitive tender procedure. This is subject to exceptions which apply mostly to in-house awards and rail services. Article 6 and the Annex specify the detailed rules on how compensation may be calculated. Article 7 contains publication obligations.

Comparing the conditions contained in the Regulation with the conditions of the 2012 SGEI decision, there are two main differences: the Regulation requires a competitive tender and compensation is more closely linked to efficiency. The first difference is that the Regulation requires compliance with the applicable rules on public procurement, and prescribes the use of a competitive tender also for concessions. The use of competitive tenders is therefore made mandatory also for concessions. State aid control in this instance is used as a tool to enforce compliance with public procurement rules. In contrast to this, the 2012 SGEI decision refers to 'the requirements flowing from the Treaty or from sectoral Union legislation'. This would appear to include the *Telaustria* case law[15] and the public procurement Directives.[16] However, the *Telaustria* case law leaves more discretion to the public authority awarding a concession than the Regulation, which requires not only transparency and non-discrimination, but also a competitive tender.

The second difference is that the Annex stipulates that the method of compensation must promote the maintenance or development of effective management by the public service operator, which can be the subject of an objective assessment. This is similar to the efficiency incentives prescribed under the 2012 SGEI

---

[15] CJEU, Case C-324/98 *Telaustria Verlags GmbH and Telefonadress GmbH* v *Telekom Austria AG* [2000] *ECR* I-10745, para 60.

[16] This is also supported by an *e contrario* with comparison to the 2012 SGEI Framework. The Framework applies 'without prejudice to' the requirements flowing from the Treaty or from sectoral Union legislation, which therefore do not constitute a condition for compatibility, but makes the compliance with Union public procurement rules a condition for compatibility (point 2.6).

framework,[17] but goes even further: it implies that the compensation is reduced over time so as to comply with the fourth *Altmark* criterion.

With regard to the scope of application of the Regulation, it is important to note that it only applies where the operator of the service has been granted an exclusive right and/or compensation. Article 3(1) holds:

> Where a competent authority decides to grant the operator of its choice an exclusive right and/or compensation, of whatever nature, in return for the discharge of public service obligations, it shall do so within the framework of a public service contract.

It therefore does not apply to completely deregulated markets such as the United Kingdom with the exception of London,[18] or Poland outside the major conurbations.[19]

The Commission has thus far adopted two final Decisions on the basis of Regulation (EC) No. 1370/2007, namely *Danske Statsbaner*[20] and *Verkehrsverbund Rhein Ruhr.*[21] In both cases, the Commission applied the Regulation to public service contracts that had been concluded before its entry into force. This application *ratione temporis* has been hotly debated with Member States, beneficiaries[22] and in the academic literature.[23] It is currently also the object of a case pending before the General Court.[24]

It should be noted that there is divergence not only with regard to the question as to whether Regulation (EEC) No. 1191/1969 (in force at the time of the conclusion of the contract) or Regulation (EC) No. 1370/2007 should apply to these contracts, but also with regard to the question as to what the precise content of Regulation (EEC) No. 1191/1969 is. This is illustrated by the fact that both the complainant in the *Danske Statsbaner* case and the beneficiary claimed in the

---

[17] 2012 SGEI framework, recital 39–43.

[18] Decision N 588/02, recital 47–49. Note, however, that the Commission concludes in this Decision that the measure at stake, the grant for long-distance coach services, does constitute a public service concession compatible on the basis of Article 93 TFEU.

[19] The Commission has recently adopted a number of restructuring aid Decisions concerning regional bus undertakings in Poland; in this context, it has stated that the Polish legislation provides neither for exclusive rights nor for compensation payments; see Decision SA.34088, recital 5; SA.33042, recital 5; SA.32612, recital 5.

[20] Commission Decision 2011/3/EU of 24 February 2010 concerning public transport service contracts between the Danish Ministry of Transport and Danske Statsbaner, *OJ* 2011 L 7/1.

[21] Commission Decision 2011/501/EU of 23 February 2011 on Aid for the Bahnen der Stadt Monheim (BSM) and Rheinische Bahngesellschaft (RBM) companies in the Verkehrsverbund Rhein Ruhr, *OJ* 2011 L 210/1.

[22] See the positions expressed by Denmark, Germany and the beneficiaries in the administrative procedure in the cases mentioned in the two previous footnotes.

[23] See for example: Maxian Rusche and Schmidt (2011); Linke (2010); Saxinger (2009a, b).

[24] GC, Case T 92/11 *Andersen v Commission*, notice of application published in *OJ* C 103/28. This application concerns Commission Decision 2011/3/EU of 24 February 2010 concerning public transport service contracts between the Danish Ministry of Transport and Danske Statsbaner, *OJ* 2011 L 7/1.

course of the administrative procedure that the Commission should have applied Regulation (EEC) No. 1191/1969. According to *Danske Statsbaner*, this would have resulted in the disputed aid being exempt from notification, whereas according to the complainant, the aid would have to be declared incompatible under that Regulation.

In the meantime, the Court has, in the context of a different case, clarified the temporal application of State aid rules. It has found that unlawful State aid[25] is to be considered as an *on-going* situation, rather than an *existing* situation, and that therefore, the Commission—in absence of any transitional rules—has to apply the new rules to all pending cases involving illegal aid.[26] Therefore, it is now beyond doubt that the Commission has rightly decided to apply Regulation (EC) No. 1370/2007 to all pending cases of unlawful aid.

11.3.1.2 Regulation (EC) Nr. 1192/1969 on Common Rules for the Normalisation of the Accounts of Railway Undertakings

Regulation (EC) 1192/1969,[27] which is based—just like Regulation (EC) No. 1370/2007—on Articles 75 and 94 EEC (now Articles 91 and 108 TFEU), obliges Member States to determine the financial burden on, or benefits for, railway undertakings imposed by any laws, regulations or administrative acts. Member States then need to compare them to other transport undertakings, and pay railway undertakings compensation for any discrepancies (Article 2). This combined action is referred to as 'normalisation', as it has the purpose of creating a level playing field between railways and the other modes of transport (recital 1).

The Regulation distinguishes between three categories of burdens: those for which compensation must be paid (Article 4 (1)); those which must be abolished by 1971 or 1973 (Article 4 (2) and (3)); and those which may be subject to normalisation (Article 4 (4)). Compensation paid pursuant to the Regulation is exempted from prior notification under Article 108(3) TFEU (Article 13 (2)).

It is remarkable that this Regulation—just like its today defunct 'sister' Regulation (EEC) No. 1191/1969 (repealed and replaced by Regulation (EC) No. 1370/2007)—was based on a joint legal basis, and that potential State aid issues were in the mind of the Union legislator back in 1969. Indeed, back then, railway markets were still closed to competition, and therefore, the rationale for State aid control was a concern for intermodal competition.

---

[25] That is, aid that has been granted in violation of the stand still obligation of Article 108(3) TFEU, see Article 1 letter f of Regulation (EC) Nr. 659/1999 on laying down detailed rules for the application of Article 93 of the EC Treaty, *OJ* 1999 L 83/1.

[26] CJEU, Joined Cases C-465/09 P -C-470/09 P *Territorio Histórico de Vizcaya a.o. v Commission* [2011] *ECR*-I 0000, paras 124–127. This has been recently confirmed in CJEU, Case C-167/11 *De Poli v Commission* [2012] *ECR*-I-0000, para 51.

[27] Regulation (EC) 1192/1969, *OJ* 1969 L 156/8.

Based on the more recent case law in *Deutsche Bahn*[28] and *Antrop,*[29] it appears doubtful whether compensation paid under Article 4(1) actually constitutes State aid in the first place. It would seem—just as for compensation paid under Regulation (EEC) No. 1191/1969—that Member States have an obligation by virtue of Union law to pay the compensation, without any discretion.[30] In such a situation, the payments are not imputable to the State.[31]

The notification exemption remains of a certain importance until today for certain national railway undertakings. They mainly cover costs for social benefits and excessive staff levels, as well as costs resulting from political decisions to keep open certain establishments.

11.3.1.3 SGEI *de minimis* Regulation

Scope: Exclusion of Road Freight Transport

The rationale behind the new SGEI *de minimis* Regulation is to simplify the bureaucratic effort surrounding SGEI that are too small to distort competition or affect trade.[32] This is in line with Vice President Almunia's efforts to streamline State aid procedures.

This Regulation complements rather than replaces Regulation (EC) No. 1998/2006,[33] and Regulation 1998/2006 will remain in force until 31 December 2013.[34] It should be noted that the two Regulations are complimentary as the new Regulation will only apply where there is an SGEI: This Regulation applies to 'aid granted to undertakings providing a service of general economic interest within the meaning of Article 106(2) of the Treaty' (Article 1). In other words, the first *Altmark* condition (entrustment) has to be met.

The legal basis for the 2012 SGEI *de minimis* Regulation is Regulation (EC) No. 994/1998 on the application of Articles 92 and 93 of the Treaty establishing the European Community to certain categories of horizontal State aid (hereafter: the Enabling Regulation),[35] which in turn is based on Article 94 EEC (now Article

---

[28] GC, Case T-351/02 *Deutsche Bahn* v *Commission* [2006] *ECR* II-1047, para 102.

[29] CJEU, Case C-504/07 *Antrop* [2009] *ECR* I-3867.

[30] This has been held by the Court for Regulation (EEC) No. 1191/1969, which contains comparable wording, see CJEU, Case C-504/07 Antrop [2009] *ECR* I-3867, paras 19 and 20.

[31] GC, Case T-351/02 *Deutsche Bahn* v *Commission* [2006] *ECR* II-1047, para 102.

[32] Press release from 20 December 2011: State aid: Commission adopts new rules on services of general economic interest, IP/11/1571.

[33] Commission Regulation (EC) No 1998/2006 of 15 December 2006 on the application of Articles 87 and 88 of the Treaty to *de minimis* aid, *OJ* 2006 L 379/5.

[34] Commission Regulation (EC) No 1998/2006 of 15 December 2006 on the application of Articles 87 and 88 of the Treaty to de minimis aid, *OJ* 2006 L 379, Article 6.

[35] *OJ* 1998 L 142/1.

109 TFEU). Therefore, there is no legal obstacle to its application to land transport.

The first *de minimis* Regulation of 2001[36]—in force at the time of the *Altmark* ruling—had nevertheless excluded transport from its scope of application (recital 3 and Article 1a). This is one of the reasons why the Court found in *Altmark* that there was—despite the rather small amount at stake (0.25 EUR per person-kilometre) and the rather local nature of the transport services (within a rural district in Eastern Germany)—an effect on trade.[37]

In the 2006 *de minimis* Regulation, transport is included, but aid for the acquisition of road freight transport vehicles is forbidden, and a lower *de minimis* threshold of 100,000 EUR applies to road transport undertakings. The 2012 SGEI de minimis Regulation excludes undertakings active in road *freight* transport (Article 1(2)(g)). The threshold for other transport undertakings is the same as for all other undertakings, i.e. 500,000 EUR.

Content of the New Regulation

According to this new Regulation on *de minimis* aid, if compensation granted to an undertaking for discharging SGEI fulfils the conditions set out in the Regulation, then the compensation does not need to be notified under 108(3) TFEU.[38] This notification exemption applies to compensation which does not exceed EUR 500,000 over any period of three fiscal years, no matter which form (i.e. a grant, loan, capital injection etc.) the aid takes.[39] If the aid does not come within the threshold of this Regulation, it needs to be assessed by the Commission.[40] Member States are charged with monitoring the correct application of this Regulation.[41] The Regulation entered into force on 28 April 2012 and will apply until 31 December 2018; however it already applies to aid complying with Articles 1 and 2 before its entry into force, and aid complying with it can continue to be implemented for six months after its expiry.[42]

The major differences to Regulation 1998/2006 are that the threshold for the notification exemption has been raised from EUR 200,000 generally and EUR 100,000 for road transport[43] over any period of three fiscal years to EUR 500,000 (Article 2(2) of the new Regulation).

---

[36] Commission Regulation (EC) No 69/2001, *OJ* 2001 L 10/30.

[37] CJEU, Case C 280/00 *Altmark* [2003] *ECR* I-7727, para 80.

[38] Article 2(1).

[39] Articles 2 (2) and (3).

[40] Article 4.

[41] Article 3.

[42] Articles 4 and 5.

[43] Commission Regulation (EC) No 1998/2006 of 15 December 2006 on the application of Articles 87 and 88 of the Treaty to *de minimis* aid, *OJ* 2009 L 379/5, Article 2(2).

In the case of aid in the form of a guarantee, the guaranteed part of the underlying loan must not be above EUR 3,750,000 in order to benefit from this Regulation. In Regulation 1998/2006, the loan is not permitted to exceed EUR 1,500,000 per undertaking in general and EUR 750,000 per undertaking in the transport sector.[44]

As a result of the new SGEI *de minimis* Regulation, in particular small local transport undertakings, which—for whatever reason—fail to comply with Regulation (EC) No. 1370/2007 may not have to fear any negative consequences on the State aid side of things, as long as their compensation does not exceed EUR 500,000 over three years.

11.3.2 Guidelines and Frameworks

The Commission has also adopted guidelines and frameworks on the basis of Article 93 TFEU. According to the case law of the Court, by adopting such pieces of soft law, the Commission auto-limits the broad discretion it enjoys when assessing the compatibility of State aid with the internal market.[45] Before presenting very briefly these guidelines and frameworks (which do not directly deal with public services), it is worth pausing on the general question whether the Commission actually enjoys discretion under Article 93 TFEU, so that it can adopt these texts without overstepping its powers.

11.3.2.1 Discretionary Power for the Commission Under Article 93 TFEU?

As set out above, Article 93 TFEU contains no equivalent to the second sentence of Article 106(2) TFEU. This could be understood as meaning that the Commission, in the application of Article 93 TFEU, is limited to a mere verification of the necessity of aid (i.e to a verification of the absence of an over-compensation). However, at the same time, Article 93 TFEU relies on two rather vague notions, namely 'coordination of transport' and 'reimbursement for the discharge of certain obligations inherent in the concept of a public service'. In order to assess whether a certain measure can be justified as 'coordination of transport' or whether a certain obligation is 'inherent in the concept of a public service', the Commission needs to carry out a complex economic assessment of the transport system. This is a first indication that the Commission, in the application of that provision, needs to enjoy a certain degree of discretion.

The Court was confronted with the challenge of interpreting Article 77 EEC (now Article 93 TFEU) relatively early on. In *Commission* v *Belgium*, it

---

[44] Ibid, Article 2(4)(d).

[45] See for example: CJEU, Case C-313/90 *CIRFS v Commission* [1993] *ECR* I-1177, para 36; CJEU, Case C-464/09 P *Holland Malt v Commission* [2010] *ECR* I-0000, para 47.

'imported' the missing second sentence of Article 106(2) TFEU into Article 93 TFEU (emphasis added)[46]:

> Moreover, the effect of the application of Article 77 of the Treaty, which acknowledges that aid to transport is compatible with the Treaty only in well-defined cases *which do not jeopardise the general interests of the Community*, cannot be to exempt aid to transport from the general system of the Treaty concerning aid granted by the States and from the controls and procedures laid down therein. (emphasis added).

After this ruling, it is clear that the Commission, when assessing an aid measure under Article 93 TFEU, not only has to establish the necessity, but also the proportionality of the aid. The guiding principle is—as under Article 106(2) TFEU—the interest of the Union. Therefore, it must be concluded that the Commission enjoys a certain amount of discretion also under Article 93 TFEU, and can adopt instruments of soft law on this basis.

11.3.2.2 Community Guidelines for State Aid to Railway Undertakings

The Community guidelines for State aid to railway undertakings[47] are based mainly on Article 93 TFEU, but deal only with the alternative 'coordination of transport', and do not contain any rules for transport infrastructure. They are therefore of little interest for the present chapter.

11.3.2.3 Community Guidelines for Cableways

In 2002, the Commission adopted Community guidelines for cableways.[48] These guidelines are different from the standard Community guidelines, as they are part of a 'no objection' Decision. Nevertheless, the Commission decided to publish the full text of that Decision in the Official Journal, and to give auto-limiting character to these guidelines. The guidelines distinguish between, on the one hand, cableways designed for a specific economic category of users (mainly ski installations), and on the other hand, cableways used for general mobility needs. With regard to the former, the guidelines provide for (generous) transitional rules for the full application of the regional aid guidelines; these rules are no longer of any practical relevance, as the transition period has expired.

With regard to the latter, the guidelines clarify, based on *Aeroports de Paris* (Case C-82/01, *ECR* 2002, I-9297), that 'private or public transport infrastructure manager, separate from the State administration, will always meet the definition of

---

[46] CJEU, Case 156/77 *Commission v Belgium* [1978] *ECR* 1881, para 10.

[47] Commission Communication C(2008) 184, Community guidelines on State Aid for railway undertakings, *OJ* 2008 C 184/13.

[48] Commission communication concerning State aid N 376/01—Aid scheme for cableways—Authorisation of State aid under Articles 87 and 88 of the EC Treaty, *OJ* 2002 C 172/2.

"undertaking"'.[49] They go on to explain that aid for cableways meeting general transport needs may also threaten to distort competition and affect trade.[50] As for the compatibility of aid for cableways, the guidelines suggest the use of Article 93 TFEU in its alternative 'coordination of transport'. However, it has to be noted that the dividing line between 'coordination of transport' and 'obligation inherent in the notion of public service' is sometimes difficult to draw in the field of transport infrastructure. It is therefore worth briefly quoting the compatibility criteria set out in these guidelines[51]:

- state contribution towards total financing of the project is necessary to enable the realisation of the project or activity in the interest of the Community,
- access to the aid is granted on non-discriminatory terms,
- the aid does not give rise to distortion of competition to an extent contrary to the common interest.

11.3.3 Direct Application of Article 93 TFEU

In *Altmark*, the Court held that since the adoption of Regulation (EEC) No. 1107/1970[52] (in the meantime repealed by Regulation (EC) No. 1370/2007), it was no longer possible to apply Article 77 EEC (now Article 93 TFEU) directly[53]:

> Regulation No 1107/70 lists exhaustively the circumstances in which the authorities of the Member States may grant aids under Article 77 of the Treaty.

This presented a certain challenge for the Commission, which had relied in a number of situations not covered by Regulation (EEC) No. 1107/1970 directly on Article 77 EEC, in particular for transport infrastructure, combined transport and inland waterway transport. The Commission relied, following the *Altmark* ruling, in its decision practice for these cases on Articles 86(2)EC and 87(3)(c) EC.

Nevertheless, the Union legislator felt that the Commission should be freed from the straightjacket. When adopting Regulation (EC) No. 1370/2007, it repealed Regulation (EEC) No. 1107/1970, and justified this with explicit reference to *Altmark*[54]:

> [Regulation (EEC) No. 1107/70] is considered obsolete while limiting the application of Article 73 of the Treaty without granting an appropriate legal basis for authorising current investment schemes, in particular in relation to investment in transport infrastructure in a

---

[49] Ibid, recital 16.

[50] Ibid, recital 18–28.

[51] Ibid, recital 39.

[52] *OJ* L 130/1.

[53] CJEU, Case C-280/00 *Altmark* [2003] *ECR* I-7747, para 108.

[54] Recital 37.

public private partnership. It should therefore be repealed in order for Article 73 of the Treaty to be properly applied to continuing developments in the sector.

The Commission has not (yet) adopted any framework or guidelines on the application of Article 93 TFEU to reimbursement for the discharge of certain obligations inherent in the concept of a public service. Therefore, the Commission enjoys in principle full discretion for its application. The Union legislator has given the Commission some 'guidance' on this question in recital 36 of Regulation (EC) No. 1370/2007:

> Any compensation granted in relation to the provision of public passenger transport services other than those covered by this Regulation which risks involving State aid within the meaning of Article 87(1) of the Treaty should comply with the provisions of Articles 73, 86, 87 and 88 thereof, including any relevant interpretation by the Court of Justice of the European Communities and especially its ruling in Case C-280/00 Altmark Trans GmbH. When examining such cases, the Commission should therefore apply principles similar to those laid down in this Regulation or, where appropriate, other legislation in the field of services of general economic interest.

The main scope of application for this recital would seem to be passenger transport on inland waterways and cableways. Whether a recital of the Union legislator can legally bind the Commission in the exercise of its State aid competence appears doubtful; however, it would seem logical to treat all modes of land transport the same when it comes to public passenger transport.

Apart from this clear consequence, this recital raises more questions than it answers. First of all, it appears to imply that public passenger transport services covered by the Regulation can only be declared compatible with the internal market if it complies with the conditions set out in the Regulation. This conclusion is not the only possible interpretation: for block exemption regulations, the General Court has decided that the Commission may declare compatible any aid not covered by the notification exemption on the basis of Article 107(3)(c)TFEU, provided that its conditions are met. The Court came to this conclusion rather than any others because of the wording of a recital which hinted into that direction.[55] However, recital 36 appears to exclude this possibility. It would therefore seem that the situation is the same under Regulation (EC) No. 1370/2007 as it was under its predecessor, Regulation (EEC) No. 1191/1969: any aid which falls within its scope of application—but does not meet the conditions set out in it—cannot be declared compatible with the internal market on any other legal basis.[56]

Secondly, it leaves the question open as to what criteria shall be applied to compensation payments for public services outside public passenger transport services. This concerns in particular public service compensation for freight (for which Regulation (EEC) No. 1191/1969 has been grandfathered until the end of 2012, see Article 10(1)) and transport infrastructure. Ultimately, it would appear

---

[55] GC, Case T-357/02 RENV *Freistaat Sachsen v Commission* [2011] *ECR* II-0000, paras 43 and 44.

[56] CJEU, Case C-504/07 *Antrop* [2009] *ECR* I-3867, para 28.

that in the absence of any secondary legislation, guidelines and frameworks, the Commission enjoys in this regard its full discretion.

11.4 Maritime and Air: On the Way to Normality... and Beyond!

Article 93 TFEU applies only to land transport; the Council and the Parliament could in theory extend, based on a proposal by the Commission, its application to air and maritime transport.[57] The Commission has, however, never made such a proposal—probably for the same reason for which turkeys do not vote for Thanksgiving. The Commission would actually weaken its competence and discretion if it was to make such a proposal, as it would mean that rather than applying the restrictive rules of Article 106(2) TFEU, it would have to apply the more permissible rules of Article 93 TFEU, and lose the possibility to create secondary law itself based on Article 106(3) TFEU.[58]

The new Communication on the notice of State aid and the new *de minimis* Regulation (see above) do apply to air and maritime transport without any limitation or particularities. There are, however, particularities with regard to the SGEI Decision and the SGEI framework, which merit closer assessment.

11.4.1 SGEI Decision 2005 Versus 2012

11.4.1.1 Tighter Thresholds in 2012

The new 2012 SGEI Decision (hereafter: 2005 Decision) [59] replaces Decision 2005/842/EC which formed part of the so-called 'Monti-Kroes-Package'. Both Decisions foresee situations in which State aid is deemed 'compatible' with the internal market and thereby avoids the notification obligation under Article 108(3) TFEU.[60] However, there are important differences as to the thresholds which need to be met in order to avoid notification.

Under the 2005 Decision, aid for SGEI was exempted from notification if the compensation was less than €30 million annually and the undertaking entrusted

---

[57] Article 100 TFEU.

[58] CJEU, Joined Cases 209–213/84 *Asjes* [1986] *ECR* 1425, paras 39 and 42.

[59] Commission Decision of 20 December 2011 on the application of Article 106(2) of the Treaty on the Functioning of the European Union to State aid in the form of public service compensation granted to certain undertakings entrusted with the operation of services of general economic interest (notified under document C(2011) 9380), 2012/21/EU.

[60] Article 3 of both the 2005 and the 2012 Decision.

with the SGEI had an annual turnover of less than EUR 100 million during the two financial years prior to the award of the SGEI.[61] This general threshold was also applicable to undertakings entrusted with maritime and air connections qualified as SGEI, as well as to ports and airports entrusted with SGEI.

The 2005 Decision foresaw a second alternative specific to air and maritime transport: air and maritime links to islands were exempt from notification if the 'average annual traffic during the two financial years preceding that in which the service of general economic interest was assigned does not exceed 300,000 passengers'.[62] Aids for airports were exempted if the average annual traffic did not exceed one million passengers and aids for ports were exempted if the annual traffic did not exceed 300,000 passengers.[63]

Under the 2012 SGEI Decision, it remains the case that State aids for SGEI which fulfil the conditions of the Decision constitute 'compatible' State aids (i.e. compatible with the internal market and therefore do not need to be notified to the Commission according to 108(3).[64] However, the 2012 SGEI Decision declares that the general notification threshold—which is lowered from €30 million to €15 million[65]—no longer applies to transport and transport infrastructure.

The only threshold applicable to air and maritime links to islands is now that they must not exceed 300,000 passengers.[66] The only threshold for State aids to ports is that they do not exceed 300,000 passengers. There is no direct link between the number of passengers and the amount of compensation paid, as the amount of compensation paid may depend on many other factors (distance to be travelled; efficiency of the undertaking entrusted; geographic situation;...). However, it is certain that many air and maritime services as well as ports which exceeded 300,000 passengers received less than EUR 30 million in compensation. This means that, whereas there has in general been a tightening of conditions, this has been particularly harsh for the air and maritime transport sector.

The strongest tightening of the screw took place with regard to airports. Here, not only did the EUR 30 million alternative threshold disappear, but at the same time, the threshold for the annual traffic changed from not exceeding 1 million passengers to 200,000 passengers.[67] The 2012 SGEI Decision itself states that lowering the threshold is appropriate 'due to the development of intra-Union trade, of multinational providers within the internal market and the amount should be calculated as an annual average.'[68]

---

[61] Commission Decision 2005/842/EC, Article 2.1(a).

[62] Ibid, Article 2.1(c).

[63] Ibid, Article 2.1(d).

[64] SGEI Decision, Article 3.

[65] Ibid, Article 2.1(a).

[66] Commission Decision C(2011) 9380 final, Article 2.1(d).

[67] Ibid, Article 2.1(e).

[68] Ibid, para 10 of the preamble.

Apart from these thresholds, the other condition for this Decision to apply is that the State aid must not exceed ten years, except for cases where the amortisation period is longer.[69] This is often going to be the case for ports and airports.

This means that, while more social services (see the chapter by van de Gronden and Rusu) are exempt from notification, more SGEI in the air and maritime transport sector are obliged to notify the Commission, once the two year grace period expires. This will significantly increase the number of cases that are subject to the notification obligation.

11.4.1.2 Compliance with Treaty Rules

Furthermore, Article 3 of the 2012 SGEI Decision holds that the State aid must also comply 'with the requirements flowing from the Treaty or from sectoral Union legislation.' This reference to Treaty requirements is new—the 2005 Decision only referred to 'stricter provisions relating to public service obligations contained in sectoral Community legislation.'[70] The Treaty requirements include in particular the so-called *Telaustria* case law on the minimal requirements for the awards of concessions, which are of particular importance for airports and ports.

11.4.1.3 Compliance with Air and Maritime Regulation

As was the case for the 2005 Decision, for the 2012 SGEI Decision to apply, the State aid in question needs to also comply with sectoral legislation. These are Regulation 1008/2008 on air services (which repealed Regulation 2408/92)[71] and Regulation 3577/92 on maritime transport. These Regulations are also expressly mentioned in both the 2005 and the 2012 SGEI Decision.

Regulation 1008/2008, the so-called 'Air Services Regulation', applies to licensing Union air carriers, air services and the pricing of intra-Union air services (Article 1.1). This Regulation sets out the conditions under which Member States can impose public service obligations for air services to airports in peripheral regions or on other thin routes.

The basic requirement is that the route has to be 'vital for the economic and social development of the region which the airport serves.' In ensuring the 'minimum provision' necessary on those routes, Member States may impose conditions such as standards of continuity, regularity, pricing, minimum capacity

---

[69] Ibid, Article 2.2.

[70] Commission Decision 2005/842/EC, Article 3.

[71] Regulation (EC) No 1008/2008 of the European Parliament and of the Council of 24 September 2008 on common rules for the operation of air services in the Community, *OJ* 2008 L 293/3.

which would not otherwise be assumed by air carriers.[72] If no air carrier takes over the route, then the Member State may limit access to one carrier for up to four or five years.[73]

Importantly, Member State will have to organise a call for tender if they decide to award the route to one carrier.[74] The now repealed Regulation (EC) No. 2408/92 did set out (in its Article 4) circumstances under which Member States were obliged to call for a public tender. However, it did not specify the particularities of such a tender. In contrast to this, the new Regulation, in Article 17, sets out detailed tender requirements: the invitation to tender has to be communicated to the Commission and published in the *OJ*. In it, the Member States need to specify the following points: necessary standards, conditions for amendment or termination, contractual duration, penalties for non-compliance and objective parameters for the compensation.[75] Selection should 'take into consideration' the following factors: adequacy of the service, prices and conditions and the amount of compensation.[76]

In order to be permissible, the compensation paid in accordance with Regulation (EC) No. 1008/2008 still needs to be assessed by the Member States according to the *Altmark* criteria.[77] While it is the Member States who are responsible for ensuring compatibility, the Commission may still examine the public service obligations (PSO) and suspend them if they do not comply with the Regulation. Therefore, this does not constitute a 'full' notification exemption: the Commission needs to be kept informed of the PSO procedure and a notice needs to be published in the OJ.[78]

The equivalent of Regulation (EC) No. 1008/2008 for maritime transport is Regulation (EC) No. 3577/92 on maritime cabotage. This Regulation applies to maritime transport and also allows for PSO to be imposed 'for the provision of cabotage services, on shipping companies participating in regular services to, from and between islands.'[79] The obligation has to be imposed on a 'non-discriminatory basis'.[80] The Court of Justice also found that in order to be permissible, there needs to be a 'real public service need', the 'prior administrative authorisation scheme [has to be] necessary and proportionate to the aim pursued' and the

---

[72] Ibid, Article 16(1).

[73] Ibid, Article 16(9).

[74] Ibid, Article 16(10).

[75] Ibid, Article 17(3).

[76] Ibid, Article 17(7).

[77] Commission staff working paper: The Application of EU State Aid rules on Services of General Economic Interest since 2005 and the Outcome of the Public Consultation. Brussels, 23.03.2011, SEC (2011) 397, pp. 11–12.

[78] Ibid, p. 9.

[79] Regulation EEC 3577/92, Article 4(1).

[80] Ibid, Article 4(1).

'scheme' has to be based 'on objective, non-discriminatory criteria which are known in advance to the undertakings concerned.'[81]

The Member State may impose the following requirements on public service obligations: 'ports to be served, regularity, continuity, frequency, capacity to provide the service, rates to be charged and manning of the vessel.'[82] There is also a long list of exemptions for certain coastal services mainly in the Mediterranean area in Article 6; the last one of these exemptions expired on 1 January 2004.[83]

Consequences of Non-compliance

If the conditions of the 2012 SGEI Decision and of the Regulations are not met, then the Commission will assess the State aid 'in accordance with the principles contained in the Commission Communication on a framework for State aid in the form of public service compensation.'[84] Equally, if during the course of the State aid, the conditions change, then it needs to be notified according to Article 108(3) TFEU.[85]

11.4.1.4 Impact of the 2012 SGEI Decision

Based on the country reports which Member States submitted to the Commission before the adoption of the 2012 SGEI package and publicly available information, we try to gauge the impact of the 2012 SGEI Decision.

Airports

It is as of yet unclear to what extent the 2012 SGEI Decision has had an impact. However, it is conceivable that it will be taken under consideration during some of the ongoing investigations for State aid to airports. To take but one example: the airport Erfurt-Weimar in Germany has traditionally benefitted from State aid.[86] However, as it never reached more than 500,000 passengers a year, these State aids would not have needed to be notified: In 2010 the airport served 323,000 passengers.[87] On the other hand, Thuringia's second largest airport, Altenburg-

---

[81] CJEU, Case C-205/99 *Asociación Profesional de Empresas Navieras de Líneas Regulares (Analir) and Others* [2001] *ECR* I-1271, para 40.

[82] Regulation EEC 3577/92, Article 4(2).

[83] Ibid, Article 6.

[84] Commission Decision 2012/21/EU, para 26 of the preamble.

[85] Ibid, Article 2(3).

[86] *Das teure Sorgenkind der Landesregierung*, MDR Thüringen, available at: http://www.mdr.de/thueringen/mitte-west-thueringen/hintergrundflughafen100.html.

[87] *Flughafen Erfurt erhält Zusatz "Weimar"*, published 21/03/2011 http://www.airliners.de/management/marketing/flughafen-erfurt-erhaelt-zusatz-weimar/23685.

Nobitz, formally serviced by the low-cost carrier Ryanair, could still potentially benefit from block-exempted SGEI compensation as it only processed 140,000 passengers in its busiest year in 2009.[88] Ryanair stopped serving the airport in March 2011[89] and there are currently no other lines serving it. In spite of Altenburg falling below the passenger threshold, the European Commission is investigating potentially illegal State aid under Article 108(2) TFEU for alleged State aid for infrastructure, operational State aid for Altenburg Nobitz GmbH and rebates for Ryanair. Therefore, airports analysing the potential threat of being investigated, should not only focus on the laws outlined above but also take into account the rules and guidelines applying to general State aid and competition law. Rostock-Laage is also far below the 500,000 passenger threshold. It may, however, be affected by the 2012 SGEI Decision: in 2010, it carried 219,489 passengers.[90] The German airport of Leipzig also received public service compensation..[91]

There might be other category D airports which will be similarly affected. For example, Nîmes Airport, 176 521 passengers in 2010, is being investigated for State aid, marketing arrangements and rebates for Ryanair.[92] Similarly, the airport of La Rochelle, 191,599 passengers in 2010 is also being investigated for its financial arrangements with the public authorities, rebates and marketing arrangements and some of the airlines servicing it.[93] Again, according to the press releases, emphasis seems to be mostly on the market economy investor principle and in particular, rebates on airport charges, infrastructure and operating aid and arrangements which potentially create an unfair economic advantage for certain airline carriers. These principles were outside the scope of this chapter but these investigations show the variety of laws and regulations that can be of importance in the transport sector.

---

[88] Bekanntmachung, 25/05/2012, Europäische Kommission: Staatliche Beihilfe SA.26500 (ex 227/2008)—Flughafen Altenburg-Nobitz—Beihilfe zugunsten von Ryanair (Beschwerde des Bundesverbandes der Deutschen Fluggesellschaften), (2012/C 149/02), p. 2.

[89] *Ryanair gibt Altenburg auf*, published 07/01/2011, available at: http://www.airliners.de/verkehr/netzwerkplanung/ryanair-gibt-altenburg-auf/23041.

[90] *Flughafen Rostock-Laage mit Rekord-Passagierzahlen im Jahr 2010*, Reisenews Online, 04/01/2011, available at http://www.reisenews-online.de/2011/01/04/flughafen-rostock-laage-mit-rekord-passagierzahlen-im-jahr-2010/

[91] This one had not been notification-exempted and was assessed in Commission Decision 2009/948/EC, *OJ* 2008 L 346/1.

[92] Press release: *State aid: Commission opens in-depth investigation into potential State aid at Nîmes airport in France*, 25/04/2012, IP/12/400.

[93] Press release: *State aid: Commission investigates potential state aid at La Rochelle airport in France*, 08/02/2012, IP/12/108. For similar investigations see the following Press releases on State aid: *Commission opens in-depth investigations in air transport sector in Germany and Austria*, 22/02/2012, IP/12/156; *Commission opens in-depth investigation in air transport sector in Belgium, France and Germany*, 21/03/2012, IP/12/265; *Commission investigates potential State aid at Carcassonne airport in France*, 04/04/2012, IP/12/350; *Commission opens in-depth investigations in air transport sector in France, Germany and Sweden*, 25/01/2012, IP/12/44; *Commission opens in-depth investigations in air transport sector in Belgium, France and Germany*. 21/03/2012, IP/12/265.

Looking further at the country reports, the Irish airports of Knock, Kerry and Galway might be affected as figures from 2006 to 2008 show that the total amount of passengers at these airports was above 200,000 which is the new threshold for airports.[94] None of the compensation receiving Swedish airports carry more than 200,000 passengers a year and will therefore not be affected.[95] The same holds true for Portuguese airports on the Azores. Luxembourg informed the Commission of a Media Plan for Luxembourg airport, which it considered a public service compensation in compliance with *Altmark*.

Ports

Ireland subsidises its harbours for maintenance works but there are no ongoing public service compensation being paid.[96] The Walloon region in Belgium finances infrastructure investment in its ports, which it considers to be services of general economic interest, with 80 % of infrastructure investment costs. It appears questionable whether this is in line with the Commission's decision practice, which usually relies on Article 107(3)(c) TFEU for port infrastructure, see the recently authorised aid for a new ferry terminal in Lithuania co-financed from the Cohesion Fund and 107(3)(c).[97]

Maritime and Air Links

As far as maritime and air links are concerned, in Germany, there was no compensation for maritime and air links to islands of fewer than 300,000 passengers a year.[98] Similarly, Sweden did not pay any compensation for maritime and air links to islands.[99] In France there were 11 air links to islands in 2005, carrying less than

---

[94] Public consultation: State aid rules on services of general economic interest, Member States reports on the application of the SGEI package. Ireland: *Report on the implementation of the Commission Decision of 28 November 2005*, available at http://ec.europa.eu/competition/consultations/2010_sgei/reports.html.

[95] Ibid, Sweden: *Regeringskansliet, Rapport om genomförandet av kommissionens beslut av den 28 november 2005 om tillämpningen av artikel 86.2 i EG-fördraget på statligt stöd i form av ersättning för offentliga tjänster som beviljas vissa företag som fått i uppdrag att tillhandahålla tjänster av allmänt ekonomiskt intresse*, p. 4.

[96] Report on the implementation of the Commission Decision of 28 November 2005, comprising a detailed description of the conditions of application in all sectors, including the social housing and the hospital sectors, to be submitted to the Commission by each Member State every three years.

[97] Press release: Commission authorises €18 million public financing for new ferry terminal in Lithuania, 22/02/2012, IP/12/155.

[98] Supra at 110: Germany: *Bericht der Bundesrepublik Deutschland zum, "Altmark-Paket" der Europäischen Kommission*, p. 22.

[99] Ibid, Sweden: *Regeringskansliet, Rapport om genomförandet av kommissionens beslut av den 28 november 2005 om tillämpningen av artikel 86.2 i EG-fördraget på statligt stöd i form av*

300,000 passengers—10 to Corsica and one to Ouessant.[100] The UK pays compensation for a few flights to Scottish islands but they would remain included in the exemption as they carry fewer than ten thousand passengers/year.[101] In Romania, there are two links to the Delta peninsula which carried both less than 200,000 passengers/year; one of them was awarded a public service obligation and complies with *Altmark* according to the Romanian authorities. It is not easy to decide whether these links in the Delta of the Danube are inland waterway or maritime transport.[102] In Spain, links to the canary islands are financed, in Portugal links to the Azores.

Germany paid compensation for several air routes originating from the airports Erfurt, Hof and Rostock-Laage.[103] These were based on Regulation (EC) No. 2408/92 (see above) and assessed to be compatible with it by Germany. The benefitting airports are Erfurt, Hof and Rostock-Laage. As stated above, Erfurt never reached the 500,000 passengers/year mark. State aid for an air route from Hof was discontinued as of 31 March 2010[104] and there are currently no air routes servicing that airport.[105] The CEO of the Hof airport stated as one of the reasons for the discontinuance the lack of passenger numbers who found it easier, through improved infrastructure, to access other, bigger, airports in the region.[106] The airline carrier in charge of two of those lines, Cirrus-Airlines, has since become insolvent.[107] Rostock-Laage is the only one of the three that was able to keep its air route despite of State aid being discontinued on 31 October 2009. The air route under State aid was carried out by OLT and is now being serviced by Lufthansa.

Conclusion

For airports, the 2012 SGEI Decision means a considerable tightening of the screw. For ports and maritime and air links, even if they are not directly affected by the

---

(Footnote 99 continued)
ersättning för offentliga tjänster som beviljas vissa företag som fått i uppdrag att tillhandahålla tjänster av allmänt ekonomiskt intresse, p. 3.

[100] Ibid, France, Rapport sur les compensations de services d'intérêt économique général : mise en œuvre de la décision de la Commission européenne du 28 novembre 2005.

[101] Ibid, UK: Letter to the State Aid Greffe, 18 February 2009.

[102] Ibid, Romania: Department for reporting, monitoring and control of State aid, Raport privind ser viciile de interes economic general din Romania, pp 20–25.

[103] Ibid, Annex 15.

[104] Ibid and see: *Stadt Plauen will Zuschuss kürzen*, Studio Franken, published 23/05/2012, available at: http://www.br.de/franken/inhalt/aktuelles-aus-franken/flughafen-hof-cirrus100.html

[105] http://www.airport-hof-plauen.de/

[106] Hanel (2012).

[107] *Europe loses four airlines in an unhappy start to 2012*, Centre for Aviation, published on 31/01/2012, available at http://www.centreforaviation.com/analysis/europe-loses-four-airlines-in-an-unhappy-start-to-2012-67001.

changes, the new Decision will bring more clarity as the thresholds and method of calculation have been streamlined. This was necessary, as a lot of Member States found that the 2005 rules were not correctly applied as many of the regional and local stakeholders were unaware of the obligations.[108] This should be easier with the 2012 SGEI package. This is particularly important, as monitoring the implementation/observance of the Decision is the responsibility of the Member States.

11.4.2 SGEI Framework

The 2005 SGEI framework excluded the entire transport sector, including air and maritime transport, from its scope of application. The 2012 SGEI framework,[109] on the contrary, applies to air and maritime transport.

The 2012 SGEI framework applies to those public service contracts in the air and maritime transport sector which are not covered by the 2012 SGEI Decision and also lays down conditions under which State aid is deemed compatible with the internal market under Article 106(2) TFEU.[110] The Commission will apply the provisions contained in the 2012 SGEI Framework from 31 January 2012 and this will also include unlawful aid which has been granted before that date.[111]

This section will briefly examine the content of the 2012 SGEI Framework in general (Sect. 11.4.2.1), and then address its relationship to the compatibility rules contained in the sectoral frameworks (Sect. 11.4.2.2). It will conclude with a preliminary examination of the impact of the changes of the 2012 SGEI Framework compared to the existing rules (Sect. 11.4.2.3).

11.4.2.1 Content of the 2012 SGEI Framework

According to para 11 of the 2012 SGEI Framework, State aid which falls outside the scope of Decision 2012/21/EU may still be compatible 'if it is necessary for the operation of the service of general and economic interest concerned and does not affect the development of trade to such an extent as to be contrary to the interests of the Union.'

In order for the State aid to be compatible, the conditions of Sections 2.2–2.10 must be fulfilled: it must be a 'genuine service of general economic interest' (Section 2.2). This refers to Article 106(2) TFEU. Accordingly, the State aid must

---

[108] Commission staff working paper: The Application of EU State Aid rules on Services of General Economic Interest since 2005 and the Outcome of the Public Consultation. Brussels, 23.03.2011, SEC(2011) 397, pp 33–35.

[109] Communication from the Commission: *European Union framework for State aid in the form of public service compensation* (2011), *OJ* 2012 C 08/3.

[110] 2012 SGEI Framework, paras 7 and 8.

[111] 2012 SGEI Framework, para 67.

be awarded to undertakings entrusted with the operation of SGEI or be a 'revenue-producing monopoly' and trade may only be affected to the extent that it is not contrary to the interests of the Union.

Furthermore, there has to be an 'entrustment act specifying the public service obligations and the methods of calculating compensation' (Section 2.3). Paragraph 16 specifies the minimum content of the entrustment act, such as the content and duration of the PSO; the duration should, under Section 2.4 be justified in the entrustment act. The act must also include the undertaking, the nature of any exclusive rights assigned to the undertaking, details and parameters of the compensation mechanism (described in more detail in Section 2.8) and arrangements for avoiding and recovering overcompensation.

Under Section 2.6, aid will only be compatible if the 'responsible authority' has complied with the 'applicable Union rules in the area of public procurement.' This raises the difficult question as to whether the sectoral rules on public procurement contained in Regulations (EC) No 1008/2008 (air services) and (EC) 3577/92 (maritime services) constitute 'applicable Union rules in the area of public procurement'. A literal interpretation would suggest that this is the case, as they prescribe detailed rules for public procurement of these services. At the same time, one can make the argument that whereas the 2012 SGEI Decision explicitly mentions compliance with these Regulations as a condition for the notification exemption,[112] there is no equivalent compatibility condition in the SGEI Framework. Following this interpretation, the two Regulations would merely constitute 'sectoral rules', which apply 'without prejudice' to the 2012 SGEI Framework.[113] Given that compliance with the two Regulations is a requirement for compatibility under the sectoral State aid guidelines (see Sect. 11.3.2.2), an interpretation of Section 2.6 in the broader context would point towards the view that the public procurement rules contained in these two sectoral regulations constitute public procurement rules in the sense of Section 2.6 of the SGEI Framework. Therefore, the Commission cannot declare State aid to be compatible if it was contained in a PSO contract that has been awarded in violation of Regulations (EC) No. 1008/2008 (air services) or (EC) 3577/92 (maritime services).

According to Section 2.5, State aid falling under this Communication must comply with Directive 2006/111/EC on the transparency of financial relations between Member States and public undertakings. This Directive is beyond the scope of this chapter. Furthermore, under Section 2.7, when compensating several undertakings for the same SGEI, this must be done without any discrimination. In order to monitor that the Communication's provisions have been complied with, Section 2.10 holds that Member States must publish certain information, such as details on the PSO, the undertaking and territory and the aid amount. This is mirrored by Section 3 which holds that Member States have a reporting obligation towards the Commission.

---

[112] 2012 SGEI Decision, Article 2 (4).

[113] SGEI Framework, recital 10.

Section 2.9 leaves room for the Commission to intervene in the award of PSO. This is the case when aid falls within the scope of the Communication and should therefore be compatible with the internal market but still affects 'trade to such an extent as would be contrary to the interest of the Union' (para 52). However, the power of the Commission to intervene in such cases, giving it an unusually broad leeway, is restricted to exceptions and serious distortions having a 'significant' effect on other Member States and the internal market (para 54). This section is re-enforced by Section 4 explaining that conditions and obligations may be necessary to ensure that SGEI do not unduly distort competition (para 66).

11.4.2.2 Relationship to Rules on SGEI in Sectoral Guidelines and Frameworks

Prior to the extension of the general SGEI Framework to maritime and air transport, there was no 'legal vacuum' with respect to the compatibility of compensation payments for SGEI in the air and maritime field. On the contrary: the 1994 Aviation Guidelines,[114] which remain in force until today, were arguably the first framework to deal with SGEI compensation payments under State aid rules. The 2004 Maritime Guidelines (*OJ* 2004 C 13/3) and the 2005 Airport Guidelines[115] also contain detailed rules on this question.

The co-existence of these different texts raises the question as to what the precise relationship between these texts is. The two classical rules of interpretation, namely *lex specialis derogat legi generali* and *lex posterior derogat legi priori*, lead to conflicting results in the present case. As will be shown in this section, the dilemma can be overcome, as there is no direct contradiction between the different sets of rules.

The 1994 Aviation Guidelines address compensation payments for public service obligations in their recitals 15–23. It is important to keep in mind that they pre-date the Court's ruling in *Altmark*. They are also based on Regulation (EC) No. 2408/92, which left much more discretion to Member States for the organisation of tenders for public service obligations than Regulation (EC) No. 1008/2008. However, it would seem that the essential statement of the 1994 Aviation Guidelines, which can be found in Recital 20 and 21, is still valid. There, the Commission holds that where the Member State has not selected the best offer, the chosen operator has most likely received State aid, and that the best offer is usually the offer requiring the lowest financial compensation. It would seem that, where the Commission finds that aid has been granted, because the Member State did not select the best offer, the Commission would deem such aid to be incompatible with the internal market. In other words: if Regulation (EC) No. 1008/2008 is not

---

[114] *OJ* 1994 C 350/5.

[115] Communication from the Commission, Community guidelines on financing of airports and start-up aid to airlines departing from regional airports, 2005/C 312/01.

complied with, because the Member State does not select the best offer, the compensation cannot be declared compatible. Therefore, a coherent application of both the 1994 Aviation Guidelines and the 2012 SGEI Framework is possible, if Regulation (EC) No. 1008/2008 is to be considered as a public procurement rule in the sense of Section 2.4 of the 2012 SGEI Framework.

A similar conclusion can be drawn with regard to the 2004 Maritime Guidelines. These stipulate in Section 9 with regard to public service compensations:

> In the field of maritime cabotage, public service obligations (PSOs) may be imposed or public service contracts (PSCs) may be concluded for the services indicated in Article 4 of Regulation (EEC) No 3577/92. For those services, PSOs and PSCs as well as their compensation must fulfil the conditions of that provision and the Treaty rules and procedures governing State aid, as interpreted by the Court of Justice.
> [...]
> The duration of public service contracts should be limited to a reasonable and not overlong period, normally in the order of six years, since contracts for significantly longer periods could entail the danger of creating a (private) monopoly

As for aviation, compliance with the sectoral rules on public service obligations is a precondition for compatibility of the aid. Coherence between the Maritime Guidelines and the 2012 SGEI Framework can be ensured by considering that Regulation (EEC) No 3577/92 constitutes a public procurement rule in the sense of Section 2.4 of the 2012 SGEI Framework. With regard to the maximum duration of the entrustment, it would seem appropriate to regard the six years contained in the Maritime Guidelines as *lex specialis* compared to the longer period foreseen in the 2012 SGEI Framework.

The 2005 Airport Guidelines contain special rules for public service compensation for airports in their recitals 34 and 64–67. Member States may impose public service obligations for airports 'to ensure that the general public interest is appropriately served'.[116] In exceptional cases, this can be extended to the overall management of an airport if it is considered an SGEI. This is permissible for example if the airport is in an 'isolated region'. Activities subject to a public service obligation may not be those which are not directly linked to its management. Paragraph 53(iv) lists as those unrelated activities: 'pursuit of commercial activities not directly linked to the airport's core activities.'

The conditions for permissible compensation in this case are the *Altmark* criteria: compensation will not constitute State aid if it complies with *Altmark*.[117] If compensation does not come within these guidelines, then it constitutes State aid under then Article 87(1) EC 'if it has an effect on intra-Community competition and trade.'[118] Compensation to airports that falls into category A or B[119] would 'normally' be considered to have an effect on trade. Airports with an annual passenger

---

[116] Communication from the Commission, 2005/C 312/01, para 34.

[117] Ibid, para 36.

[118] Ibid, para 37.

[119] Ibid, para 15.

volume of less than 1 million, so-called category D airports, are 'unlikely to distort competition'. As no detailed conditions can be determined from the outset, any compensatory measure, also within category C and D, has to be notified to the Commission.[120] The only notification exemptions are category D airports which are carrying out a mission of general economic interest.[121]

The 2012 SGEI Framework goes beyond these requirements, as it also requires compliance with the *Telaustria* case law for the award of any public service concession. The two sets of rules do not, however, openly contradict each other. Therefore, it would in this case seem the most convincing to apply both texts in parallel.

11.4.3 Court Cases and Commission Decision Practice

As far as aviation in general is concerned, no public service obligation has ever been notified to the Commission. The only (negative) Decision that the Commission has taken was a case where a PSO was granted without a prior call for tender.[122] Similarly, the Commission has not taken any final decisions on public service compensation for airports.[123]

There has been a number of Commission Decisions in the cases field of maritime transport, which have often led to Court challenges. While the cases do not consider transport law specific issues, the breadth of potentially important areas which must be considered by transport undertakings, is telling of the complexity in this sector. The most important ones are summarised below and range from the question of new/existing aid to restructuring aid.

In *Tirrenia*[124] the GC decided on the partial annulment of Decision 2005/163/EC which concerned State aid given by Italy to certain maritime companies. In the Decision, the Commission had declared most aids to be compatible with the internal market if certain conditions were going to be met. Those provisions which declared the aid to be incompatible with the internal market were attacked by the concerned undertakings. The GC first considered whether the subventions constituted State aid, whether they constituted existing or new aid and then, whether they were compatible with the internal market. On the question of new and existing aid, the GC held that legislative changes to an aid regime constitute new aid in certain circumstances (para 124). In this instance, the Commission's

---

[120] Ibid, para 39.

[121] Ibid, para 41.

[122] C 79/2002, Commission Decision 2005/351/EC, *OJ* 2005 L 110/56.

[123] Commission staff working paper: The Application of EU State Aid rules on Services of General Economic Interest since 2005 and the Outcome of the Public Consultation. Brussels, 23.03.2011, SEC(2011) 397, pp 11–12.

[124] GC, Joined Cases, T-265/04, T-292/04, T-504/04, *Tirerenia di Navigazione v Commission* [2009] *ECR* II-21.

qualification of the aids as new aids was held to be insufficiently supported by arguments. As insufficient reasons were given by the Commission, the GC was unable to verify the legality of the Decision and this part was consequently annulled (para 134). The GC also considered 3577/92 and again pointed to the lack of reasons provided by the Commission (para 151). As far as the public service obligations are concerned, the GC considered that the Decision should be partially annulled to the extent that it qualifies aids given to maritime lines as new aids (para 146). The GC points out that the Commission had held the entirety of the aid measures to the maritime lines as compatible as they were necessary and proportional to the additional cost incurred by the public service obligation (para 146).

In the *Corsica Ferries*[125] case, the then CFI considered Decision 2004/166/EC on State aid for the restructuring of a shipping company which operates regular maritime services from mainland France to Corsica. These services are operated as public service obligations. The Corsican authority called for a tender on services from Corsica to Marseille in 2001 and awarded this jointly to two undertakings. One of these undertakings, SNCM, received rescue aid for restructuring. The Commission found that the aid granted until 2001 as compensation for discharge of public service obligations was compatible with the common market. In addition to this aid, the Commission also investigated restructuring aid granted to SNCM, registered under C-58/2002. With regard to the restructuring aid, the Commission found in its Decision 2004/166/EC[126] that it was compatible with the internal market under certain conditions, including the disposal of certain properties. This Decision was challenged by Corsica Ferries. The Court of First Instance only found for the appellant with regard to the condition imposed by the Commission that the aid must be kept to a minimum. In particular, the Commission ought to have had regard for the actual net proceeds of a proposed property sale within the restructuring plan, rather than only the estimated proceeds, particularly as the figure was already available. In not doing so, the Commission breached the guidelines on State aid for restructuring[127]

In the case of *Fred Olsen*,[128] the Court considered State aid in the maritime sector under Regulations 3577/92 EC, 659/1999, Community guidelines on State aid to maritime transport, and the Communication on services of general economic interest in Europe. The Court looked into subsidies paid by Spain to an undertaking for the operation of maritime services of national interest between 1978 and 1997. A competitor complained about the contract, and in particular the subsidy that was paid towards the end of the contractual period to settle past expenses.

---

[125] GC Case T-565/08, *Corsica Ferries France v Commission* [2005] *ECR* II-2197.

[126] Commission Decision 2004/166/EC on aid which France intends to grant for the restructuring of the Société Nationale Maritime Corse-Méditerranée (SNCM), *OJ* 2004 L 61/13.

[127] Community Guidelines on State aid for rescuing and restructuring firms in difficulty, *OJ* 1999 C 288/2, applicable from 9 October 1999.

[128] GC, Case T-17/02, *Fred Olsen* [2005] *ECR* II-2031. This judgment has been confirmed on appeal:C-320/05 P *Fred Olsen* [2007] *ECR* I-131.

The competitor alleged that this subsidy was new aid but the Commission held that it was within the existing scheme and therefore existing aid. However, the Court found with Spain and the Commission that the later subsidies fell within existing aid and therefore dismissed the application.

In a Decision to raise no objections, the Commission considered a public service contracts on a maritime line between Italy, Slovenia and Croatia.[129] This decision is based on the 2005 SGEI Decision.

The Decision N 265/2006[130] concerned public service obligations for maritime lines to Sicily and the surrounding minor islands. In its Decision to raise no objections, the Commission considered that the maritime links to islands constitute State aid (para 40) which should be assessed in the light of the 2005 SGEI Decision. It further considered that, under Article 86(2) EC, the compensation serves a general economic interest, is necessary and proportionate and is not contrary to the Union's interests.

Furthermore, the Commission found that the existing State aid granted under public service contracts for maritime links to Scottish islands was compatible under Article 86(2) EC was compatible. However, this time, it imposed certain conditions with regard to one of the routes operated by one of the operators.[131]

11.5 In Lieu of a Conclusion...

This chapter has illustrated the specificities of SGEI and public services in transport and its rich history in terms of legislation, decisions and Court cases. Despite this rich history, many legal questions remain open. The interpretation of Regulation (EC) No. 1370/2007 has been debated extensively already by scholars, and there is already a certain amount of litigation in national Courts. This may in the near future trigger interesting references to the CJEU. The Commission has announced in its 2011 Transport White Paper further market opening in the railway sector, which will certainly as well raise important State aid questions...

References

Bayreuther F (2009) Konzessionsvergabe im öffentlichen Personenverkehr—Betriebsübergang durch behördliche Anordnung? [Procurement of Concessions for public transport—transfer of business by administrative order?], NZA 582

---

[129] Case N 62/2005, contrat de service public sur une ligne maritime Frioul-Vénétie-Juliennes et Slovénie et Croatie, *OJ* 2007 C 90/10.

[130] Case N 265/2006, *Aide au transport maritime-Società Ustica Lines e Società N.G.I. OJ* 2007 C 196/3.

[131] Commission Decision 2011/98/EC *OJ 2011* L 45/33.

Deuster J (2009) Endspurt zur VO (EG) Nr. 1370/2007: Handlungsbedarf für die Liniengenehmigung (Teil 1) [Final sprint to Regulation (EC) No 1370/2007: in need of action for line concessions (Part 1)], IR 2009, 202

Deuster J (2010) Vom Auskunftsanspruch zur Veröffentlichungspflicht [From the right of information to the publication requirement] DÖV 591

Haats J, Richter N (2010) Auswirkungen des Inkrafttretens der EU-Verordnung 1370/2007 auf die ertragsteuerliche Behandlung der Leistungen der Gesellschafter bzw. Träger öffentlicher Verkehrsunternehmen an kommunale Verkehrsbetriebe [Implications of the entry into force of EU Regulation 1370/2007 on the income tax treatment of benefits of members or representatives of public transport companies to municipal transport companies], IR 149

Hanel T (2012) *Die Gründe für das Ende der Hofer Linie* [Reasons for the end of the route to Hof airport line] Frankenpost, 22/05/2012, p 20. http://www.pro-flughafen-hof-plauen.de

Hübner A (2009) Neue Vergaberegeln für den ÖPVN unter der Verordung (EG) Nr. 1370/2007 [New procurement rules for public local passenger transport under Regulation (EC) No 1370/2007], VergabeR 2009, 363

Jasper U, Seidel J, Telenta V (2009) Direktvergaben vs. Grundrechte im Schienenpersonennahverkehr [Direct awards vs. Fundamental rights in rail transport] IR 2008, 346

Kaufmann M, Lübbig T, Priess H-J (2010) Kommentar EG VO 1370/2007 [Commentary on Regulation 1370/EC]

Kekelekis M, Rusu E (2010) The Award of Public Contracts and the Notion of 'Internal Operator' under Regulation 1370/2007 on Public Passenger Transport Services by Rail and by Road PPLR 198

Kramer J (2010) Abwehrrechte gegen das Marktverhalten interner Betreiber und privilegierter Unternehmen nach der neuen VO (EG) 1370/2007 [Rights of defence against the market conduct of internal operators and privileged undertakings under the new Regulation (EC) 1370/2007] IR 2010, 80

Linke B (2010) Altaufträge im Personenbeförderungsrecht und die Übergangsregelung der neuen Verordnung 1370/2007/EG [Old contracts in passenger transport legislation and transitional arrangements of the new Regulation (EC) 1370/2007] NZBau 2010, 207

Maxian Rusche T, Schmidt S (2011) The post-Altmark era of State aid control in public passenger transport has started: 15 months of application of Regulation (EC) No. 1370/2007 to public transport services EStAL 249

Nettesheim M (2009) Das neue Dienstleistungsrecht des ÖPNV—Die Verordnung (EG) sNr. 1370/2007 [The new law of public transport services—Regulation (EC) No. 1370/2007] NVwZ 2009, 1449

Olgemöller U, Otting O (2009) Verfassungsrechtliche Rahmenbedingungen für Direktvergaben im Verkehrssektor nach Inkrafttreten der Verordnung (EG) Nr. 1370/2007 [The constitutional framework for direct awards in the transport sector following the entry into force of Regulation (EC) No 1370/2007] DÖV 364

Polster J (2009) Die Zukunft der (Direkt-)Vergabe von SPNV-Aufträgen [The future of (direct) local railway passenger services orders] NZBau 2011, 209

Polster J (2010) Der Rechtsrahmen für die Vergabe von Eisenbahnverkehrsleistungen [The legal framework for the procurement of railway services] NZBau 662

Pünder H (2010a) Die Vergabe von Dienstleistungsaufträgen im Eisenbahnverkehr. [Procurement of service contracts in rail transport] EuR 2010:774

Pünder H (2010b) Beschränkungen der In-house-Vergabe im öffentlichen Personenverkehr [The limitations of in-house awards for public transport] NJW 263

Pünder H (2010c) Die Vergabe von Dienstleistungsaufträgen im Eisenbahnverkehr [The award of service contracts in the rail sector]. EuR 2010:774

Röbke M, Rechten S (2010) Voraussetzungsfreie Direktvergabe von SPNV-Leistungen möglich? [Possible unconditional direct awards of local passenger rail services?]. NZBau 2010:680

Saxinger A (2009a) Das Verhältnis der Verordnung (EG) Nr. 1370/2007 zum nicht an sie angepassten deutschen Personenbeförderungsrecht [The relationship between Regulation (EC) No 1370/2007 to as of yet unamended German passenger law] GewA 350

Saxinger A (2009b) Übergangsregelungen, Legisvakanz und Vorwirkungen der Verordnung (EG) Nr. 1370/2007 [Transitional arrangements, vacation legis and the advance effect of Regulation (EC) No 1370/2007] EuZW 449

Scheps C, Otting O (2008) Direktvergabe von Eisenbahnverkehrsdienstleistungen nach der neuen Verordnung (EG) Nr. 1370/2007 [Direct award of railway transport services in accordance with the new Regulation (EC) No 1370/2007] NVwZ 2008, 499

Schmitz J-V, Winkelhüsener B (2009) Vergaberechtliche Handlungsoptionen und deren beihilferechtliche Konsequenzen [Options under procurement law and their legal consequences] EuZW 2011, 52

Schön D (2009) Die neue ÖPNV-Verordnung und ihre Auswirkung auf die interkommunale Zusammenarbeit [The new public transport regulation and its impact on inter-municipal cooperation] KommJur 334

Schröder H (2008) Inhalt, Gestaltung und Praxisfragen des wettbewerblichen Vergabeverfahrens nach der neuen europäischen ÖPNV-Verordnung, [Content, design and practical issues of the competitive tendering process in accordance with the new European public transport regulation] NVwZ 2008, 1288

Schröder H (2010) Die Direktvergabe im straßengebundenen ÖPNV—Selbsterbringung und interne Betreiberschaft [Direct award in road-based public local passenger transport—internal self-provision and operatorship] NVwZ 862

Skovgaard Oelykke G (2008) Regulation 1370/2007 on Public Passenger Transport Services. PPLR NA84

Stickler T, Feske I (2010) Die In-House-Vergabe von ÖSPV-Dienstleistungen nach der VO (EG) 1370/2007, [The in-house procurement of public road transport services under Regulation (EC) 1370/2007] VergabeR 2010, 1

Tegner H, Wachinger L (2010) Ausgleichsberechnung und Überkompensationskontrolle nach dem Anhang zur VO 1370/07—Eine juristisch-ökonomische Beleuchtung (nicht nur) für den SPNV, [Compensation calculation and control of overcompensation under the annex to Regulation 1370/07—A legal and economic view (not only) for the rail-based public local passenger transport rail] IR 2010, 264

Winnes M (2009) Der Begriff der gemeinwirtschaftlichen Verpflichtung im Rahmen der Verordnung 1370/07 [The concept of public service obligation under Regulation 1370/07] DÖV 2009, 1135

Winnes M, Schwartz A, Mietzsch O (2009) Zu den Auswirkungen der VO 1370/07 für den öffentlichen Nahverkehr in Deutschland [The Impact of Regulation 1370/07 for public transport in Germany] EuR 290

Wittig O, Schimanek P (2008) Sondervergaberecht für Verkehrsdienstleistungen—Die neue EU-Verordnung über öffentliche Personenverkehrsdienste auf Schiene und Straße [Special Procurement of Transport Services—The new EU regulation on public passenger transport services by rail and road] NZBau 222

Ziekow J (2009) Die Direktvergabe von Personenverkehrsdiensten nach der Verordnung (EG) Nr. 1370/2007 und die Zukunft eigenwirtschaftlicher Verkehre [The procurement of passenger services in accordance with Regulation (EC) No 1370/2007 and the future of economic self-governance] NVwZ 865

Chapter 12
This Won't Hurt a Bit: The Commission's Approach to Services of General Economic Interest and State Aid to Hospitals

Leigh Hancher and Wolf Sauter

Abstract The exemption regime for healthcare services that constitute SGEI as part of the 2011 Decision under the new SGEI Package has been broadened considerably to cover not just hospital care but all (curative) healthcare as well as long-term care, irrespective of the amount of aid or turnover concerned. The IRIS-H decision concerning the financing of public hospitals in the Brussels capital region of Belgium, although adopted by the Commission prior to the 2011 SGEI Package, proves a useful illustration of the way the Commission applies the rules on State aid and SGEI compensation in practice. Both the new 2011 SGEI Package and the State aid practice show that the Commission is content to do without a stringent application of the State aid rules based on economic analysis in the hospital sector—or indeed in healthcare and long-term care at large: net costs are assumed as given, and only the scope for reasonable profits is restrained. The Commission could presumably reverse this trend by bringing its own practice into line with a more ambitious interpretation of its recent legislation, and insisting that Member States do the same.

The views expressed here are personal.

L. Hancher (✉) · W. Sauter
Tilburg Law School, Warandelaan 2, 5037 AB Tilburg, The Netherlands
e-mail: i.l.hancher@tilburguniversity.edu

W. Sauter
e-mail: w.sauter@tilburguniversity.edu

E. Szyszczak and J.W. van de Gronden (eds.), *Financing Services of General Economic Interest*, Legal Issues of Services of General Interest, DOI: 10.1007/978-90-6704-906-1_12, © T.M.C. Asser Press, The Hague, The Netherlands, and the authors 2013

Contents

12.1 Introduction

The hospital sector in the European Union is organised on various lines, both in terms of public and private provision and in terms of the degree of solidarity or competition in respect of the sector's regulation. Hospitals can be large or small and the former are not only providers of intra- and extramural care but are also major employers and major purchasers of often complex and expensive goods and services. As with most social services in Europe, the provision of hospital services is primarily a matter of national competence,[1] subject to the Treaty rules on free movement and competition, including the State aid rules.[2]

The provision of medical services and the acquisition, and subsequent use of, complex medical devices and equipment are market activities that can have

---

[1]   Article 168 TFEU.

[2]   See also Hancher and Sauter 2012; Sauter and van de Gronden 2011, p. 615.

important spillover effects on upstream and downstream markets. It therefore follows that national funding for the hospital sector, although critical for social welfare, can also have important competition implications. This makes the practice of 'deficit funding'—that is ex post compensation for shortfalls in hospital budgets—a particularly sensitive issue.[3] The application of the EU State aid regime to this type of ex post funding is the focus of this chapter.

Following the codification of the so-called compensation approach that was pioneered in the 2003 *Altmark* case,[4] hospital financing has been recognised as an explicit candidate for a 'Services of General Economic Interest (SGEI) exemption' based on Article 106(2) TFEU, both under the original 2005 SGEI Package and again under the recently adopted second SGEI Package of 2011.[5] In this chapter we will outline both SGEI regimes for hospital services in general terms before discussing one of the few Commission State aid rulings on the merits in this field: the Commission's 2009 IRIS-H Decision concerning hospitals in the Brussels region.[6] Because this Decision is so far available only in French and in Dutch we believe a more detailed discussion in English may be useful for a broader audience.

The three main questions that we will address here are:

- What is the SGEI regime for hospital services and how has it changed between the first and second *Altmark* packages, if at all?
- How strictly does the Commission apply the *Altmark* criteria and those of the SGEI Package (block exemption Decision) to hospital services in practice?
- What lessons can be learned for national authorities assigning or entrusting SGEI concerning hospital services?

Our conclusion will briefly summarise our findings on these points.

12.2 The 2005 *Altmark* Package Decision

As is extensively discussed elsewhere in this volume the Commission adopted its first *Altmark* Package in 2005 consisting of a Decision, a Framework Communication and an amendment and codification of the Directive on financial transparency in 2006.[7] The 2005 Decision contained a block exemption both for specific

---

[3] See also Koenig and Paul 2010, p. 755.

[4] CJEU, Case C-280/00 *Altmark Trans GmbH and Regierungspräsidium Magdeburg v Nahverkehrsgesellschaft Altmark GmbH, and Oberbundesanwalt beim Bundesverwaltungsgericht* (Altmark) [2003] *ECR* I-7747.

[5] Sauter W 2012.

[6] European Commission, Decision of 28 October 2009, State aid measure NN 54/2009 (ex CP244/2005)—Belgium. Financing of public hospitals of the IRIS-network of the Brussels capital region. (Available in Dutch and in French only).

[7] Commission Decision of 28 November 2005 on the application of Article 86(2) of the EC Treaty to State aid in the form of public service compensation granted to certain undertakings

types of services without any restrictions on the amount of aid or on their turn-over—including hospital services—as well as for all services provided by undertakings with an annual turnover threshold of less than € 100 million and subject to a maximum aid of € 30 million. Hence we will focus our discussion on the 2005 Decision and we will not deal at length with the other aspects of the *Altmark* Package, which are relevant to different types of services.

The Decision first sets out the types of services that may qualify for exemption and then details the conditions under which they are exempted, notably the need for an explicit act of entrustment and specification of the parameters for compensation and the mechanism for retrieving overcompensation. Services that are exempted need not be notified to the Commission nor does the otherwise standard standstill obligation apply: aid can thus be awarded immediately and lawfully without further action by the Commission. Services that may be exempted but which do not meet the conditions on the other hand are subject to notification for an individual exemption decision under the Framework, which applies substantively largely identical conditions.

Article 2(1)b of the 2005 Decision covered 'public service compensation granted to hospitals (…) carrying out activities qualified as SGEI by the Member State concerned.' The nature of the activities concerned is left to the Member States. Recital 16 stated as follows:

> Hospitals (…) which are entrusted with tasks involving services of general economic interest have specific characteristics that need to be taken into consideration. In particular, account should be taken of the fact that at the current stage of development of the internal market, the intensity of distortion of competition in those sectors is not necessarily proportionate to the level of turnover and compensation. Accordingly, hospitals providing medical care, including, where applicable, emergency services and ancillary services directly related to the main activities, notably in the field of research (…) should benefit from the exemption from notification provided for in this Decision, even if the amount of compensation they receive exceeds the thresholds laid down in this Decision, if the services performed are qualified as services of general economic interest by the Member States.

It was, therefore, not sufficient to provide hospital services: in addition it was necessary that the services concerned were designated as SGEI. The conditions that must be met were, first, that the act or acts concerned must specific (i) the nature and the duration of the public service obligations; (ii) the undertaking and territory concerned; (iii) the nature of any exclusive or special rights assigned to the undertaking; (iv) the parameters for calculating, controlling and reviewing the compensation; and (v) the arrangements for avoiding and repaying any over-compensation. Second, compensation could not amount to more than the costs of

---

(Footnote 7 continued)

entrusted with the operation of services of general economic interest *OJ* 2005 L312/67; Community framework for State aid in the form of public service compensation *OJ* 2005 C297/4; Commission Directive 2006/111/EC of 16 November 2006 on the transparency of financial relations between Member States and public undertakings as well as on financial transparency within certain undertakings *OJ* 2006 L318/17.

the services concerned and a reasonable profit. A mechanism to control for overcompensation with annual checks had to be in place although a maximum of 10 % excess financing could be carried forward to a following year. In addition the Decision imposed information (records kept for 10 years) and transparency requirements with three yearly reporting to the Commission.

12.3 The 2011 SGEI Package Decision

In December 2011 the Commission comprehensively updated its SGEI Package.[8] The basic structure with block exemptions in a Decision and dealing with individual notifications under the Framework was not changed although the aid threshold in the 2011 Decision is now lowered from € 30 million to € 15 million. A change in emphasis has been that the Decision now targets social services in a much broader sense than before, leaving the Framework to deal mainly with the utilities sectors (e.g. energy, water and waste disposal services, transport and electronic communications) where the Commission expects there is more scope for liberalisation and less risk of political controversy—at least less than when exposing social services to the State aid and competition rules. This new Framework is dealt with in depth in various other chapters and we do not go into detail here nor do we provide a full critical assessment of it.

The new definition of the healthcare services covered in Articles 2(1)b and 2(1)c of the 2011 Decision is now much broader:

> (b) compensation for the provision of SGEI by hospitals providing medical care, including, where applicable, emergency services; the pursuit of ancillary activities directly related to the main activities, notably in the field of research, does not, however, prevent the application of this paragraph;
>
> (c) compensation for the provision of SGEI meeting social needs as regards health and long-term care, childcare, access to and reintegration into the labour market, social housing and the care and social inclusion of vulnerable groups;

The relevant recital (11) is substantively unchanged although in part the text is now incorporated in Article 2(1)b. The most significant extensions are obviously

---

[8] Commission Decision of 20.12.2011 on the application of Article 106(2) of the Treaty on the Functioning of the European Union to State aid in the form of public service compensation granted to certain undertakings entrusted with the operation of services of general economic interest *OJ* 2012 L7/3; Communication Commission European Union framework for State aid in the form of public service compensation, *OJ* 2012 C8/15; Communication from the Commission on the application of the European Union State aid rules to compensation granted for the provision of services of general economic interest Brussels, [2012] C8/4. A draft Commission Regulation on the application of Articles 107 and 108 of the Treaty on the Functioning of the European Union to *de minimis* aid granted to undertakings providing services of general economic interest was scheduled for adoption in April 2012, *OJ* 2012 C8/23 and was adopted as Regulation No 360/2012 on 25 April 2012: *OJ* 2012. L 114/8.

the unlimited inclusion of 'health and long term care' in Article 2(1)c which sits uneasily with the specifications in Article 2(1)b as regards the various types of medical services and the status of ancillary activities. Indeed it raises the question whether the more general phrasing in Article 2(1)c could not have sufficed. However, it may be that the link between health and long-term care with social needs is construed as a restriction, the scope of which is yet unclear.

The obligations in relation to the act of entrustment, its contents, the parameters for compensation based on cost plus reasonable profits, controls on overcompensation are the same as under the 2005 regime, except for the addition of a more extensive elaboration on how to determine what a reasonable profit entails. This latter is based on a rate of return on capital that takes into account the degree of risk incurred. The rate of return on capital should be defined as the internal rate of return that the undertaking obtains on its invested capital over the duration of the period of entrustment based on a benchmark of the relevant swap rate plus 100 basis points.

There is so far no experience of the application of the 2011 Decision in this sector, given that it only came into force on 31 January 2012. Instead we will take a closer look at the only substantive SGEI ruling concerning hospital services, the Commission's 2009 IRIS-H Decision.

12.4 Commission Decisions in the Hospital Sector

The Commission Decision of October 2009 concerning the financing of public hospitals in the so-called IRIS network of public hospitals in Brussels was groundbreaking (the IRIS-H Decision).[9] This is because it was, and remains, the first full Decision at EU level concerning the application of the State aid rules to the hospital sector. The Commission concluded that the Belgian measures were indeed State aid. However, in so far as these measures came into effect after November 2005, they were both exempted from notification and compatible with the internal market under Article 108(3) TFEU because they were in accordance with the formal and substantive conditions of the 2005 SGEI Decision. Moreover the Commission declared those measures which had entered into force before that date and that had not been notified to be compatible with the internal market as well, because they met the conditions of Article 106(2) TFEU. Both aspects will be discussed in detail further below.

It may be noted that the Commission had considered a system of capital allowances for hospitals in Ireland and found it to be compatible with Article 108(3) (c) TFEU.[10] In general, the Commission appears reluctant to be drawn into

---

[9] Above n 6.

[10] European Commission, Decision of 27 February 2002, State aid measure N 543/2001—Ireland. Capital allowances for hospitals.

detailed analysis of hospital sector aid. Notably, the Commission has rejected several complaints concerning hospital financing in various Member States,[11] or it came to the conclusion that the measure concerned did not constitute aid.[12]

In the German hospitals case *Asklepios Kliniken* (2007) a number of private hospitals had complained that German public hospitals received State aid by way of regional support—mostly in the form of unlimited guarantees.[13] The complaint asked the Commission in January 2003 to look into the allegedly unlawful conduct on the basis of the information which it had provided to the Commission and to take measures to suspend the aid until such time as the Commission had taken a final decision. The Commission initially refused to take a decision, and ultimately informed the complainants that its position on the matter was covered by the then draft Decision of 2005 on Compensation for SGEI. The complainants challenged the Commission's approach before the General Court. They argued that the Commission had used an unreasonable delay in responding to their complaint, and further that the final position taken by the Commission was not a legitimate method of dealing with their complaint.

The General Court confirmed that the general rules on legal review provided legal standing not just against decisions but against refusals to take a Decision as well. Nevertheless, the General Court dismissed the action, as the adoption by the Commission of a decision of general scope setting out abstract criteria for assessing the legality of State financing does not by itself constitute a definition of its position by the Commission on a complaint concerning that financing. Only the actual application of those criteria by the Commission to the situations complained of can constitute a definition of position that creates legal standing.[14] Finally the Court held that the reasonableness of the duration of the investigation of a State aid complaint must be determined in relation to the particular circumstances of each case, its context, the various procedural stages and the complexity of the case. Uncertainty about the (national) legal framework concerned may justify the Commission deferring its proceedings pending clarification.[15]

In the meantime, the Commission has ruled twice on the financing of health insurers in Ireland and once in The Netherlands (all three cases concerned more specifically risk equalisation systems)[16] while the General Court has handed down

---

[11] CJEU, Case T-167/04 *Asklepios Kliniken GmbH v Commission* [2007] *ECR* II-2379.

[12] GC, Case T-397/03 *Fédération de l'hospitalisation privée*, *OJ* 2006, C22/25. This case was withdrawn and removed from the register.

[13] Case T-167/04 *Asklepios Kliniken GmbH v Commission* [2007] *ECR* II-2379.

[14] Ibid, paras 77–78.

[15] Ibid, para 81.

[16] Decision of the Commission of 13 May 2003 with regard to State aid N 46/2003—Ireland—risk equalisation scheme in the Irish health Insurance market; Decision of the Commission of 3 May 2005 with regard to State aid N 541/2004 en N 542/2004—The Netherlands—risk equalisation system and retention of reserves; Decision of the Commission of 17 June 2009 with regard to State aid N 582/2008 (IP/09/961)—Ireland—health insurance intergenerational solidarity relief.

an important ruling concerning the first Irish Decision in the *BUPA* case.[17] However, the case that we will discuss here is the first in which the Commission directly tackles the often opaque world of hospital financing.

12.5 The IRIS-H Decision

The Commission's approach in the IRIS-H Decision suggests that it opened its investigation only reluctantly. Two associations representing private hospitals in Brussels first filed a complaint in September 2005. After 3 years of discussion, the Commission effectively rejected the complaint (see below). The plaintiffs appealed to the General Court but in the meantime—and after an informal meeting convened by the General Court in July 2009—the Commission published a comprehensively motivated decision in October 2009. (The General Court had meanwhile dismissed the appeal by the plaintiffs against the earlier putative decision.[18]) As a result, after 4 years of proceedings the plaintiffs were left with a first phase State aid decision—as the Commission did not think it was necessary to open the second (contentious) phase. The plaintiffs have appealed against the Commission decision, and this appeal is now pending before the General Court.[19]

12.5.1 Background

12.5.1.1 The Beneficiaries

The IRIS-H Decision concerns the five public hospitals in the Brussels capital region jointly identified as the IRIS-H (hospitals). From 1996 onward the organisation and the operations of these five hospitals including their financing has been elaborated in plans that were decided upon by the IRIS framework body in which the five hospitals cooperate. This IRIS body is subject to public supervision and itself mainly consists of communal representatives of the public centres for social security in Brussels (which administratively is made up of 20 separate communes) alongside representatives of physicians' organisations and of the two university hospitals in Brussels.

---

[17] GC, Case T-289/03 *British United Provident Association Ltd (BUPA)* et al. *v Commission* [2008] *ECR* II-81.

[18] GC, Joined Cases T-128/08 and T-241/08 *Coordination bruxelloise d'Institutions sociales et de santé (CBI) and Association bruxelloise des institutions des soins de santé privées asbl (ABISP) v Commission, OJ* 2010, C195/17.

[19] GC, Case T-137/10 *Coordination bruxelloise d'Institutions sociales et de santé (CBI) v Commission*, Pub 2010, C148/38.

The IRIS concept was the result of fundamental restructuring of the financing and supervision of hospitals in Belgium dating back to 1995. Briefly summarised, the Brussels' government has decided to balance the budgets of the hospitals concerned by means of a € 100 million loan extended to the IRIS hospitals via the Brussels' communes.[20]

12.5.2 Sources of Financing

The system of public financing for all hospitals in Belgium remains complex, even after the above-mentioned reforms. During the period covered by the Commission's investigation the Belgian hospitals received six different types of financing for carrying out their SGEI, as formulated at national level (discussed further below).

The relevant sources and volumes of the financing are set out in the Decision:[21]

- Sickness- and invalidity insurance payments, which cover only part of hospital costs;
- Full or partial restitution of the compensation paid to hospital doctors (the entire amount paid by patients to reimburse the interventions of medical doctors is collected centrally and redistributed);
- Operating costs through a special budget that is based on reimbursement per standard day of care provided. This also covers additional costs for hospitals that care for patients who are challenged socially and/or economically;
- Investment subsidies—intended to cover the building and (interior) remodelling of hospitals including investments in medical devices;
- An indemnity awarded for costs with regard to construction projects or closing down hospitals.

The sixth source of financing only relates to public hospitals including the IRIS-H, and constitutes additional funding by the Brussels communes that can be used to cover the budget deficits of the public hospitals.[22]

12.5.3 The Public Service Obligations

Apart from the pso which applies to all hospitals and is set out at national level in the Law on Hospitals, the IRIS-H are also subject to a supplementary pso that is formulated by the IRIS framework body itself (and thereby, by the representatives of the social services of the communes who have a majority there). This concerns

---

[20] As was the case on 31 December 1999, compared to a cumulative deficit of almost € 200 million on 31 December 1995, the year of the above-mentioned aid.

[21] IRIS-H Decision, above n 6, points 29–48.

[22] Ibid., points 43–48.

(i) the duty to treat everyone (also for services other than emergency services) and (ii) the duty or maintaining a full range of hospital services at every location operated by the IRIS-H.

The IRIS-H are also required to fulfil a number of non-healthcare of 'social' pso that are carried out by the IRIS framework body. These tasks are delegated to the hospitals by the public centres for social security of the relevant Brussels' communes and are financed based on agreements between the communes and the IRIS-H that regulate the grant of specific subsidies.

Finally the IRIS-H are under an obligation to ensure that a large proportion of their staff is bilingual (as the region of Brussels is both French and Dutch-speaking). This obligation is not imposed on the private hospitals in Brussels or any other hospitals in Belgium and the annual costs are estimated at € 4 million.

12.5.4 The Complaint

The plaintiffs did not contest all six of these subsidies—they only contest the subsidy for social public service obligations, the subsidy to make up for budget deficits (i.e. the sixth source of hospital funding listed above) and the one-off restructuring subsidy in 1995.

According to the plaintiffs there are no public service obligations that are specific to the IRIS-H. The only such obligations that exist are imposed by the Law on Hospitals,[23] which apply to all hospitals without distinction regarding their public or private status and regarding both emergency care and elective treatment. The complaint focuses on the fact that at federal level the system is the same for public and private hospitals whereas at local level only the deficits of public hospitals are compensated, while at regional level supplementary ad hoc subsidies are also exclusively reserved for public hospitals. The plaintiffs assert that the private hospitals are consequently forced to reduce their capacity or may even be forced to close down. By contrast, studies carried out for the Belgian government show that the costs of hospitalisation in a public hospital are € 21 per day higher than in a private hospital.[24]

---

[23] Loi sur les hôpitaux coordonnée du 7 août 1987 (coordinated law on hospitals of 7 August 1987), Moniteur Belge (Belgian offical journal) 7 October 1987, in force from 17 October 1987.

[24] According to a report by the Belgian Mutualités Chretiennes discusssed by Lienard 2004, p. 10 (with statistical annexes). This was the difference between a hospital day in public (€ 258) and private hospitals (€ 237) in 2003.

12.6 The Evaluation by the Commission

Because the original complaint dated back to October 2005—and as according to Article 15 of Regulation 659/1999[25] the competence of the Commission to recover aid expires after 10 years—the fact that the original restructuring took place in 1995 is significant. The limitation on recovery does not however affect the powers of investigation of the Commission, and as such the Decision focuses on the aid granted from October 1996 onward, but including the aid that was granted in the restructuring of 1995.

The Commission considered it necessary to investigate all the sources of financing that the IRIS-H received by way of pso compensation (i.e. for intramural and extramural care and including social services) in view of the requirements set out in the *Deutsche Post* Case,[26] where the General Court has ruled that the Commission is required to carry out a comprehensive and thorough investigation in order to establish whether the total amount of aid by way of compensation of a SGEI was not in excess of the net costs of providing the services concerned.

The Commission's approach was to investigate first whether the funding at issue constituted State aid in the sense of Article 107(1) TFEU before addressing the defence of the Belgian state that was based on the *Altmark* case.[27] The Commission investigated in turn whether (i) undertakings were involved in (ii) a transfer of state resources that (iii) conferred a selective advantage on them (iv) to the detriment of trade between the Member States.

12.6.1 The Concept of Undertaking

The Belgian authorities adopted the position that the hospitals were not involved in economic activities as they were fully based on the solidarity principle.

The Commission found that in view of established case law,[28] the economic nature of the hospitals' activities was without doubt. The main activities of the IRIS-H, which consist of elective and emergency medical care (intramural care), are activities that were also carried out by other institutions including private hospitals. This confirms that although the solidarity aspect plays a role in the

---

[25] Council Regulation (EC) No 659/1999 of 22 March 1999 laying down detailed rules for the application of Article 93 of the EC Treaty, *OJ* 1999, L83/1.

[26] CJEU, Case T-266/02 *Deutsche Post v Commission* [2008] *ECR* II-1233.

[27] CJEU, Case C-280/00 *Altmark Trans* above n 4.

[28] CJEU, Case C-237/04 *Enirisorse SpA v Sotacarbo SpA* [2006] *ECR* I-2843; CJEU, Case C-41/90 *Klaus Höfner and Fritz Elser v Macrotron GmbH* [1991] *ECR* I-1979; CJEU, Joined Cases C-180/98—C-184/98 *Pavel Pavlov et al. v Stichting Pensioenfonds Medische Specialisten* [2000] *ECR* I-6451.

Commission's assessment it is not decisive,[29] especially where private hospitals are providing the same type of intramural care (even if this is possibly not identical).

The Commission did not consider it necessary to engage in a further analysis whether the extramural activities of a social nature constituted economic activities or not because it considered that the subsidies involved would in any event qualify as aid that was compatible with the internal market.[30]

12.6.2 State Resources

As the measures concerned and their financing (at federal as well as regional and local level) originate with the responsible public authorities the Commission ruled that it was not contestable that they could be attributed to the State.

12.6.3 Selectivity

Regarding intramural care the Commission considered the measures to be selective because only the IRIS-H had been charged with the relevant pso—and also they were the only undertakings receiving compensation for these obligations. Other healthcare providers were excluded from this scheme. The Commission did not deal with the question whether this was a case of economic advantage or, as was claimed by the Belgian authorities based on the *Altmark* case,[31] purely a matter of compensation for pso. This point was dealt with separately after the assessment of the other elements of State aid had been completed.

12.6.4 An Effect on Trade Between the Member States

As regards this point the Commission pointed out that several undertakings are present on the market and the position of the undertakings that benefited from the contested measures was strengthened so the existence of a negative effect on trade could not be excluded. Moreover it pointed out there was some limited cross-border provision of services to patients for both intramural and extramural care.

---

[29] CJEU, Case C-244/94 *Fédération française des sociétés d'assurances* et al. [1995] *ECR* I-4013.

[30] IRIS-H Decision, above n 6, point 111. This is remarkable because it would appear that market entry by means of public procurement would be a private alternative to the IRIS-H network.

[31] CJEU, Case C-280/00 *Altmark Trans*, above n 4.

Hence the Commission concluded that the contested financing constituted State aid in the meaning of Article 107(1) TFEU. Next it addressed the application of the *Altmark* criteria.

12.6.5 The Altmark Criteria: State Aid or Compensation?

The well-known four cumulative *Altmark* criteria can be summarised as follows:

- being charged with a clearly defined pso
- objective and transparent parameters for compensation;
- no overcompensation;
- compensation based on public procurement procedure or the costs of an efficient undertaking

Based on the 2008 *BUPA* case the rule is that these *Altmark* criteria must be applied ex tunc,[32] i.e. retroactively to the IRIS-H subsidies that were granted before the *Altmark* ruling took place, as the CJEU had chosen not to limit the applicability of its *Altmark* judgment in time. The Commission next tried to simplify the analysis by considering only two of the four *Altmark* criteria, and went on:

- first, to analyse whether the undertakings involved had indeed been entrusted with an SGEI (the first criterion);
- and second whether the selection of the undertakings involved had been based on the fourth criterion

12.6.6 Entrustment

The Commission recalled the broad discretion enjoyed by the Member States in this sector—as had been confirmed in the *BUPA* case:[33]—the organisation of the healthcare sector largely remains the domain of the Member States. The role of the Commission is limited to checking for a manifest error of judgment.

As regards intramural care the Commission considered that the EU law requirements had been met. The federal system with regard to the SGEI had been well defined in the Law on Hospitals and in particular their obligatory and social character was clear. Regarding the specific pso of the IRIS-H the Commission established that these had been imposed on the basis of a law on social security services[34] and in the strategic IRIS plans that were set out by the IRIS framework

---

[32] GC, Case T-289/03 *BUPA*, above n 17.

[33] Ibid., para 165.

[34] Loi organique des Centres Publics d'Action Sociale du 8 juillet 1976 (Organic law on the public centres for social security), Belgian official journal 5 August 1976.

body (and 'which should be regarded as equivalent to the act of a public authority'). The IRIS-H are under the obligation to provide all types of hospital care to everyone on demand in a framework in which all types of hospital care must be available at all locations. In contrast to the private hospitals which are free to select their patients and to organise their activities the IRIS-H do not have any choice as regards the definition and the scope of the said obligations.[35] This means that the existence of a pso has been established: the territorial limitation of the users/beneficiaries involved does not affect this conclusion.[36]

As regards the non-hospital tasks of the IRIS-H (social care, alongside medical care to patients) the obligatory character of these social tasks likewise has a legal basis and can also be found in the fact that those charged with these tasks have no room for manoeuvre with regard to its definition and scope. In what appears to be circular reasoning, the social character of these tasks flows from the fact that the additional costs that are incurred by the IRIS-H to fulfil these tasks are charged to the public authorities in the context of their responsibility for setting social policy.

The first *Altmark* criterion was therefore met both for intra- and extramural care as well as the social services concerned.

12.6.7 Public Procurement or Efficient Undertaking

The Commission first established for all intramural and extramural SGEI with which the IRIS-H had been entrusted that these had not been attributed on the basis of a public procurement procedure (and noted this aspect might become the subject of separate proceedings under the enforcement of the public procurement rules).[37] In addition, neither the Belgian State nor the plaintiffs had provided sufficient evidence to determine whether the compensation mechanisms for intramural and extramural care provided by the IRIS-H actually and fully met the requirement of matching an efficient undertaking in the sense of the fourth *Altmark* criterion:

> According to the Commission it is not possible, based on the arguments provided by the parties, to establish with absolute certainty whether when setting the level of the necessary compensation, the actual costs of an average undertaking with the characteristics demanded by the case law were really taken into account and whether the IRIS-H and the private hospitals that have filed the complaint are actually such representative or average well run undertakings as the *Altmark* Case requires.[38]

---

[35] 'The obligatory nature of the service and therefore the existence of a service of general economic interest are proven if the service providers is obliged to conclude agreements on fixed terms.' IRIS-H Decision, para 149.

[36] GC, Case T-289/03 *BUPA*, above n 17, para 186.

[37] Directive 2004/18/EC of the European Parliament and of the Council of 31 March 2004 on the coordination of procedures for the award of public works contracts, public supply contracts and public service contracts, *OJ* 2004 L134/114.

[38] IRIS-H Decision, above n 5, para 161.

Moreover, according to the Commission compensation for providing an SGEI that is awarded to several undertakings and that is based on their average costs without requiring any evidence of sound management would inevitably lead to overcompensation. Note that at a later stage of the decision the Commission would adopt the opposite point of view: compensation based on average costs can lead to under-compensation.) Hence the Commission held that the fourth *Altmark* condition had not been met so that the measures constituted State aid in the sense of Article 107(1) TFEU on the basis of the *Altmark* analysis. It was therefore stricter in its approach on this count in *IRIS-H* than the General Court had been in *BUPA*—where it held that the fourth *Altmark* condition could not be applied because in the system of risk equalisation the beneficiaries could not be identified in advance and compared with an efficient operator, but the requisite standard was nevertheless held to be met because the Commission had otherwise tested for inefficiencies. This brought the Commission to the third and final branch of its analysis: the question whether the contested measures were compatible with the internal market based on Article 106(2) TFEU. This required it to apply the criteria set out in the 2005 SGEI Package (cast as a specification of the general requirements of necessity and proportionality that apply under Article 106(2) TFEU).

12.6.8 Services of General Economic Interest

Article 106(2) TEFU can only be relied upon if the measure concerned respects the requirements of necessity and proportionality as well as the following conditions:

> (i) the services in question must be an SGEI that is clearly defined as such by the Member State; (ii) the undertaking provided the SGEI must have been formally charged with doing so by the Member State; (iii) application of the competition rules set out in the Treaty must obstruct the fulfilment by the undertaking of the special tasks with which it has been charged and an exemption from these rules may not affect trade to an extent that this is at odds with the Community interest.[39]

Because of the repetitive nature and the overlap of the criteria deployed as part of the various tests at both the procedural and substantive stages in this case (and similar cases) it is at times difficult to keep sight of the larger picture. The main substantive difference between the SGEI test in Article 106(2) TFEU as elaborated in the 2005 Decision and the *Altmark* criteria is that the fourth *Altmark* criterion (tender or efficiency test) is not included in the criteria of the SGEI package. In addition, there is an important procedural difference: the SGEI package and its more detailed substantive assessment criteria that elaborate on Article 106(2) TFEU only applied from November (the Framework) respectively December (the Decision) of 2005 whereas, as mentioned, the *Altmark* Case applies *ex tunc*.[40]

We shall address first the Commission's test of necessity and proportionality.

---

[39]   Ibid., para 165.
[40]   Cf. Grespan 2008, 4.1140ff.

12.6.9 Necessity

As the General Court had already indicated in the *BUPA* Case the Member State enjoys a broad margin of appreciation not just with regard to the definition of an SGEI but also when determining the compensation of the costs involved.[41] The authorities must specify the parameters of the compensation involved so the Commission may determine whether the compensation awarded is in line with what is necessary. This is a marginal standard of review: the act of assignment must contain the necessary basic elements that enable the future compensation to be calculated. However the Member States retain the freedom to set the parameters of their choice.

The first part of the necessity criterion regarding the definition of and the entrustment of the SGEI obligations largely covers the same ground as the first *Altmark* criterion. The Commission also pointed out that based on consistent case law the fact that parts of the entrustment are found in different legal acts and/or have to be derived from the legal context does not raise any doubts as to whether these criteria (an act of assignment specifying the SGEI etc.) are met. This may be in line with the recent practice but it is perhaps surprising if we look at the list of elements that are set out in the SGEI package which must be covered by a 'clear' act of assignment.

It is less surprising that the Commission subsequently reaches the conclusion that the legal basis for compensation of the IRIS-H by the responsible authorities is clearly set out in law and regulation. As regards the compensation of deficits as a result of public service obligations that have exclusively been imposed upon public hospitals (including the IRIS-H) the Commission notes that the Law on Hospitals clearly sets out the criteria for compensation in advance and also sets out specific provisions for the compensation of SGEI-related deficits of the public hospitals. This compensation is not based on actual costs but on the average costs of a group of comparable hospitals.

Next the Commission, without any further reference to a significant investigation into the costs involved, concludes that this system can lead to undercompensation. Consequently the compensation is regarded as necessary and not just in order to compensate for the actual costs of carrying out the pso set out in the Law on hospitals. The 'ex post' compensation of deficits is also considered to be necessary from a health perspective and for social reasons in order to guarantee the continuity and the viability of the system that in all probability could not function if only a limited number of private hospitals were available.[42] It would seem that from this perspective there can never be overcompensation. What makes this observation questionable is the fact that earlier in the same decision the same compensation based on average costs was interpreted as proof that overcompensation was possible, and hence the fourth *Altmark* condition was not met.

---

[41] GC, Case T-289/03 *BUPA*, above n 16, para 214.

[42] IRIS-H Decision, above n 4, para 177.

As regards the social tasks the Commission concluded, based on a succinct analysis, that here the cost parameters can likewise be determined in advance.

The Commission then tackles the question whether the provisions to prevent and/or correct for overcompensation are adequate. As regards the compensation for deficits due to pso of the public hospitals awarded by the national (federal) government the Commission concludes that this compensation is limited to the balance of the net costs of the relevant public services. Hence the compensation remains within the limits of the 2005 SGEI package: 100 % of the net costs plus a reasonable profit margin. The regional restructuring aid that had been provided by the Brussels capital region related to pso that had already been fulfilled and in accordance with parameters for compensation that were adequately defined. In addition, the region only provides temporary credits while awaiting the calculation and payment (10 years later) of the definitive deficit with regard to the public service obligations by the federal authorities. Finally the cost for the public service obligations and social tasks that are delegated by the public centres for social security via the IRIS-Z framework body are not reimbursed automatically but only when (unspecified) further demands set by the public centres for social security are met, which are designed to avoid overcompensation.

Hence the Commission concluded that these measures are adequate to meet the first compatibility criterion in the SGEI package; necessity.

12.6.10 Proportionality

Here too the Commission cites the *BUPA* case:

> As regards, more particularly, review of the proportionality of the compensation for discharging an SGEI mission, as established by an act of general application, it has further been specified in the case law that that review is limited to ascertaining whether the compensation provided for is necessary in order for the SGEI in question to be capable of being performed in economically acceptable conditions (...), or whether, on the other hand, the measure in question is manifestly inappropriate by reference to the objective pursued (...).[43]

The Commission also applies the provisions of the SGEI package and recalls that for purposes of substantive compatibility assessment (in contrast to the *Altmark* procedural test) the amount of compensation does not have to be established by means of a comparison of the costs of an efficient undertaking. If the state shows that the amount of compensation is equal to the projected net costs based on the parameters that are clearly defined in the act of assignment there will be no finding of overcompensation and the compensation involved will be regarded as compatible aid. In other words: the public authorities may compensate the

---

[43] GC, Case T-289/03 *BUPA*, above note 17, para 222. Most likely the GC only intended to juxtapose the necessity and the proportionality test in order to highlight that the latter test is whether the means used are manifestly inappropriate.

undertaking that has been charged with carrying out an SGEI for 100 per cent of the costs involved plus a reasonable profit margin, and ignore any consideration of efficiency in respect of how these costs are incurred. Based on its investigation of the annual accounts of the IRIS-H (i.e. the results regarding hospital services and social services, excluding non-SGEI activities) the Commission reached its conclusion that no overcompensation was involved.

This point is all the more important to the extent that the test to which the financing is subjected is less strict: this means more financial room for manoeuvre is left that could be (ab) used for cross subsidies for competitive services. The Belgian state had provided information demonstrating that the EU requirement of separate accounts had been met and this provided evidence that the division between the economic and the non-economic activities of the hospitals had been respected. The Commission considered this satisfactory. Hence the measures involved were considered not to be manifestly inappropriate, and therefore proportional.

12.7 Some Implications of the IRIS-H Decision

12.7.1 The Application of the Altmark Criteria

The Commission appears to use the approach of applying only two of the four (cumulative) *Altmark* criteria more frequently.[44] Nevertheless the question arises why the Commission has decided not to use the second (clear parameters for compensation) and/or the third (no overcompensation) criteria. Apparently, this served to simplify the analysis. The nature of the complaint may also have been decisive: the plaintiffs' position is that the IRIS-H has not been charged with distinctive pso. In addition, they are claiming that the way in which the services concerned are financed is inefficient. Perhaps the Commission did not wish to tackle the same issue twice? In addition the plaintiffs claim that even if the intervention at federal level is organised in such a way that it is compatible with the second *Altmark* criterion, the same does not apply to the regional and local levels of intervention where the system is not transparent. Because the deficits at local and regional levels are financed ex post this would mean that the system as a whole does not meet the second criterion (otherwise the second and third criteria would become indistinct—i.e. no overcompensation). Hence the plaintiffs in their appeal claim that the Commission has not applied the criteria for evaluating overcompensation properly and that transparency is also lacking.

At the same time, as we have seen, the Commission does not follow the approach taken by the General Court in the *BUPA* Case either, where it watered

---

[44] The Commission examined all four criteria in its Decision of 17 June 2009, State aid No N 582/2008—Ireland. Health Insurance intergenerational solidarity relief.

down the *Altmark* criteria to a considerable degree. The approach by the Commission which seems laudable leads to the finding of aid in the sense of Article 107(1) TFEU that takes place because the fourth *Altmark* criterion is not met.

12.7.2 The Application of Article 106(2) TFEU and the SGEI Package

The criteria of the 2005 SGEI Package with regard to the act of assignment are disregarded by erroneously assuming that these had been met when applying the *Altmark* test. There is no clear legal basis for the additional services that the Commission assumes must be performed exclusively by the public hospitals, while the requirement of such a basis does exist. The general pso at national level is moreover not set out in line with the requirements of the SGEI package (which may explain why *Altmark* is relied upon at this point).

In addition, there is an important distinction between the application of the *Altmark* criteria and the application of the SGEI Package: *Altmark* serves to decide whether an economic advantage was enjoyed in the sense of Article 107(1) TFEU whereas Article 106(2) TFEU is about balancing interests. This means that when carrying out the latter test the Commission omits several of the *Altmark* criteria (especially the fourth criterion) on public procurement and efficiency. This is in line with the 2005 SGEI Package, based on Article 106(2) TFEU and adopted in line with Article 106(3) TFEU. Only the first three *Altmark* criteria are repeated, with additional tests regarding overcompensation. Is this the correct approach?[45]

The efficiency test is replaced by a test in the 2005 SGEI Package that allows full compensation of costs without any considerations of value for money. It is clear that this is undesirable from a perspective of competition. The instruments of the Commission are thereby limited to checking the financing mechanisms for overcompensation (i.e. where more than actual costs incurred plus a reasonable profit) and competitors cannot compete for the market based on public procurement. This gives the providers of SGEI perverse incentives to run up costs and releases the Member States form the obligation of replacing inefficient incumbents and controlling costs. It will also not help to lower State aid levels in line with the 2005 State aid action plan.[46]

In the IRIS-H Decision the total amount of compensation for SGEI has become a crucial component of the balancing of interests when Article 106(2) TFEU is applied to establish the compatibility of the aid: the Commission does not consider the underlying costs in any detail at all. Nevertheless, this is the crucial element of this Decision which, after all, is about ex post financing of deficits. Perhaps,

---

[45] GC, Case T-289/03 *BUPA* (above n 17), also assumes overlap. Cf. GC, Case T-8/06 *FAB Fernsehen aus Berlin GmbH v Commission* [2009] *ECR* II-196, paras 64 and 65–69.

[46] COM (2005) 107 final of 7 June 2005.

therefore, the relevant question is not whether the efficiency criterion has been met but what method is used to ensure that only actual costs are reimbursed. As one of us has argued elsewhere however, this is a different test.[47]

Arguably, it is not up to the Commission to develop its own standard of efficiency in the hospital sector, and even if it could take a more stringent approach to inputs it is highly questionable whether it has the power to determine outputs—the quality of service is determined by the Member States.[48] Nevertheless, it could have taken the costs in the private sector as a benchmark in order to determine whether the public hospitals were obliged to incur additional expenses in order to be able to deliver additional services. The Commission avoids using this model by claiming that the public and private hospitals have different tasks, but it is not clear from its analysis whether this distinction is wholly justified.

The plaintiffs moreover rightly point out that Article 106(2) TFEU must, because it is an exception, be interpreted restrictively and therefore (arguably, we believe) in line with the proportionality test in this provision an efficiency test is required. At a minimum the Commission could have addressed this element of the complaint.

12.7.3 Recent Developments

The 2010 Monti Report on the internal market[49] saw possibilities for establishing SGEI at EU level for specific services i.e. bank accounts (current accounts) and access to broadband services. It also pleaded in favour of aligning public procurement and the rules on SGEI and, as such, in favour of applying the fourth *Altmark* criterion more rigorously. A greater emphasis on compliance with the EU public procurement regime has been adopted with the 2011 SGEI Package, albeit that in the context of the block exemption Decision the Commission recalls that the procurement principles deriving from the Treaty free movement principles should be respected. An important innovation of the new framework which applies to aid which would not fall within the scope of the exemption Decision, is the requirement for Member States to hold a public consultation to establish public service needs.[50]

State aid to the hospital sector is unlikely to be evaluated under the new framework as this will be primarily applicable to aid measures above the EUR 15 million

---

[47] Cf. Hancher and Larouche 2010.

[48] GC, Case T-442/03 *SIC—Sociedade Independente de Comunicação, SA v Commission* [2008] *ECR* 1161, at para 212.

[49] A new strategy for the single market: at the service of Europe's economy and society. Report to the President of the European Commission, José Manuel Barroso, by Mario Monti, 9 May 2010 (especially point 3.3. Social services and the single market.

[50] Commission Communication, European Union framework for State aid in the form of public service compensation, C (2011) 9406 final.

threshold. As explained, this threshold does not apply to the hospital sector. If a measure cannot be brought under the conditions set out in the Decision then it is unlikely that it could be declared compatible with the Framework, following notification, given that the latter imposes similar and indeed stricter conditions for assessing the compatibility of the aid. This leaves open the question of whether the Commission would nevertheless consider a justification based on Article 106(2) TFEU, for example where there are perhaps only weak provisions for controlling compensation levels ex ante, but where ex post controls can be satisfactorily applied.

Finally, in the Communication published along with the new 2011 Decision and Framework, the Commission considers that contracts for the performance of SGEI should be awarded in compliance with the procurement principles, as well as the EU procurement Directives in so far as these apply.[51] If adequate procedures have not been followed, then the aid cannot be deemed compatible. If in its subsequent enforcement of the new 2011 *Altmark* Package, the Commission succeeds in its attempt to restrict 'gold plating' of public services by the Member States, this may indicate that the Commission is prepared to embark on a more economic approach to examining the trade off between national public interests on the one hand and competition and free movement objectives on the other.

12.7.4 Procurement

At the time of writing the Commission has proposed a fundamental revision of the procurement regime which would provide an exemption for social services. On the same date as the Second *Altmark* package was adopted, the Commission announced its proposed reforms to the EU procurement regime.[52]

The new proposals can be summarised as follows:

- First, the Commission intends to publish a separate measure for a directive on public services concessions—albeit that social service concessions will be given special treatment.
- Second, a new 'light regime' approach to social services, including healthcare services will be introduced in the revised procurement Directive.
- Third, a new, clearer definition of contracting entity is to be adopted and the definition of the term 'bodies governed by public law' is clarified.
- Fourth, new criteria for the award of contracts will be recognised—so that a cost-effectiveness approach is firmly recognised.
- Fifth, the right of contracting authorities to deploy a strategic use of the procurement rules, for example, to improve public health will be explicitly acknowledged.
- Finally the proposal recommends the establishment of a designated national authority to monitor and review observance of procedures.

---

[51] Above n 8.

[52] http://ec.europa.eu/internal_market/publicprocurement/modernising_rules/reform_proposals_en.htm

If adopted this reform will mean that a new separate procurement regime for social services, including health services is to be introduced. The Commission considers that social, health and education services have specific characteristics which make them inappropriate for the regular procedures for the award of public service contracts. These services are considered to be typically provided within a specific context that varies widely between Member States due to different administrative organisational and cultural circumstances. Therefore, once again the Commission confirms that such services have, by their very nature, only a very limited cross-border dimension. Member States should have the discretion to organise the choice of service providers.

The proposed Directive provides:

(i) a higher threshold for social services of EUR 500,000, and
(ii) that above this threshold, the only procedural obligations that will apply are the so-called procurement principles, that is, respect for the basic 'procurement principles' of transparency and equal treatment.

12.8 Conclusion

The exemption regime for healthcare services that constitute SGEI as part of the 2011 Decision under the new SGEI Package has been broadened considerably to cover not just hospital care but all (curative) healthcare as well as long-term care, irrespective of the amount of aid or turnover concerned. As before, this exemption applies to the notification and standstill requirements but only if the conditions set out in the Decision with respect to the act of entrustment, the parameters for compensation and the controls of overcompensation are met. These latter conditions are equally applicable to all sectors, albeit the Commission appears to recognise the need for some flexibility at national level.

The IRIS-H decision proves a useful illustration of the way the Commission applies the rules on State aid and SGEI compensation in practice. The first *Altmark* case and SGEI Package criterion was once again not strictly applied: instead the Commission assumed that at least a local level, public service obligations existed and had been well-defined in the regulatory context. In addition we have seen how, the fourth *Altmark* criterion on efficiency which is applied to determine whether aid is present was trumped by the more relaxed compatibility assessment standards set out in the 2005 SGEI package where no comparable criterion exists: net costs are assumed as given, and only the scope for reasonable profits is restrained.

This may well be in line with the way the SGEI Package (2005 and 2011 versions) works, but it results in a system that perpetuates the existence of perverse incentives for SGEI incumbents which both frustrate competition in the sector and in all likelihood could lead to a suboptimal provision of the SGEI themselves. The Commission also missed a golden opportunity to apply an efficiency test where in the present case it could have had comparable data for public and private hospitals at its disposal which are, after all, subject to largely comparable regulatory requirements.

It is striking that in the Brussels hospital Decision the Commission did not carry out a detailed cost/benefit analysis even where this would be possible based on national rules. It is worrying that the fact deficits are compensated by definition is justified as evidence of the solidarity-based character of the tasks involved. If all deficits are covered *ex post* the difference between the second *Altmark* criterion (setting out parameters in advance) and the third *Altmark* criterion (no overcompensation) disappears. But, as the Court held in *BUPA*, the Member State should not fund inefficiencies and to ensure that this does not occur, this ought to require an economic analysis as part of the compatibility assessment. If the Commission decision in the IRIS hospitals case is to be deemed the standard approach, this seems to suggest that we are unlikely to see a strict discipline for public service obligations in the hospital sector in the near future.[53]

This result seems to be due to an overly cautious approach by the Commission which considers all but the grossest violations of EU law out of bounds to intervention, especially in areas such as healthcare where the EU so far lacks extensive involvement (but may have ambitions to become more involved—such as is evidenced by the 2011 Patients' Rights Directive).[54] One possible way out might be stricter application of the public procurement rules in the SGEI context.[55] For the time being, however, both the new 2011 SGEI Package and the State aid practice show that the Commission is content to do without a stringent application of the State aid rules based on economic analysis in the hospital sector—or indeed in healthcare and long-term care at large.

The lesson for the Member States is likely to be that they can remain relatively relaxed about formal SGEI entrustment of hospital services as the Commission is likely to derive public service obligations from the general regulatory context as necessary. This is relevant for Member States as it shelters them from making tough decisions on access, priorities and preferential funding. This is regrettable because apart from foregoing the salutary effects of Member States making precisely those choices explicit, this approach also curtails the possibility for third parties to point out discrepancies and contest the coherence and thereby the validity of formal SGEI entrustment—or the lack thereof. In terms of legal certainty and legal protection this is a lamentable result, even if it is one the Commission could presumably reverse, by bringing its own practice into line with its recent legislation and insisting that Member States do the same. The coming into force of the 2011 SGEI Package would be an excellent moment to start doing so.

---

[53] However, see Commission Decision 2006/513/EC of 9 November 2005 on the State Aid which the Federal Republic of Germany has implemented for the introduction of digital terrestrial television (DVB-T) in Berlin-Brandenburg, *OJ* 2006, L200/14, confirmed in GC, Case T-8/06 *FAB Fernsehen*, above n 46, paras 63ff.

[54] Directive 2011/24/EU of the European Parliament and of the Council of 9 March 2011 on the application of patients' rights in cross-border healthcare, *OJ* 2011, L88/45.

[55] Cf. Office of Fair Trading (OFT) (2010) http://www.oft.gov.uk/shared_oft/economic_research/oft1242.pdf (last accessed 15 May 2012); J. Fingleton, Reforming public services, speech of 7 July 2010. http://www.oft.gov.uk/shared_oft/speeches/689752/0810.pdf (last accessed 15 May 2012).

References

Grespan D (2008) Services of general economic interest. In: Mederer W, Pesaresi N, van Hoof M (eds) EU competition law, part IV, State aid, book 2, Claeys & Casteels, Leuven pp 1123–1208

Hancher L, Larouche P (2010) Community, state and market. In: Craig P, De Búrca G (eds) The evolution of EU law, 2nd edn. OUP, Oxford

Hancher L, Sauter W (2012) EU competition and internal market law in health care. OUP, Oxford

Koenig C, Paul J (2010) State aid screening of hospital funding—the German case. EStAL 9(4):755

Lienard D (2004) Hôpitaux privés/Hôpitaux publics: financement, déficits, patientèle sociale [Private/Public Hospitals: funding deficits, social patient base] MC informations 211:10

Office of Fair Trading (2010) Competition in mixed markets: ensuring competitive neutrality Working paper, (July) http://www.oft.gov.uk/shared_oft/economic_research/oft1242.pdf (last accessed 15 May 2012)

Sauter W, van de Gronden J (2011) State aid, services of general economic interest and universal service in healthcare. ECLR 32(12):615

Sauter W (2012) The Altmark package mark II: new rules for State aid and the compensation of services of general economic interest. ECLR 33(7):307

Chapter 13
Conclusion

Johan W. van de Gronden

- It just goes over all again, but interestingly it says that although there are things to settle, the approach is towards more competition in SGEIs

Abstract In this concluding chapter, it will be examined to what extent the update of the Monti-Kroes package has shed more light on the relationship between the Treaty provisions on State aid and Services of General Economic Interest. It will be argued that the Commission has succeeded to make considerable progress in its update and modernisation of the '*Altmark*-Monti-Kroes Package'. Although a couple of issues remain to be settled, it is apparent from the analysis carried out in the present volume that many other problems are solved. By so doing, the Commission has contributed to the development of the EU approach to SGEI. Although the EU edifice for SGEI is far from finished, some important bricks of this building are identified in the updated '*Altmark*-Monti-Kroes package'. Competition and principles of good governance should play a key role. If these values are not satisfactorily adhered to by the Member States, the Commission is likely *not* to approve their measures to finance particular SGEI. As a result, the updated '*Altmark*-Monti-Kroes Package' should be regarded as an important development, which could, eventually, lead to convergence of the national policies for the provision of SGEI.

Contents

J. W. van de Gronden (✉)
Department of International and European, Law, Radboud University Nijmegen,
P.O. Box 9049, 6500 KK Nijmegen, The Netherlands
e-mail: j.vandegronden@jur.ru.n

E. Szyszczak and J.W. van de Gronden (eds.), *Financing Services of General Economic Interest*, Legal Issues of Services of General Interest, DOI: 10.1007/978-90-6704-906-1_13, © T.M.C. ASSER PRESS, The Hague, The Netherlands, and the authors 2013

13.1 Introduction

As was already pointed out in the **Introduction**, with handing down its landmark decision in *Altmark*[1] the CJEU has acknowledged the important role that State aid plays for guaranteeing access to SGEI for all. As is rightly pointed out by *Vedder* and *Holwerda*, to this acknowledgment there is even a constitutional dimension: the Member States' competences to organise these services should be respected. However, *Altmark* has also given rise to many complicated questions and issues that were hard to tackle. It did not come as a surprise that in 2005 the Commission issued the so-called 'Altmark-Monti-Kroes Package'[2] in order to clarify and work out the approach adopted by the CJEU and even to extend it. These measures did not prevent litigation from occurring[3] and, therefore, it was clear that a reform was necessary. The consultation started by the Commission eventually resulted in the publication of the Commission Communication on the application of the European Union State aid rules to compensation granted for the provision of services of general economic interest (hereafter the 'Commission Communication'),[4] the Commission Decision on the application of Article 106(2) of the Treaty to State aid in the form of public service compensation granted to certain undertakings entrusted with the operation of services of general economic interest (hereafter the 2011 Commission Decision),[5] the Commission Communication on the framework for State aid in the form of public service compensation (hereafter: 'EU Framework')[6] and Commission Regulation 360/2012 on the application of Articles 107 and 108 of the Treaty to *de minimis* aid granted to undertakings providing services of general economic interest (hereafter '*De Minimis* Regulation').[7]

In its Press Release of 20 December 2011[8] the Commission contended that the update of the '*Altmark*-Monti-Kroes Package' would provide the Member States with a simpler, clearer and more flexible framework for financing SGEI. In this volume many scholars and practitioners have explored the measures taken by the Commission, an overview of which is given by *Szyszczak* in the **Introduction**. These contributions have revealed the improvements achieved by the Commission but also the flaws of its measures. Below, it will be examined to what extent the

---

[1] CJEU, Case C-280/00 *Altmark* [2003] *ECR* I-7747.

[2] See the Community framework of the Commission for State aid in the form of public service compensation, OJ 2005 C 297/4; the Commission Decision on the application of Article 86(2) of the EC Treaty to State aid in the form of public service compensation granted to certain undertakings entrusted with the operation of services of general economic interest, OJ 2005 L312/67 and.

[3] See e.g. Case T-289/03 *British United Provident Association* [2008] *ECR* II-81.

[4] *OJ* 2012 C8/4.

[5] *OJ* 2012 L7/3.

[6] *OJ* 2012 C8/15.

[7] *OJ* 2012 L114/8.

[8] IP/11/1571.

Commission has kept the promise and has given more guidance on matters of State aid and SGEI. At first the issues that have been clarified will be identified. Subsequently, the issues that still remain unclear will be discussed. This conclusion will end by making some final observations.

13.2 Issues Clarified

Article 106 (3) TFEU gives the Commission the authority to adopt Directives or Decisions in order to ensure the application of the other sections of this Treaty provision. The 2005 Monti-Kroes package was based on Article 106 (3) TFEU. However, since the entry into force of the Treaty of Lisbon in 2009, Article 14 TFEU contains an explicit basis for EU regulations setting the principles and conditions for SGEI. These regulations shall be adopted by the Council and the European Parliament in accordance with the ordinary legislative procedure. Despite this new legal basis for EU action regarding SGEI the Commission has decided to base the updated Monti-Kroes package on Article 106 (3) TFEU. *Maxian Rusche* argues that this decision is not contrary to EU law, as, inter alia, Article 14 TFEU does not refer to the Treaty provisions on State aid.[9] Additionally, Article 106 (3) TFEU provides for an exclusive competence for the Commission to adopt Decisions and Directives, whereas Article 14 TFEU confers the power upon the European Parliament and the Council to enact only regulations.[10] In the view of *Maxian Rusche,* these systematic arguments justify the choice of the Commission for making use of the legal basis of Article 106 (3) TFEU.[11] If *Maxian Rusche* is correct, the issue of legal basis is settled and does not give rise to uncertainties. In any event, as is argued by *Maxian Rusche*, the position of SGEI is reinforced by the Treaty of Lisbon and, therefore, the measures taken by the Commission are in line with the wish of the *Herre der Vertrage*, as these measures respect the role SGEI play in modern society.

An important improvement brought about by the '*Altmark*-Monti-Kroes Package' concerns the rules for calculating the level of reimbursement. The point of departure of both the 2005 and 2011 package is to avoid overcompensation. Furthermore, it is permitted for the Member States to allow the undertakings funded to realise a reasonable profit. The crucial question was *how* the level of costs and the reasonable profits should be calculated. It is apparent from the analysis of the case law subsequent to *Altmark* carried out by *Vedder* and *Holwerda* that the CJEU and the GC have offered only little guidance on this issue.

---

[9] See Sect. 5.1.2.2.

[10] Cf. also Krajewski 2008, p. 392.

[11] Cf. also Van de Gronden and Rusu 2012, pp. 431 and 432.

The 2011 package contains specific rules for calculating the costs and reasonable profit.[12] *Kavanagh* argues that the Commission has drawn on the experiences in the network sectors (such as the telecommunication sector) when setting these standards. By basing the standards on various cost calculating tests developed in economics the Commission has given considerable guidance in its updated '*Altmark-Monti-Kroes Package*' in *Kavanagh*'s view. For example, the Commission has explained how to interpret the notion of 'reasonable profit' by referring to the rate of return on invested capital over the duration of the entrustment period and by outlining several methods of calculation.[13] In addition, as is argued by *Maxian Rusche*, the matter of cost calculation is further simplified by the adoption of an 'SGEI specific' *De Minimis* Regulation. According to this Regulation aid (except for a few specific aid measures concerning, inter alia, agriculture and transport) not exceeding EUR 500,000 over any period of three years is exempted from the notification requirement, provided that the aid concerned is given in order to finance the provision of SGEI. In order words, the financing of small SGEI operators is immune from the Treaty provisions on State aid.

Additionally, as is pointed out by *Rusu* and *Van de Gronden*, a safe harbour is created for social services.[14] The 2011 Commission Decision respects greatly the competences of the Member States to organise and deliver these services. Consequently, the Commission has made clear that it is for the Member States to decide on matters of financing services that are essential for the social welfare state. Therefore, it could be argued that Decision 2011 gives shape to the concept of 'social market economy', on which the EU is based pursuant to Article 3 TEU. Given its ambiguous wording this concept definitely needs such concrete EU measures that set out how to strike a balance between market forces and social values.[15]

Furthermore, it should be pointed out that in EU State aid law it is not only social services that have a special status. Remarkably, *Maxian Rusche* and *Schmidt* argue that to a certain extent the EU regulations adopted in the field of transport have introduced a safe harbour for various transport services as well. The 2011 Commission Decision also exempts the financing of particular medium and small-sized SGEI operators from the State aid rules. In comparison with the 2005 package, the exemption is less generous, as the threshold is set at EUR 15 million, whereas under the old rules the threshold was EUR 30 million. Nevertheless, the threshold is drafted in clear wording and does not cause any legal uncertainty.

As for aid given to small- and medium-sized companies, in fact a three-tiered system of regulation is in place. Aid not exceeding EUR 200,000 continues to benefit from the general *De Minimis* block exemption, even if this aid might

---

[12] The EU Framework sets out a comprehensible test for calculating the costs and the reasonable profit. See paras 21–59.

[13] Sinnaeve 2012, p. 357.

[14] For a wider discussion and a contextual approach to the use of safe havens for SSGI see Szyszczak 2012b.

[15] Costamanga 2012, p. 397.

concern SGEI.[16] For this kind of aid a Member State is not under the obligation to prove that the company concerned is entrusted with an SGEI mission, since aid of this size given to any undertaking is exempted. For aid, the amount of which is between EUR 200,000 and EUR 500,000, the *De Minimis* Regulation for SGEI constitutes the adequate framework. In order to benefit from this exemption the Member States must prove that the operator concerned is entrusted with the operation of an SGEI. If aid exceeds EUR 500,000 but is below EUR 15 million, the 2011 Decision comes into play. For this Decision to be applicable, a particular operator must not only be assigned with an SGEI mission, but the act of entrustment must also meet particular procedural standards set out in Article 4 of this Decision.[17] The larger the amount of State aid, the stricter the standards set by the *De Minimis* rules. The rationale of this approach of increasing control is crystal clear: State aid of a relatively considerable size is capable of distorting competition more than smaller amounts of State aid.

All in all, the updated 'Monti-Kroes package' has led to much clarification and even to simplification (especially for *De Minimis* aid). As is pointed out by *Maxian Rusche*, the consulation process running up to the adoption of this package was very extensive and comprehensive. The input given by the Member States and the stakeholders has enabled the Commission to identify the issues that were not clear and to shed more light on resolving problematic areas. In other words, the experience of the consultation of the 'Monti-Kroes package' shows that involving stakeholders in the adoption process pays off.

13.3 Issues Still to Be Settled

Although the 2011 package has clarified many issues, a few problems remain unsolved. *Maxian Rusche* and *Klasse* point to the importance of the explicit act of entrustment. The Commission adheres to its (firm) position that SGEI missions must be granted by explicit acts of entrustment. Both the 2011 Commission Decision[18] and the EU Framework[19] set out comprehensive standards that must be met by Member States when designating SGEI missions.

On first sight, this approach enhances legal certainty, as the Member States know which specific requirements they have to observe. But on second thoughts,

---

[16] Commission Regulation 998/2006 on the application of Articles 87 and 88 of the Treaty to *de minimis* aid, *OJ* 2006 L379/5.

[17] This provision requires that the act of entrustment specifies the content and duration of the SGEI concerned, the undertaking to which the special task is assigned, the nature of any exclusive or special rights granted to this undertaking, a description of the compensation mechanism and the arrangements made for tackling problems of overcompensation. Furthermore, the act should even make a reference to the 2011 Decision.

[18] See Article 4 of the 2011 Commission Decision.

[19] See paras 15–17 of the EU Framework.

the strict Commission approach to the explicit act of entrustment is not in line with the case law of the CJEU and the GC. As is pointed out by *Rusu* and *Van de Gronden* the European Courts have increasingly relaxed the requirements for entrustment. In cases such as *BUPA*[20] and *AG2R*[21] the Courts have derived SGEI missions from the general obligations (related to, for example, solidarity and access for all) laid down in national legislation. This approach, which comes down to acknowledging 'implicit acts of entrustment', is not in line with the strict view of the Commission as expressed in the updated '*Altmark*-Monti-Kroes Package'.[22] As a result, it is difficult for national public bodies financing the provision of SGEI and domestic courts confronted with litigation resulting from this financing to find out whether the EU State aid rules are observed. As the condition of entrustment is one of the core requirements of invoking the exceptions contained in *Altmark*, the 2011 Decision and Article 106(2) TFEU, fierce debates and litigation are likely to occur in cases, where SGEI are financed by the State. It is a pity that the Commission has failed to clarify how its measures relate to the recent developments in case law.

Another requirement that continues to cause problems is the fourth condition of the *Altmark* judgment. According to this condition, in the absence of a public procurement procedure the level of the costs the compensation is permitted to cover must be calculated on the basis of the expenses of a well-run company. Since *Altmark* the State aid rules are closely interlinked with EU public procurement law. Moreover, the European Courts have interpreted EU State aid and public procurement law in accordance with the overall purpose of the prevention of distortion of competition on the internal market.[23] The question is, however, whether the tendering of the grant of an SGEI mission automatically entails that the State aid rules do not apply. *Clarke* argues that the old *Altmark* package failed to clarify whether public procurement procedure in itself could ensure that no overcompensation was granted. This is an important issue for Member States that have privatised the provision of various SGEI. Should they only rely on public procurement? Or must they base their decisions also on complicated compensation benchmarking mechanisms? From the analysis of the decisional practice of the Commission under the old *Altmark* package carried out by *Klasse* it is apparent that in some cases the presence of public procurement did not prevent the Commission from finding that the national compensatory measure under review

---

[20] GC, Case T-289/03 *British United Provident Association* [2008] *ECR* II-81.

[21] CJEU, Case C-437/09, *AG2R Prévoyance* v. *Beaudout Père et Fils SARL*, judgment of 3 March 2011 (n.y.r.).

[22] See also Sauter 2012, p. 313. He even argues that the emphasis on the entrustment act that runs as a red thread through the updated Monti-Kroes package stands in stark contrast with the own decisional practice of the Commission. In some cases, the Commission itself has derived SGEI missions from general obligations of national law. See e.g. the decision of the Commission of 22 December 2005 on the introduction of a risk equalisation system in the Dutch Health Insurance, N541/2004 and N542/2004 – C (2005) 1329 fin.

[23] Karayigit 2009, p. 563.

constituted State aid. In this regard, it should be noted that, as pointed out by *Sanchez Graells*, a public procurement procedure does not automatically lead to the lowest possible costs, as such a procedure could also amount to the selection of a provider that offers the best value of money in terms of quality. Consequently, in a tendering procedure it is not clear from the outset on which level the costs will be fixed, and this could have its bearing on the question of whether the State aid rules apply. In *Clarke's* view it is a missed opportunity that the Commission did not elaborate on the role that public procurement could play in the new package. In this regard, it should be noted that according to the Commission Communication an open or restricted procedure within the meaning of Article 1 (11)[24] can satisfy the fourth *Altmark* condition. Whereas a competitive dialogue or a negotiated procedure, with prior publication in the sense of this Directive, is deemed acceptable *only in exceptional circumstances*. With regard to all procedures outlined in EU public procurement law this wording leaves room for calling into question whether the fourth *Altmark* condition is met in a particular case. Consequently, it remains unsettled to what extent tendering could prevent the State aid rules from being violated. In any event, *Clarke* contends that the outcome of a public procurement procedure best reflects the market value of a particular SGEI mission. He opines that these procedures should be used as often as possible by the Member States when designating SGEI.

Making the grant of SGEI subject to public procurement law would definitely lead to a stricter and more market-based approach than the majority of the Member States are used to. In this regard it should be noted that *Hancher* and *Sauter* are of the opinion that the requirements of the updated '*Altmark*-Monti-Kroes Package' are not strict enough.[25] They fear that, as a result, no stricter discipline will occur for financing the provision of SGEI in, for example, the hospital sector. Therefore, they also advocate a stricter application of the public procurement rules in order to address these flaws. Then again, as rightly pointed out by *Buendia Sierra* and *Panero Rivas*, the tendering of SGEI missions is a very delicate matter. They argue that although the preference for tendering is in line with the need to make efficient use of public money, it cannot be ruled out that the wish to apply public procurement rules to every grant of SGEI missions is overambitious. In their view, it may not be expected that the tradition in many Member States, where tendering does not play a role at all in the designation of SGEI, will change overnight. In this regard, the critical remark made by *Sanchez Graells* is also of interest. He argues that the Commission in its view on the relationship between the fourth *Altmark* condition and EU public procurement law focuses too much on the 'pure (lowest) costs'. In his view it is questionable whether such a focus does justice to the fourth *Altmark* condition. He fears that the '*Altmark*-Monti-Kroes Package' favours the use of a relatively inflexible and cost-oriented procurement procedure, which

---

[24] Directive 2004/18 on the coordination of procedures for the award of public works contracts, public supply contracts and public service contracts, *OJ* 2004 L134/114.

[25] Cf. in this regard Fiedziuk 2010, pp. 277–279.

leaves the public authorities with minimum room for manoeuvre. It goes without saying that the *quality* of SGEI is also an important concern and, therefore, the emphasis on public procurement and the lowest possible costs should not lead to a lower level of the quality of these services.

In sum, it is clear that the interpretation of the fourth *Altmark* condition is far from clear. Therefore, it is to be hoped that in the decisional practice of the Commission and in the case law of the European Courts more light will be shed on this issue.

Another issue that could cause problems of interpretation is the notion of 'social services' within the meaning of Decision 2011. As is pointed out by *Rusu* and *Van de Gronden* opinions may differ as to which tasks are covered by this notion. In the past the generous exemption from the notification obligation only applied to hospital services and social housing and, as a result, the question arose what was, inter alia, meant by social housing.[26] As the exemption is extended, the definitional problems are now shifted to the notion 'social services'. As is apparent from the analysis carried out by *Rusu* and *Van de Gronden*, an important group of social services seems to fall outside the scope of the 2011 Decision. It is questionable whether social security services satisfy the conditions of the exemption of this Decision and, therefore, these services do not escape from EU State aid law (in so far as they constitute economic activities).[27] As (economic) social security services play a significant role in national welfare states, it may be expected that the Commission, and perhaps the European judiciary, will be called upon to shed more light on this matter in the short- to middle-term run.

Another important issue concerns the relationship between the 2011 Commission Decision and the EU Framework. *Rodrigues* notes that the services (such as the social services) covered by the Decision enjoy a favourable treatment, whereas the services assessed under the EU Framework (and a as a result under Article 106(2) TFEU) are subject to a strict assessment. An important test to be applied by the Commission is whether the compensation granted by the Member State concerned introduces incentives for the efficient provision of SGEI of a high standard, unless it can be shown that it is not appropriate to take efficiency as a point of departure.[28] The objection of *Rodrigues* is that it is questionable whether it is for the Commission to assess the efficiency of the provision of SGEI or whether the EU is the right level for setting efficiency standards for these services. Additionally, he calls into question the view that enhancing efficiency in the provision of SGEI leads, as a rule, to more satisfaction on the part of the citizens/users. In other words, the EU Framework does not solve the matter of how to reconcile the need of efficiencies with values that are of great interest for citizens/users.

---

[26] Bartosch 2007, p. 570.

[27] Many social security schemes, especially the statutory schemes, however, do not amount to economic activities and are, accordingly, immune from EU State aid law for that reason.

[28] See para 39 of the EU Framework.

13.4 Final Observations: Towards an EU Approach to SGEI

In its attempt to provide more clarity and to allow for more flexibility for the Member States the Commission has succeeded to make considerable progress in its update and modernisation of the '*Altmark*-Monti-Kroes Package'. Admittedly, a couple of issues remain to be settled, as has been outlined in this Conclusion, but many other problems are solved. By so doing, the Commission has contributed to the development of the EU approach to SGEI by stressing the significance of market forces in its modernisation package. In several places in this Package the Commission encourages the Member States to introduce competition elements in the provision of SGEI. The most striking example of this approach is highlighted in the chapters by *Buendía Sierra* and *Panero Rivas* and by *Klasse*. According to the Commission Communication, it is not appropriate to attach public service obligations[29] to an activity that is already provided or can be provided satisfactorily under normal market conditions.[30] In my view, *Buendía Sierra* and *Panero Rivas* and *Klasse* rightly note that this point of view is at odds with the position, repeatedly expressed by the European Courts in their settled case law,[31] that the designation of SGEI belongs to the competences of the Member States. Although the validity of the argument made in the Commission Communication can be called into question, this argument clearly reflects the preference for using market forces in the provision of SGEI and, as a result, contains an incentive to introduce competition.[32] The role of competition is also reinforced by the EU regulations on transport and SGEI. *Maxian Rusche* and *Schmidt* note that pursuant to these regulations the grant of public transport concessions should be made subject to a competitive tender procedure. In this regard, mention should also be made of the recently adopted EU State Aid Modernisation plan of the Commission, which sets as priority, inter alia, the fostering of '...sustainable, smart and inclusive growth in a competitive internal market...'.[33] In other words, competition is inherent in the approach developed by the Commission to attain objectives of public interest.

The preference for market forces is reinforced by the standards set for the calculation of costs in the updated '*Altmark*-Monti-Kroes Package'. *Klasse* notes, for example, that in its decisional practice the Commission has contended as a matter of principle that any *ex post* discretion and room for manoeuvre for public authorities in setting parameters for calculating the level of compensation are not

---

[29] In this regard it should be noted that in the *BUPA* case (supra n 20) the GC decided that public services obligations are identical to SGEI.

[30] See para 48 of the Commission Communication.

[31] See e.g. CJEU, Case C-157/94 *Commission* v. *The Netherlands* [1997] *ECR* I-5699.

[32] Cf. Szyszczak 2012a, b, p. 1388.

[33] See the Communication of 8 May 2012 from the Commission, EU State Aid Modernisation, COM(2012) 209 final, p. 3.

in line with the *Altmark* approach.[34] *Kavanagh* claims that the SGEI markets may be shaken-up, as this package forces the SGEI operators to adopt cost-effective policies. *Kavanagh* argues that one of the main concerns of the Commission was to avoid overcompensation (which could lead to cross-subsidization of non-SGEI activities). In its update of the *Altmark* Package, the Commission is encouraging a 'light touch' form of economic regulation in relation to cost effectiveness. For the calculation of the reasonable profit, the Commission has opted for an efficiency-based approach, although other options were available.[35] These economic standards are capable of changing the tradition of the provision of SGEI in many Member States, where cost-effectiveness did not, and still does not, belong to the core values of the regulation of these services. In this regard it should be noted that measures financing social services only benefit from the exemption of the 2011 Decision, if the efficiency standards of this decision are observed.[36] As a result, efficiency is also an important value that Member States must take into account with regard to the organisation and delivery of SGEI. *Vedder* and *Holwerda* contend that Member States when making public interventions in the market should ensure the efficiency of the provision of the SGEI concerned in order to avoid litigation based on the Treaty provisions on State aid and even on the EU antitrust rules.

Next to stimulating the provision of SGEI in a market environment, the Commission has paid attention to the issue of governance in the SGEI sectors. As already pointed out, an important issue in the updated *Altmark*-Monti-Kroes Package is public procurement. Although the Commission is ambiguous on whether tendering the grant of an SGEI mission would lead to the non-applicability of the State aid rules, it clearly supports the use of the public procurement rules in shaping the provision of SGEI. In other words, transparency is a key value. Another important governance issue, pointed out by *Buendía Sierra* and *Panero Rivas*, is the role public consultation should play. The Commission requires that before entrusting an operator with an SGEI mission a Member State should have consulted the users and the providers (unless it is clear that a new consultation will not bring any added value).[37] The involvement of the most important stakeholders is presented as a condition for the designating an SGEI in line with EU law. In my view, by stressing the role of public procurement and consultation the Commission has made clear that principles of good governance should play an important role.

In sum, by shedding more light on particular issues and by elaborating on conditions formulated in the case law of the European Courts, the Commission has

---

[34] In this respect *Klasse* refers to the Commission Decision of 3 May 2005, State aid N 382/2004, Broadband Infrastructure Project Limousin (Dorsal).

[35] Kamaris 2012, p. 59.

[36] In this regard, it should be noted that Koenig and Paul have rightly pointed out that deficit funding of public hospital does not fall within the ambit of the exemption of the Commission Decision, as such funding is not based on efficiency standards. See Koenig and Paul 2010, pp. 769 and 770.

[37] See para 14 EU Framework.

further specified and articulated the EU approach to State aid and SGEI. Although the EU edifice for SGEI is far from finished, some important bricks of this building are identified in the updated '*Altmark*-Monti-Kroes package'. Competition and principles of good governance should play a key role. If these values are not satisfactorily adhered to by the Member States, the Commission is likely *not* to approve their measures to finance particular SGEI. As a result, the updated '*Altmark*-Monti-Kroes Package' should be regarded as an important development, which could, eventually, lead to convergence of the national policies for the provision of SGEI.

To conclude, the application of the State aid rules to SGEI has prompted an important constitutional development. In *Altmark* the point of view of the CJEU was to acknowledge the significant role of these services and the Member States competences to organise them. In the updated '*Altmark*-Monti-Kroes Package', the Commission mainly embarked on the significant role of SGEI by developing important principles and specific provisions. The result is the emergence of an important constitutional EU concept: SGEI. This concept impinges on the competences of the Member States and therefore, the updated '*Altmark*-Monti-Kroes package leads to a shift from the national to the EU level. What does this shift entail? The leading principles for financing SGEI are increasingly set by the Commission and the Member States are losing control over these principles. This is the price, which the Member States have to pay for the clarification of the *Altmark* approach. The adoption of the modernised package has improved the guidance given on how to balance market forces and non-economic values on the EU level. But the other side of the coin is a limitation of the Member States' room for financing the delivery of SGEI. The adoption of this package is, nevertheless, an important step in the development of the EU concept of a highly competitive social market economy.[38]

References

Bartosch A (2007) Social housing and European state aid control. ECLR 28:563–570
Costamanga F (2012) The internal market and the welfare state;anything new after Lisbon? In: Trybus M, Rubini L (eds) The Treaty of Lisbon and the future of European law and policy. Edward Elgar, Cheltenham, pp 381–397
Fiedziuk N (2010) Towards a more refined economic approach to services of general economic interest. EPL 16(2):271–288
Kamaris G (2012) The reform of EU state aid rules for services of general economic interest in times austerity, ECLR 33:55–60
Karayigit M F (2009) Under the triangle rules of competition, state aid and public procurement: public undertakings entrusted with the operation of services of general economic interest. ECLR 30:542–564

---

[38] Pursuant to Article 3 (3) TEU one of the aims of the EU is to realise such an economic order. See Szyszczak 2012a.

Koenig C, Paul J (2010) State aid screening of hospital funding exemplified by the German case. EStAL 4:755–770

Krajewski M (2008) Providing legal clarity and securing policy space for public services through a legal framework for services of general economic interest: squaring the circle? EPL 14:377–398

Sauter W (2012) The Altmark package II; new rules for state aid and the compensation of services of general economic interest. ECLR 33:307–313

Sinnaeve A (2012) What's new in SGEI in 2012? – an overview of the Commission's SGEI package. EStAL 2:347–367

Szyszczak E (2012a) Building a socioeconomic constitution;a fantastic object? Ford Int Law Jo 35:1364–1395

Szyszczak E (2012b) Soft law and safe havens. In: Neergaard U, Szyszczak E, Van de Gronden JW, Krajewski M (eds) Social services of general interest in the EU. TMC Asser Press, The Hague

van de Gronden JW, Rusu CS (2012) Services of general (economic) interest post Lisbon. In: Trybus M, Rubini L (eds) The Treaty of Lisbon and the future of European Law and policy. Edward Elgar, Cheltenham, pp 413–435

Table of Cases

General Court of the European Union

Case T-106/95 *FFSA a.o.* v *Commission* ECR [1997] ECR II-229, 55, 102
Case T-46/97 *SIC* [2000] ECR II-2125, 55
Case T-266/97 *Vlaamse Televisie Maatschappij* v *Commission* [1999] ECR II-2329, 105
Case T-613/97 *Ufex and Others* v *Commission* [2000] ECR II-4055, 62
Case T-128/98 *Aéroports de Paris* v *Commission* ECR [2000] ECR II-3929, 102, 229
Case T-53/01 R *Poste Italiane* v *Commission* [2001] ECR II-1479, 105
Case T-157/01 *Danske Busvognmaend* v *Commission of the European Communities* [2004] ECR II-917, 77
Case T-168/01, *GlaxoSmithKline Services Unlimited* v *Commission* [2006] ECR II 2969, 96
Case T-274/01 *Valmont* [2004] ECR II-3150, 59
Case T-17/02 *Fred Olsen* [2005] ECR II-2031, 19, 245
Case T-266/02 *Deutsche Post* v *Commission* [2008] ECR II-1233, 259
Case T-351/02 *Deutsche Bahn* v *Commission* [2006] ECR II-1047, 226
Case T-357/02 RENV *Freistaat Sachsen* v *Commission* [2011] ECR II-0000, 231
Case T-388/03 *Deutsche Post* [2009] ECR II-199, 60
Case T-289/03 *BUPA* [2008] ECR II-81, 7, 9, 10, 11, 40, 42, 51, 60–62, 66, 70, 164, 165, 194–197, 203, 214, 256, 261–267, 271, 278, 281
Case T-397/03 *Fédération de l'hospitalisation privée* [2006] ECR I-4429, 255
Case T-442/03 *SIC - Sociedade Independente de Comunicação SA* v *Commission* [2008] ECR II-1161, 62, 268
Case T-167/04 *Asklepios Kliniken GmbH* v *Commission* [2007] ECR II-2379, 255
Joined Cases, T-265/04, T-292/04, T-504/04, *Tirerenia di Navigazione* v *Commission*, [2009] ECR II-21, 244

E. Szyszczak and J.W. van de Gronden (eds.), *Financing Services of General Economic Interest*, Legal Issues of Services of General Interest, DOI: 10.1007/978-90-6704-906-1, © T.M.C. ASSER PRESS, The Hague, The Netherlands, and the authors 2013

Court of Justice of the European Union

Case C-244/94 *Fédération française des sociétés d'assurances et al.* [1995] ECR
  I-4013, 260
Case C-70/95 *Sodemare* [1997] ECR I-3395, 77, 192
Case C-55/96 *Job Centre* [1997] ECR I-7119, 193
Case C-67/96 *Albany* [1999] ECR I-5751, 192
Joined Cases C-115/97 Case C-219/97 *Drijvende bokken* [1999] ECR I-6121, 192
Joined Cases C-116/97 C-117/97 *Brentjens* [1999] ECR I-6025, 193
Case C-251/97 *France v Commission* [1999] ECR I-6639, 171
Case C-107/98 *Teckal Srl v Comune di Viano* [1999] ECR I-8121, 73
Joined Cases C-180/98–C-184/98 *Pavlov v Stichting Profesioenfonds Medische
  Specialisten* [2000] ECR I-6451, 190, 259
Case C-206/98 *Belgium v Commission* [2000] ECR I-3509, 219
Case C-324/98 *Telaustria Verlags GmbH and Telefonadress GmbH v Telekom
  Austria AG* [2000] ECR I-10745, 82, 117–120, 223, 234, 244
Case C-379/98 *Preussen Elektra AG v Schhleswag AG* [2001] ECR I-2099, 106
Case C-94/99 *ARGE Gewässerschutz v Bundesministerium für Land- und
  Forstwirtschaft* [2000] ECR I-11037, 73
Case C-205/99 *Asociación Profesional de Empresas Navieras de Líneas Regulares
  (Analir) and Others* [2001] ECR I-1271, 236
Case C-53/00 *Ferring v Agence Centrale des Organismes de Securite Sociale
  (ACOSS)* [2001] ECR I-9067, 6, 10, 54–58, 71, 96, 128
Case C-280/00 *Altmark Trans GmbH and Regierungspräsidium Magdeburg v
  Nahverkehrsgesellschaft Altmark GmbH, and Oberbundesanwalt beim
  Bundesverwaltungsgericht (Altmark)* [2003] ECR I-7747, 1, 3, 6–11, 13–15,
  18, 21, 36–38, 41, 42, 46–48, 50, 54, 55, 57, 58, 62, 64, 66, 69–71, 74, 77–79,
  82, 83, 88, 99, 100, 103, 106, 107, 112, 114, 115, 119–121, 127, 128, 143, 159,
  162–167, 194, 200, 205, 211, 219, 221, 227, 230, 231, 242, 243, 251, 259–263,
  270, 274, 275, 278, 283
Case C-355/00 *Freskot* [2003] ECR I-5263, 191–193, 196
Case C-34/01 *Enirisorse SpA v Ministero delle Finanze* [2003] ECR I-14243, 54,
  59, 77
Joined Cases C-83/01 P, C-93/01 P and C-94/01 P *Chronopost v Ufex and Others*
  [2003] ECR I-6993, 78, 106
Case C-126/01 *Ministre de l'économie, des finances et de l'industrie v GEMO SA*
  [2003] ECR I-13769, 55–57, 71, 165, 171
Case C-110/02 *Commission v Council* (Portuguese Pig Farms) [2004] ECR I-6333,
  56
Case C-26/03 *Stadt Halle v RPL Recyclingpark Lochau* [2005] ECR I-1, 74
Case C-234/03 *Contse SA v Instituto Nacional de Gestion Sanitaria (INGESA)
  (formerly Instituto Nacional de la Salud (INSALUD))* [2005] ECR I-9315, 77
Case C-237/04 *Enirisorse SpA v Sotacarbo SpA* [2006] ECR I-2843, 259
Case C-220/05 *Auroux v Commune de Roanne* [2007] ECR I-389, 73
Case C-295/05 *Transformación Agraria SA (Tragsa) and Administración del
  Estado* [2007] ECR I-2999, 116
Case C-320/05 P *Fred Olsen* [2007] ECR I-131, 245

Table of European Commission Decisions

1 October 1997, 98/365/EC concerning alleged State aid granted by France to SFMI- Chronopost OJ 1998 L 164/37, 62

3 July 2001, State Aid N 209/2001 Guarantee for borrowings of the Housing Finance Agency, 193

27 February 2002, State Aid N 543/2001 Capital allowances for hospitals, 254

19 February 2003, State Aid N 588/02 Grant for long-distance coach services, 224

13 May 2003, State Aid N 46/2003 risk equalisation scheme in the Irish health Insurance market, 255

9 July 2003, 2004/166/EC on aid which France intends to grant for the restructuring of the Société Nationale Maritime Corse-Méditerranée (SNCM) OJ 2004 L 61/13, 245

10 December 2003, State Aid N 282/2003 Cumbria Broadband, Project Access, Advancing Communication for Cumbria and Enabling Sustainable Services, 78

16 December 2003, State Aid N 475/2003 Public Service Obligation in respect of new electricity generation capacity for security of supply, 36, 46, 166

19 May 2004, 2005/217/EC on measures implemented by Denmark for TV2/Danmark OJ 2006 L 85/1, 59

14 July 2004, State Aid C 25/2004 DVB-T in Berlin-Brandenburg, 40

20 October 2004, C 79/2002 concerning the aid scheme implemented by the Kingdom of Spain for the airline Intermediación Aérea SL OJ 2005 L 110/56, 244

16 November 2004, State Aid N 199/2004 Broadband Project East Midlands, 48

16 November 2004, State Aid N 307/2004 Broadband Project Scotland, 48

16 November 2004, State Aid N 381/2004 Broadband Infrastructure Project Pyrénées-Atlantiques, 36, 39, 45

6 April 2005, State Aid N 244/2003 Access to Basic Financial Services, 39

3 May 2005, State Aid N 382/2004 Broadband infrastructure project Limousin (Dorsal), 36, 40, 42, 47, 48, 282

3 May 2005, State Aid N 541/2004 en N 542/2004 risk equalisation system and retention of reserves, 255, 278

E. Szyszczak and J.W. van de Gronden (eds.), *Financing Services of General Economic Interest*, Legal Issues of Services of General Interest, DOI: 10.1007/978-90-6704-906-1, © T.M.C. Asser Press, The Hague, The Netherlands, and the authors 2013

Index

A
Almunia, 3, 14, 72, 107, 112, 113, 126, 150, 218, 226
Almunia Package, 1, 3, 4, 11, 15, 26, 27, 29–31, 69, 83, 99–101, 104, 107, 109–115, 121, 125, 126, 143, 161–163, 166–169, 175, 176, 178, 222, 236, 240
Altmark-Monti-Kroes Package (see also Monti-Kroes Package), 4, 9, 11, 93, 273–276, 278, 279, 281–283
Aviation guidelines 1994, 242, 243

B
Barroso, 92, 107, 110, 114

C
Commission Decision 2005, 30, 37, 38, 44, 45, 79, 80, 129, 130, 206, 209, 220, 232–234, 246, 251–253, 263
Commission Decision 2012, 2, 26, 29, 30, 80, 94, 95, 111, 118, 119, 131, 132, 137–142, 144, 146, 150, 185, 187, 199–214, 217, 222, 223, 232–234, 236, 237, 239–241, 249, 253, 254, 269, 270, 274, 276–278, 280, 282
Commission Communication 2012, 2, 14, 17, 25, 130–132, 134–137, 142, 168–174
Commission Framework 2005, 9, 29, 37, 38, 44, 45, 79, 80, 130, 217, 240, 251, 252, 263

Commission Framework 2012, 7, 25–27, 29, 80, 83, 91, 94, 95, 111, 114, 119, 120, 127, 131, 132, 138, 139, 141–145, 147, 150–153, 158, 159, 166, 167, 169, 170, 175, 205–208, 210–212, 217, 222, 224, 232, 240–244, 253, 269, 274, 277, 280
Committee of the Regions, 14, 111, 112
Compensation for a SGEI, 15, 16, 19–30, 38, 46, 55, 57, 76, 82, 84, 93, 95, 99, 100, 104, 107, 120, 121, 128, 130, 132, 135, 138, 145, 146, 149–152, 159, 163, 170–172, 185, 190, 192, 203, 208, 210, 227, 237, 242, 246, 249, 253, 255, 259, 263, 264, 267, 270, 274
  over-compensation, 13, 19, 20, 25–27, 29, 38, 43, 44, 47, 58, 73, 78, 79, 99, 114, 122, 129, 152, 172, 185, 187, 204–206, 208, 210, 228, 241, 252, 253, 264–267, 275, 278, 282
Concessions, 81, 82, 281
  service concessions, 69, 73, 76, 82
Constitutionalisation, 102
Cost allocation methodology, 144, 153, 206
Consultation, 2, 13–15, 25, 81, 93–96, 99, 106, 107, 111, 117, 121, 142, 143, 209, 268, 274, 277, 282

D
De minimis, 6, 13, 16, 18, 79, 80, 94, 112, 118, 145, 146, 168, 277

E. Szyszczak and J.W. van de Gronden (eds.), *Financing Services of General Economic Interest*, Legal Issues of Services of General Interest, DOI: 10.1007/978-90-6704-906-1, © T.M.C. ASSER PRESS, The Hague, The Netherlands, and the authors 2013

Printed by Printforce, the Netherlands